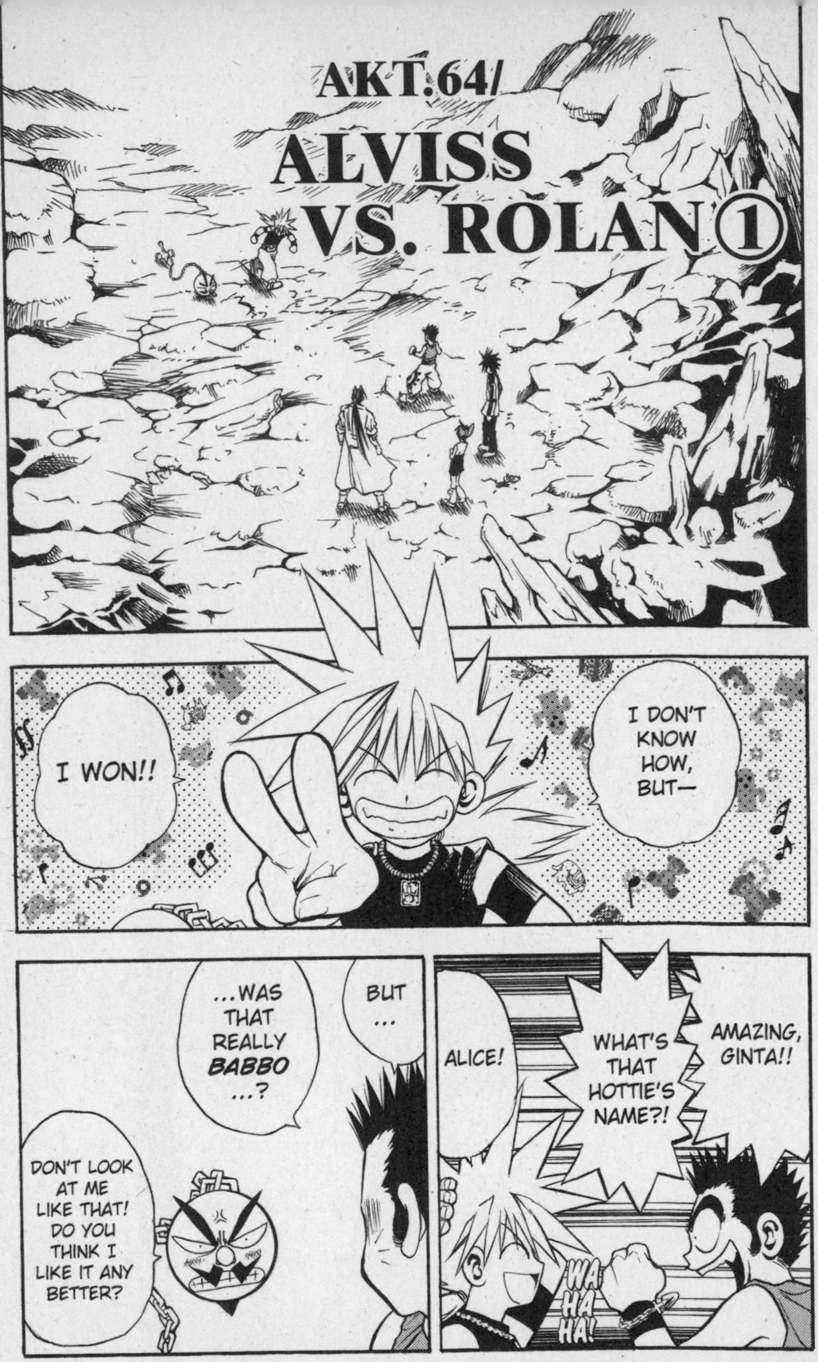
AKT.64/
ALVISS VS. ROLAN ①
I DON'T KNOW HOW, BUT—
I WON!!
AMAZING, GINTA!!
WHAT'S THAT HOTTIE'S NAME?!
ALICE!
WA HA HA!
BUT ...
...WAS THAT REALLY BABBO ...?
DON'T LOOK AT ME LIKE THAT! DO YOU THINK I LIKE IT ANY BETTER?

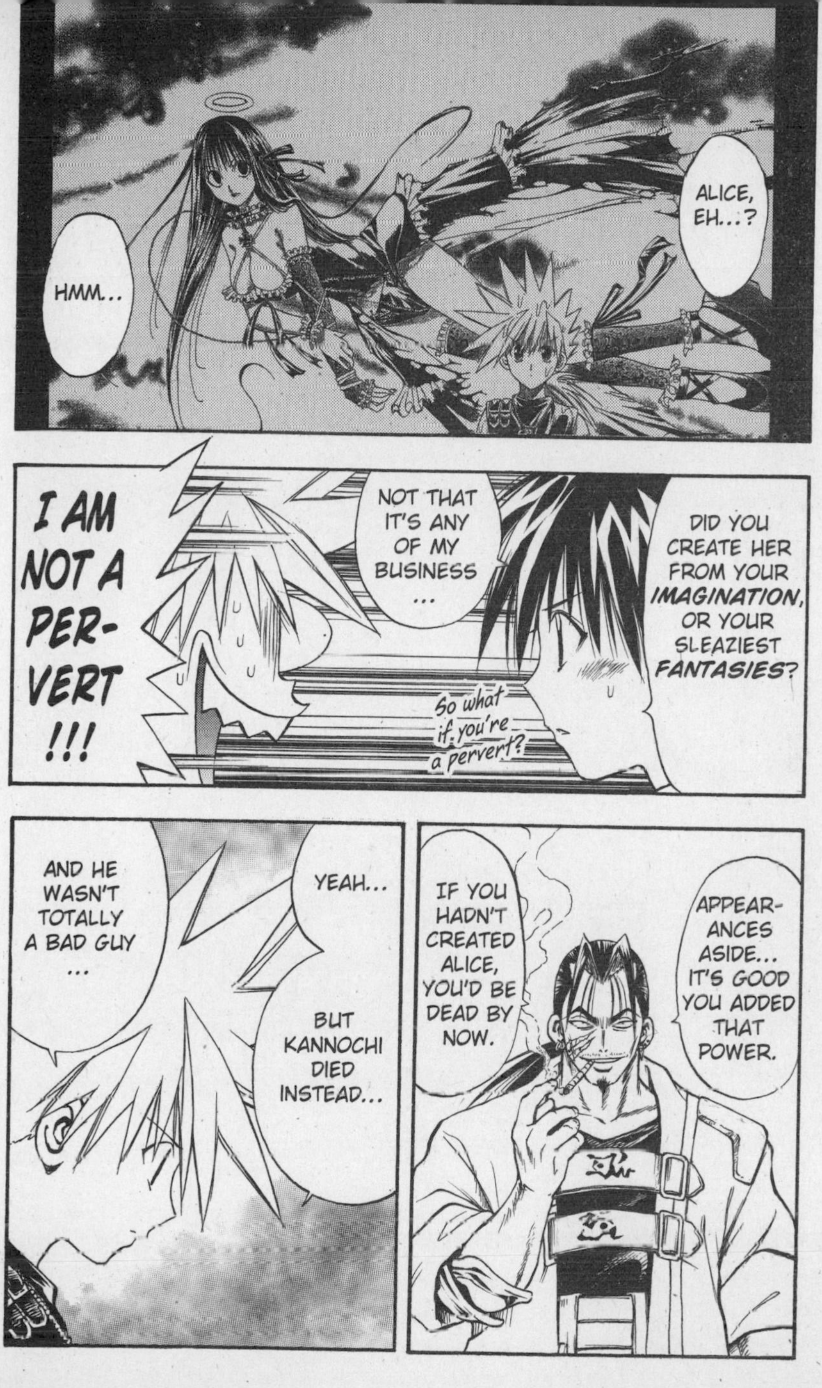

ALICE, EH...?
HMM...
DID YOU CREATE HER FROM YOUR *IMAGINATION*, OR YOUR SLEAZIEST *FANTASIES*?
NOT THAT IT'S ANY OF MY BUSINESS ...
So what if you're a pervert?
I AM NOT A PER-VERT !!!
APPEAR-ANCES ASIDE... IT'S GOOD YOU ADDED THAT POWER.
IF YOU HADN'T CREATED ALICE, YOU'D BE DEAD BY NOW.
YEAH...
BUT KANNOCHI DIED INSTEAD...
AND HE WASN'T TOTALLY A BAD GUY ...

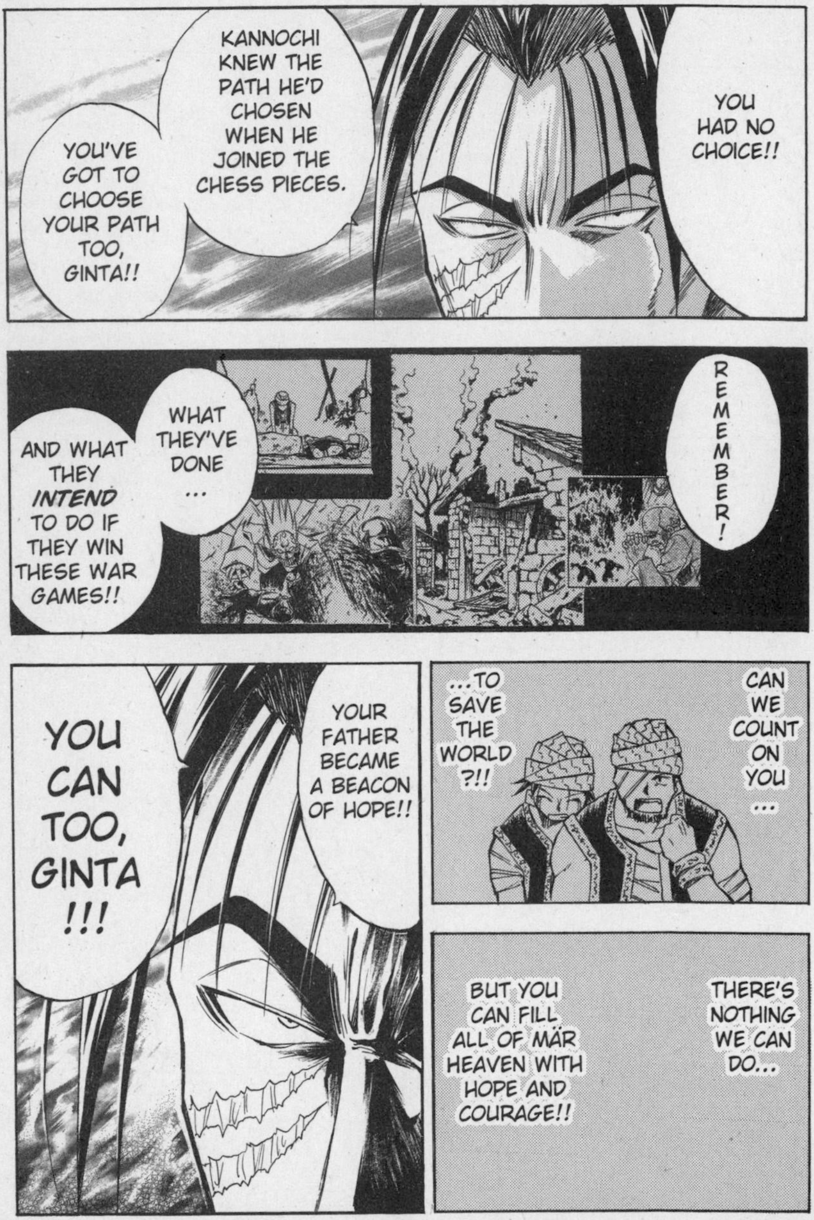
YOU HAD NO CHOICE!!
KANNOCHI KNEW THE PATH HE'D CHOSEN WHEN HE JOINED THE CHESS PIECES.
YOU'VE GOT TO CHOOSE YOUR PATH TOO, GINTA!!
REMEMBER!
WHAT THEY'VE DONE ...
AND WHAT THEY *INTEND* TO DO IF THEY WIN THESE WAR GAMES!!
CAN WE COUNT ON YOU ...
...TO SAVE THE WORLD ?!!
THERE'S NOTHING WE CAN DO...
BUT YOU CAN FILL ALL OF MÄR HEAVEN WITH HOPE AND COURAGE!!
YOUR FATHER BECAME A BEACON OF HOPE!!
YOU CAN TOO, GINTA !!!

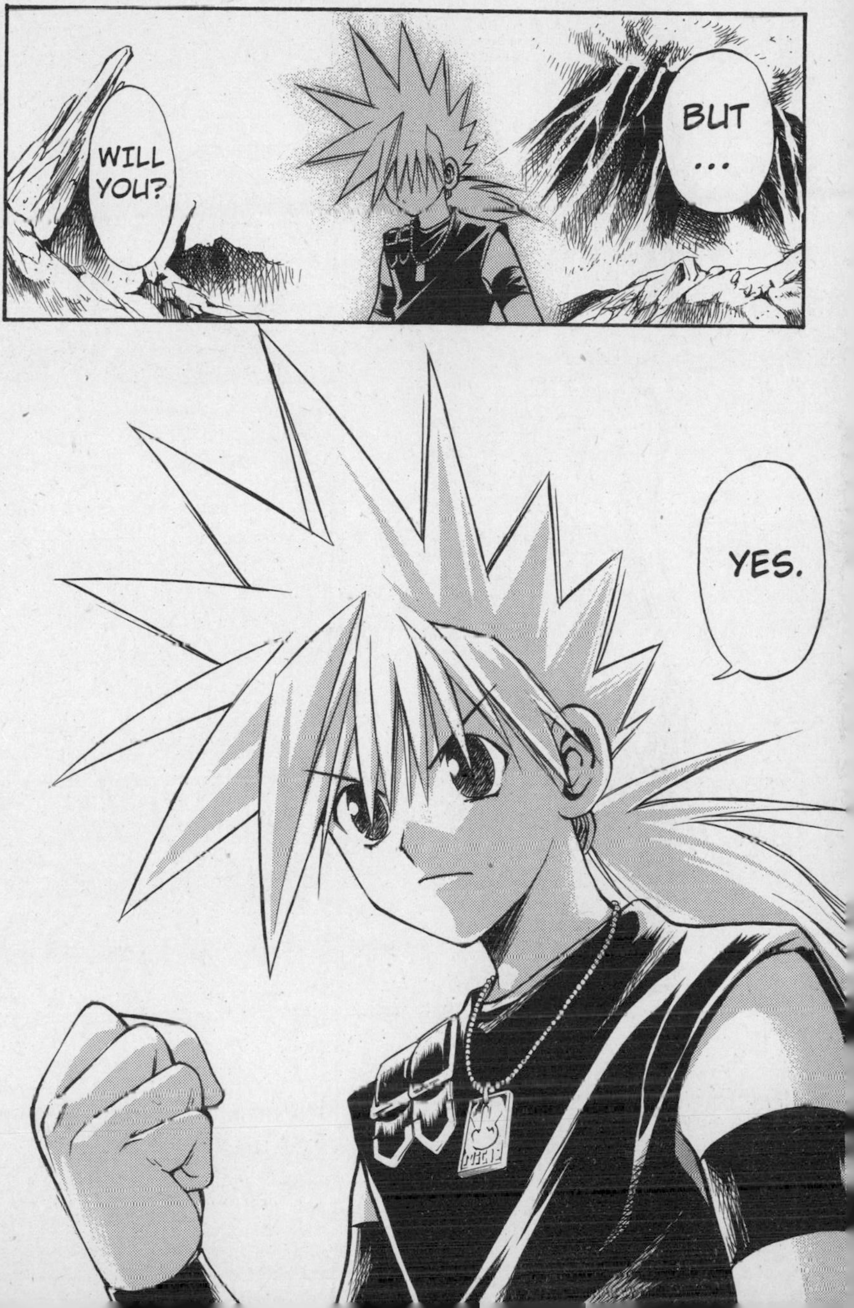
BUT ...
WILL YOU?
YES.

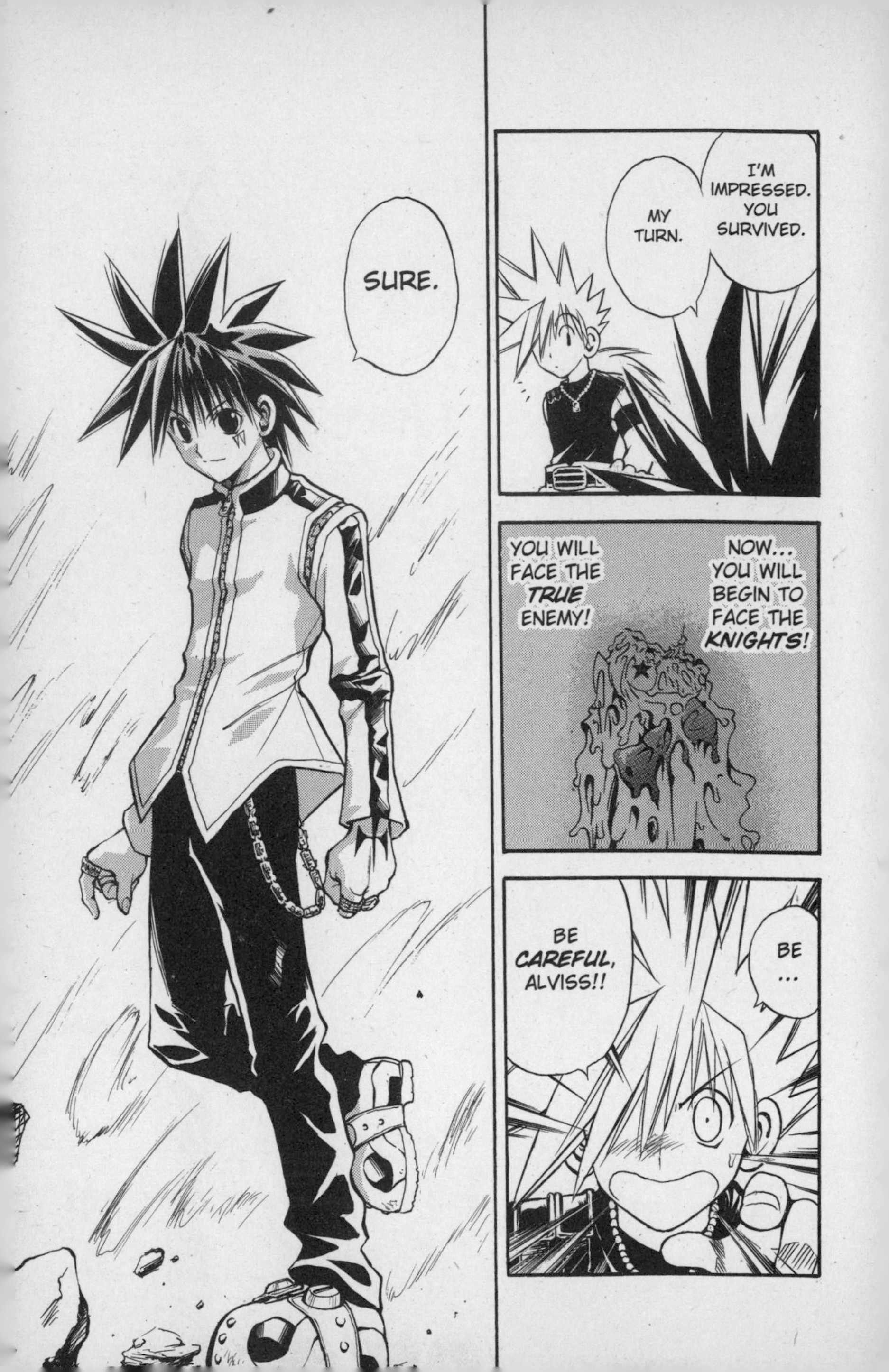
I'M IMPRESSED. YOU SURVIVED.
MY TURN.
NOW... YOU WILL BEGIN TO FACE THE **KNIGHTS**!
YOU WILL FACE THE **TRUE** ENEMY!
BE ...
BE **CAREFUL**, ALVISS!!
SURE.

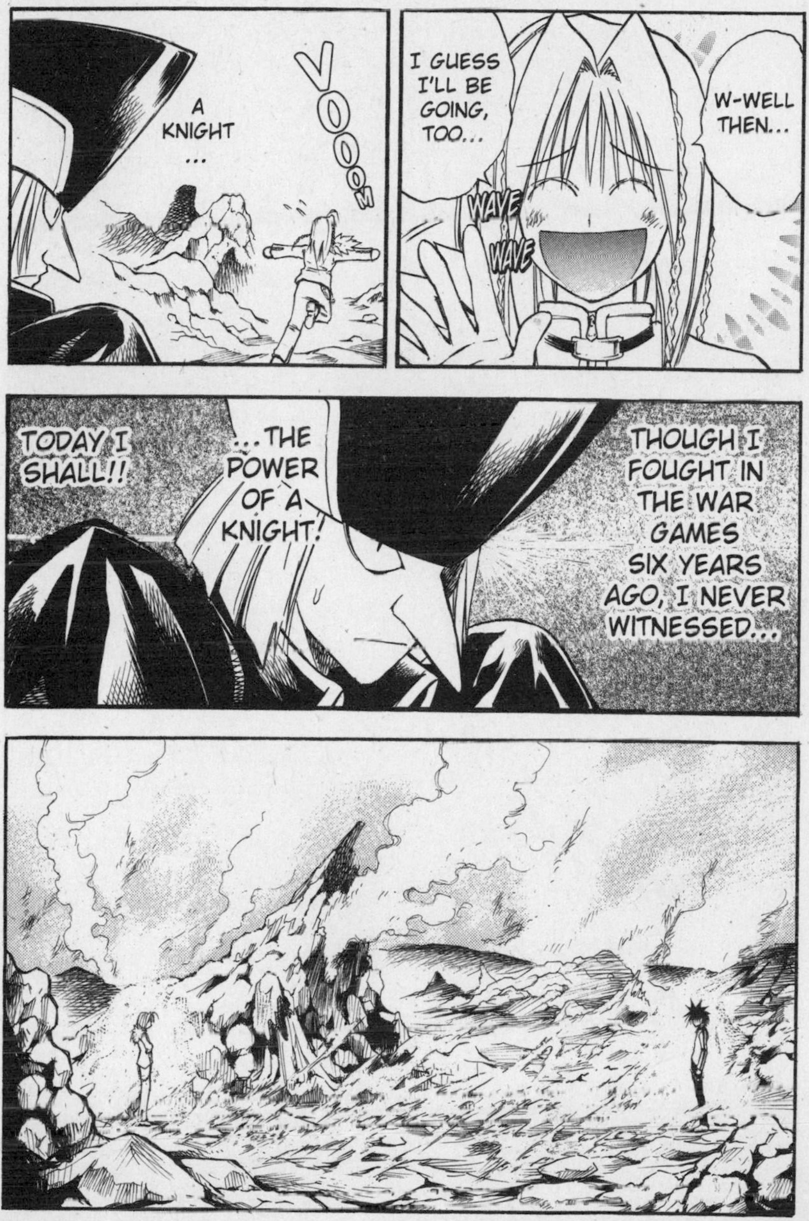
W-WELL THEN...
I GUESS I'LL BE GOING, TOO...
WAVE
WAVE
VOOOOM
A KNIGHT ...
THOUGH I FOUGHT IN THE WAR GAMES SIX YEARS AGO, I NEVER WITNESSED...
...THE POWER OF A KNIGHT!
TODAY I SHALL!!

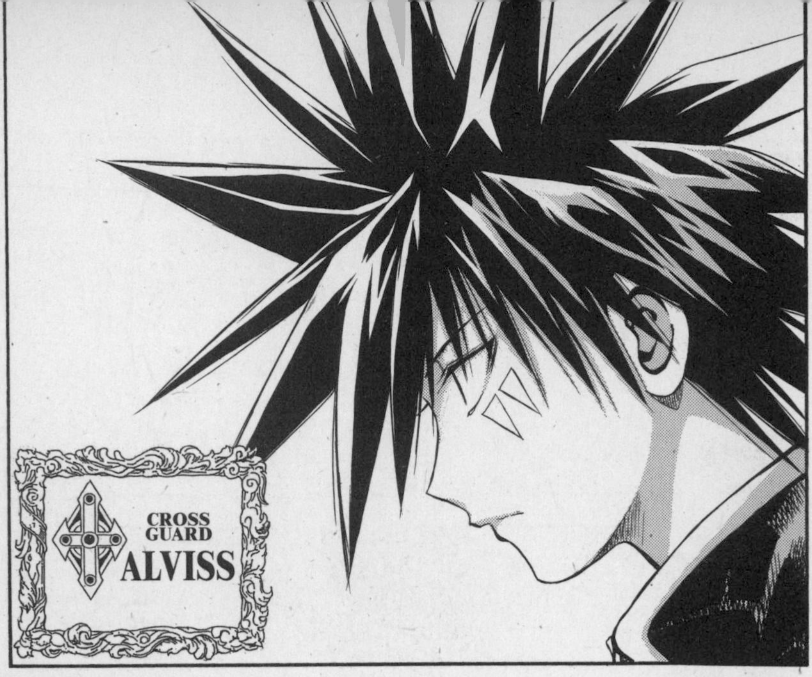
CROSS GUARD
ALVISS

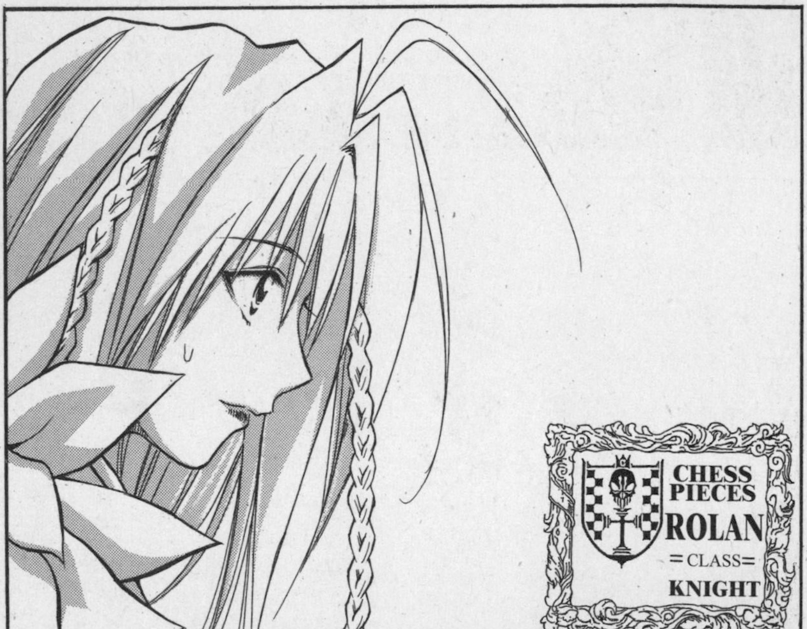
CHESS PIECES
ROLAN
=CLASS=
KNIGHT

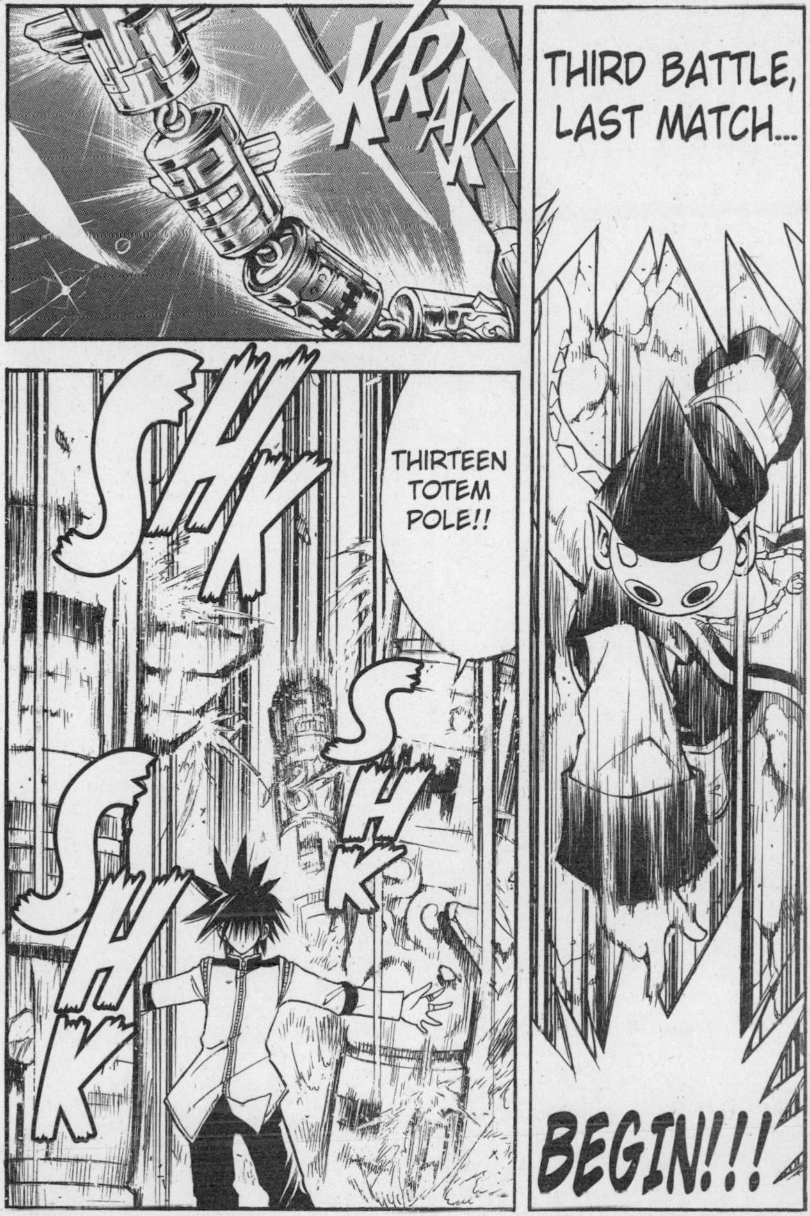
THIRD BATTLE, LAST MATCH...
BEGIN!!!
KRAK
SHK
THIRTEEN TOTEM POLE!!
SHK
SHK

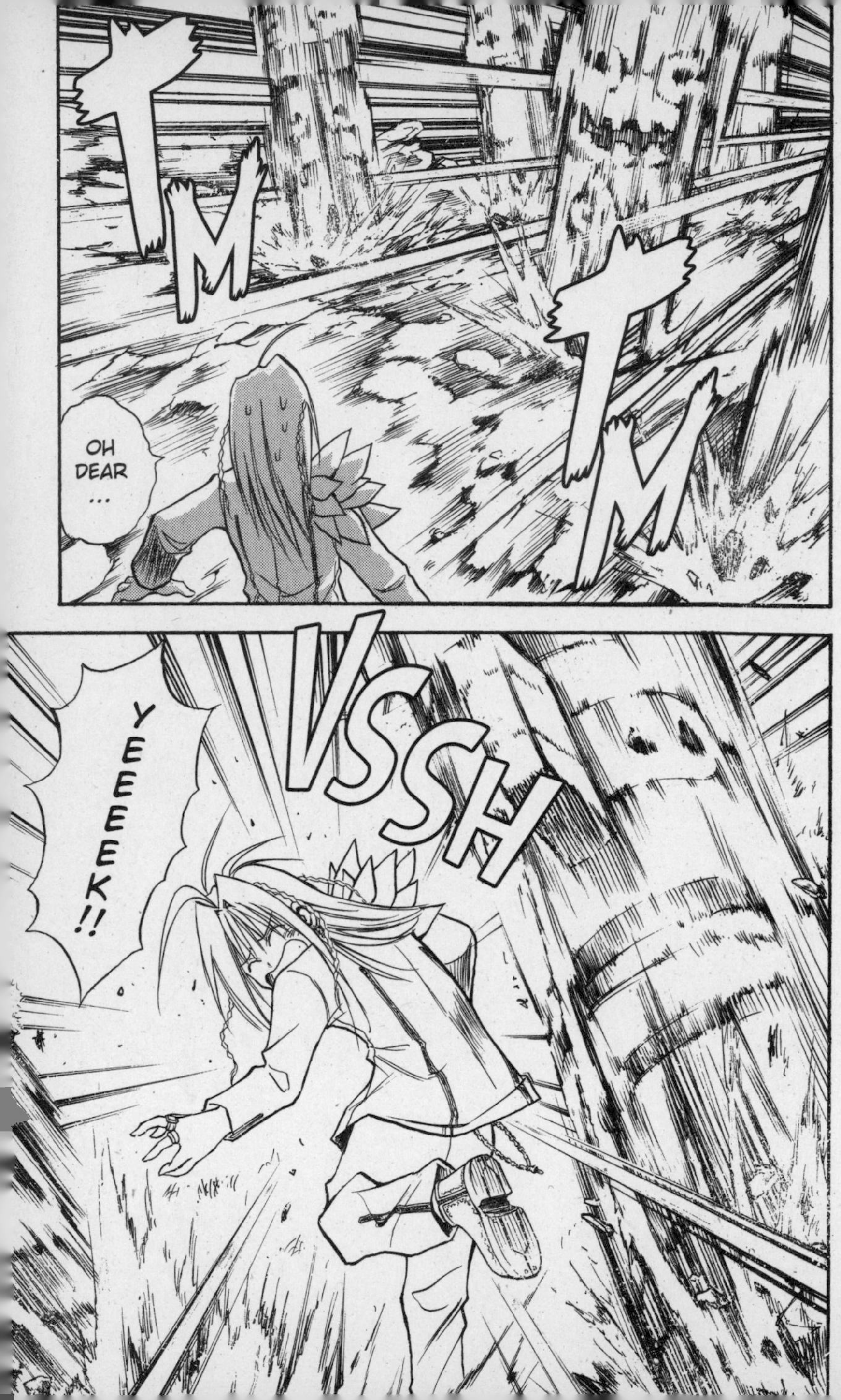
TM
TM
OH DEAR ...
VSSH
YEEEEK!!

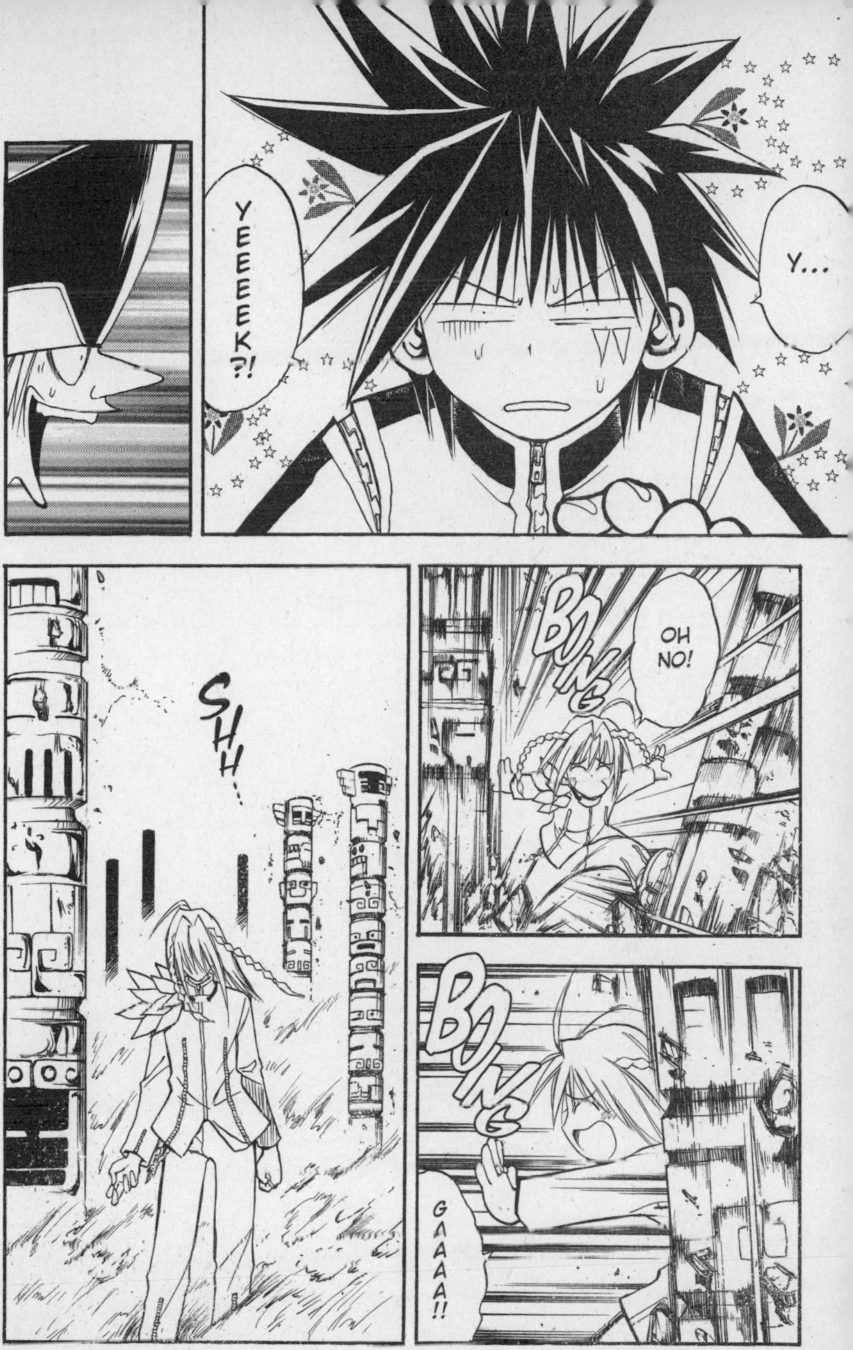
Y...
YEEEEEK?!
OH NO!
BOING
BOING
GAAAAA!!
SHH...

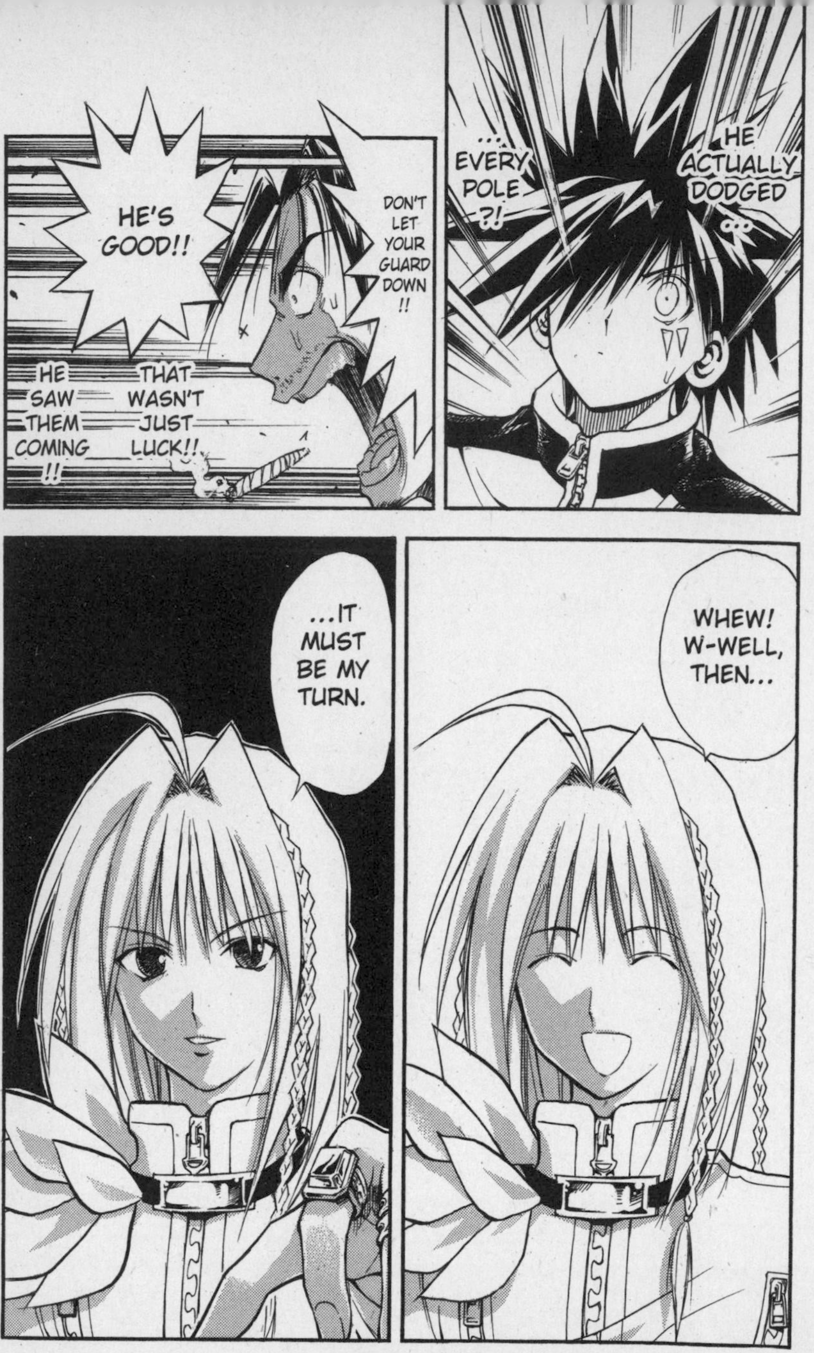
HE ACTUALLY DODGED...
...EVERY POLE?!
DON'T LET YOUR GUARD DOWN!!
HE'S GOOD!!
THAT WASN'T JUST LUCK!!
HE SAW THEM COMING!!
WHEW! W-WELL, THEN...
...IT MUST BE MY TURN.

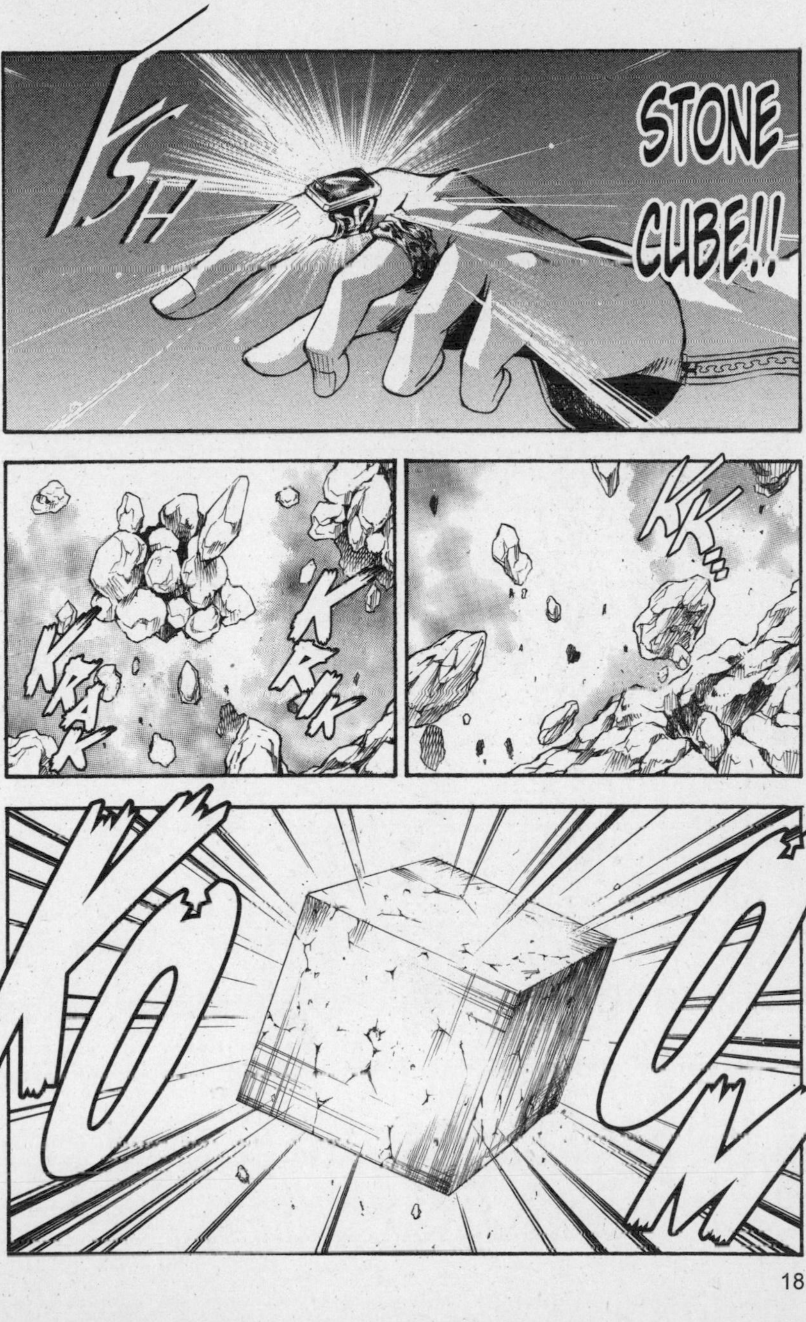
STONE CUBE!!
FSH
KK...
KRIK
KRAK
KOOM

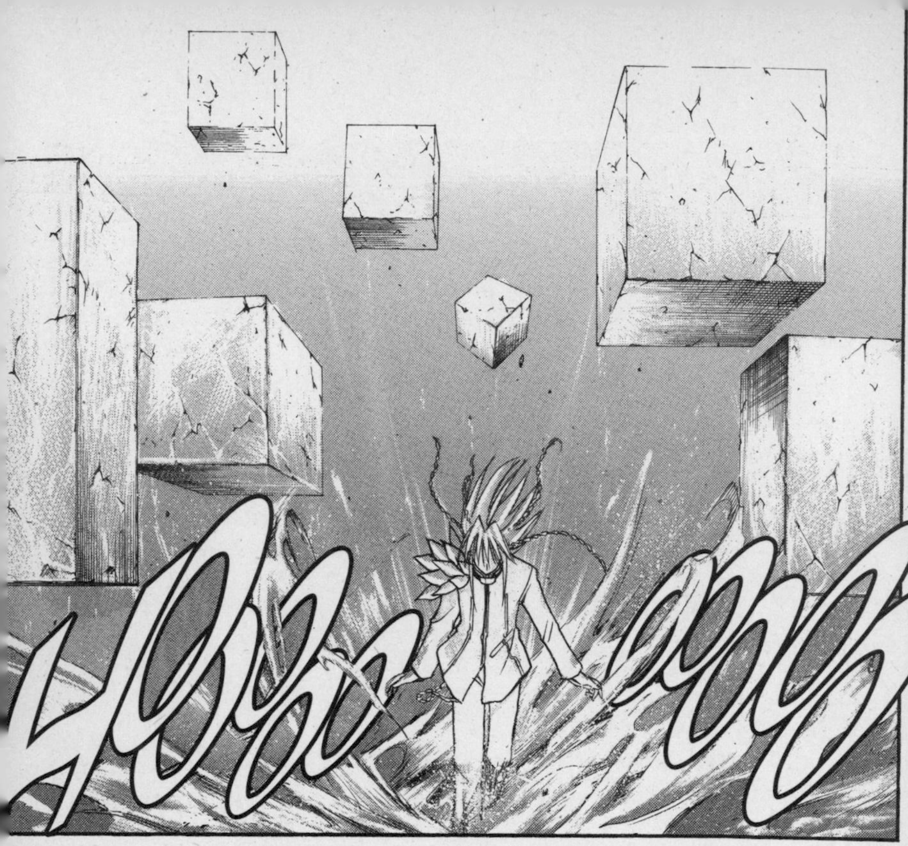

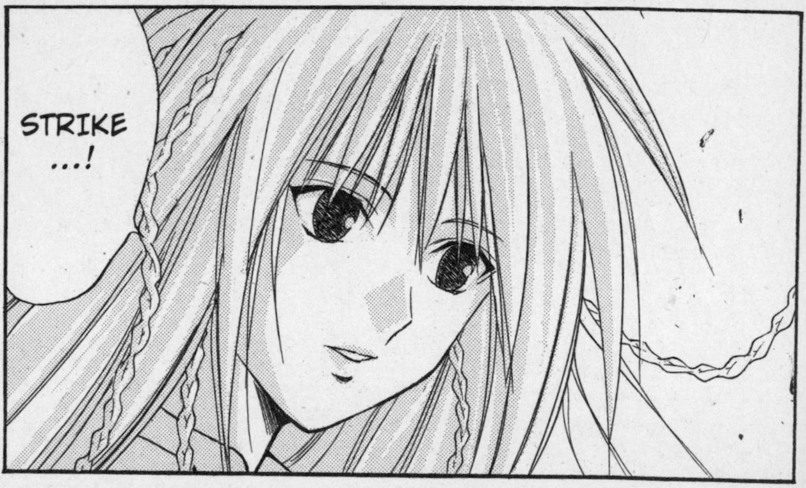
STRIKE ...!

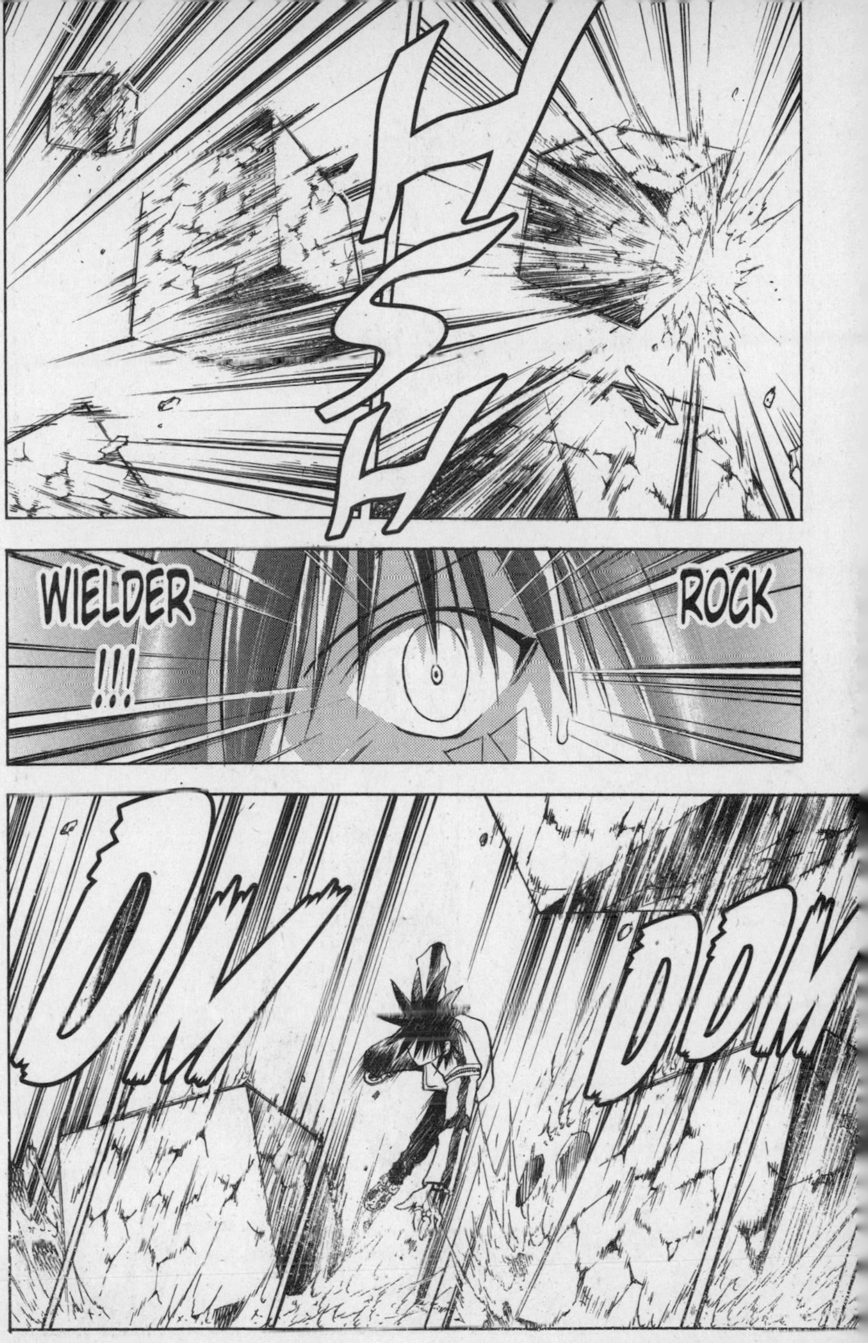
ROCK
WIELDER
!!!

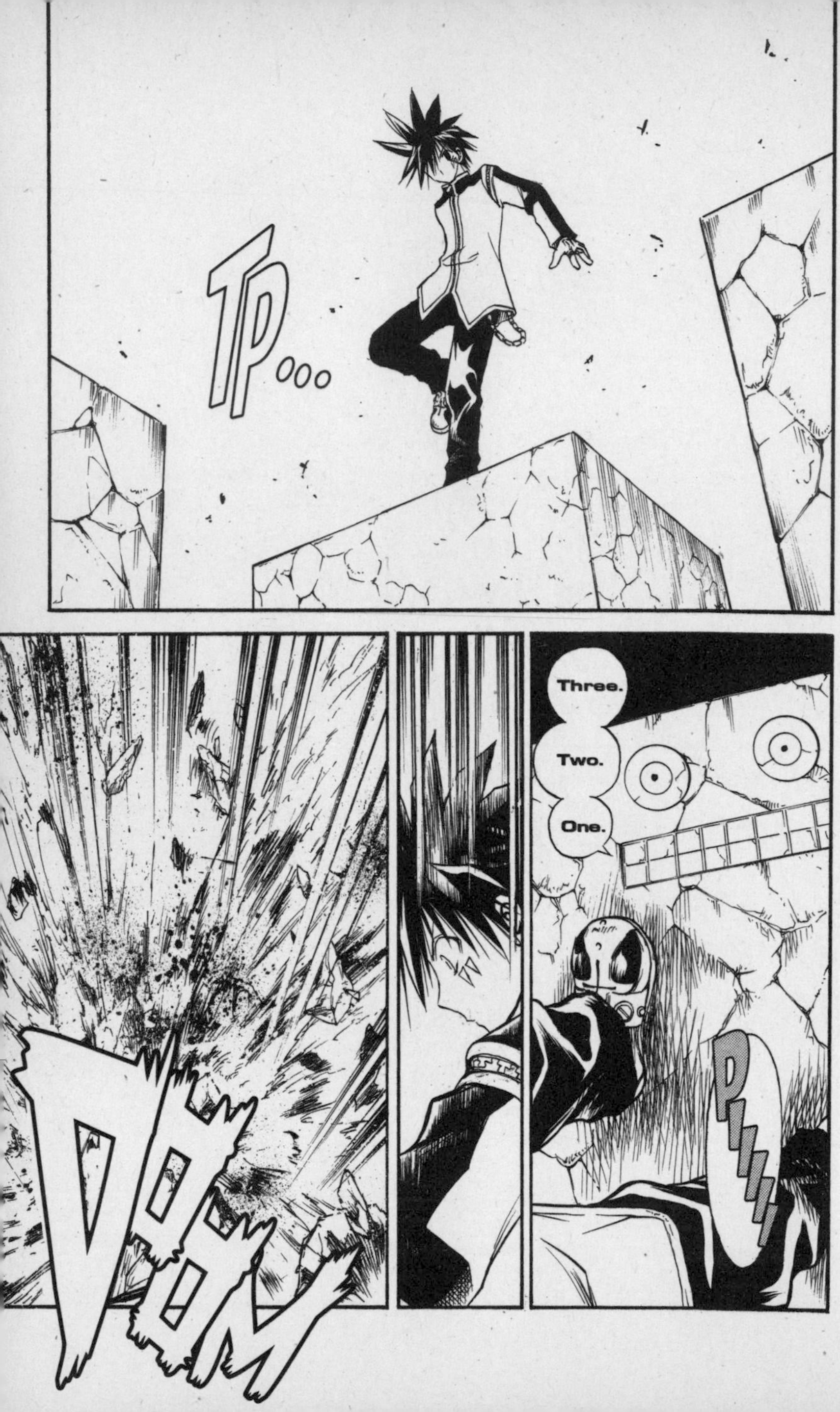
Tp ooo
Three.
Two.
One.

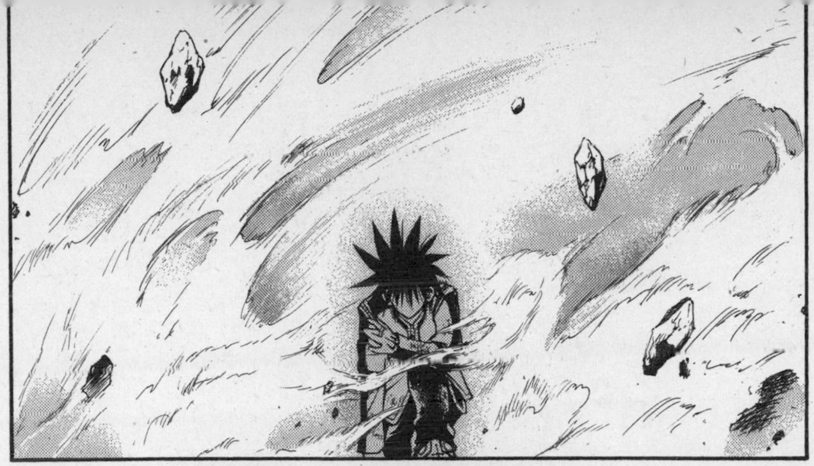

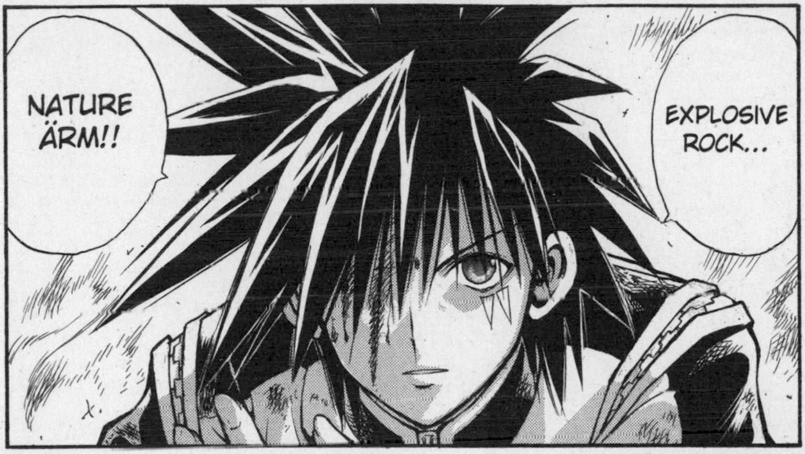
EXPLOSIVE ROCK...
NATURE ÄRM!!

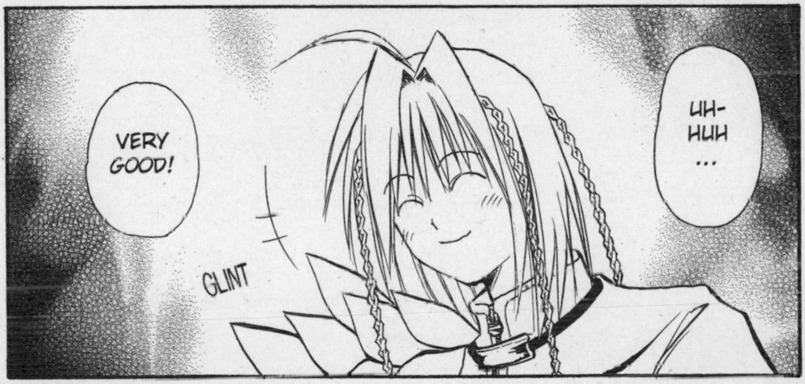
UH-HUH ...
VERY GOOD!
GLINT

AKT.65/ ALVISS VS. ROLAN②

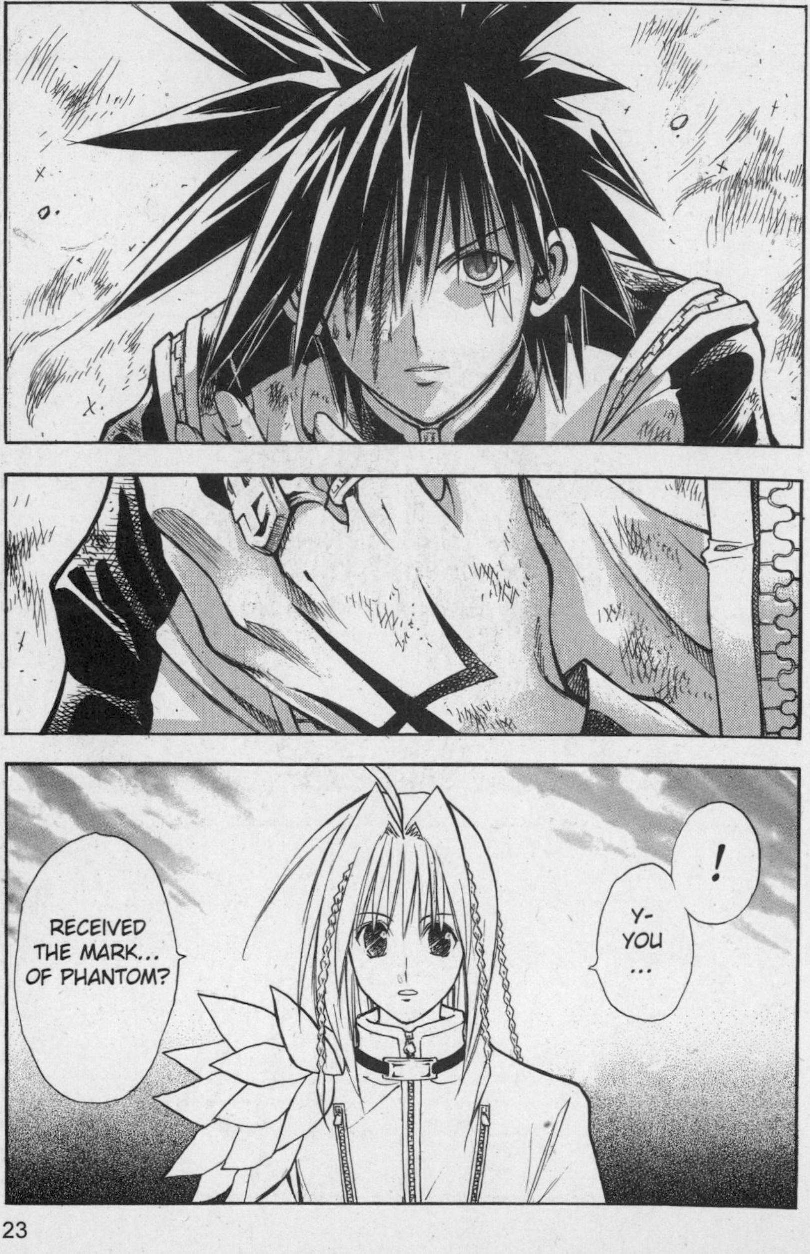
!
Y- YOU ...
RECEIVED THE MARK... OF PHANTOM?

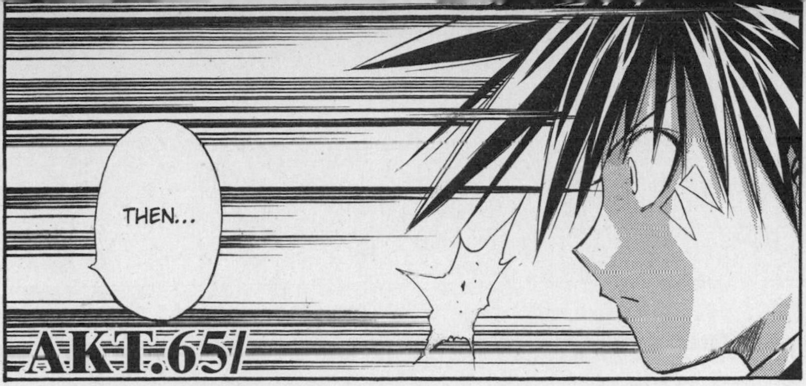
THEN...

AKT.65/ ALVISS VS. ROLAN②

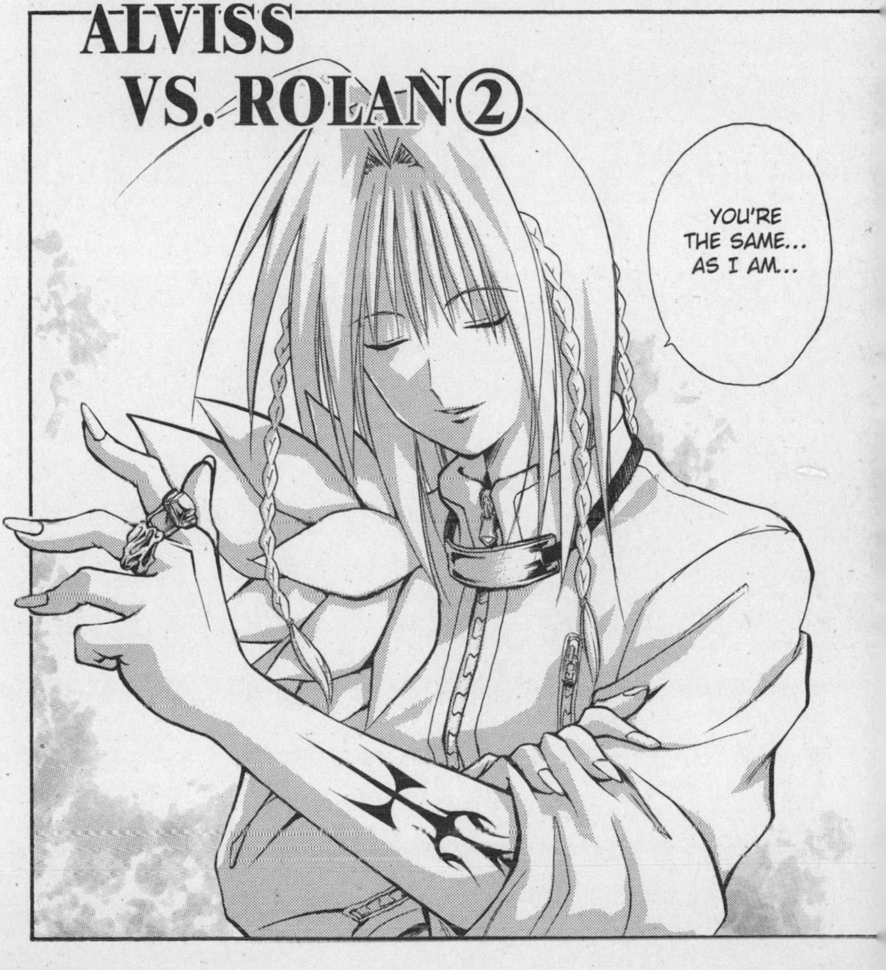
YOU'RE THE SAME... AS I AM...

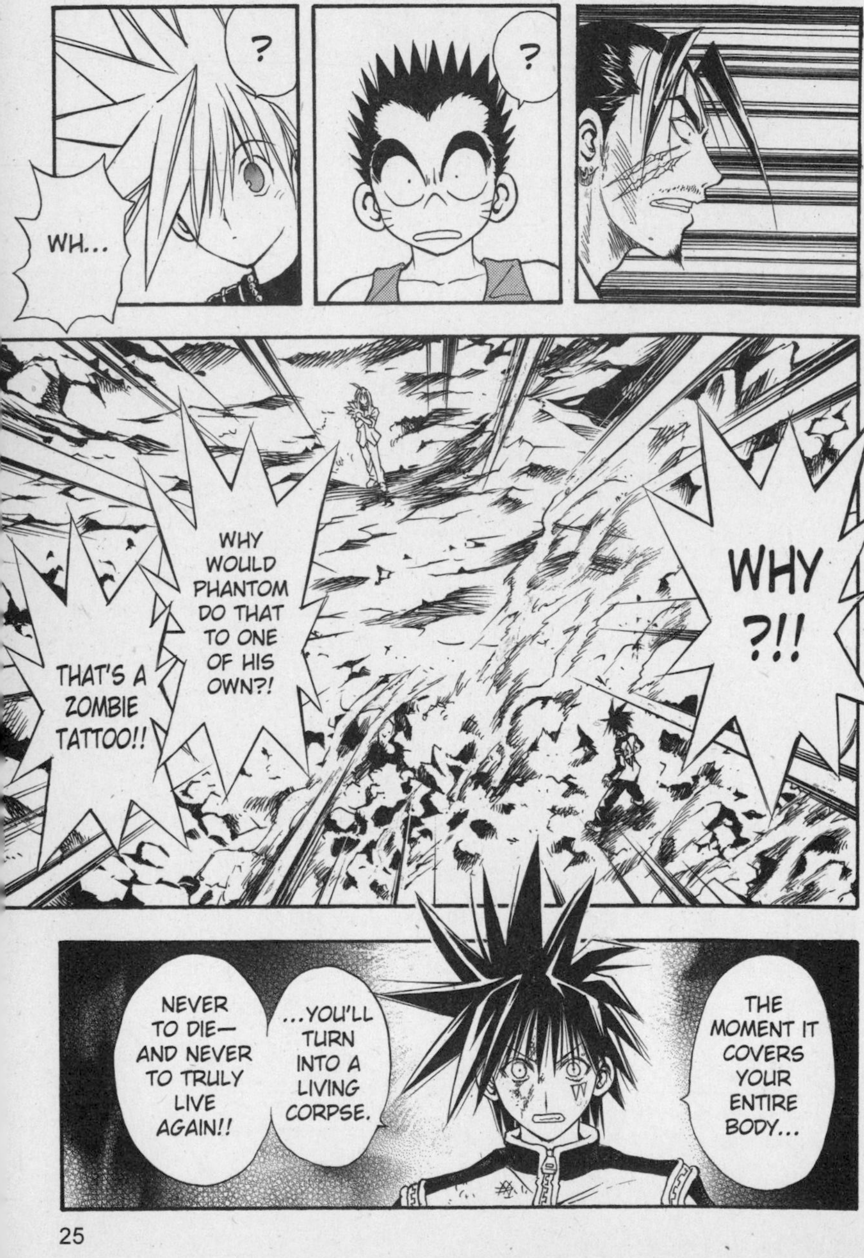
?
?
WH...
WHY ?!!
WHY WOULD PHANTOM DO THAT TO ONE OF HIS OWN?!
THAT'S A ZOMBIE TATTOO!!
THE MOMENT IT COVERS YOUR ENTIRE BODY...
...YOU'LL TURN INTO A LIVING CORPSE.
NEVER TO DIE— AND NEVER TO TRULY LIVE AGAIN!!

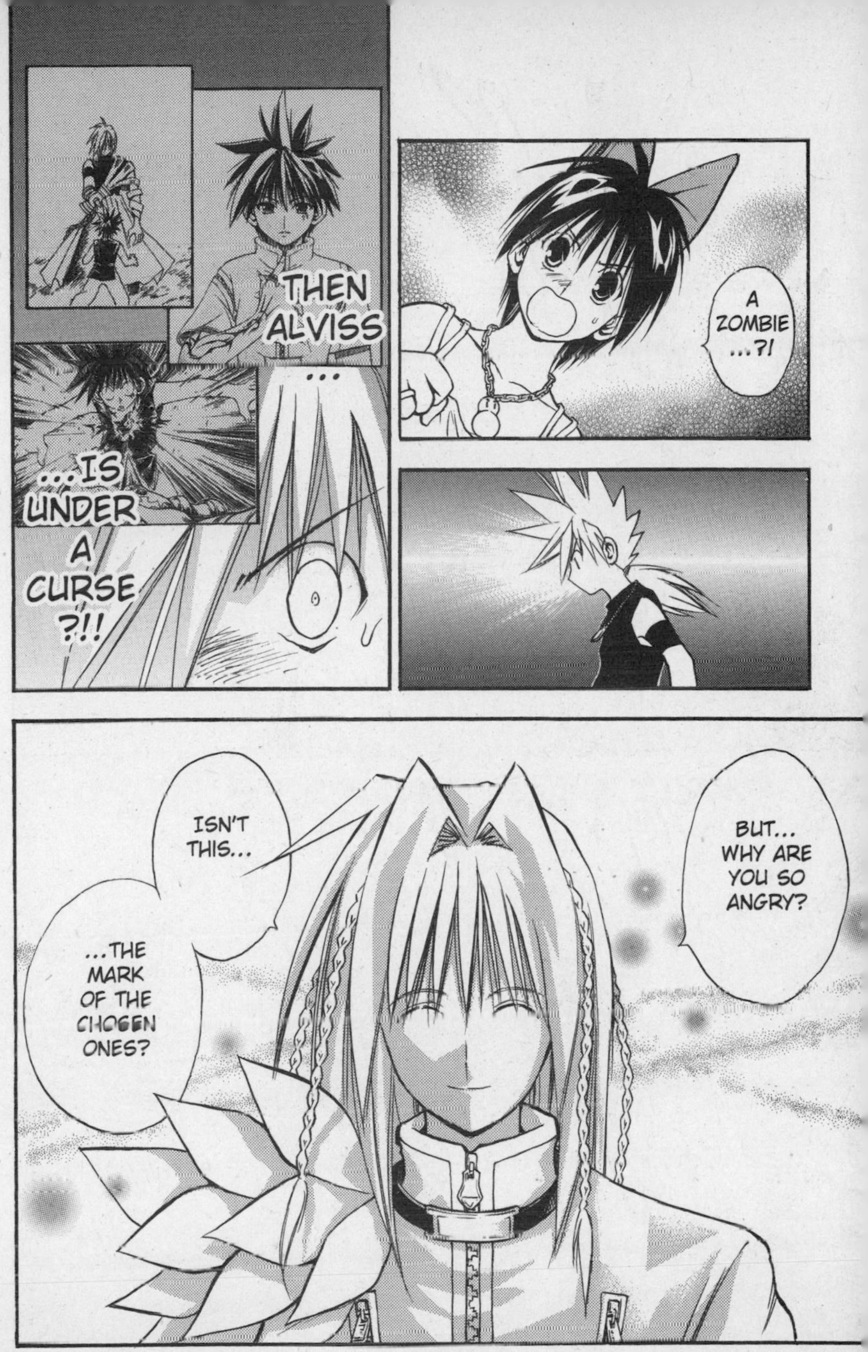
A ZOMBIE...?!
THEN ALVISS
...
...IS UNDER A CURSE?!!
BUT... WHY ARE YOU SO ANGRY?
ISN'T THIS...
...THE MARK OF THE CHOSEN ONES?

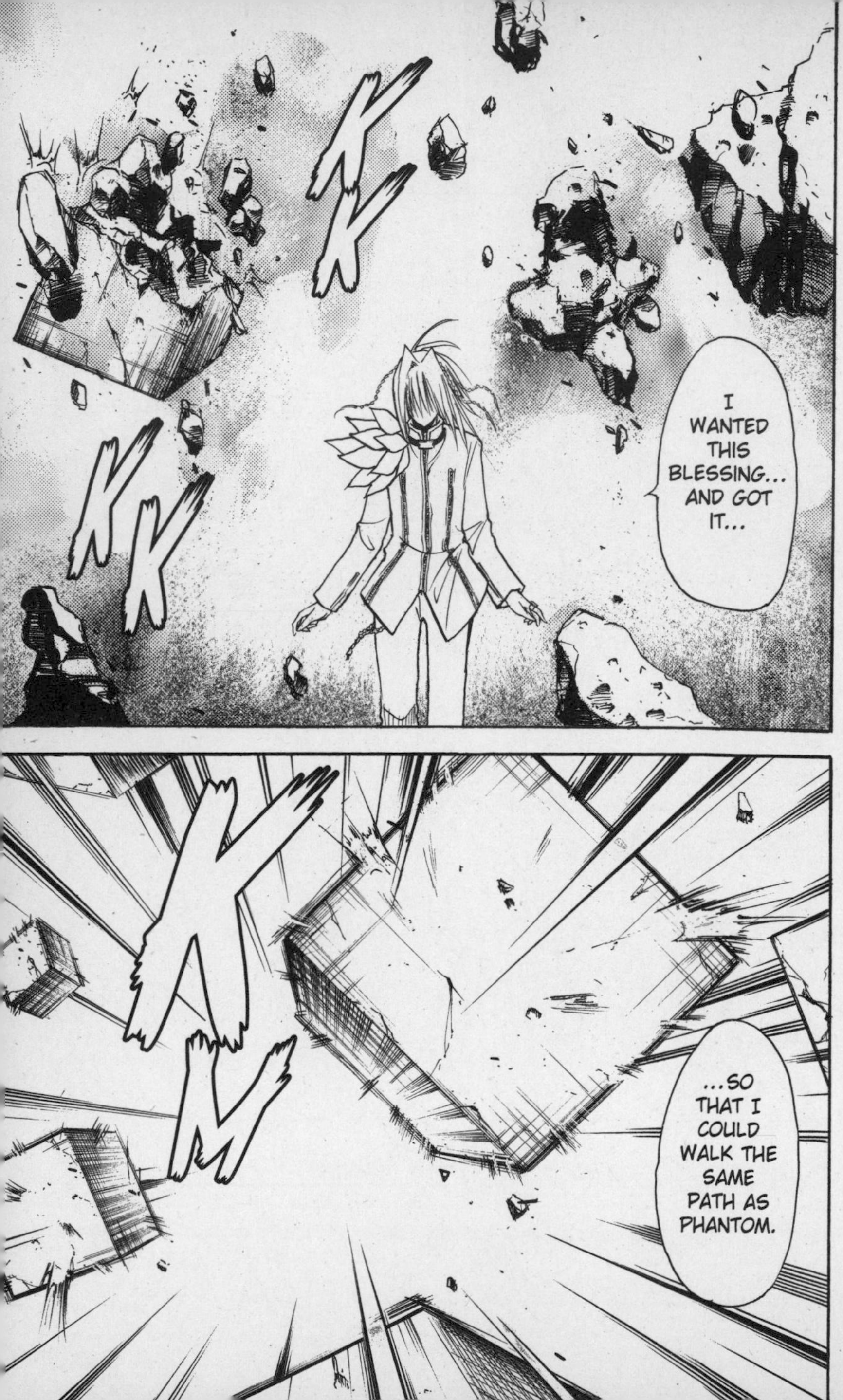
I WANTED THIS BLESSING... AND GOT IT...
KK
KK
...SO THAT I COULD WALK THE SAME PATH AS PHANTOM.

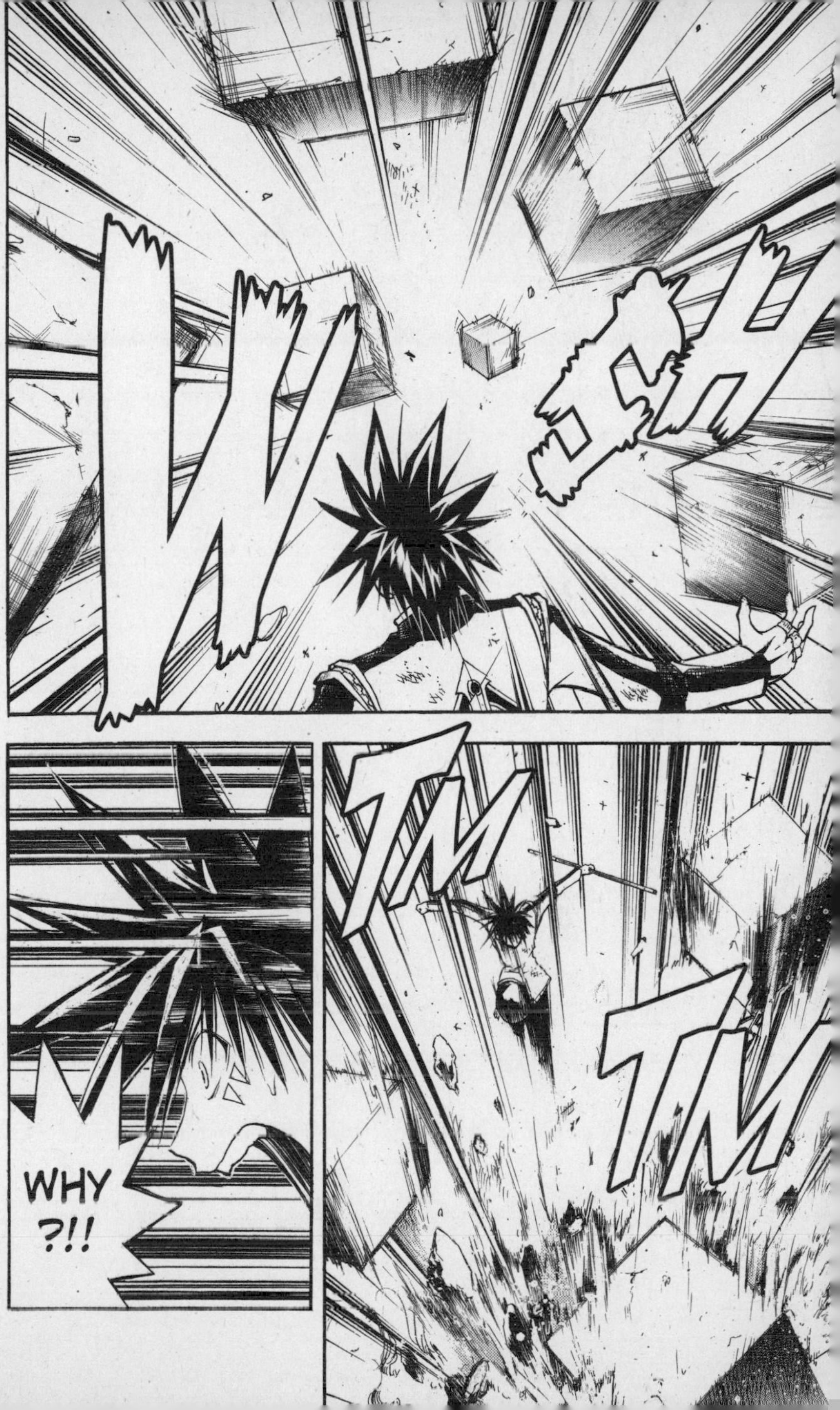
WSH
TM
TM
WHY ?!!

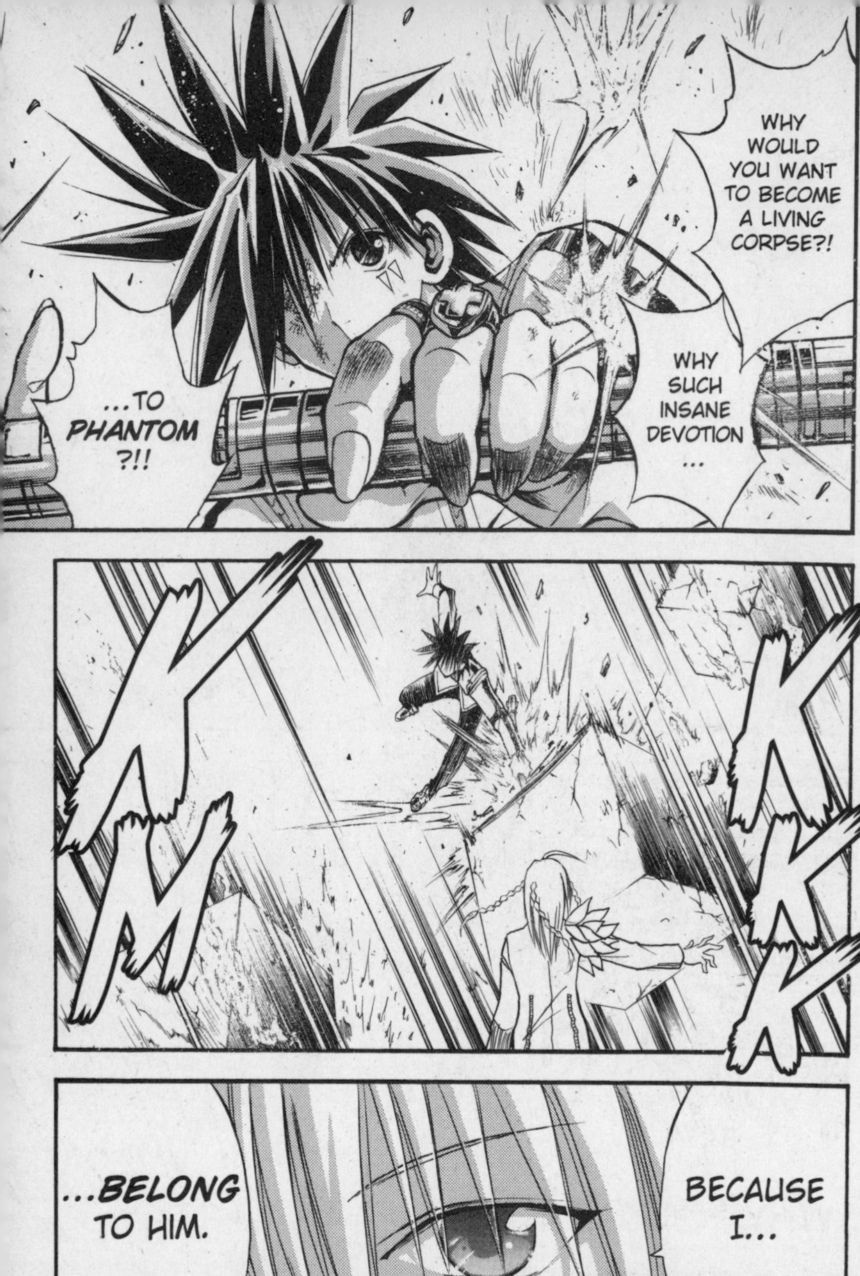
WHY WOULD YOU WANT TO BECOME A LIVING CORPSE?!
WHY SUCH INSANE DEVOTION ...
...TO *PHANTOM* ?!!
KKK
KM
BECAUSE I...
...*BELONG* TO HIM.

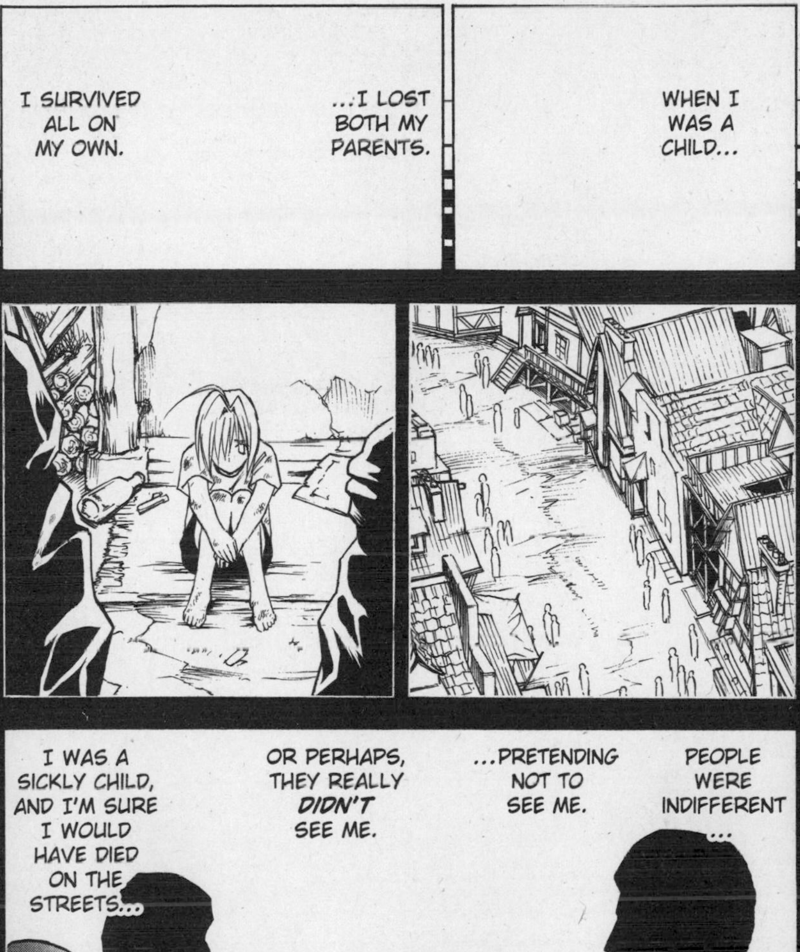
WHEN I WAS A CHILD...
...I LOST BOTH MY PARENTS.
I SURVIVED ALL ON MY OWN.
PEOPLE WERE INDIFFERENT...
...PRETENDING NOT TO SEE ME.
OR PERHAPS, THEY REALLY *DIDN'T* SEE ME.
I WAS A SICKLY CHILD, AND I'M SURE I WOULD HAVE DIED ON THE STREETS...

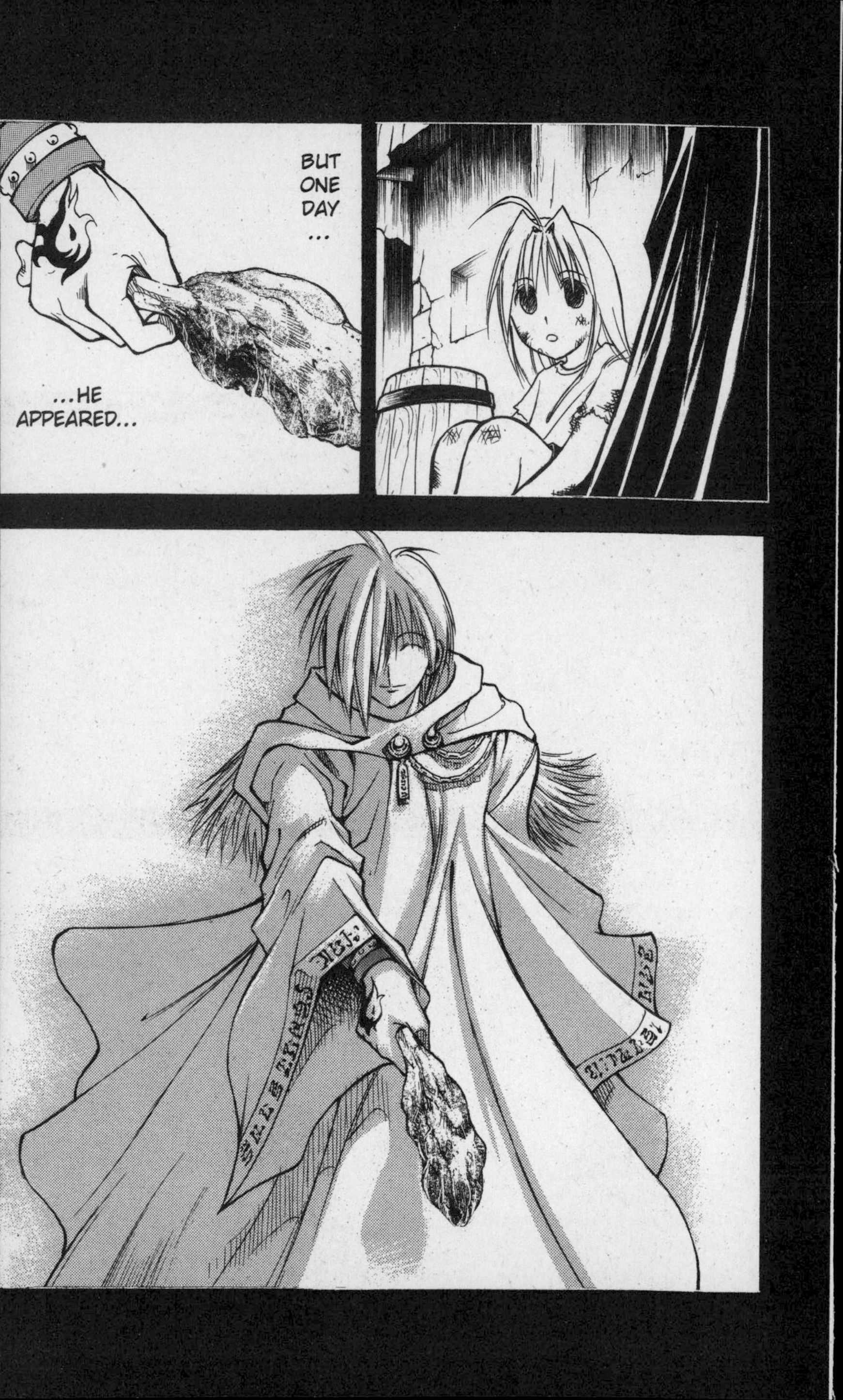
BUT ONE DAY ...
...HE APPEARED...

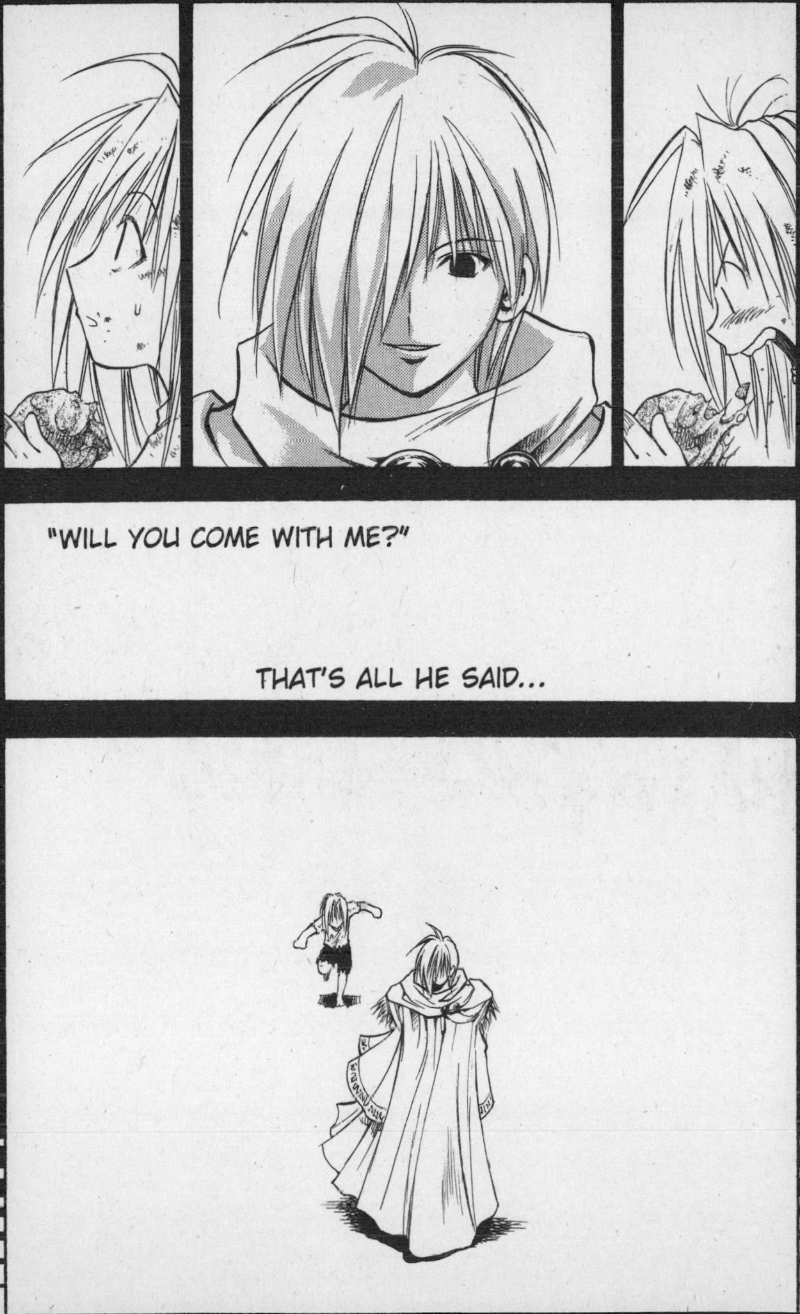
"WILL YOU COME WITH ME?"
THAT'S ALL HE SAID...

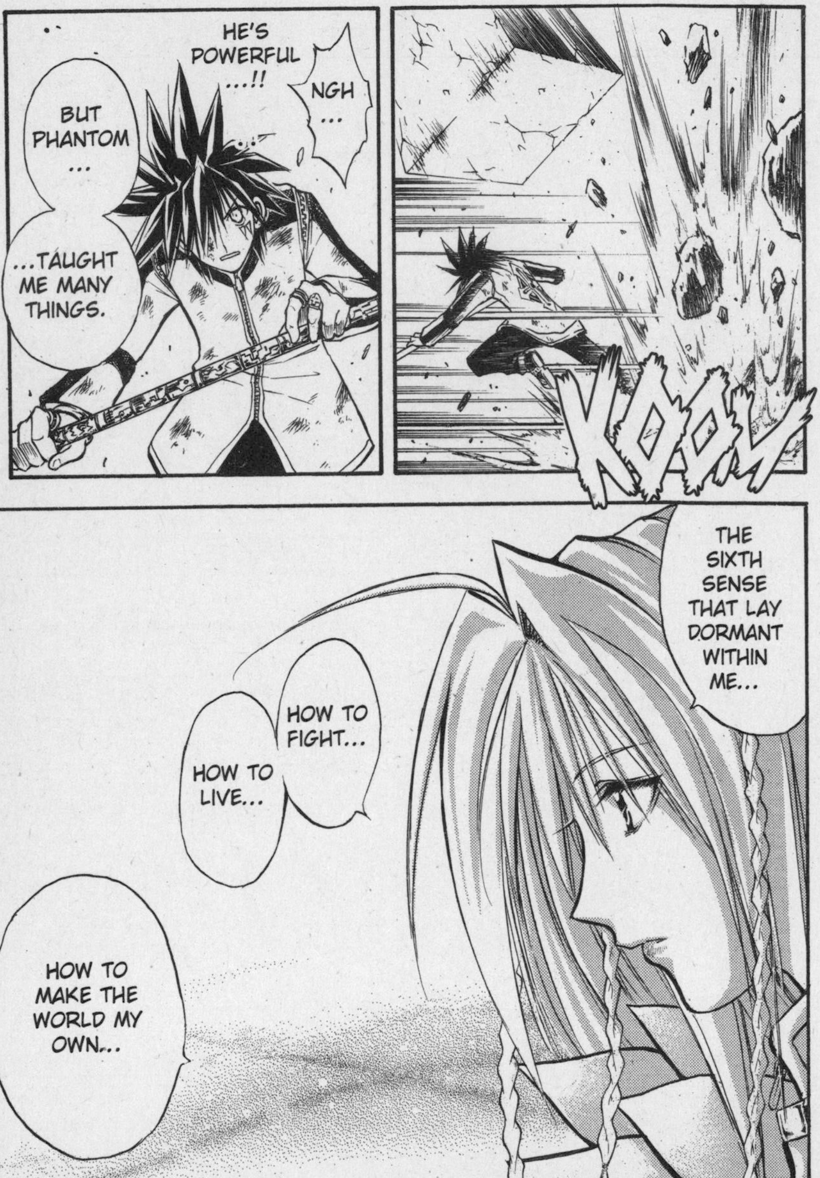
KOOM
NGH...
HE'S POWERFUL...!!
BUT PHANTOM...
...TAUGHT ME MANY THINGS.
THE SIXTH SENSE THAT LAY DORMANT WITHIN ME...
HOW TO FIGHT...
HOW TO LIVE...
HOW TO MAKE THE WORLD MY OWN...

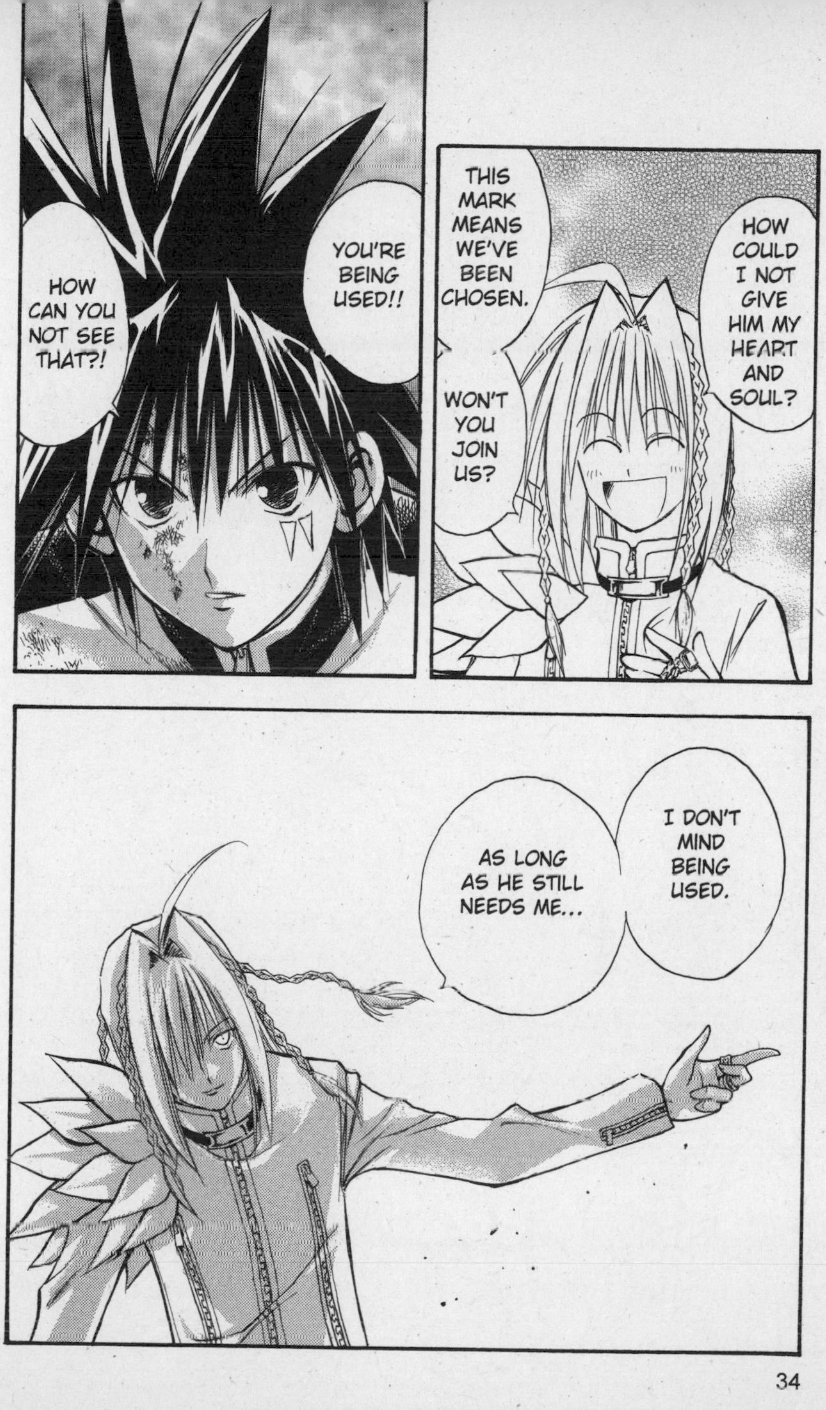
HOW COULD I NOT GIVE HIM MY HEART AND SOUL?
THIS MARK MEANS WE'VE BEEN CHOSEN.
WON'T YOU JOIN US?
YOU'RE BEING USED!!
HOW CAN YOU NOT SEE THAT?!
I DON'T MIND BEING USED.
AS LONG AS HE STILL NEEDS ME...

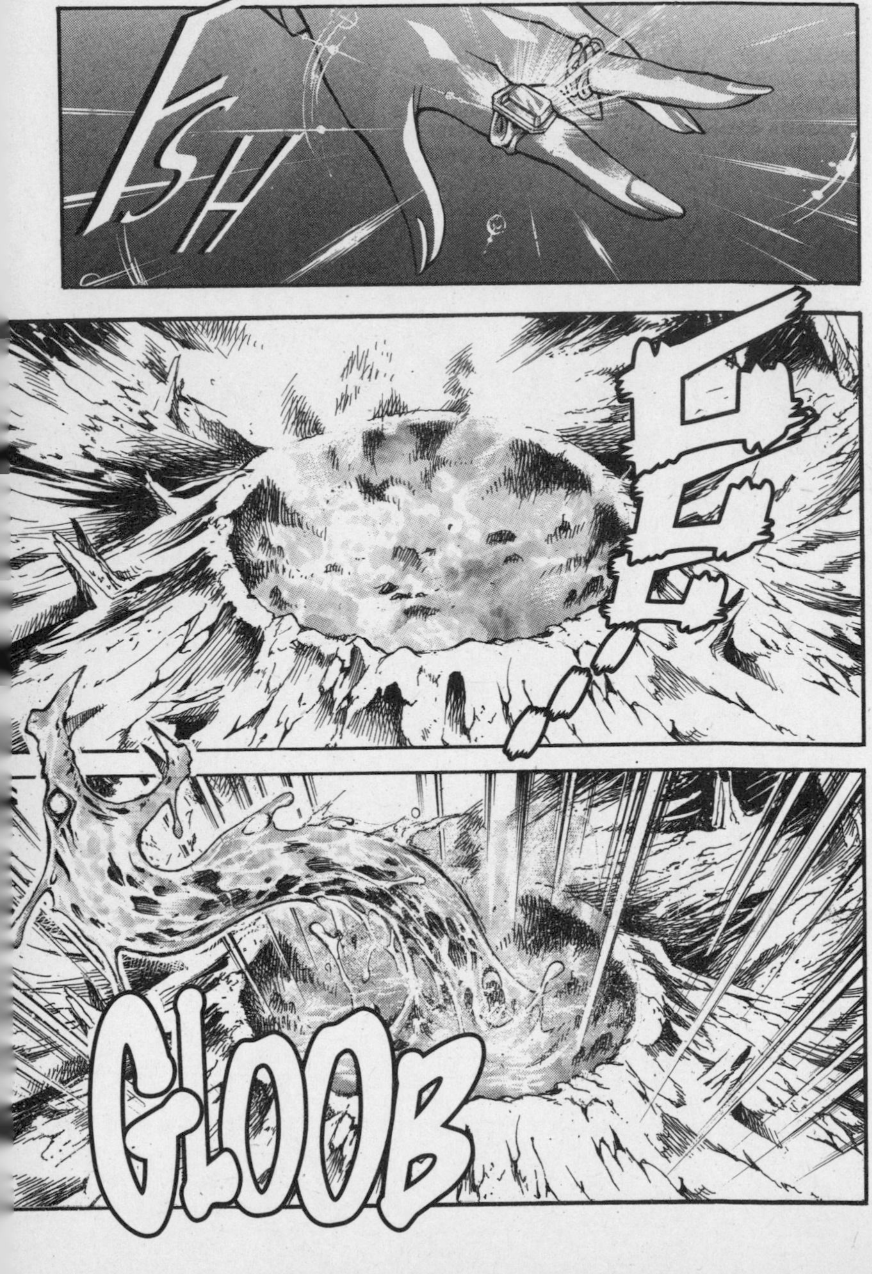
FSH
GLOOB

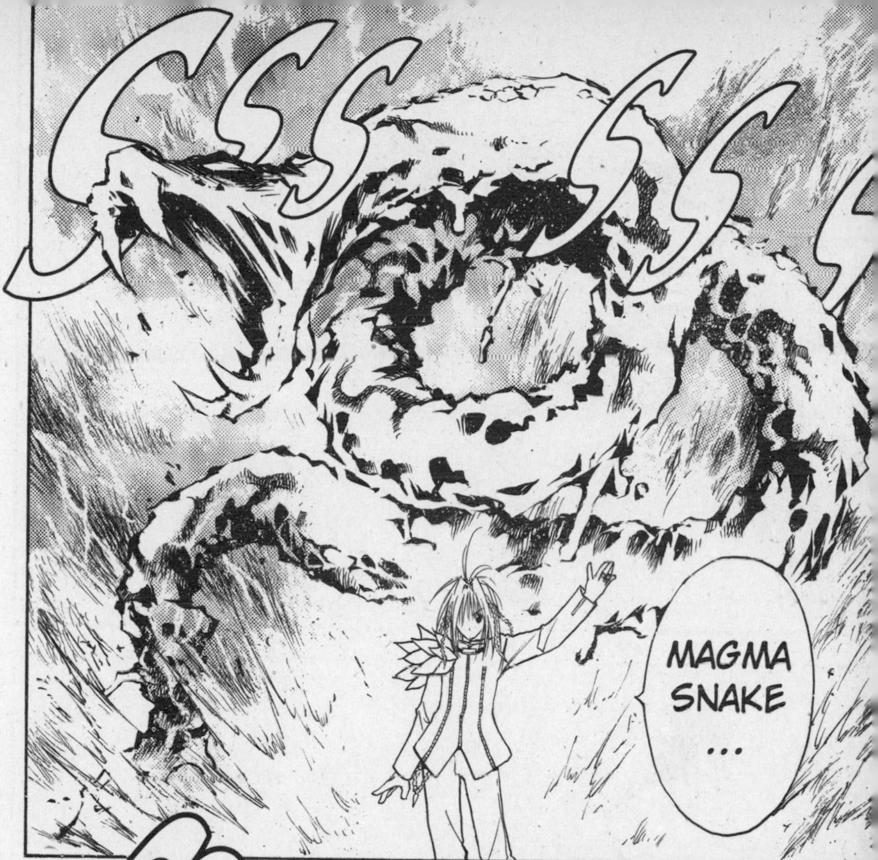
MAGMA SNAKE ...

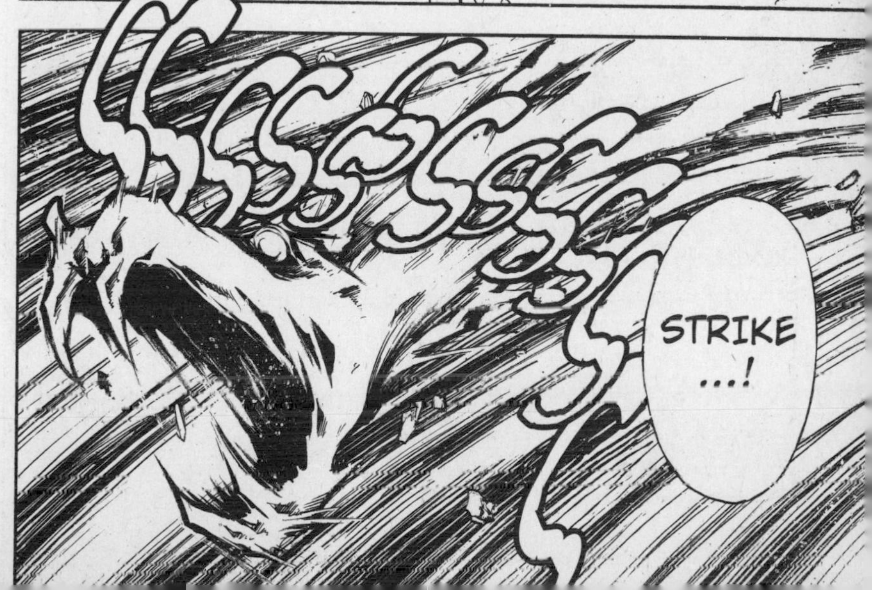
STRIKE ...!

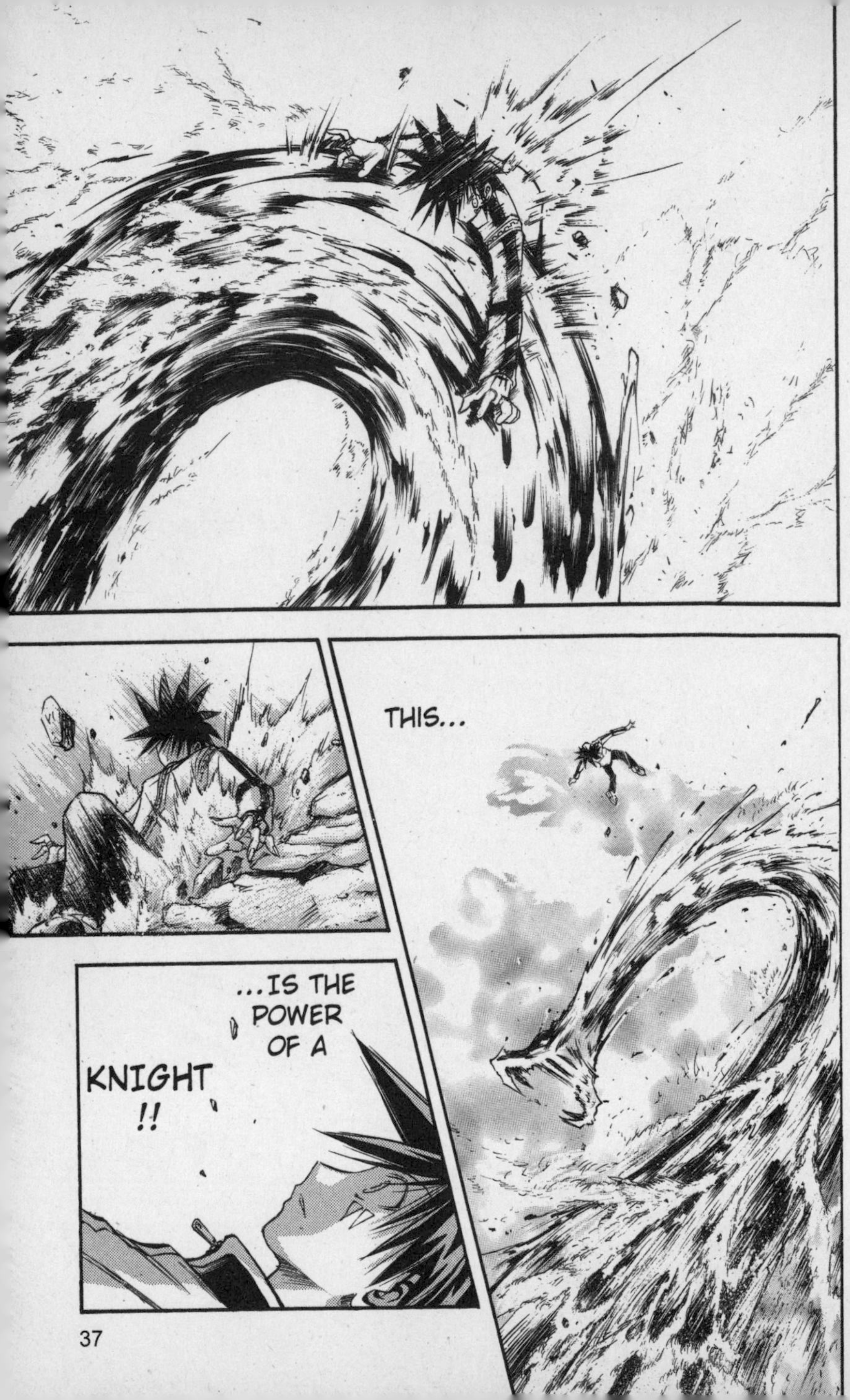
THIS...
...IS THE POWER OF A KNIGHT!!

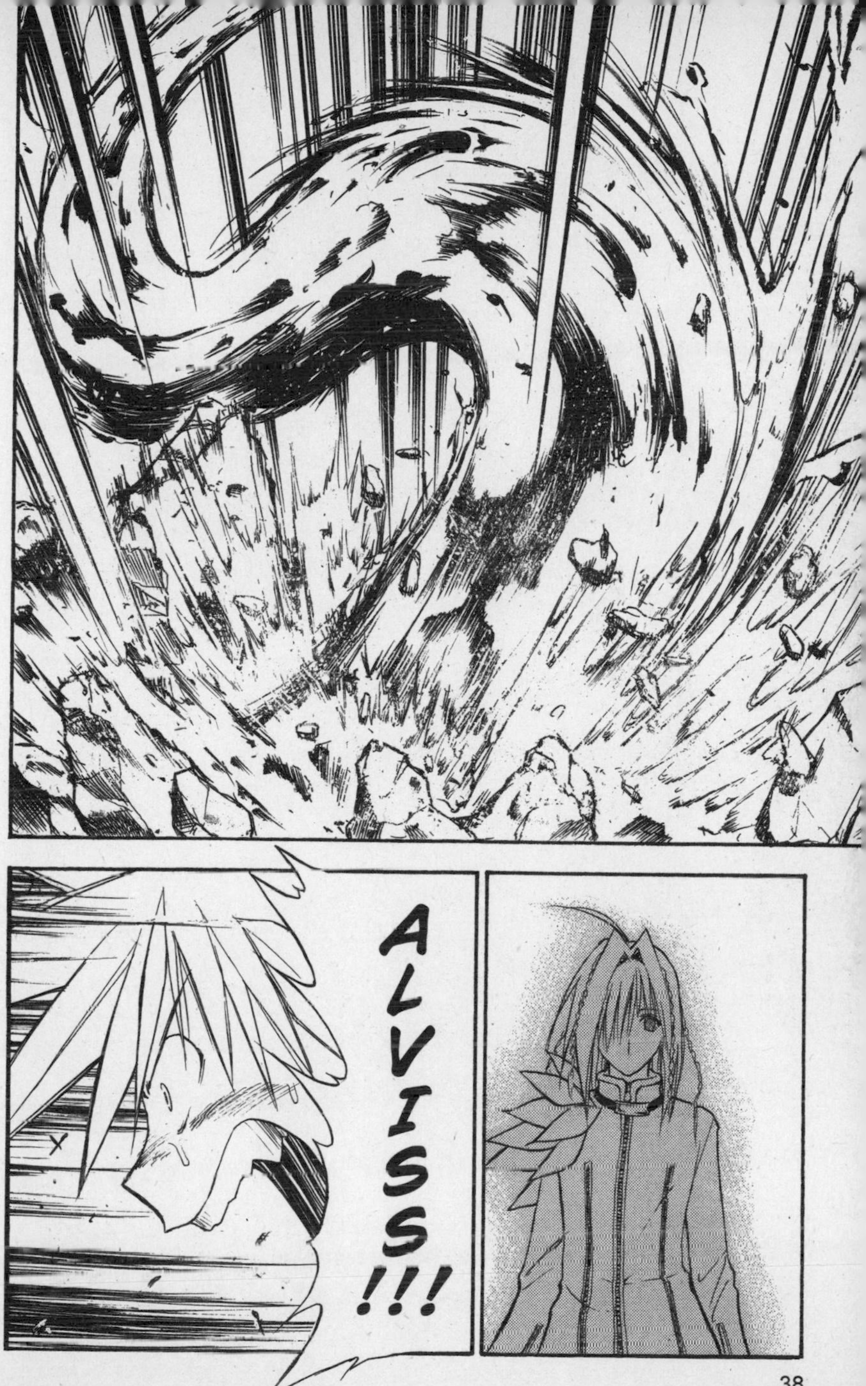
ALVISS!!!

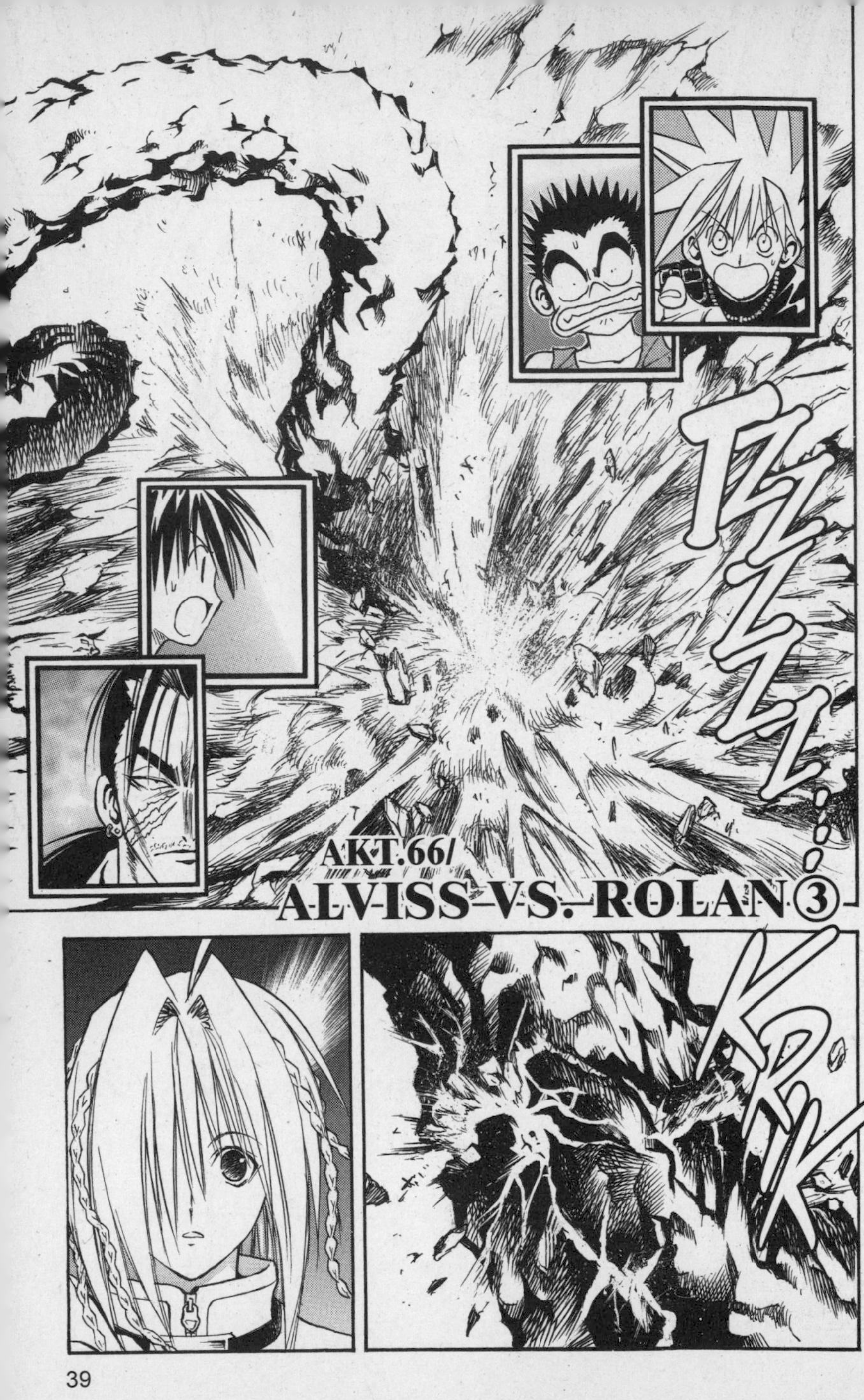
TZZZZZ...
AKT.66/
ALVISS VS. ROLAN ③
KRIK

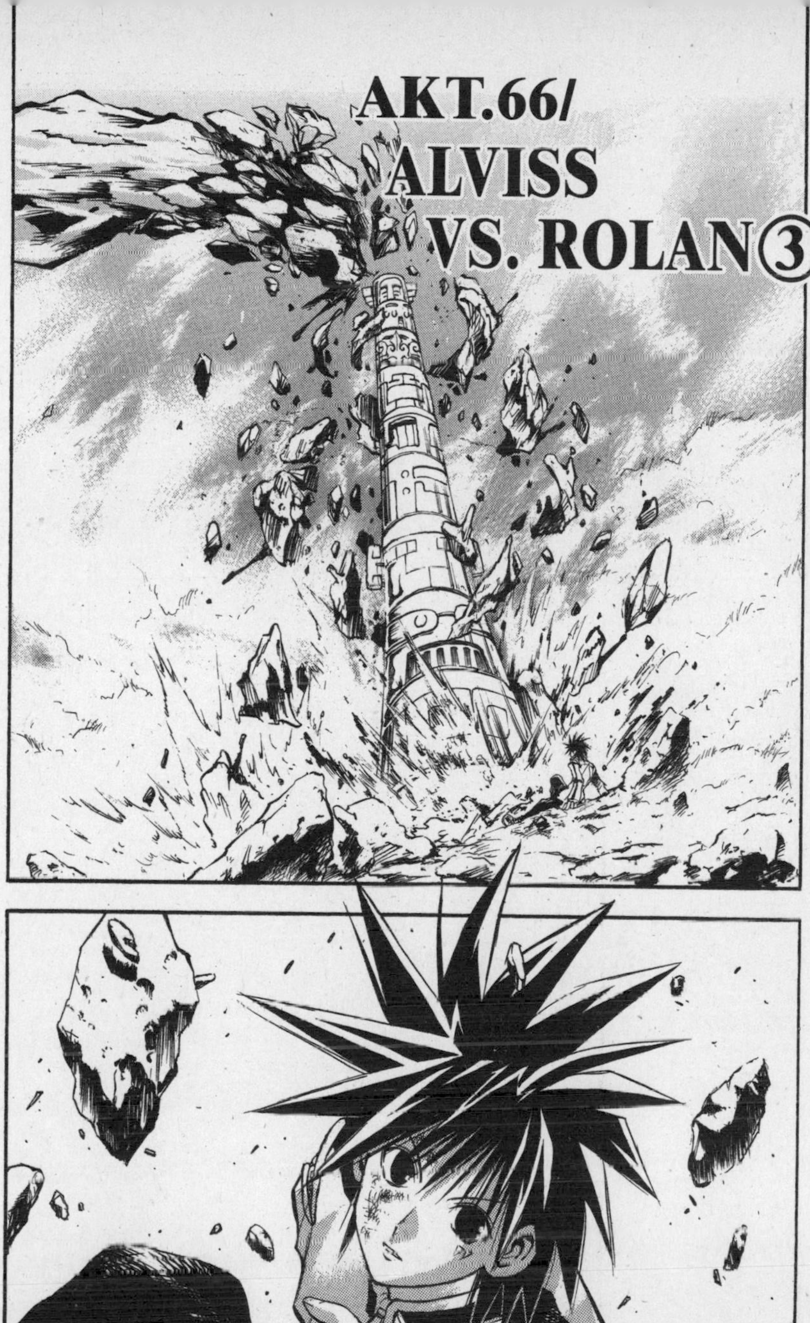
AKT.66/
ALVISS
VS. ROLAN ③

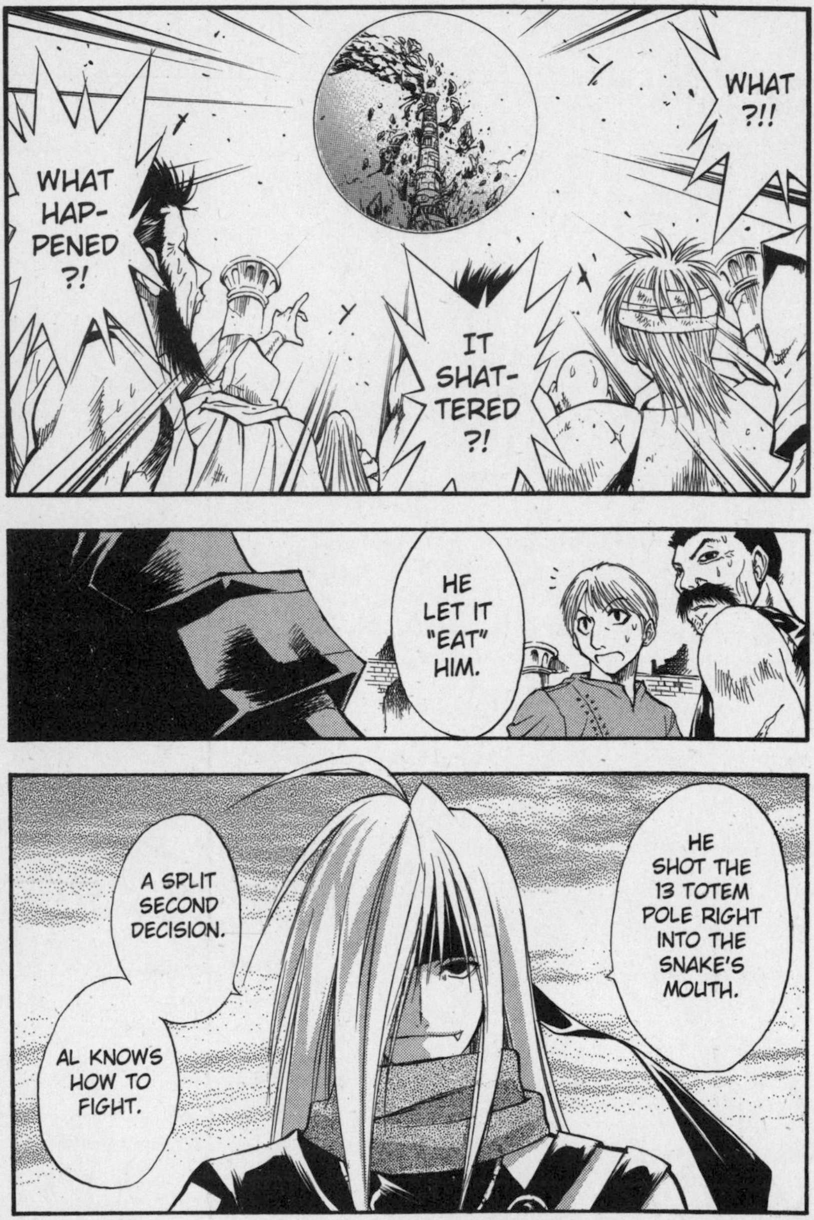
WHAT ?!!
IT SHAT-TERED ?!
WHAT HAP-PENED ?!
HE LET IT "EAT" HIM.
HE SHOT THE 13 TOTEM POLE RIGHT INTO THE SNAKE'S MOUTH.
A SPLIT SECOND DECISION.
AL KNOWS HOW TO FIGHT.

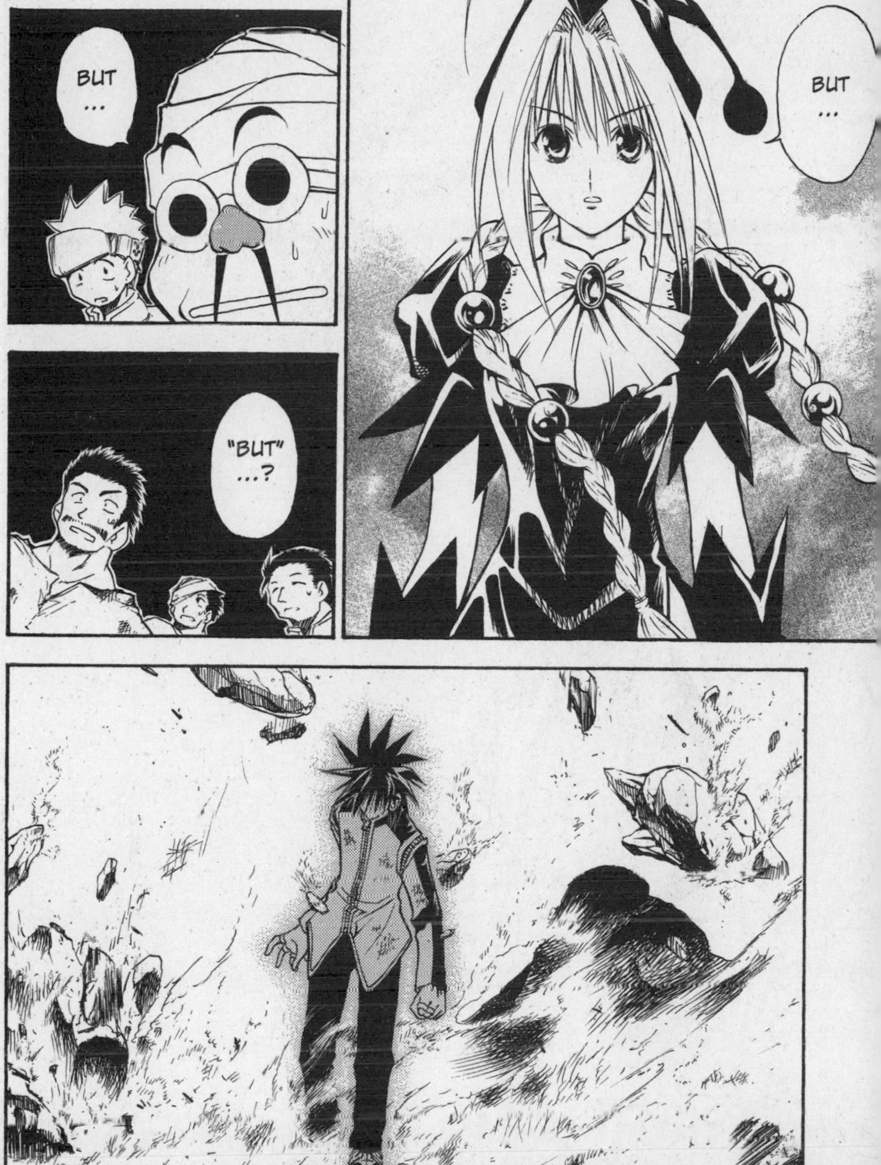
BUT ...
BUT ...
"BUT" ...?

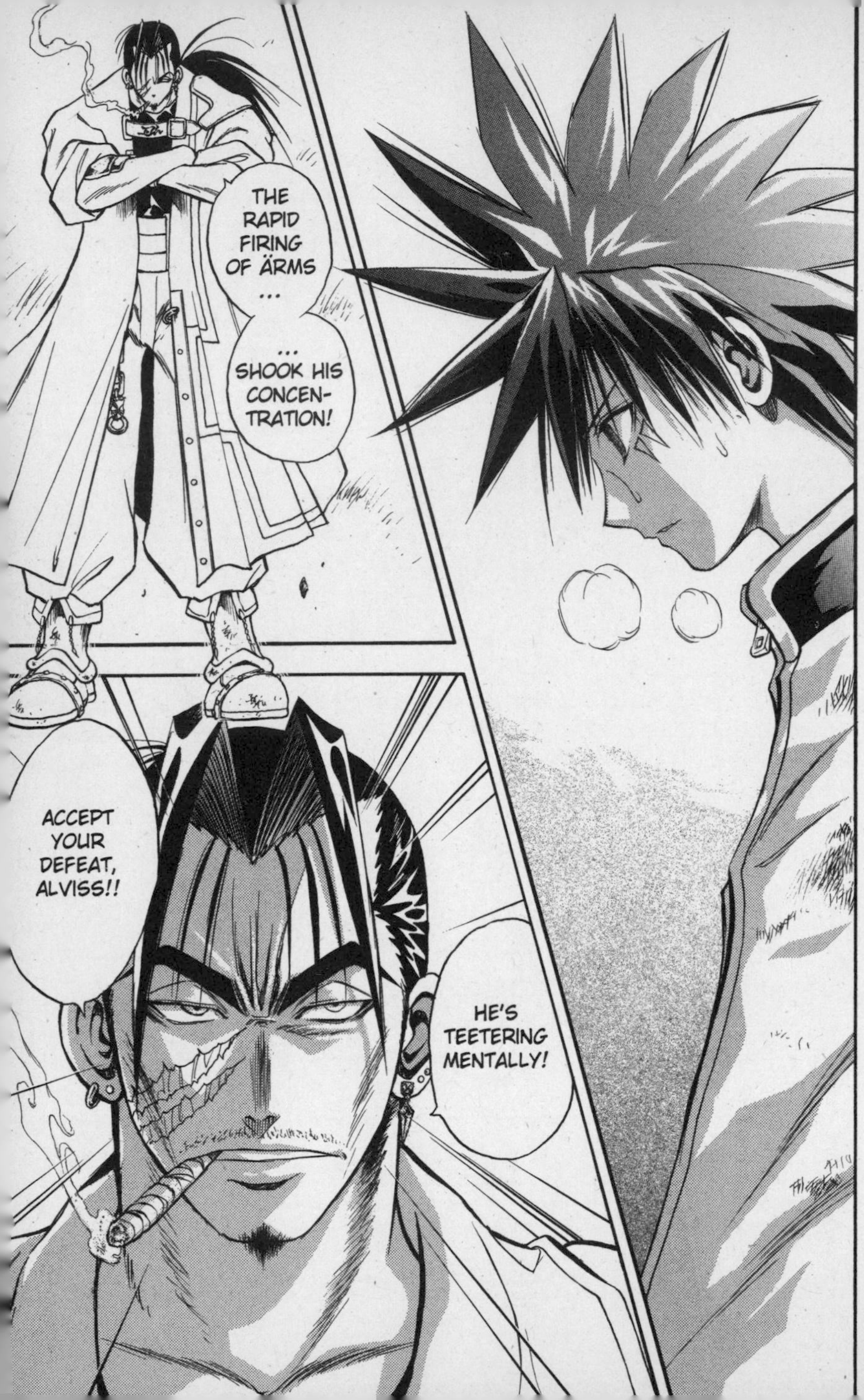
THE RAPID FIRING OF ÄRMS ...
... SHOOK HIS CONCENTRATION!
HE'S TEETERING MENTALLY!
ACCEPT YOUR DEFEAT, ALVISS!!

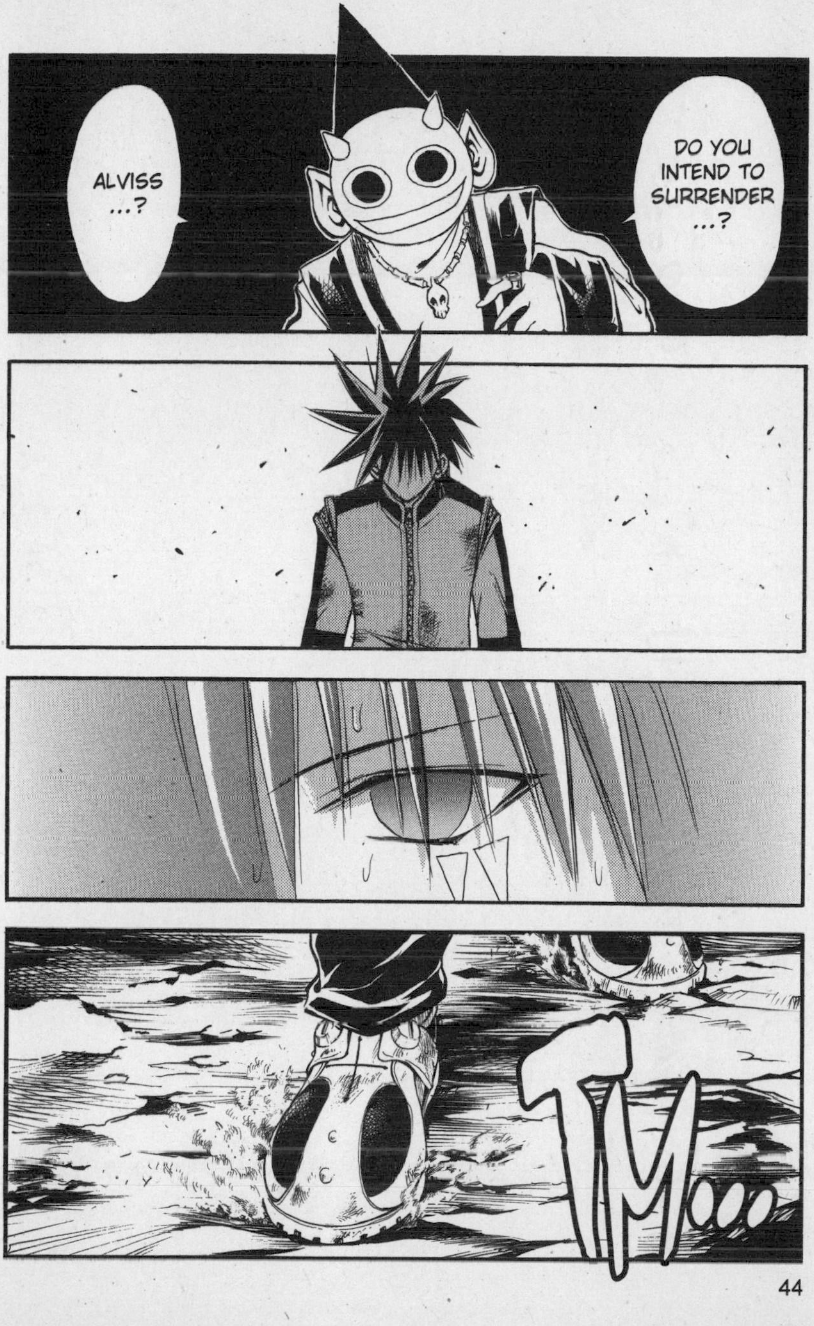
DO YOU INTEND TO SURRENDER ...?
ALVISS ...?
TM...

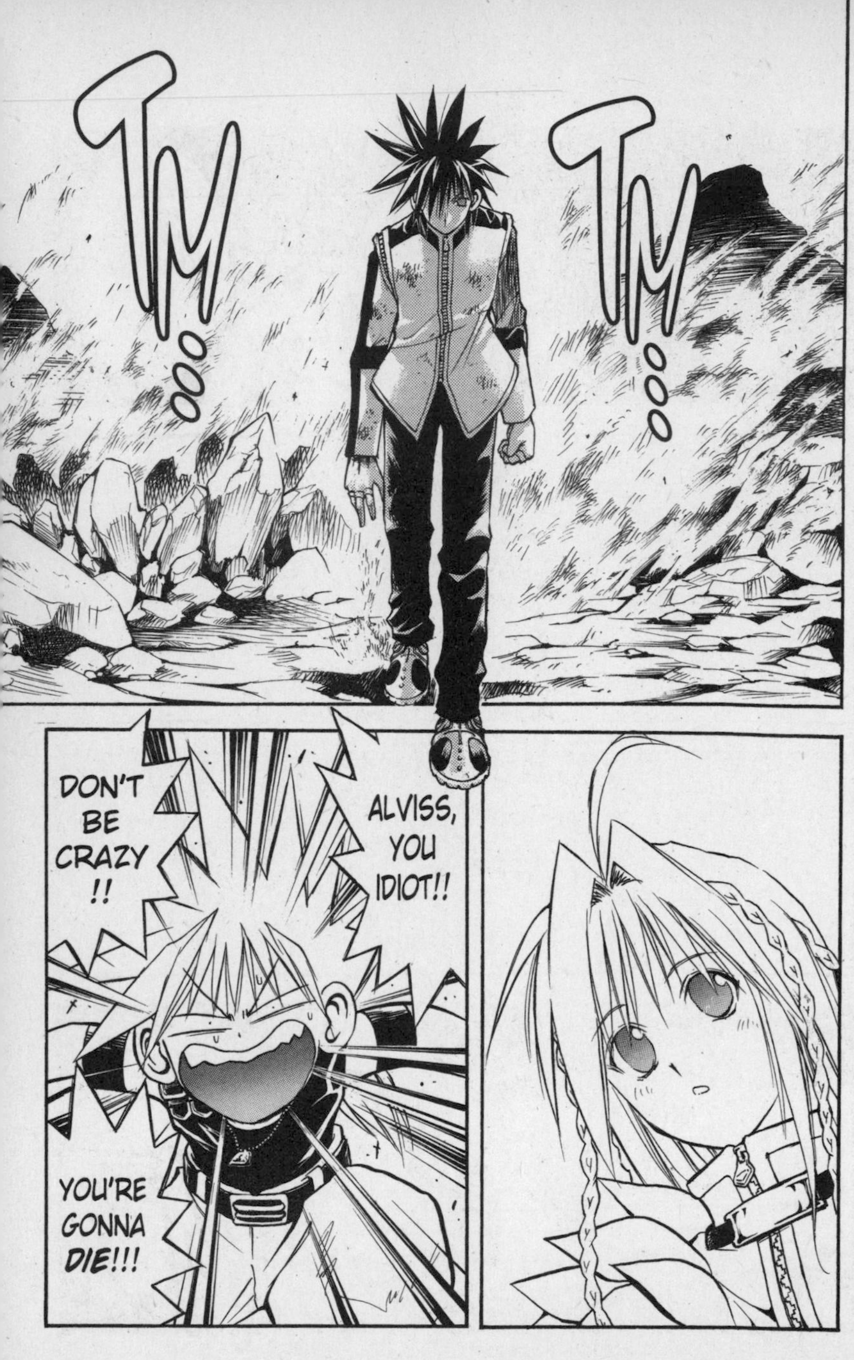
TM...
TM...
ALVISS, YOU IDIOT!!
DON'T BE CRAZY!!
YOU'RE GONNA DIE!!!

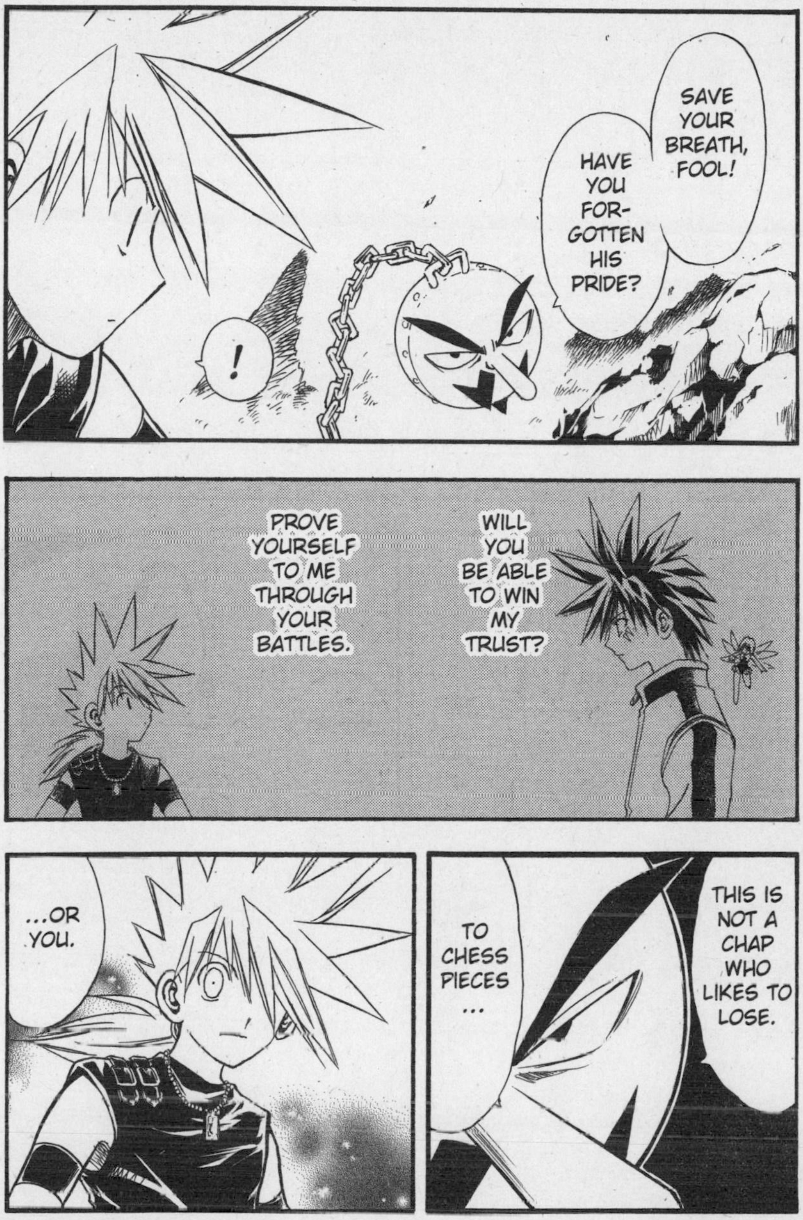
SAVE YOUR BREATH, FOOL!
HAVE YOU FOR-GOTTEN HIS PRIDE?
!
WILL YOU BE ABLE TO WIN MY TRUST?
PROVE YOURSELF TO ME THROUGH YOUR BATTLES.
THIS IS NOT A CHAP WHO LIKES TO LOSE.
TO CHESS PIECES ...
...OR YOU.

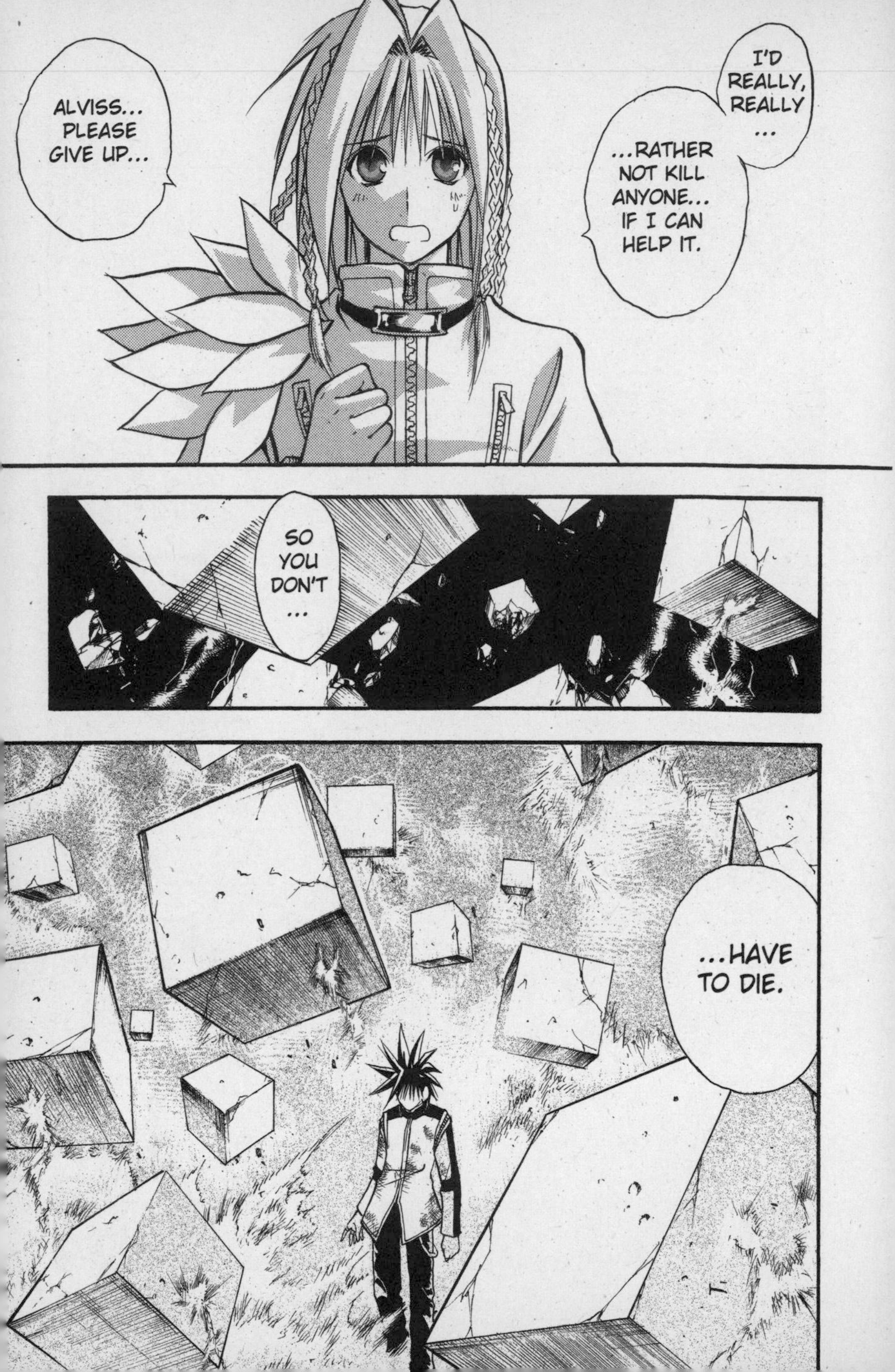
I'D REALLY, REALLY ...
...RATHER NOT KILL ANYONE... IF I CAN HELP IT.
ALVISS... PLEASE GIVE UP...
SO YOU DON'T ...
...HAVE TO DIE.

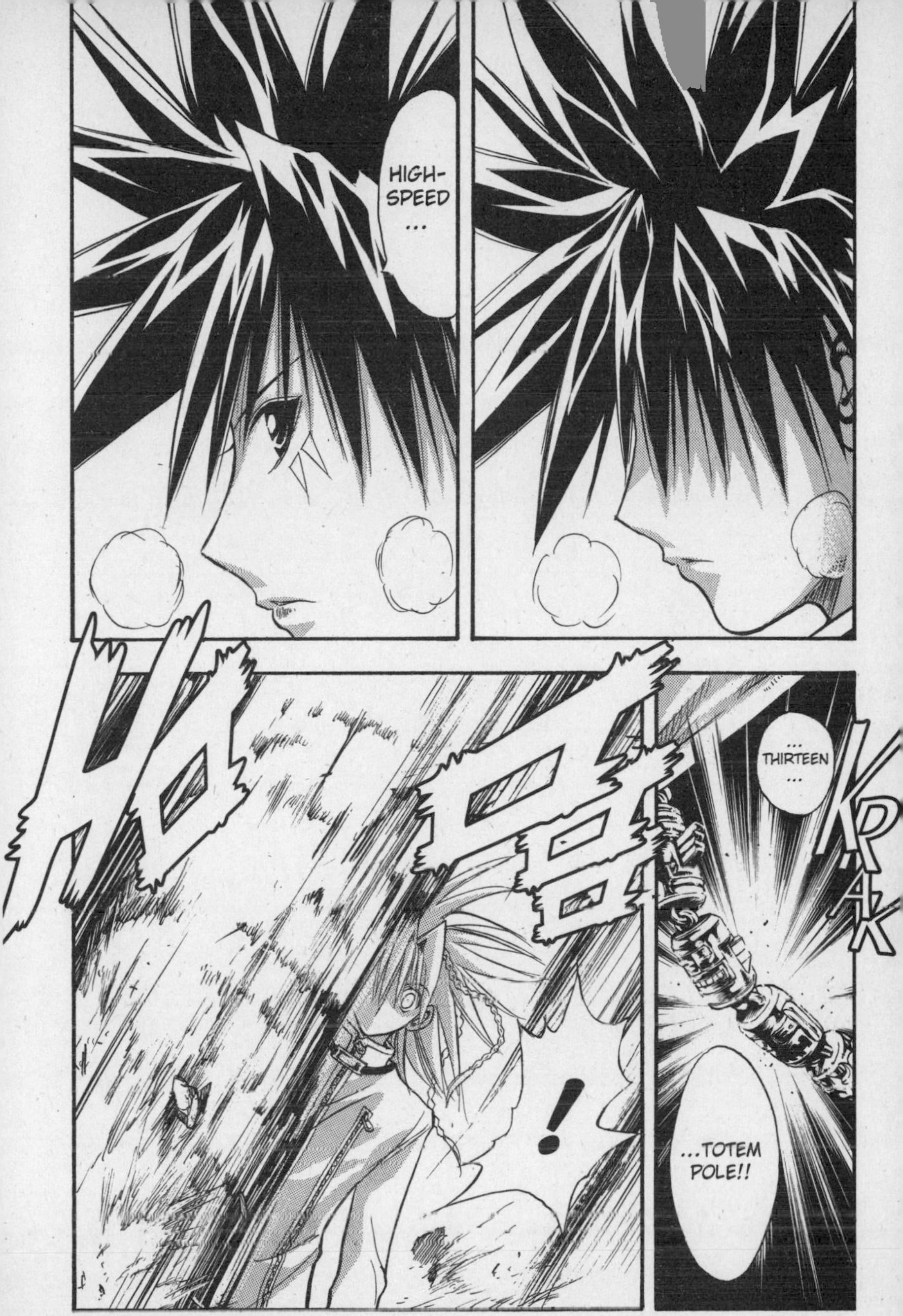
HIGH-SPEED ...
... THIRTEEN ...
KRAK
...TOTEM POLE!!

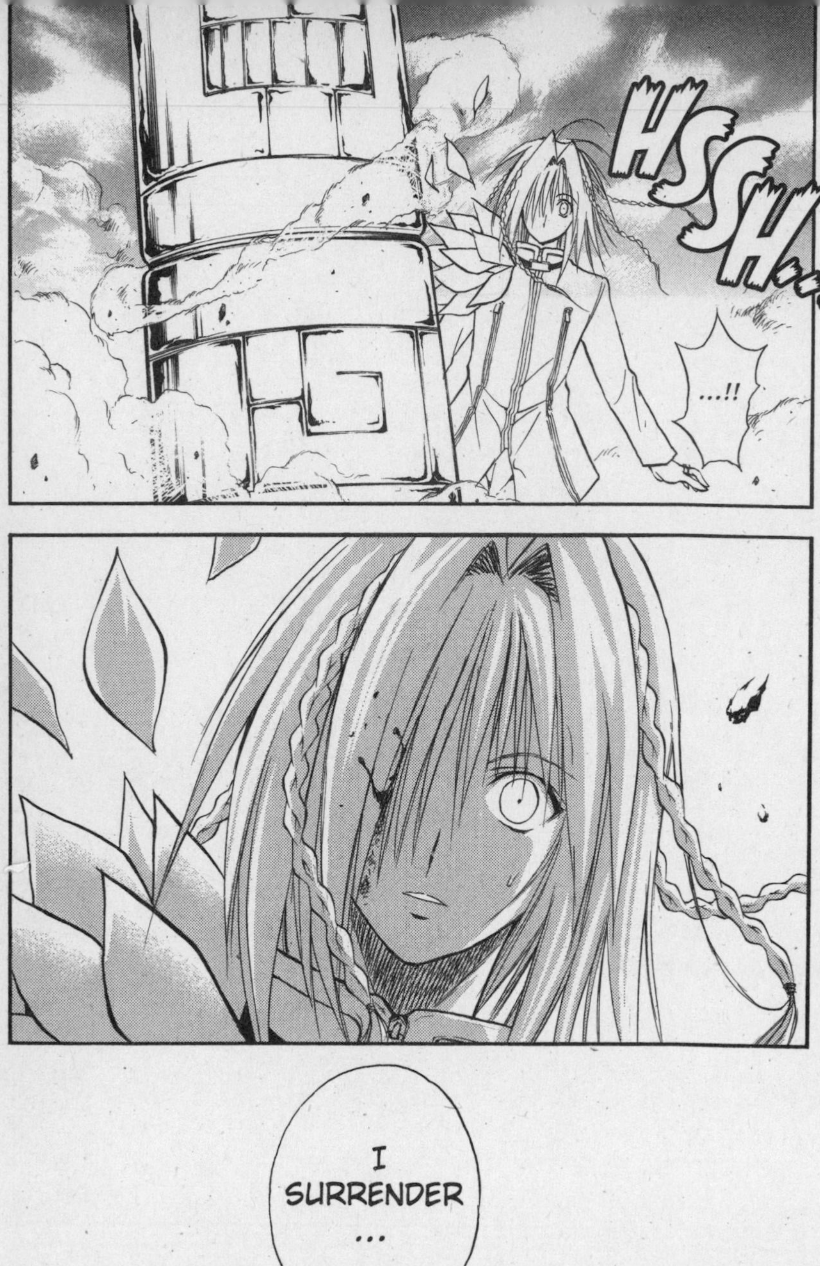
HSSH...
...!!
I SURRENDER ...

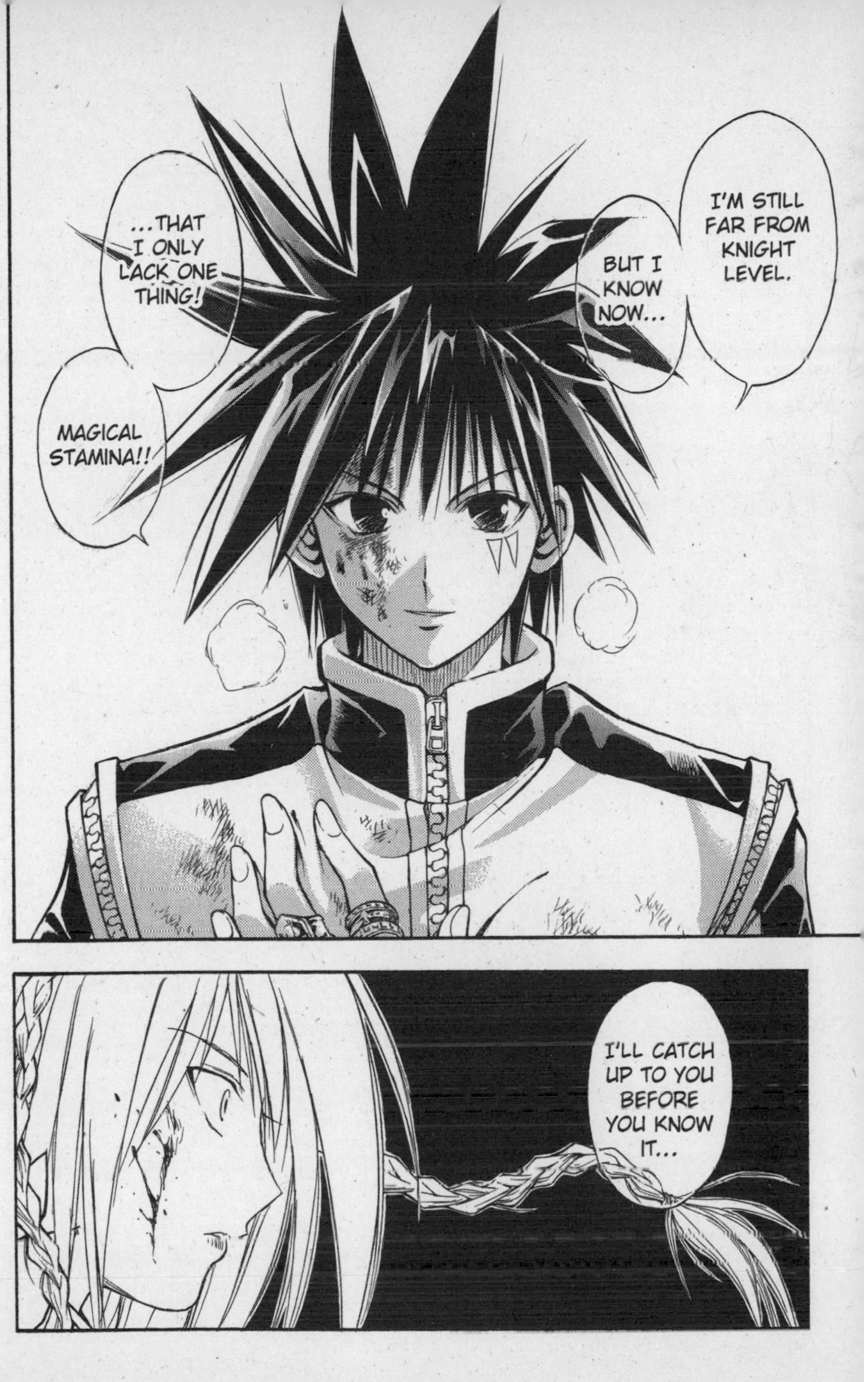
I'M STILL FAR FROM KNIGHT LEVEL.
BUT I KNOW NOW...
...THAT I ONLY LACK ONE THING!
MAGICAL STAMINA!!
I'LL CATCH UP TO YOU BEFORE YOU KNOW IT...

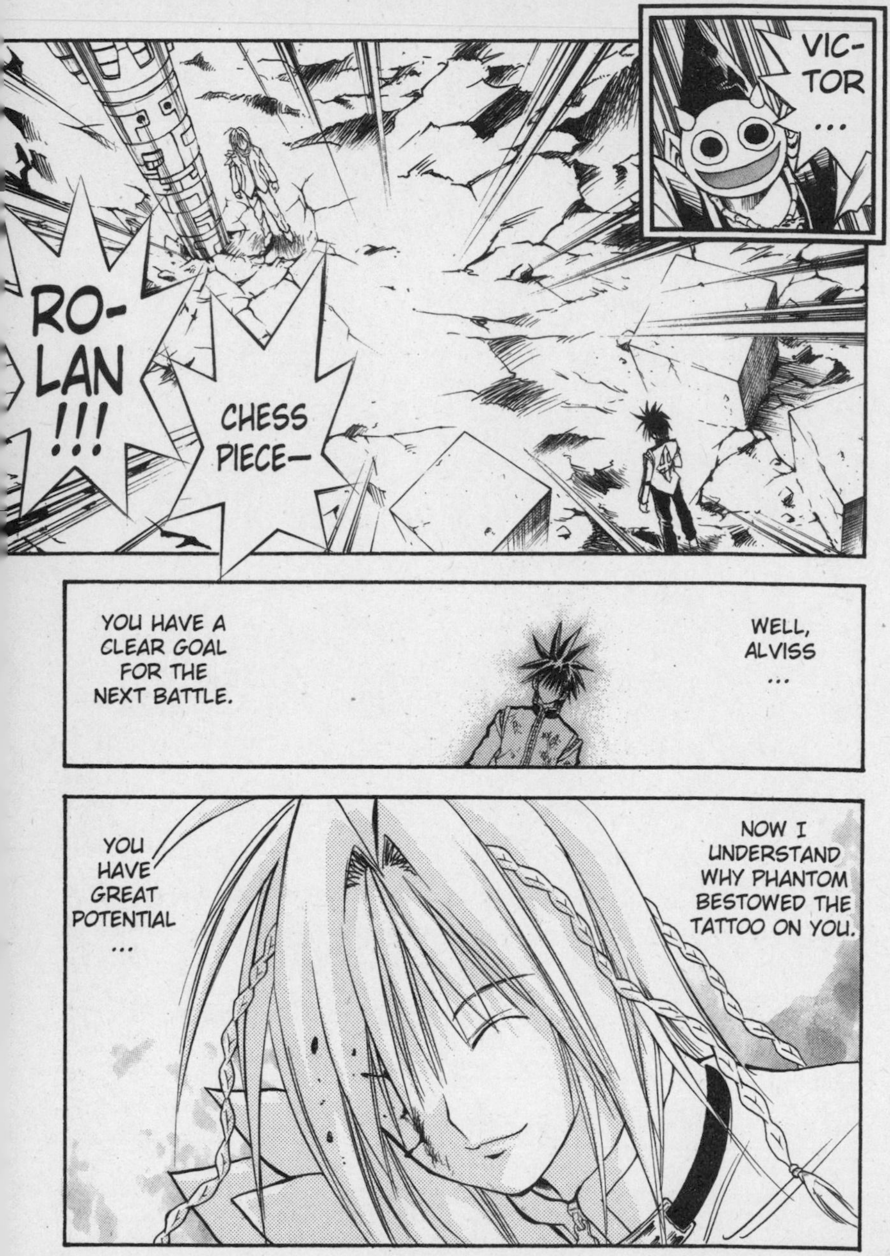
VIC-TOR ...
CHESS PIECE—
RO-LAN!!!
WELL, ALVISS ...
YOU HAVE A CLEAR GOAL FOR THE NEXT BATTLE.
NOW I UNDERSTAND WHY PHANTOM BESTOWED THE TATTOO ON YOU.
YOU HAVE GREAT POTENTIAL ...

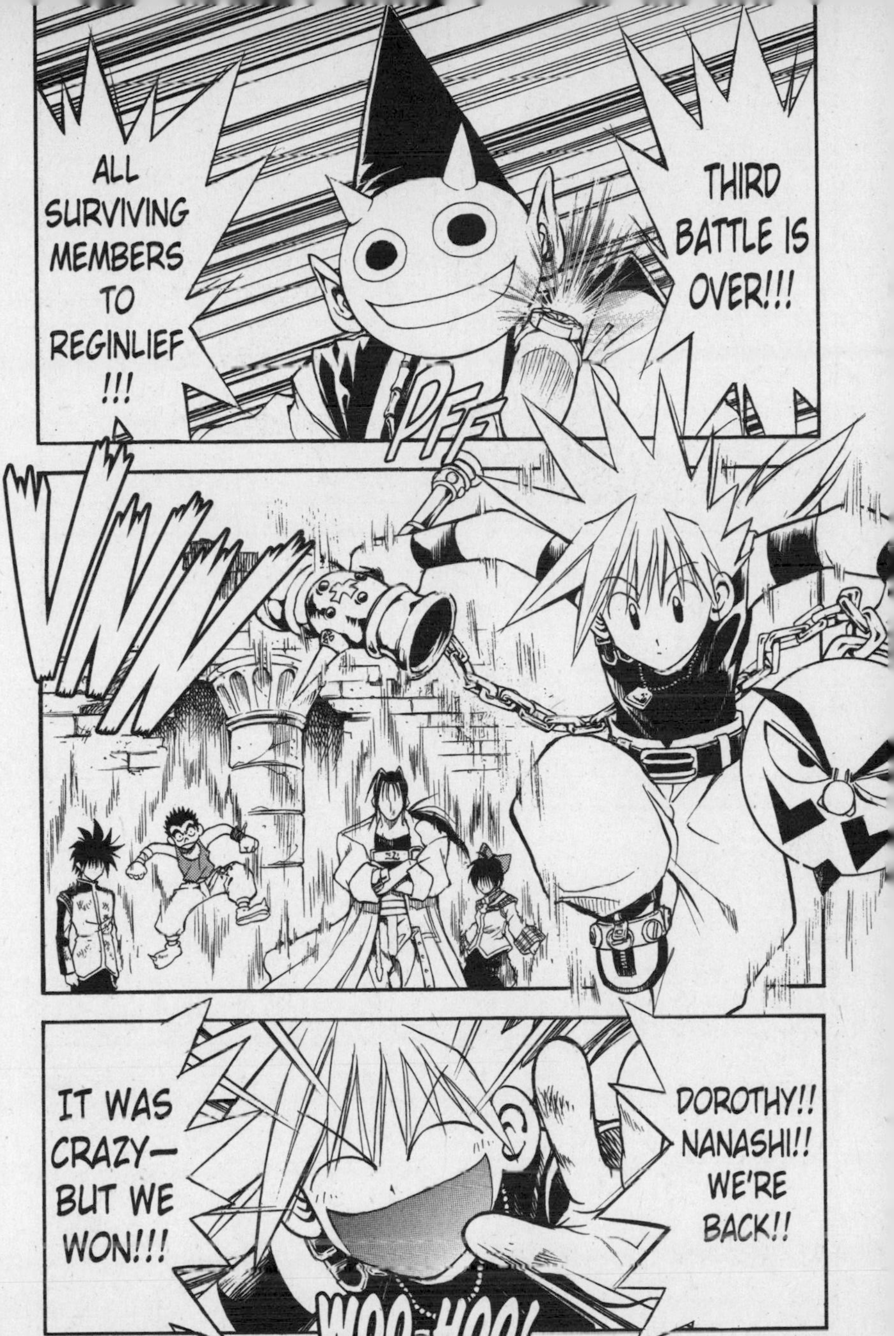
THIRD BATTLE IS OVER!!!
ALL SURVIVING MEMBERS TO REGINLIEF!!!
PFF
DOROTHY!! NANASHI!! WE'RE BACK!!
IT WAS CRAZY— BUT WE WON!!!
WOO-HOO!

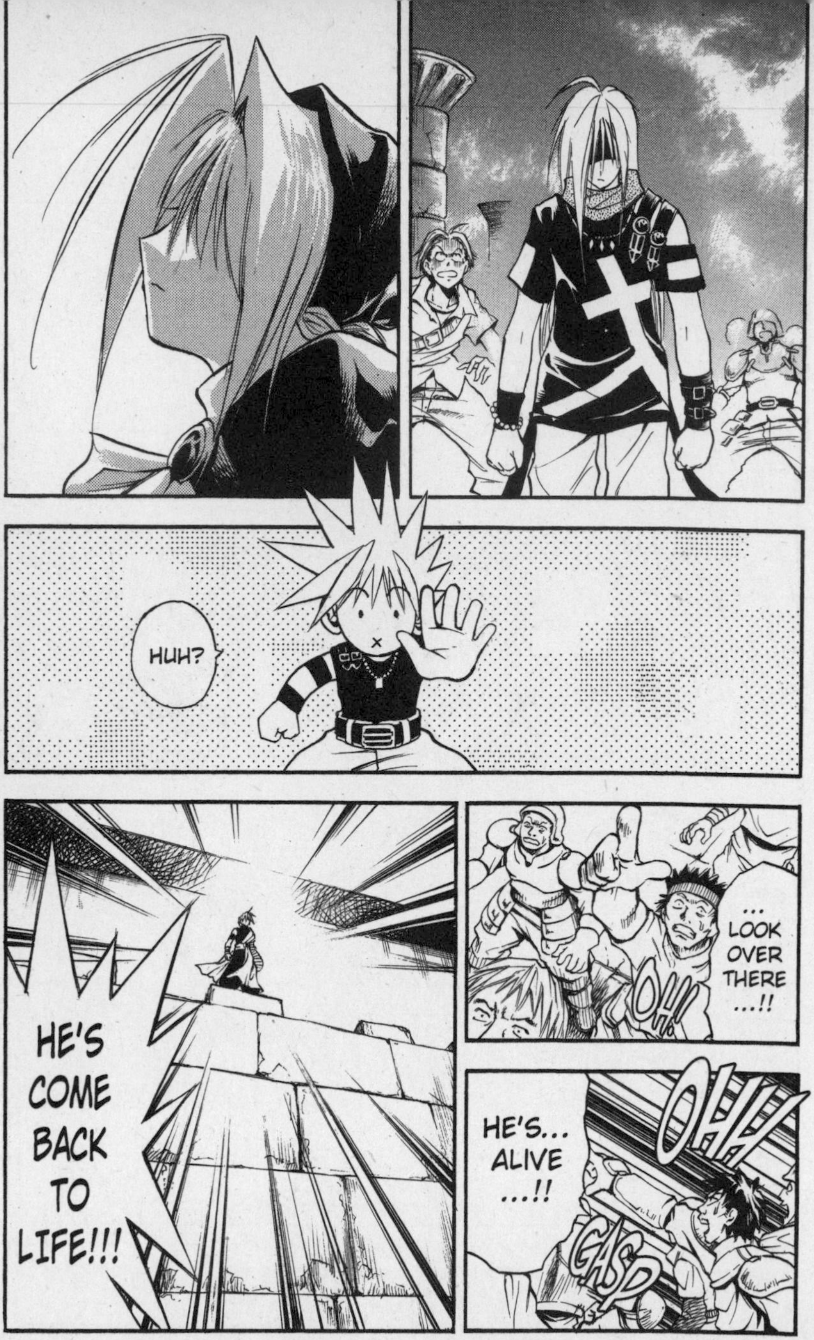
HUH?
...LOOK OVER THERE ...!!
OH!!
HE'S... ALIVE ...!!
OHH
GASP
HE'S COME BACK TO LIFE!!!

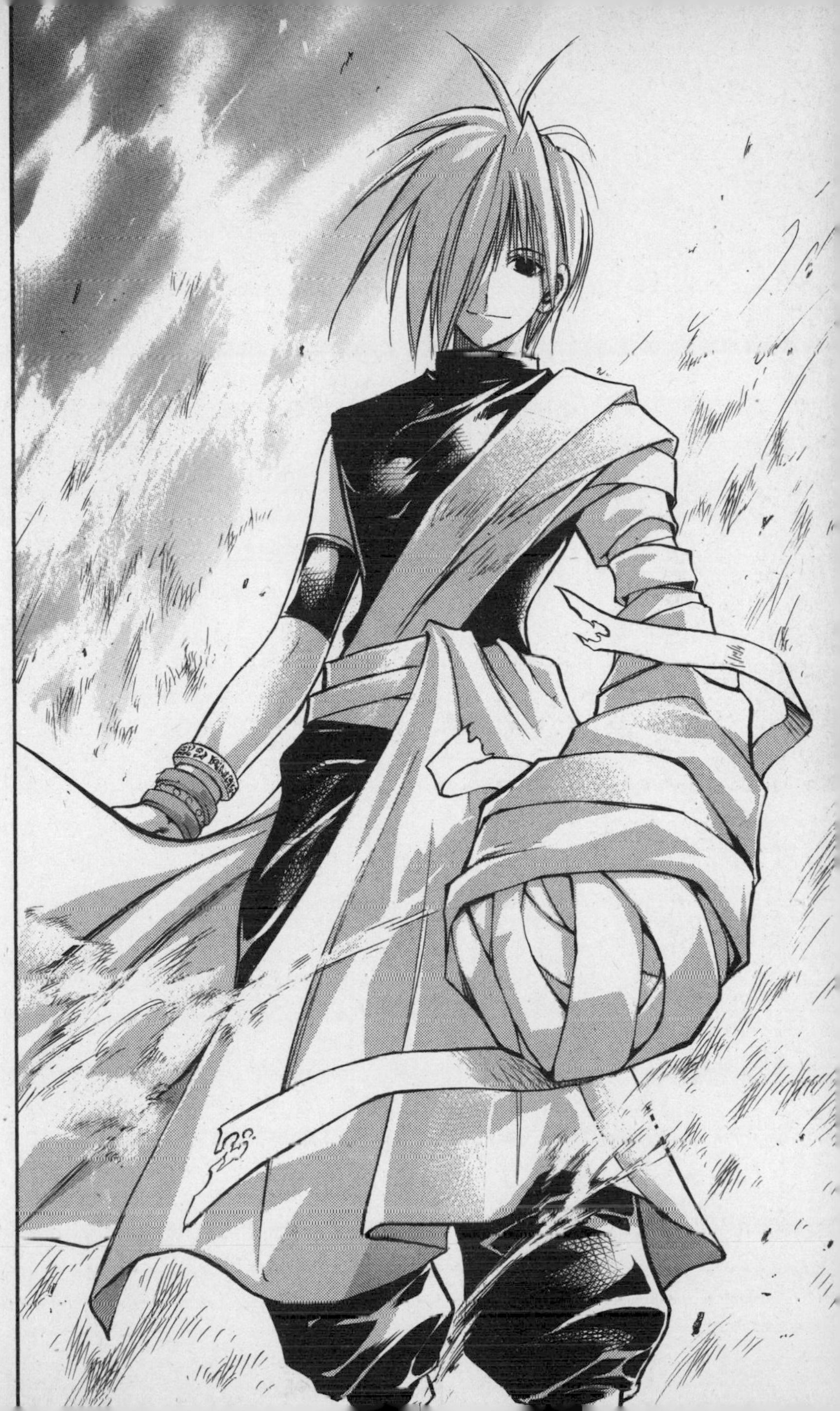

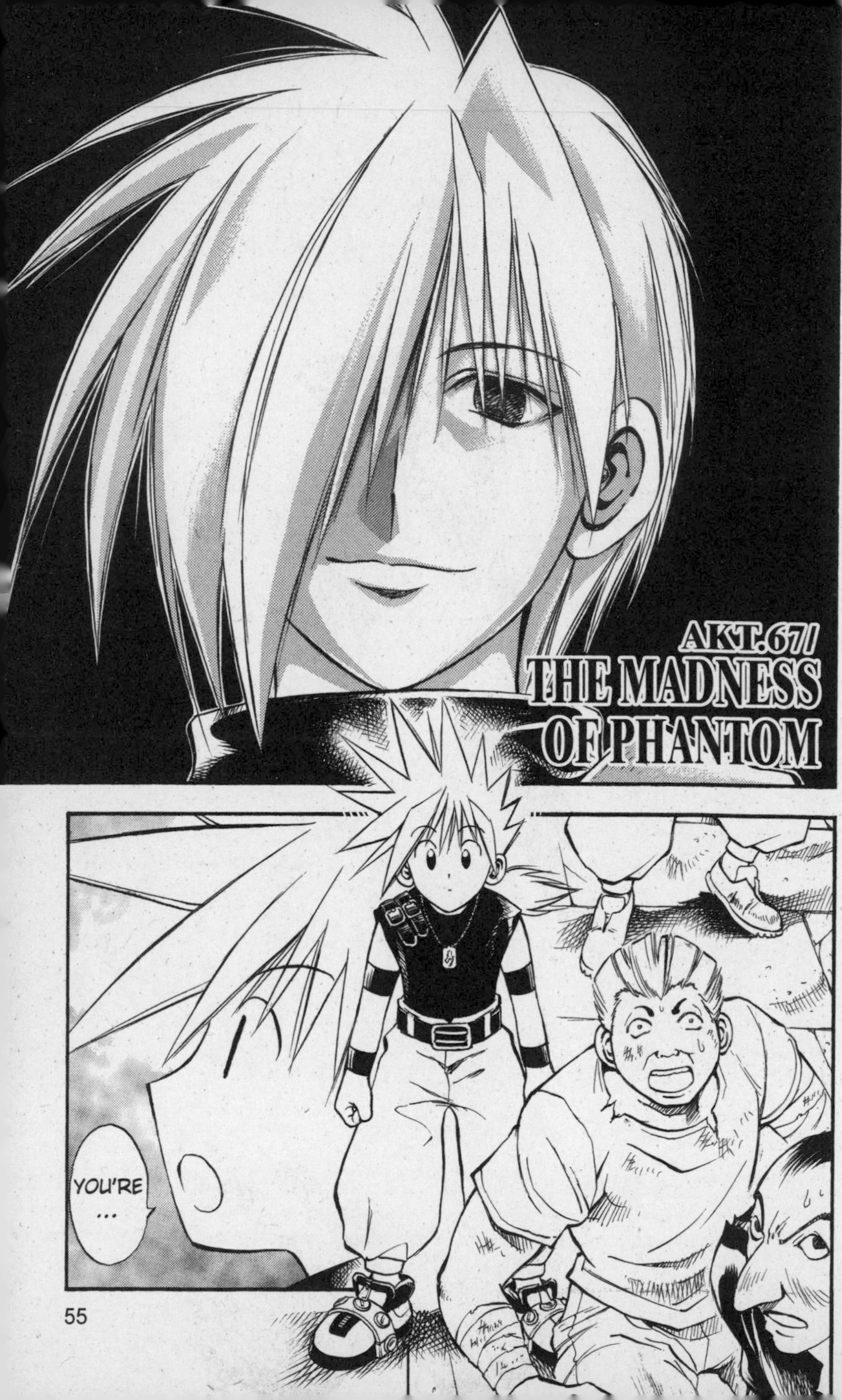
AKT.67/
THE MADNESS OF PHANTOM
YOU'RE ...

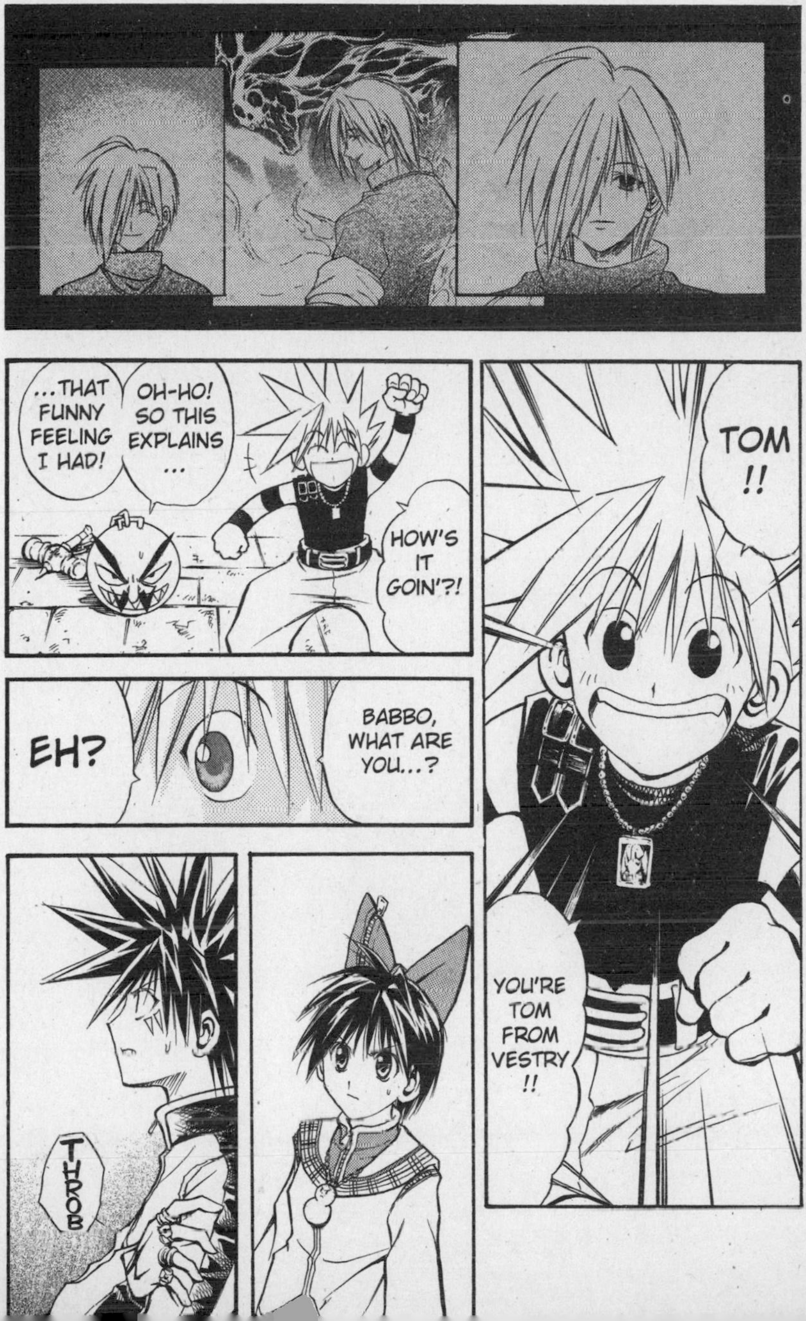
TOM !!
YOU'RE TOM FROM VESTRY !!
HOW'S IT GOIN'?!
OH-HO! SO THIS EXPLAINS ...
...THAT FUNNY FEELING I HAD!
BABBO, WHAT ARE YOU...?
EH?
THROB

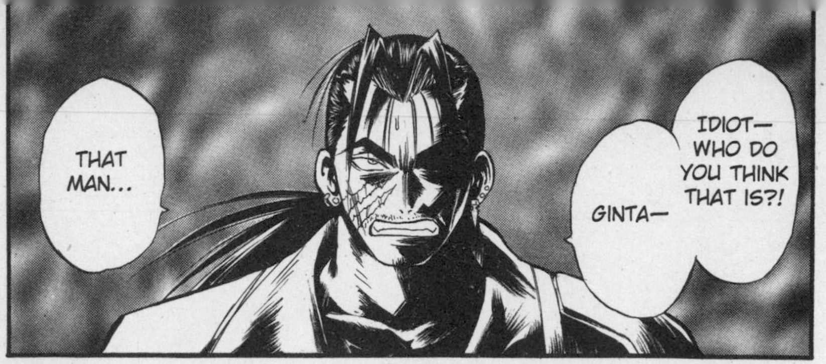
IDIOT— WHO DO YOU THINK THAT IS?!
GINTA—
THAT MAN...

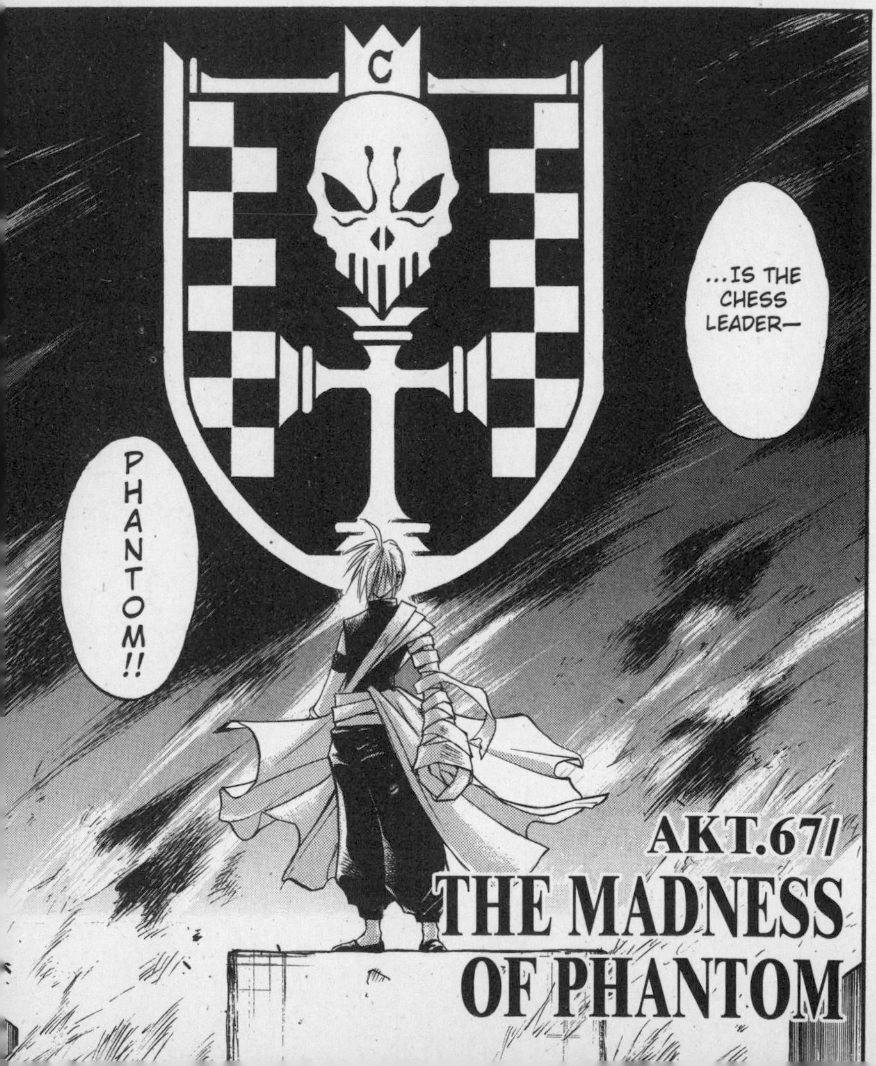
C
...IS THE CHESS LEADER—
PHANTOM!!

AKT.67/ THE MADNESS OF PHANTOM

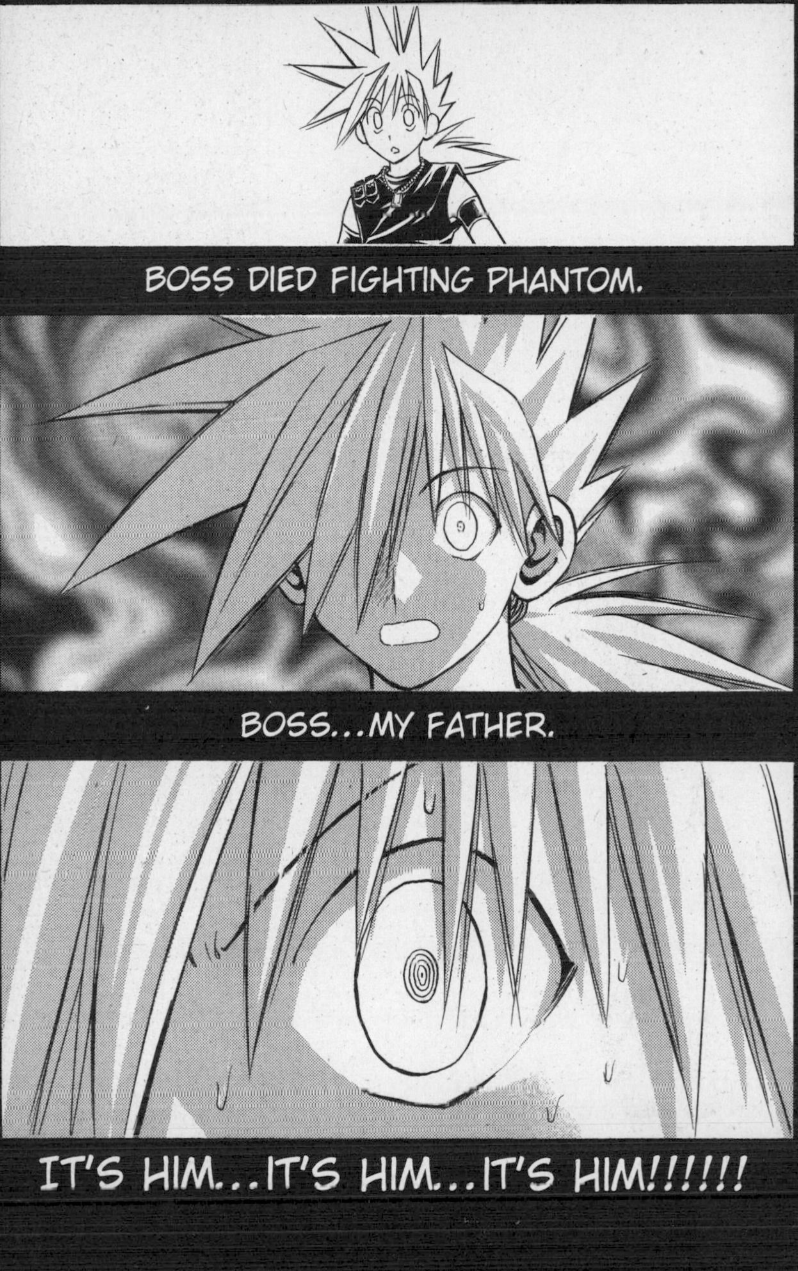
BOSS DIED FIGHTING PHANTOM.
BOSS...MY FATHER.
IT'S HIM...IT'S HIM...IT'S HIM!!!!!!

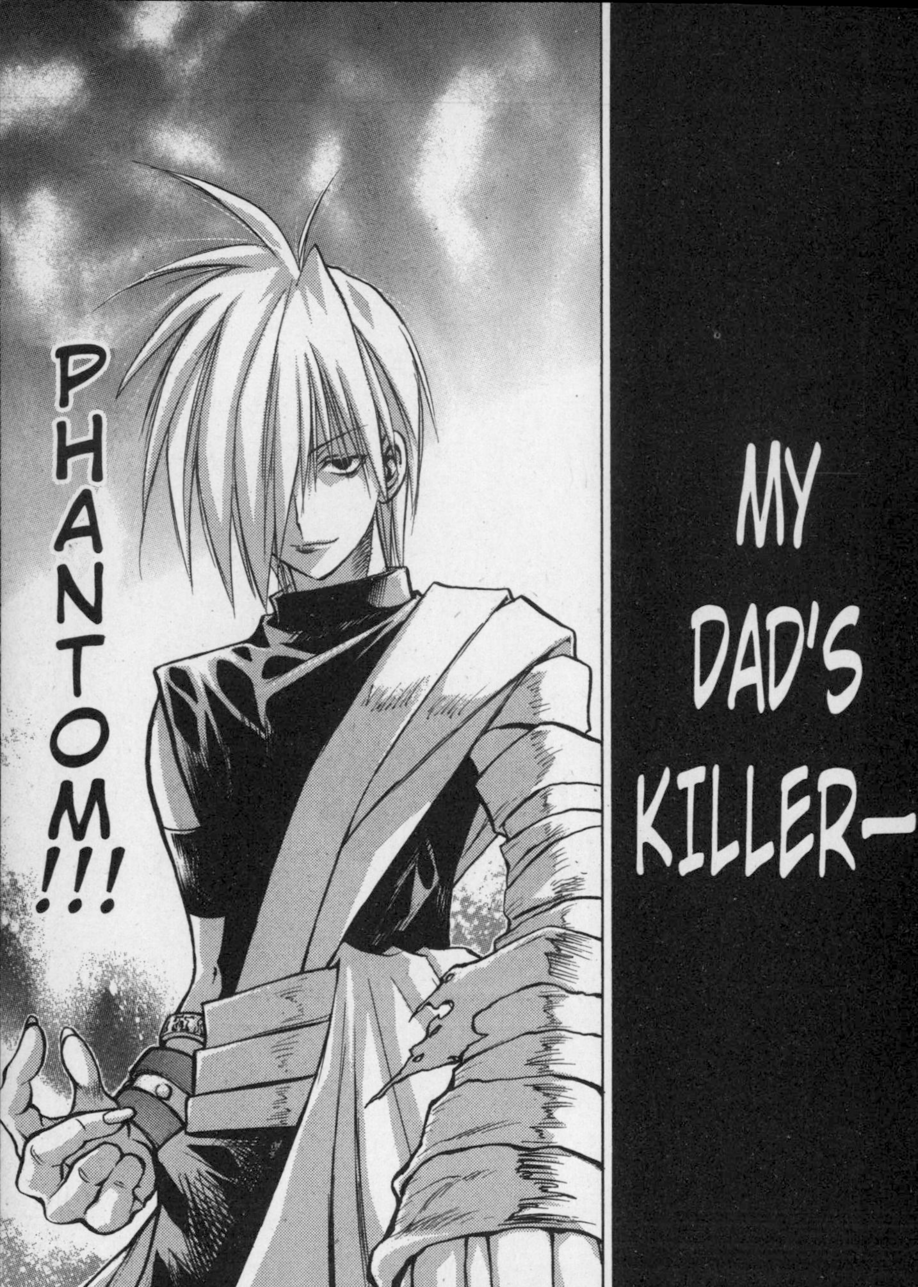
MY DAD'S KILLER—
PHANTOM!!!

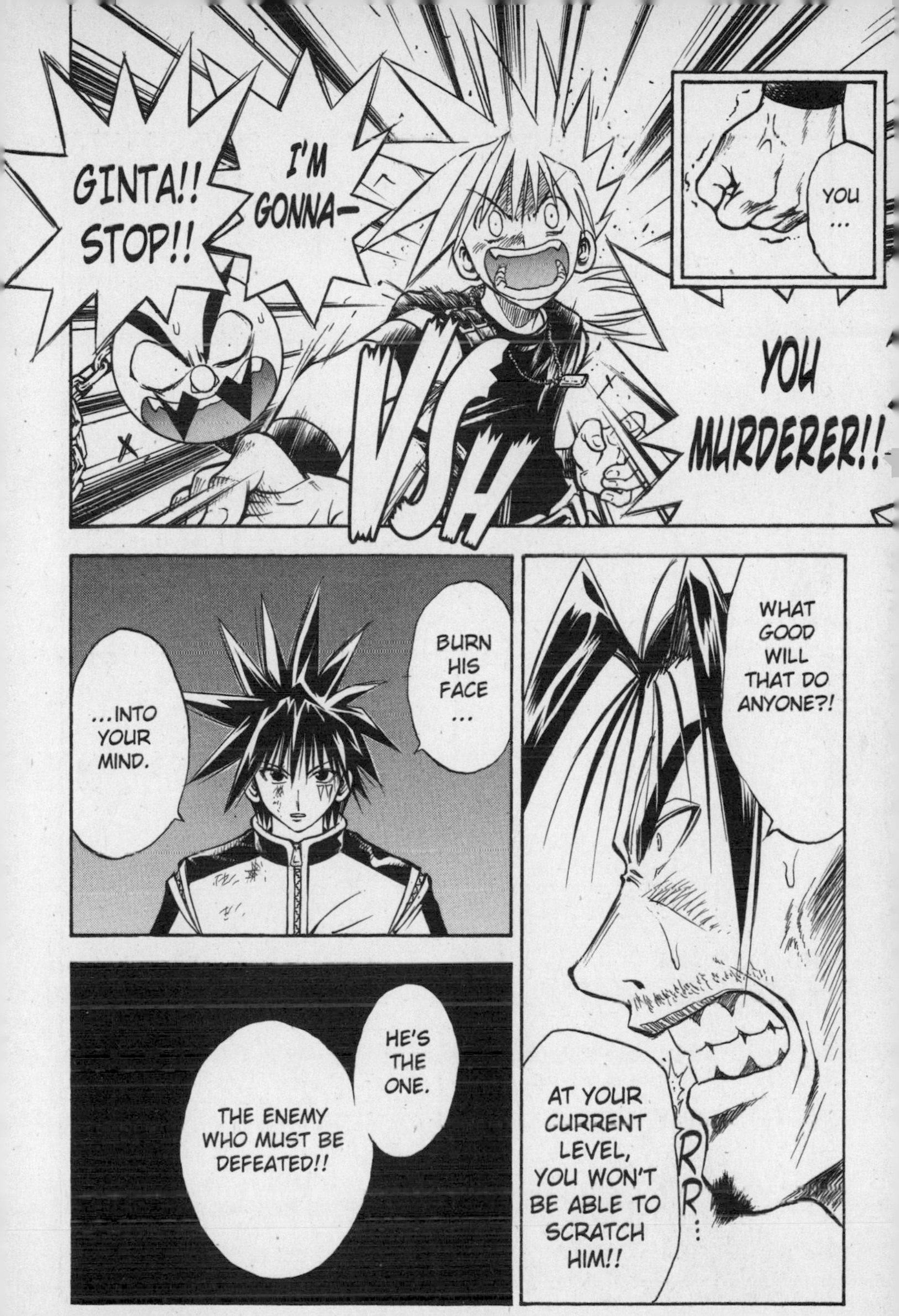
YOU ...
YOU MURDERER!!
I'M GONNA-
GINTA!! STOP!!
VSH
WHAT GOOD WILL THAT DO ANYONE?!
AT YOUR CURRENT LEVEL, YOU WON'T BE ABLE TO SCRATCH HIM!!
RR...
BURN HIS FACE ...
...INTO YOUR MIND.
HE'S THE ONE.
THE ENEMY WHO MUST BE DEFEATED!!

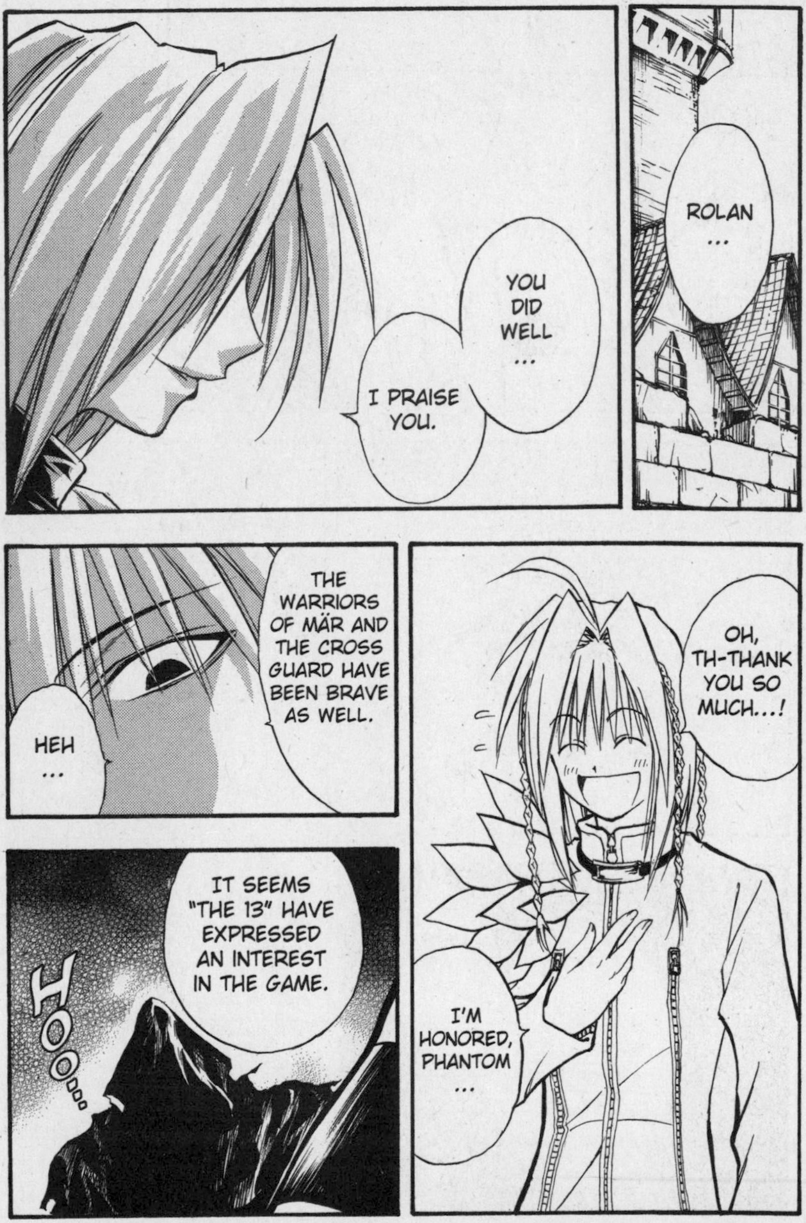
ROLAN ...
YOU DID WELL ...
I PRAISE YOU.
OH, TH-THANK YOU SO MUCH...!
I'M HONORED, PHANTOM ...
THE WARRIORS OF MÄR AND THE CROSS GUARD HAVE BEEN BRAVE AS WELL.
HEH ...
IT SEEMS "THE 13" HAVE EXPRESSED AN INTEREST IN THE GAME.
HOOooo

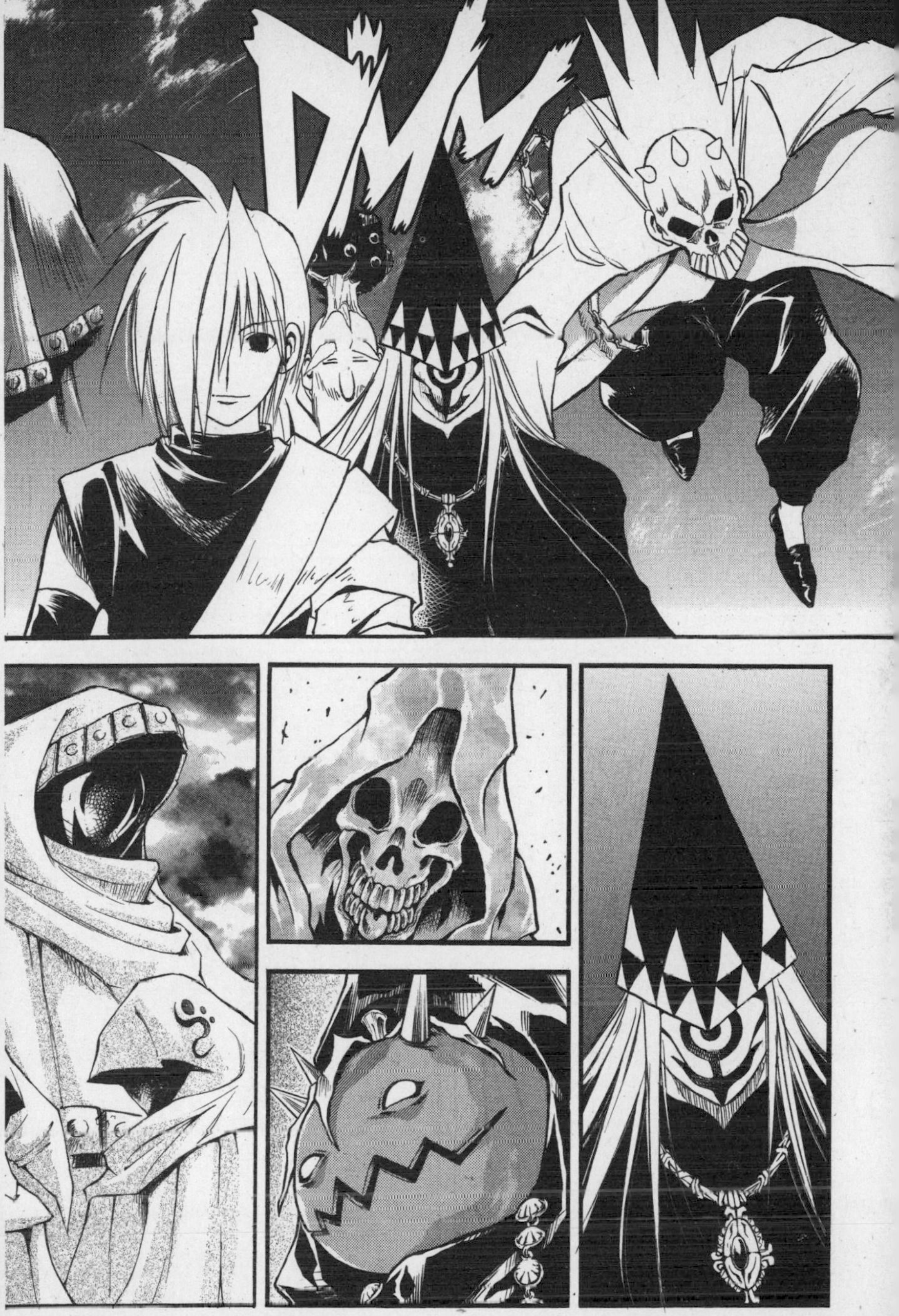
DMM

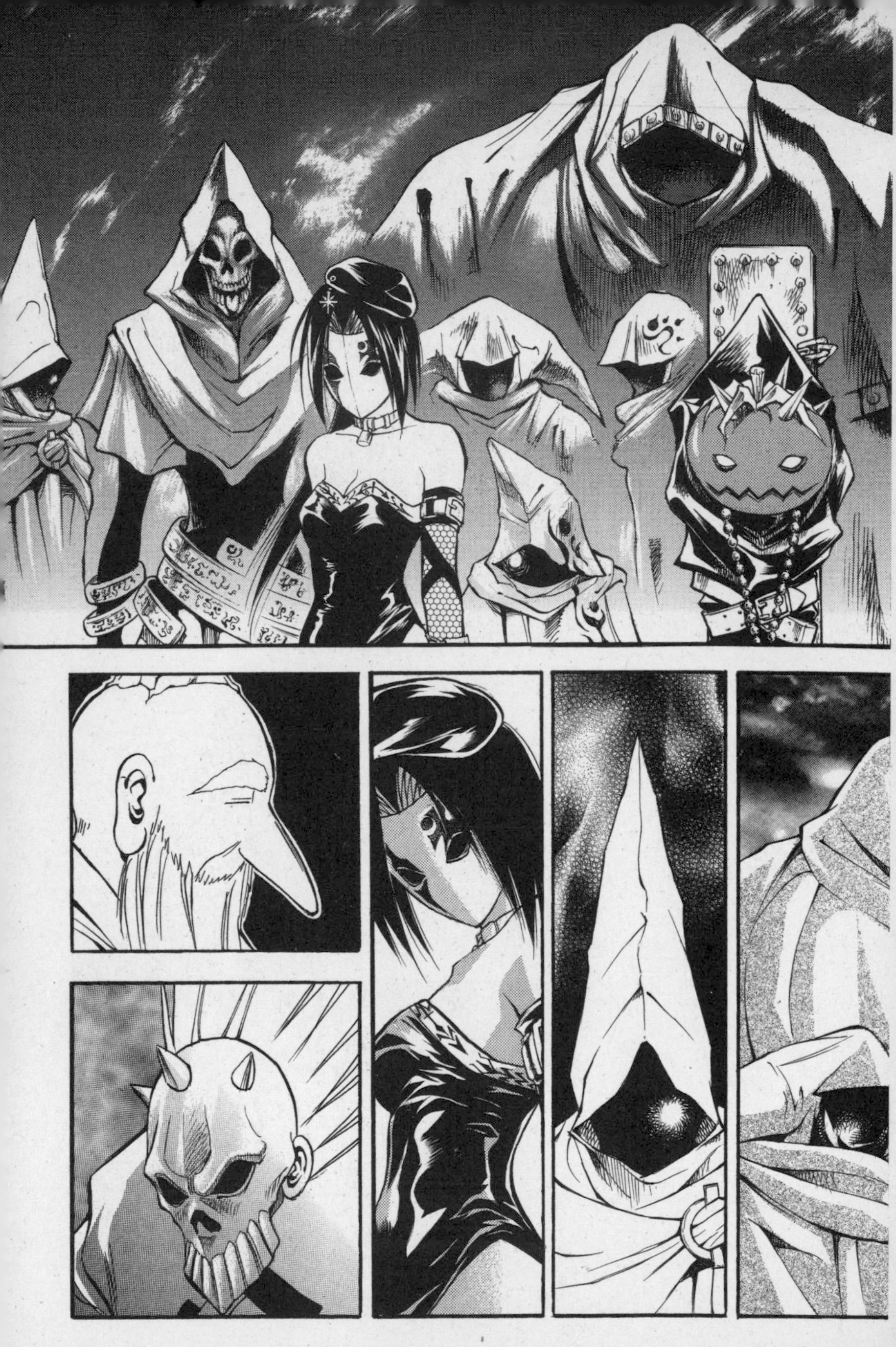

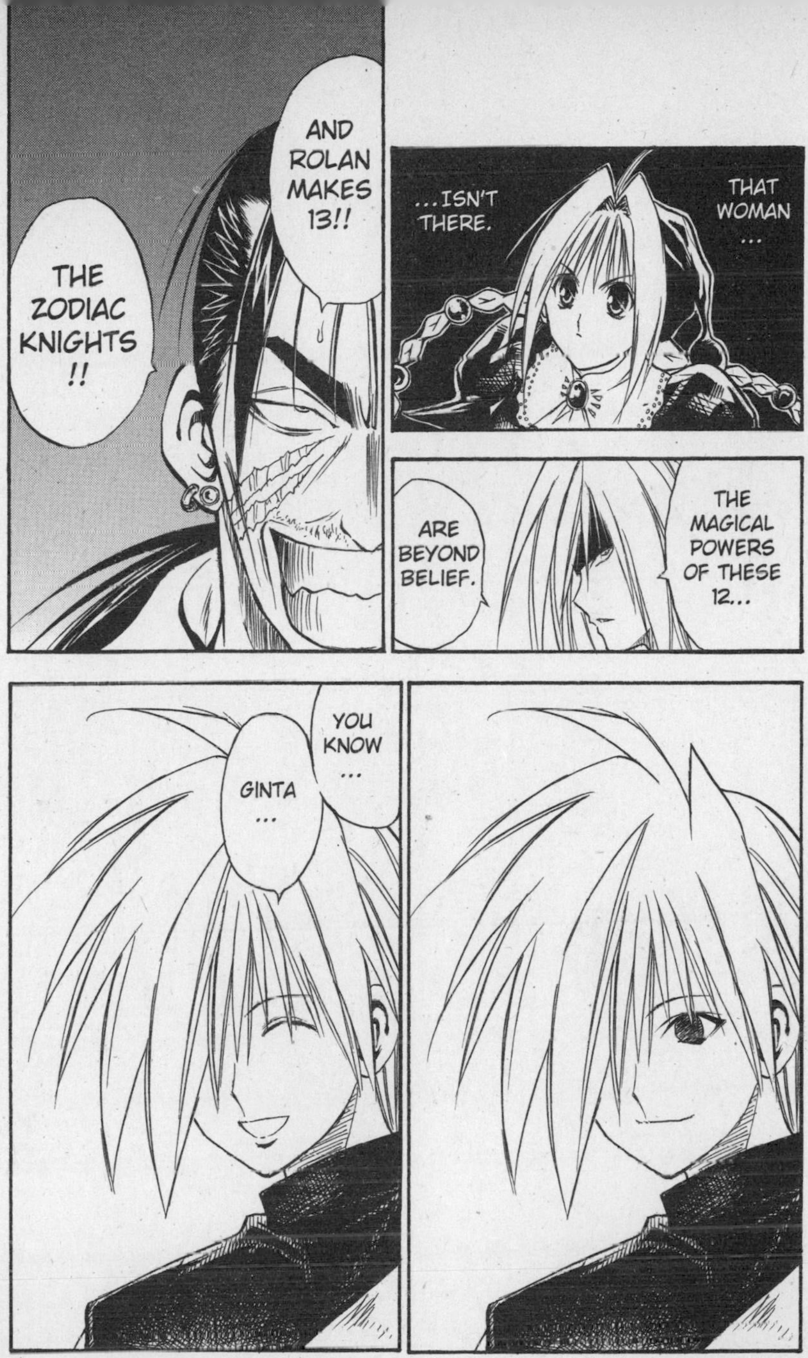
THAT WOMAN ...
...ISN'T THERE.
THE MAGICAL POWERS OF THESE 12...
ARE BEYOND BELIEF.
AND ROLAN MAKES 13!!
THE ZODIAC KNIGHTS !!
YOU KNOW ...
GINTA ...

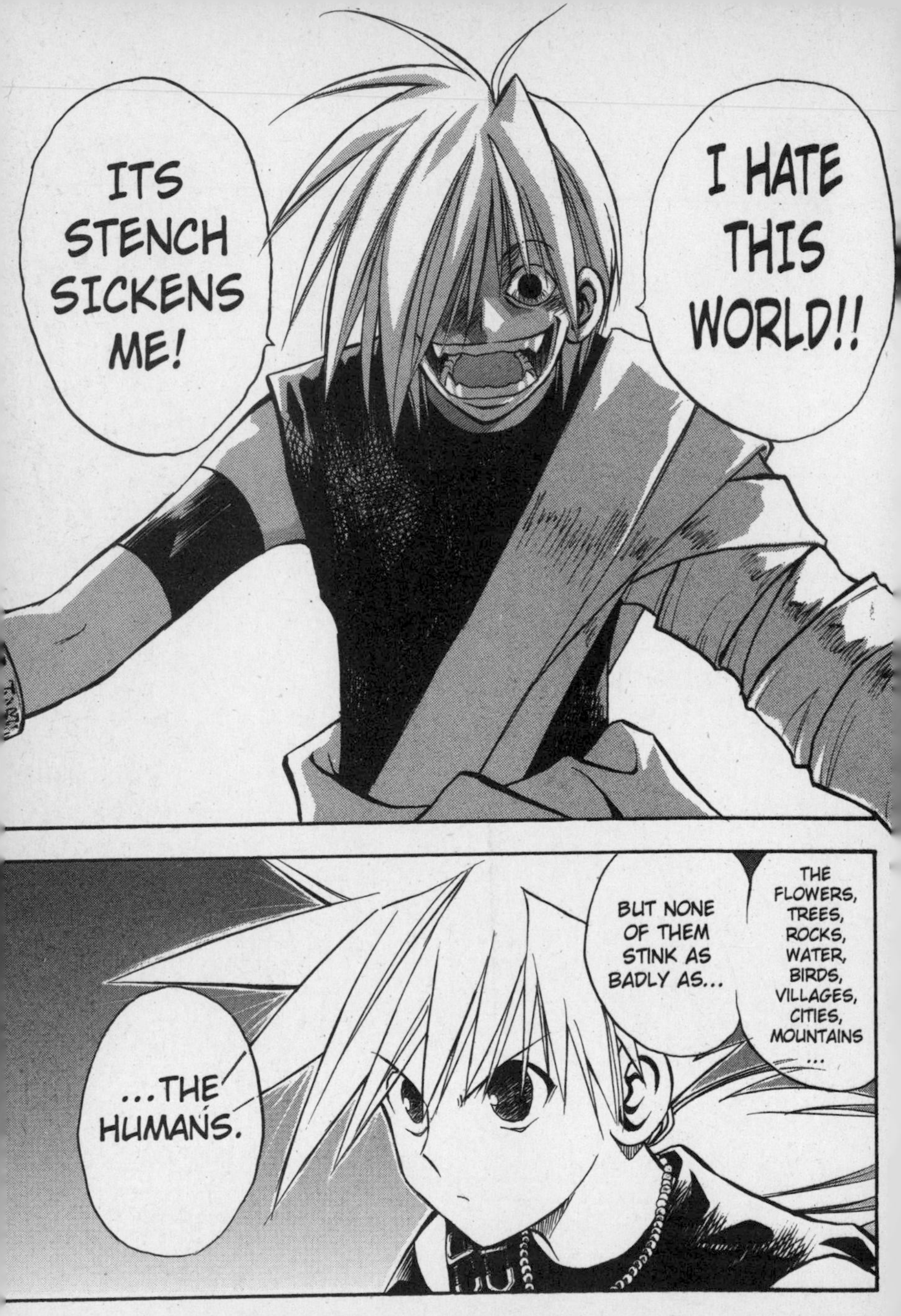
I HATE THIS WORLD!!
ITS STENCH SICKENS ME!
THE FLOWERS, TREES, ROCKS, WATER, BIRDS, VILLAGES, CITIES, MOUNTAINS ...
BUT NONE OF THEM STINK AS BADLY AS...
...THE HUMANS.

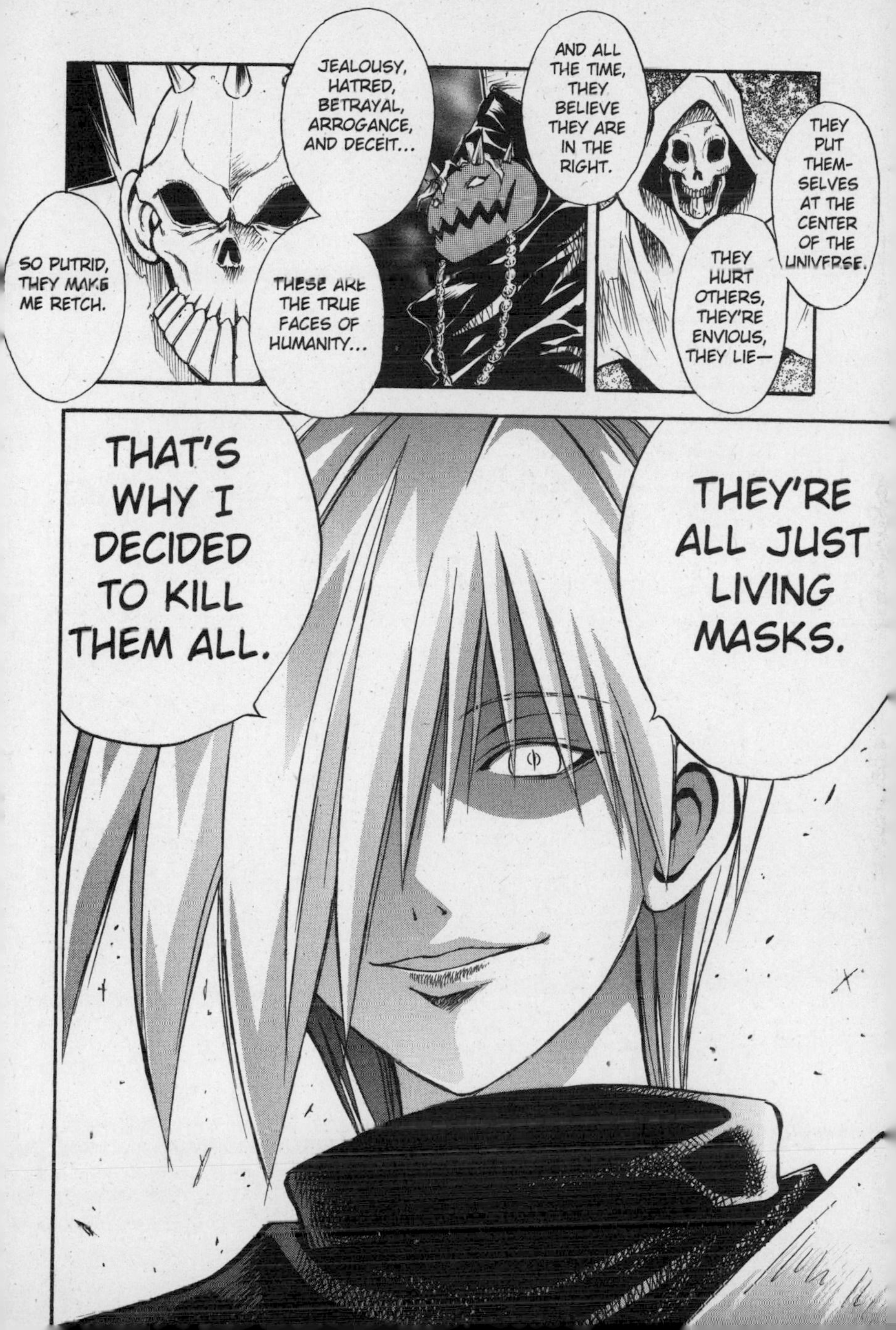
THEY PUT THEM-SELVES AT THE CENTER OF THE UNIVERSE.
THEY HURT OTHERS, THEY'RE ENVIOUS, THEY LIE—
AND ALL THE TIME, THEY BELIEVE THEY ARE IN THE RIGHT.
JEALOUSY, HATRED, BETRAYAL, ARROGANCE, AND DECEIT...
THESE ARE THE TRUE FACES OF HUMANITY...
SO PUTRID, THEY MAKE ME RETCH.
THEY'RE ALL JUST LIVING MASKS.
THAT'S WHY I DECIDED TO KILL THEM ALL.

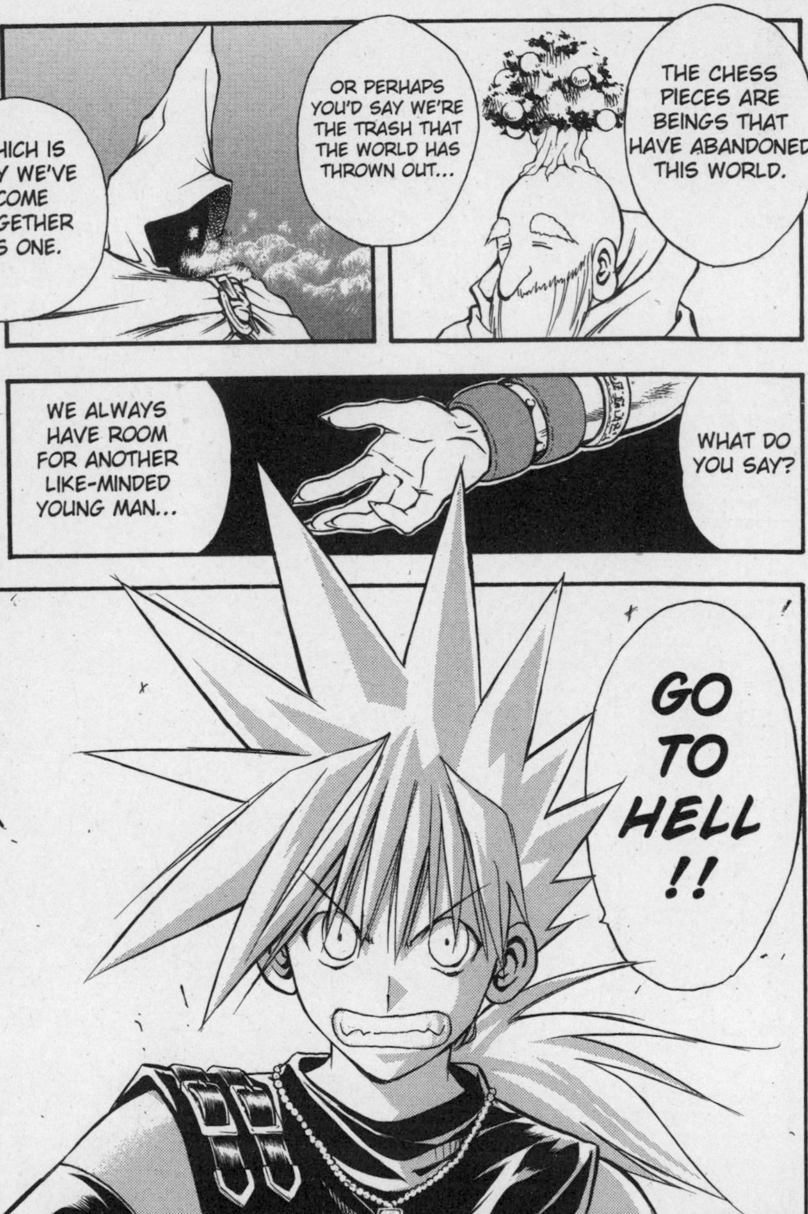
THE CHESS PIECES ARE BEINGS THAT HAVE ABANDONED THIS WORLD.
OR PERHAPS YOU'D SAY WE'RE THE TRASH THAT THE WORLD HAS THROWN OUT...
WHICH IS WHY WE'VE COME TOGETHER AS ONE.
WHAT DO YOU SAY?
WE ALWAYS HAVE ROOM FOR ANOTHER LIKE-MINDED YOUNG MAN...
GO TO HELL!!

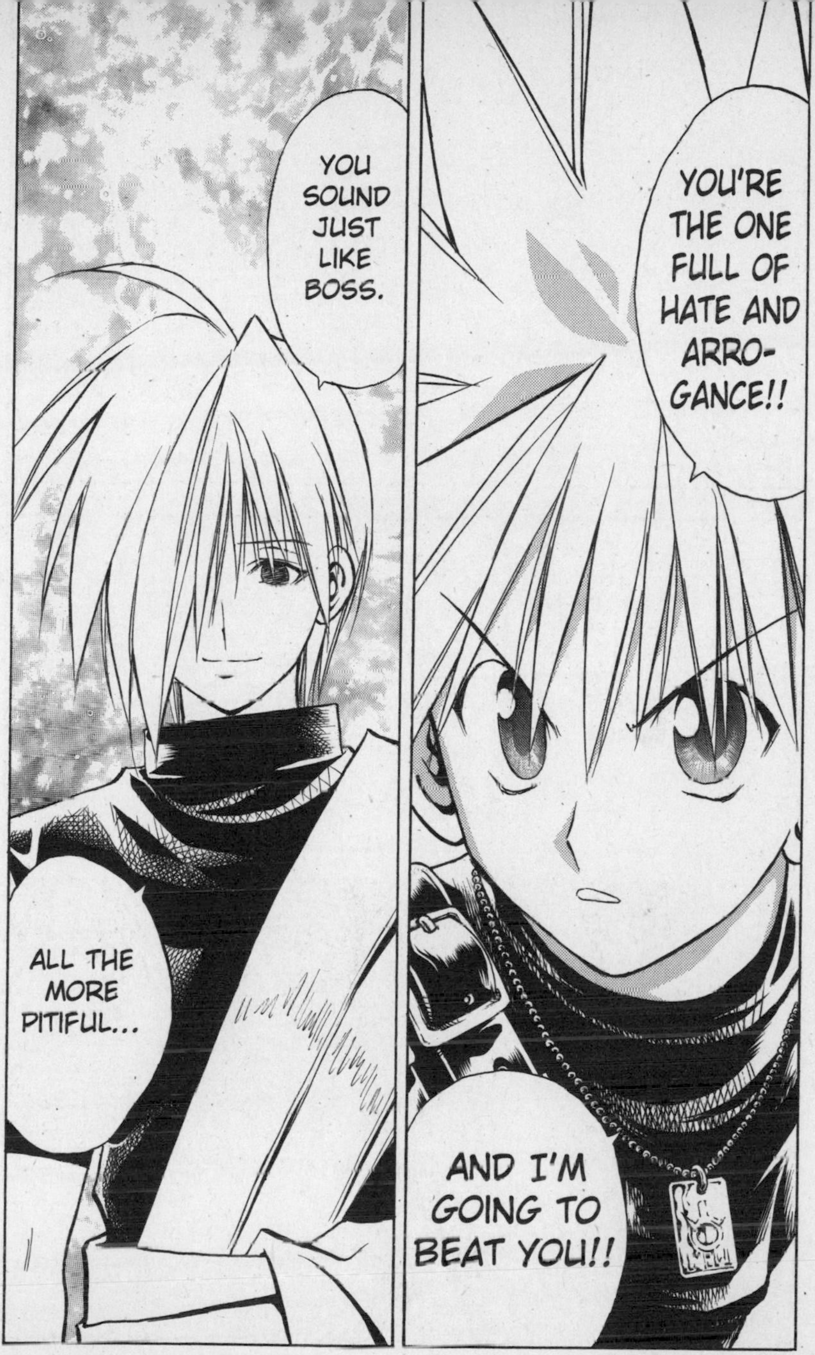
YOU'RE THE ONE FULL OF HATE AND ARRO-GANCE!!
AND I'M GOING TO BEAT YOU!!
YOU SOUND JUST LIKE BOSS.
ALL THE MORE PITIFUL...

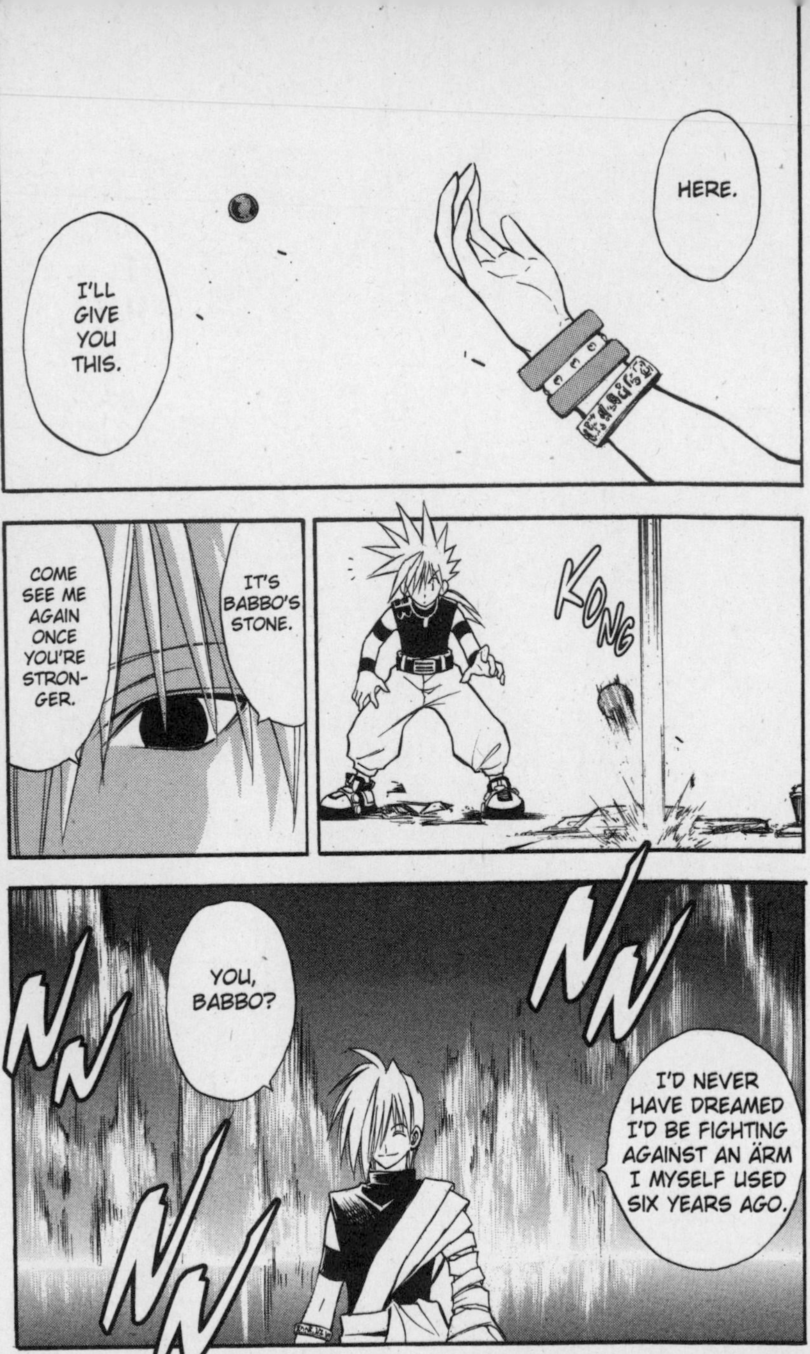
HERE.
I'LL GIVE YOU THIS.
KONG
IT'S BABBO'S STONE.
COME SEE ME AGAIN ONCE YOU'RE STRONGER.
I'D NEVER HAVE DREAMED I'D BE FIGHTING AGAINST AN ÄRM I MYSELF USED SIX YEARS AGO.
YOU, BABBO?

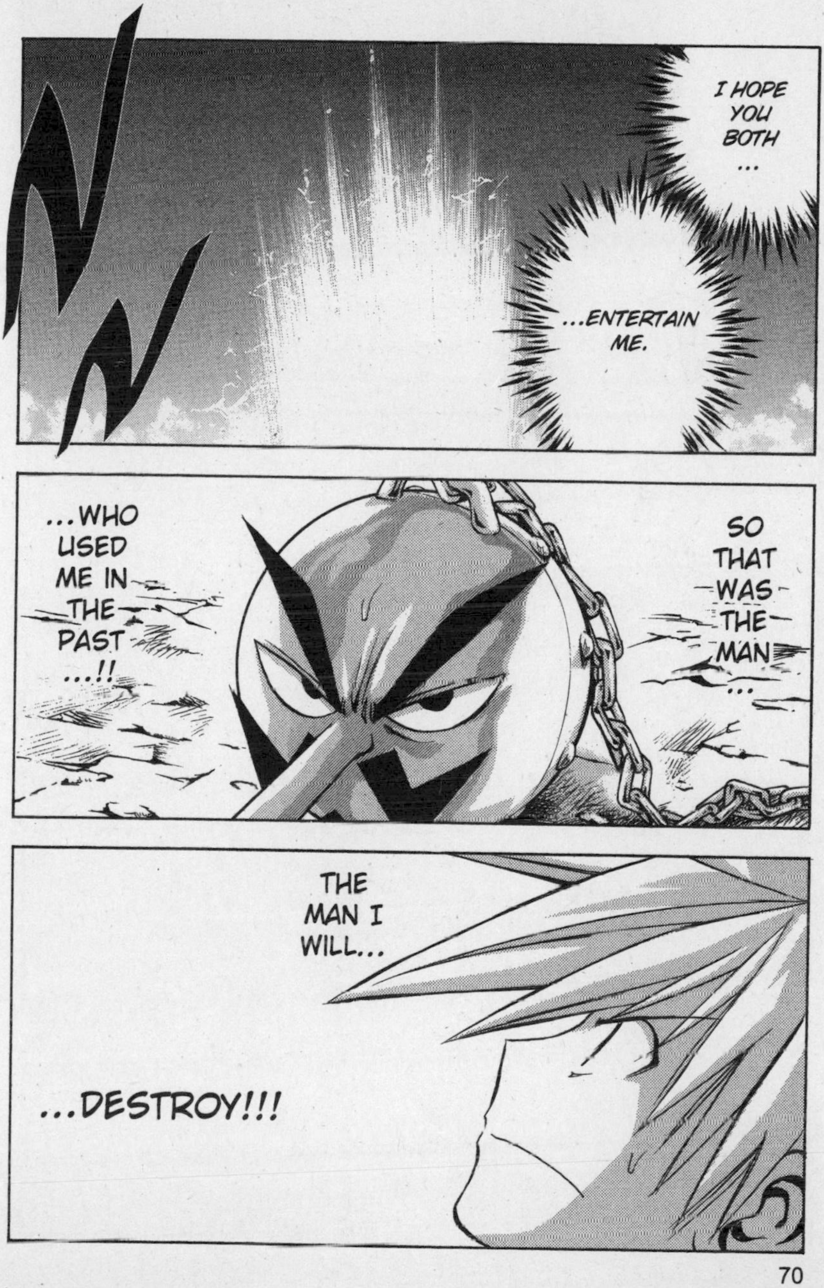
I HOPE YOU BOTH ...
...ENTERTAIN ME.
SO THAT WAS THE MAN ...
...WHO USED ME IN THE PAST ...!!
THE MAN I WILL...
...DESTROY!!!

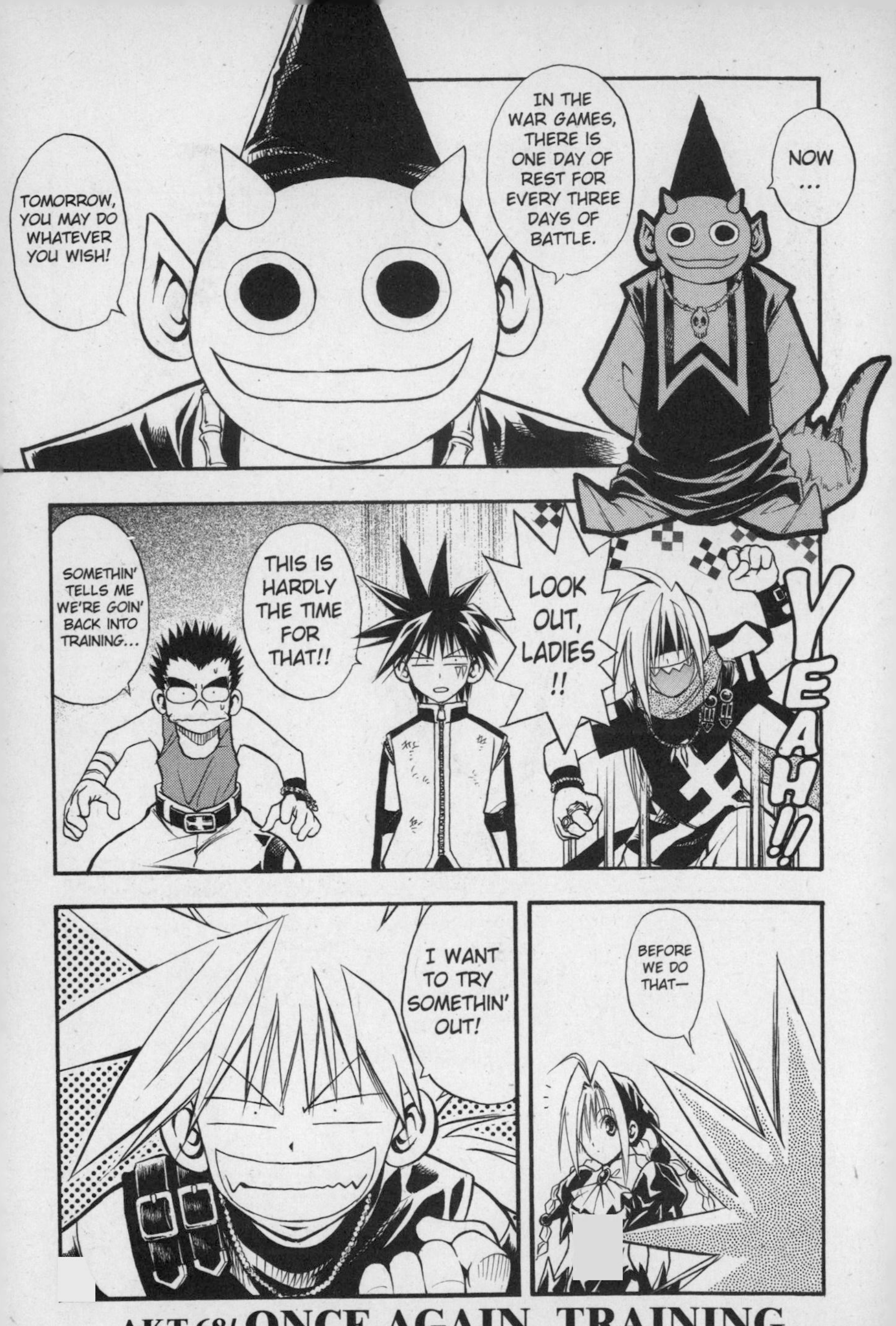
NOW...
IN THE WAR GAMES, THERE IS ONE DAY OF REST FOR EVERY THREE DAYS OF BATTLE.
TOMORROW, YOU MAY DO WHATEVER YOU WISH!
YEAH!!
LOOK OUT, LADIES!!
THIS IS HARDLY THE TIME FOR THAT!!
SOMETHIN' TELLS ME WE'RE GOIN' BACK INTO TRAINING...
BEFORE WE DO THAT—
I WANT TO TRY SOMETHIN' OUT!

AKT.68/ ONCE AGAIN, TRAINING

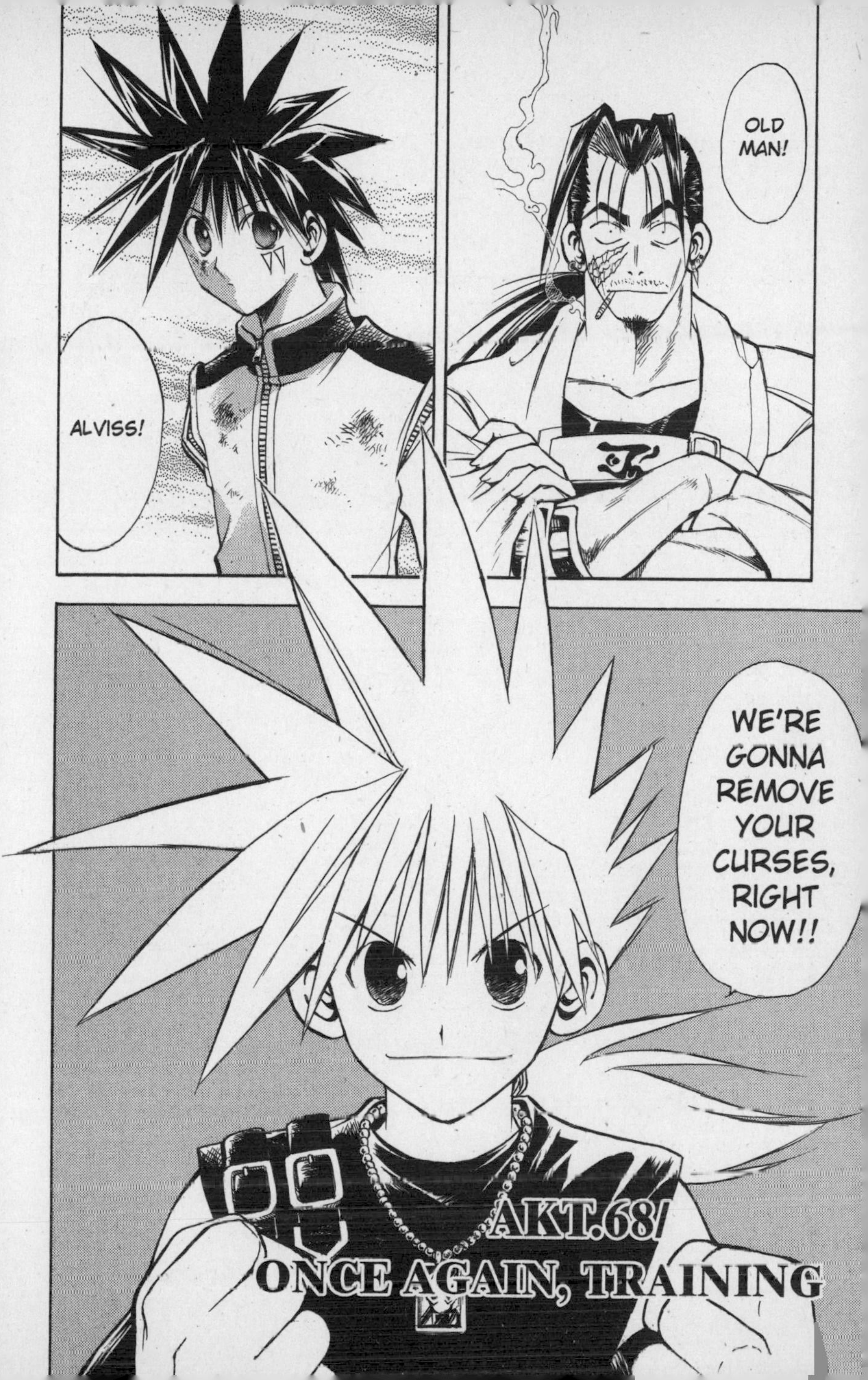
OLD MAN!
ALVISS!
WE'RE GONNA REMOVE YOUR CURSES, RIGHT NOW!!
AKT.68/
ONCE AGAIN, TRAINING

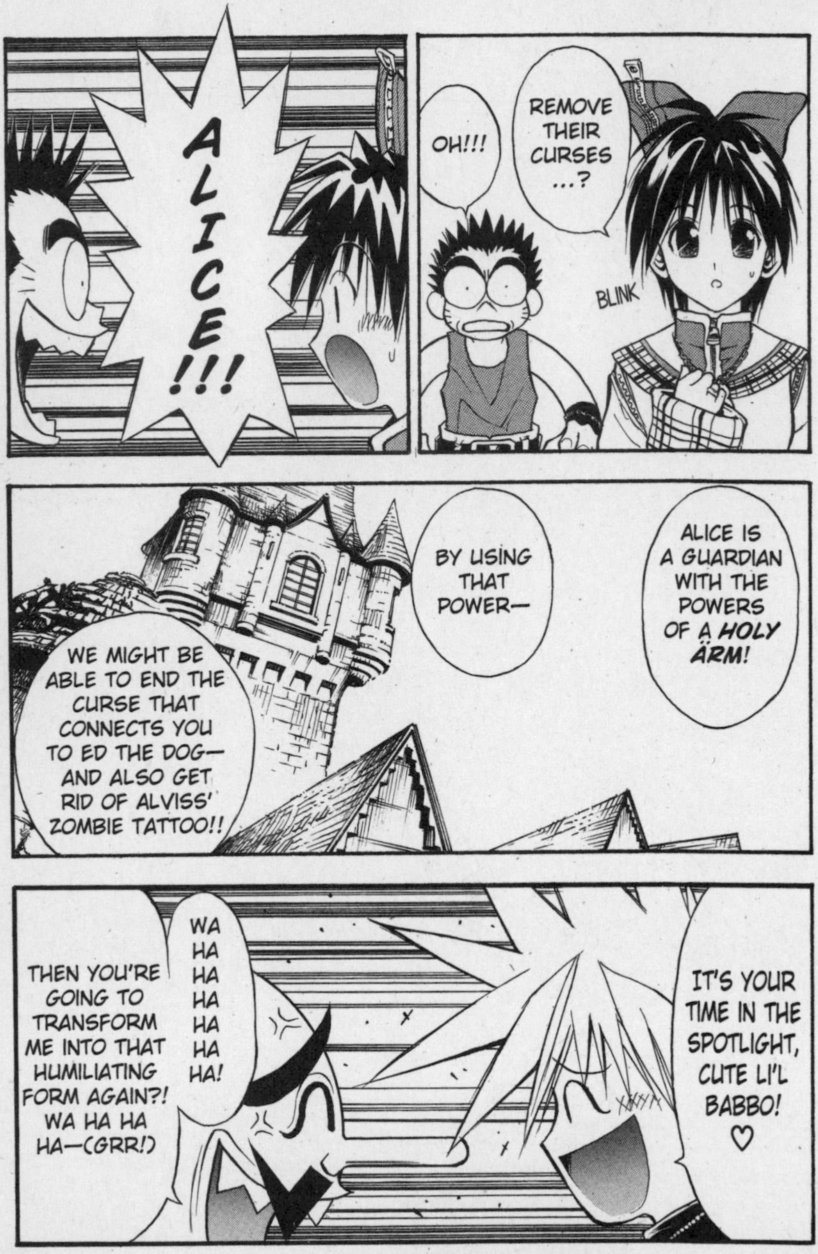

REMOVE THEIR CURSES ...?
OH!!!
BLINK
ALICE!!!
ALICE IS A GUARDIAN WITH THE POWERS OF A *HOLY ÄRM!*
BY USING THAT POWER—
WE MIGHT BE ABLE TO END THE CURSE THAT CONNECTS YOU TO ED THE DOG—AND ALSO GET RID OF ALVISS' ZOMBIE TATTOO!!
IT'S YOUR TIME IN THE SPOTLIGHT, CUTE LI'L BABBO! ♡
WA HA HA HA HA HA HA!
THEN YOU'RE GOING TO TRANSFORM ME INTO THAT HUMILIATING FORM AGAIN?! WA HA HA HA—(GRR!)

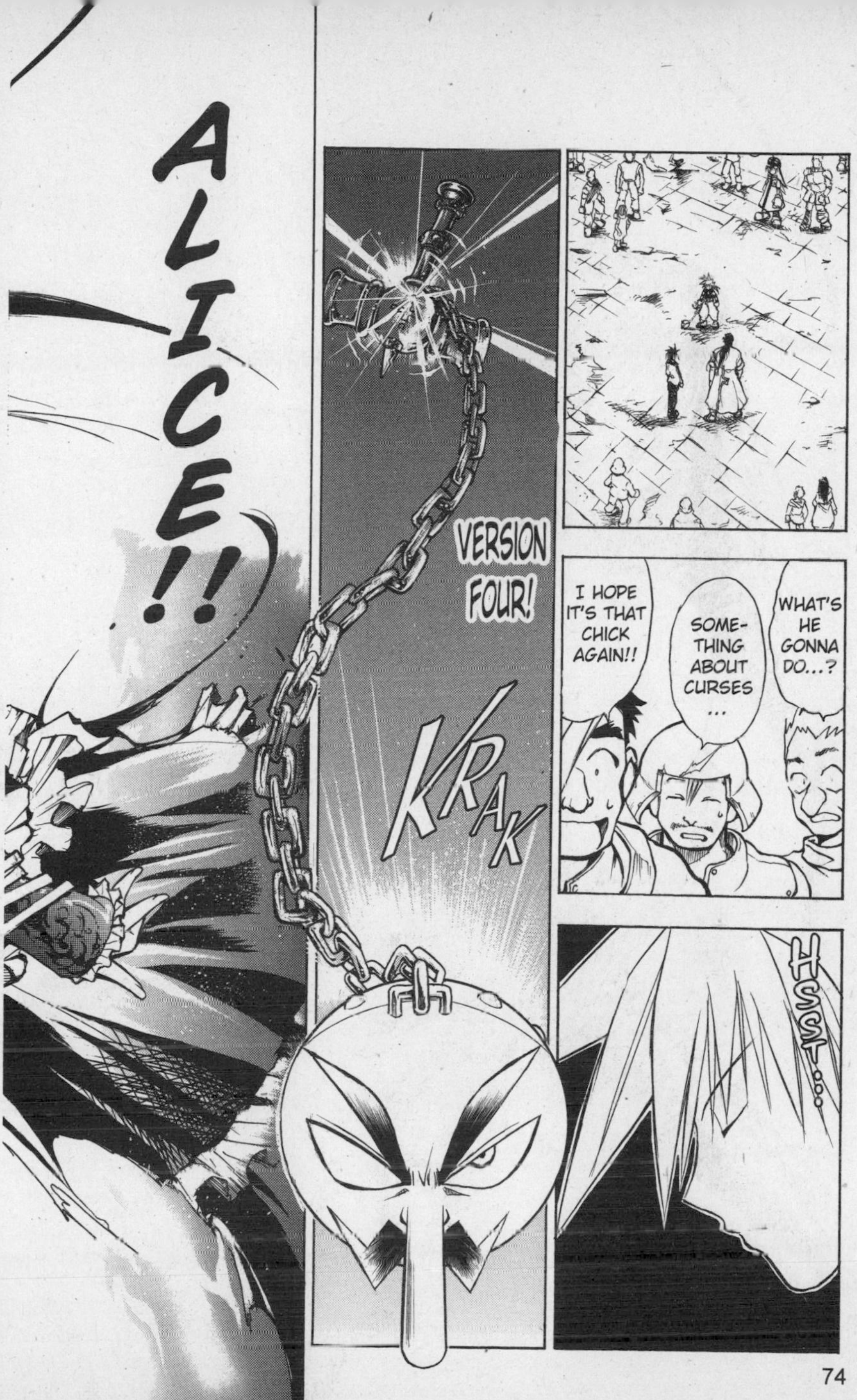
WHAT'S HE GONNA DO...?
SOME-THING ABOUT CURSES...
I HOPE IT'S THAT CHICK AGAIN!!
HSST...
VERSION FOUR!
KRAK
ALICE!!

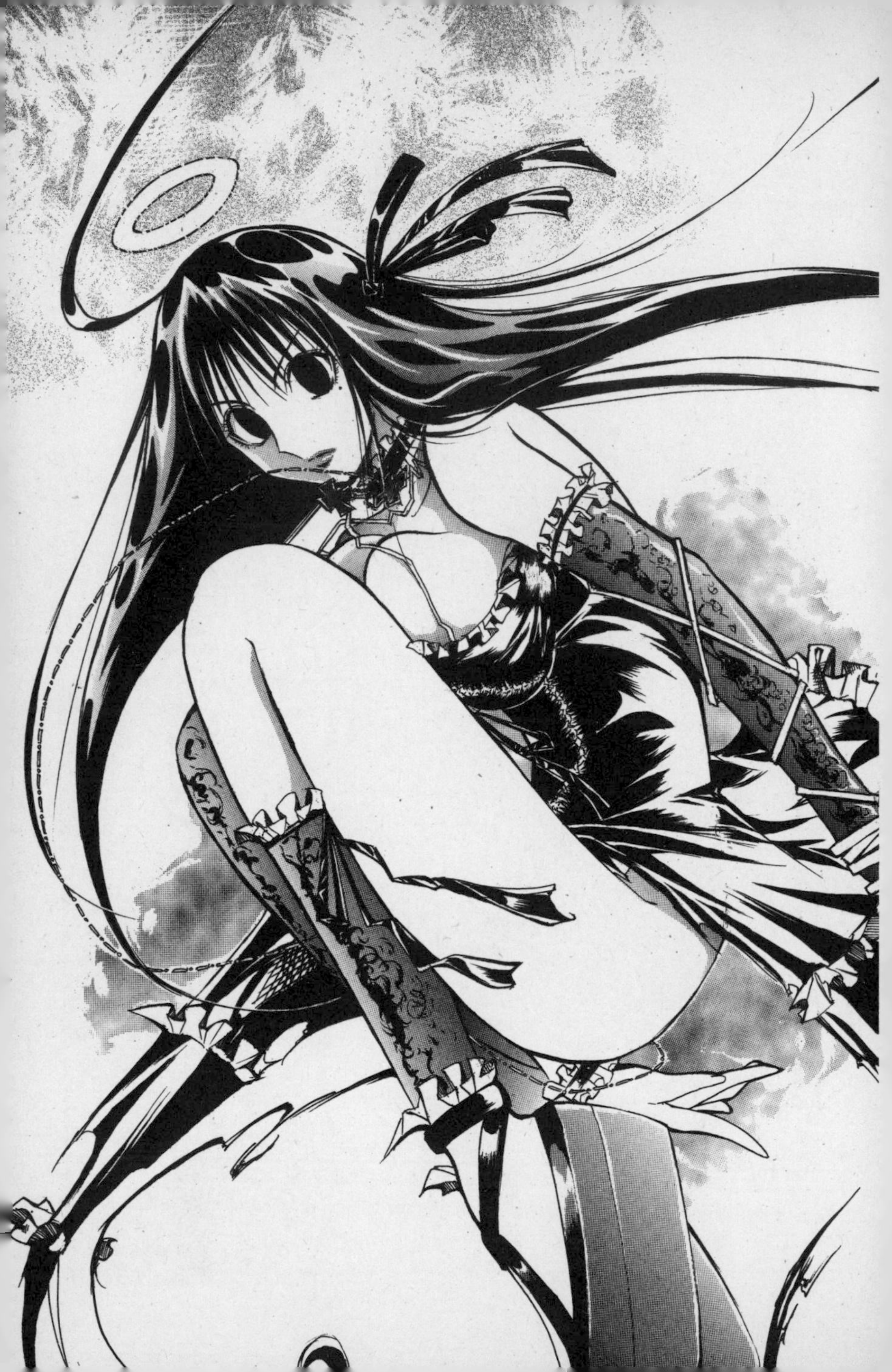

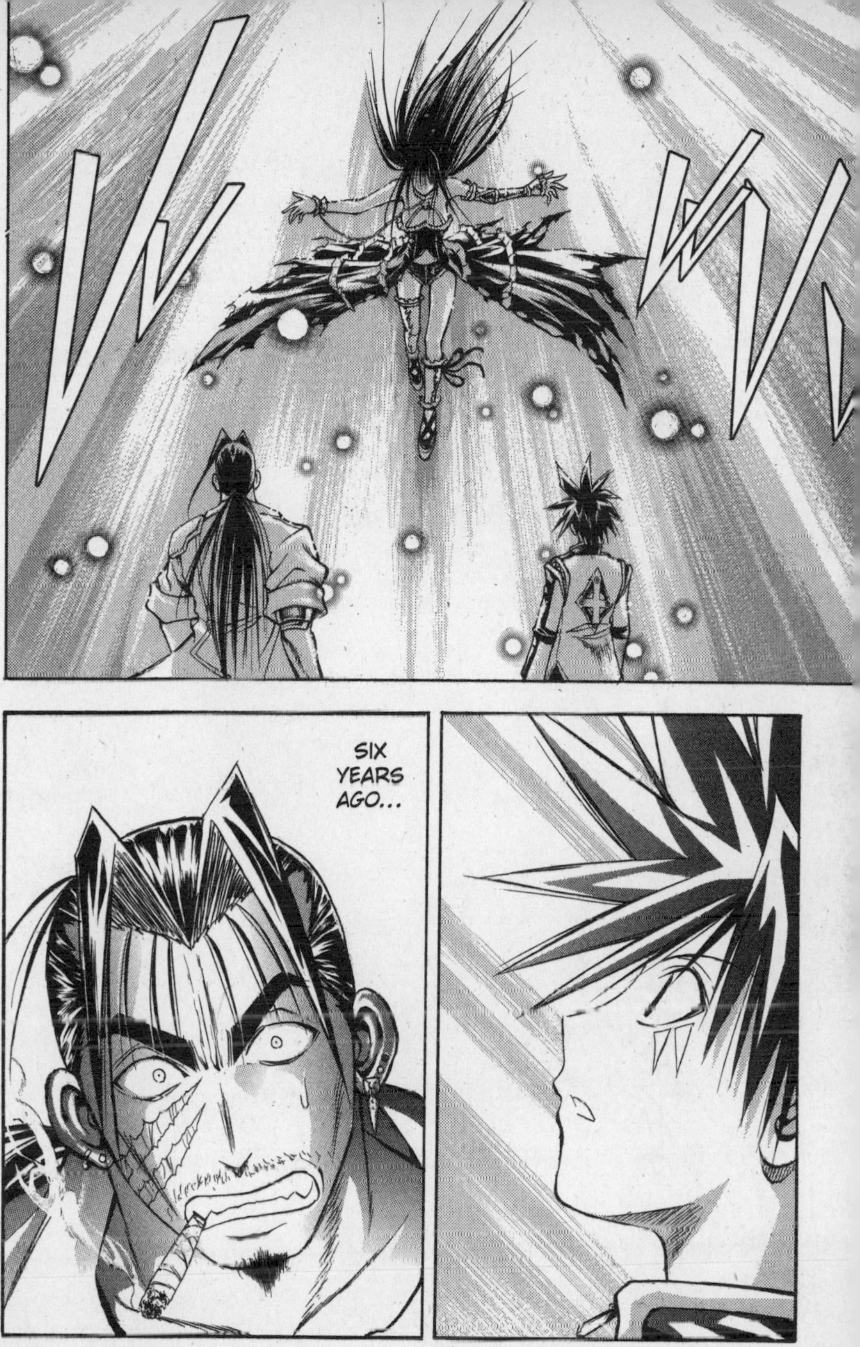
SIX YEARS AGO...

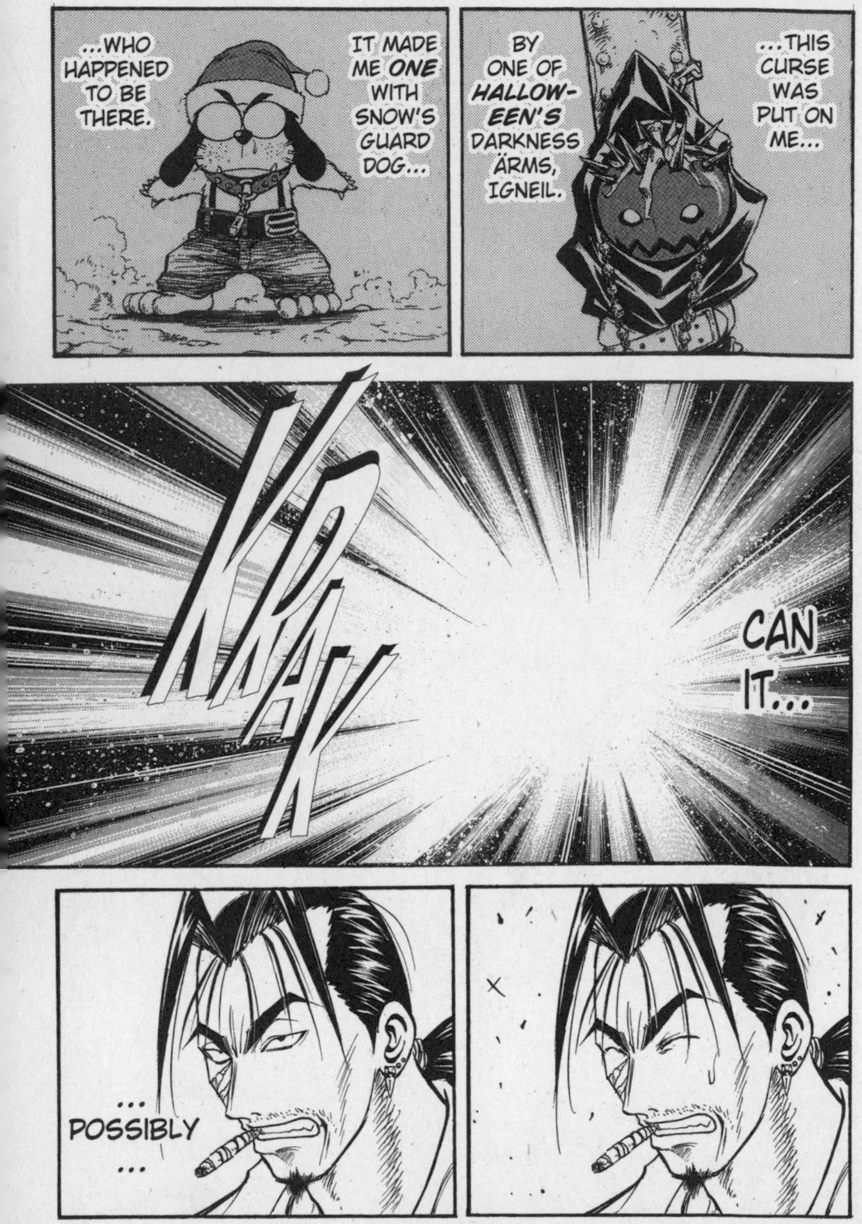
...THIS CURSE WAS PUT ON ME...
BY ONE OF HALLOWEEN'S DARKNESS ÄRMS, IGNEIL.
IT MADE ME ONE WITH SNOW'S GUARD DOG...
...WHO HAPPENED TO BE THERE.
CAN IT...
KRAK
...POSSIBLY...

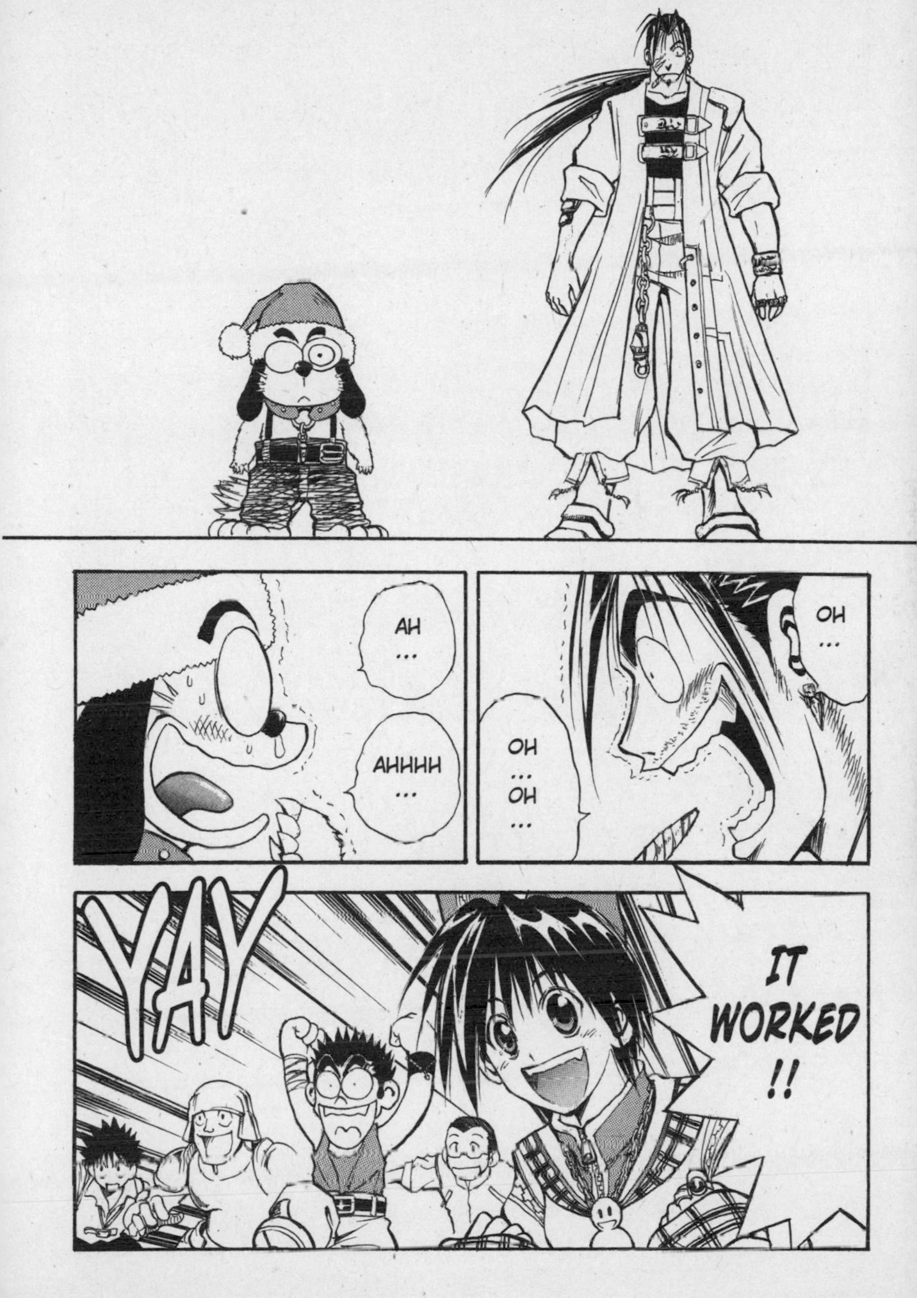
OH ...
OH ... OH ...
AH ...
AHHHH ...
IT WORKED !!
YAY

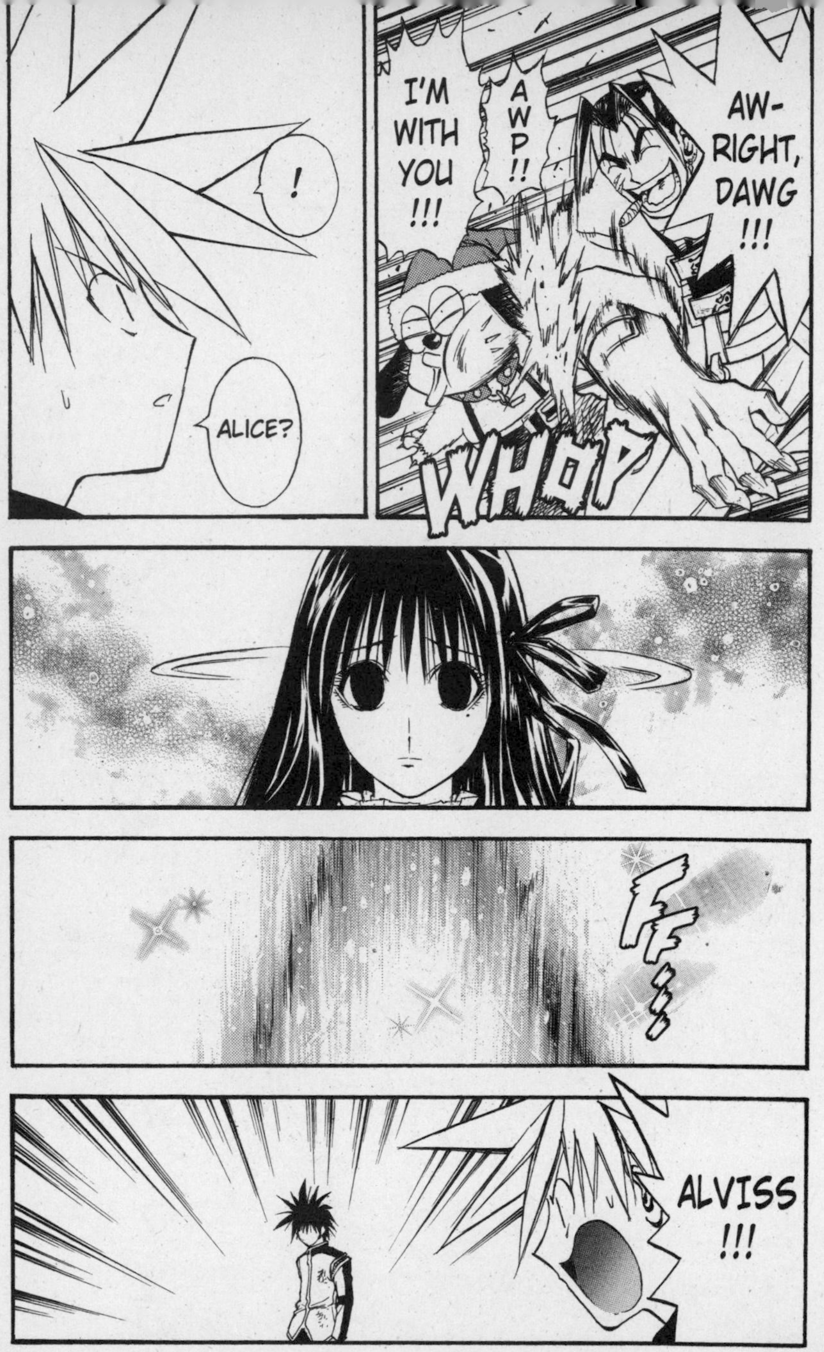
AW-RIGHT, DAWG!!!
AWP!!
I'M WITH YOU!!!
WHOP
!
ALICE?
FF...
ALVISS!!!

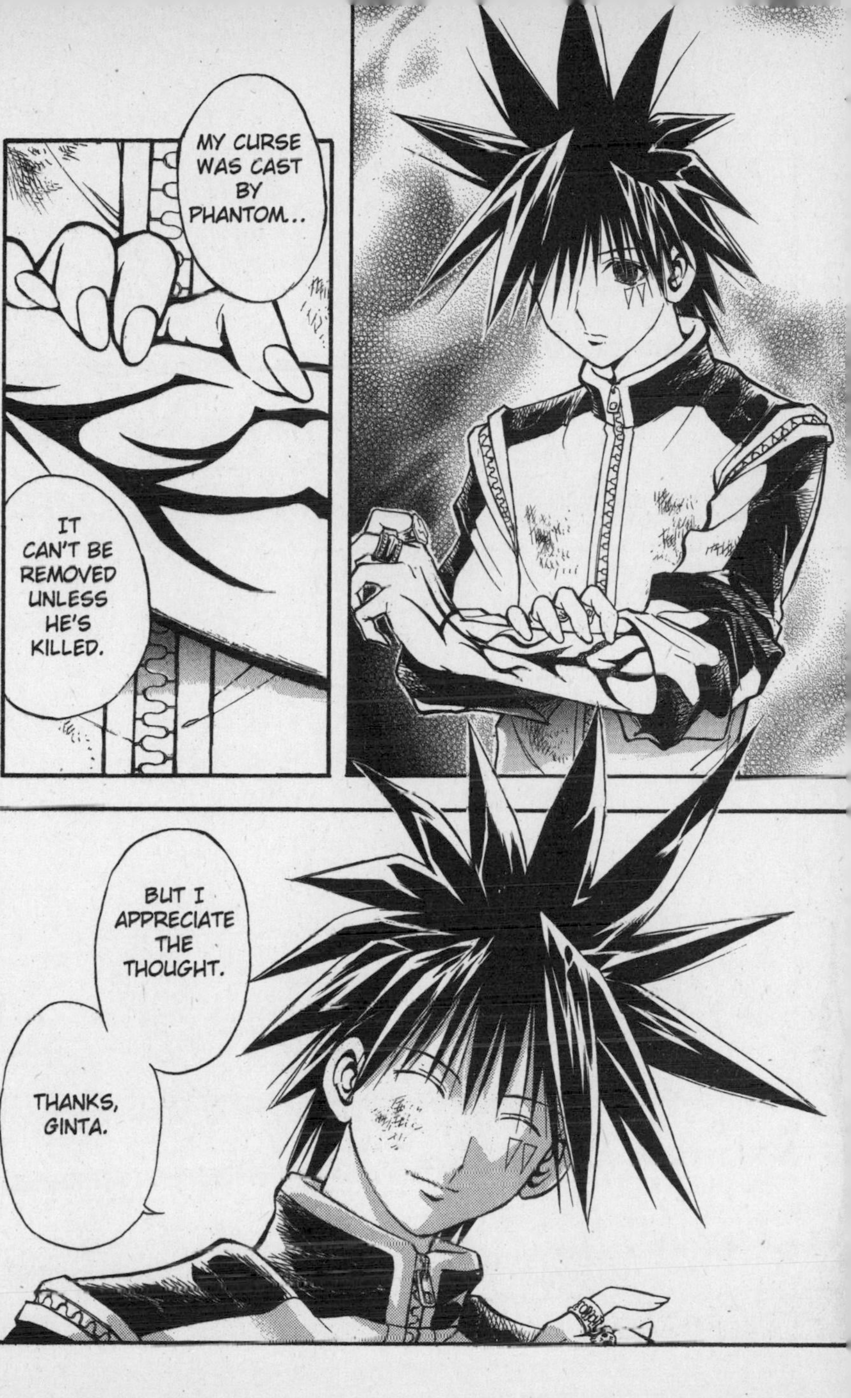
MY CURSE WAS CAST BY PHANTOM...
IT CAN'T BE REMOVED UNLESS HE'S KILLED.
BUT I APPRECIATE THE THOUGHT.
THANKS, GINTA.

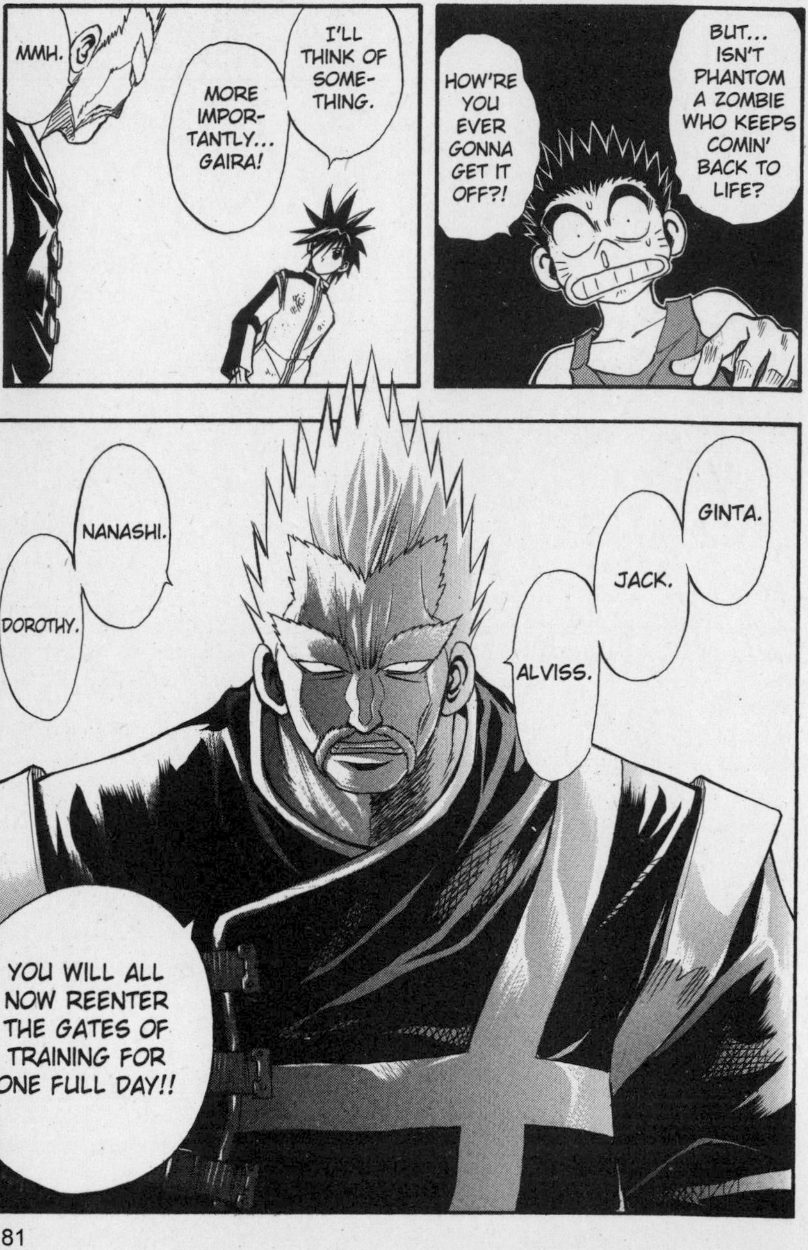
BUT... ISN'T PHANTOM A ZOMBIE WHO KEEPS COMIN' BACK TO LIFE?
HOW'RE YOU EVER GONNA GET IT OFF?!
I'LL THINK OF SOME-THING.
MORE IMPOR-TANTLY... GAIRA!
MMH.
GINTA.
JACK.
ALVISS.
NANASHI.
DOROTHY.
YOU WILL ALL NOW REENTER THE GATES OF TRAINING FOR ONE FULL DAY!!

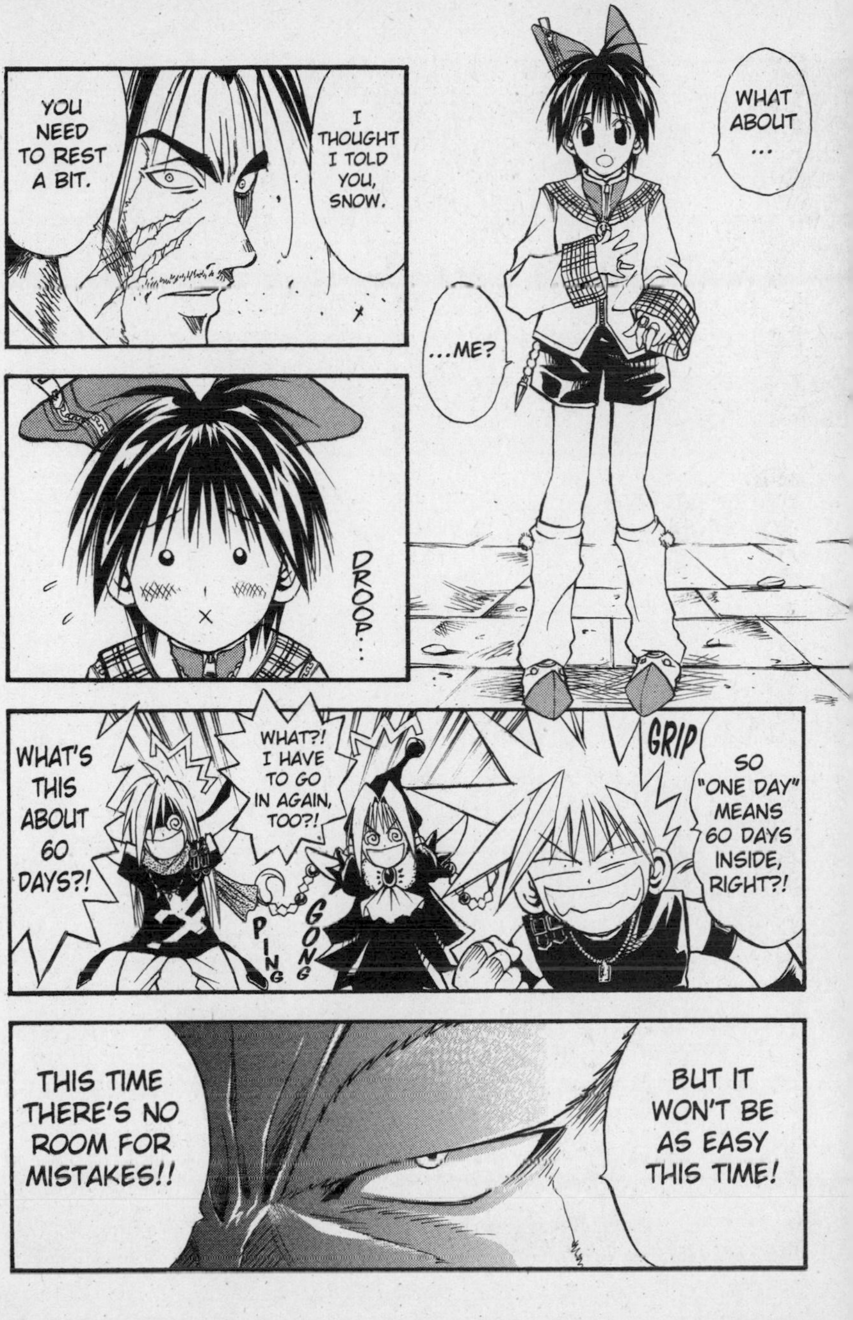
WHAT ABOUT ...
...ME?
I THOUGHT I TOLD YOU, SNOW.
YOU NEED TO REST A BIT.
DROOP...
GRIP
SO "ONE DAY" MEANS 60 DAYS INSIDE, RIGHT?!
WHAT?! I HAVE TO GO IN AGAIN, TOO?!
GONG
PING
WHAT'S THIS ABOUT 60 DAYS?!
BUT IT WON'T BE AS EASY THIS TIME!
THIS TIME THERE'S NO ROOM FOR MISTAKES!!

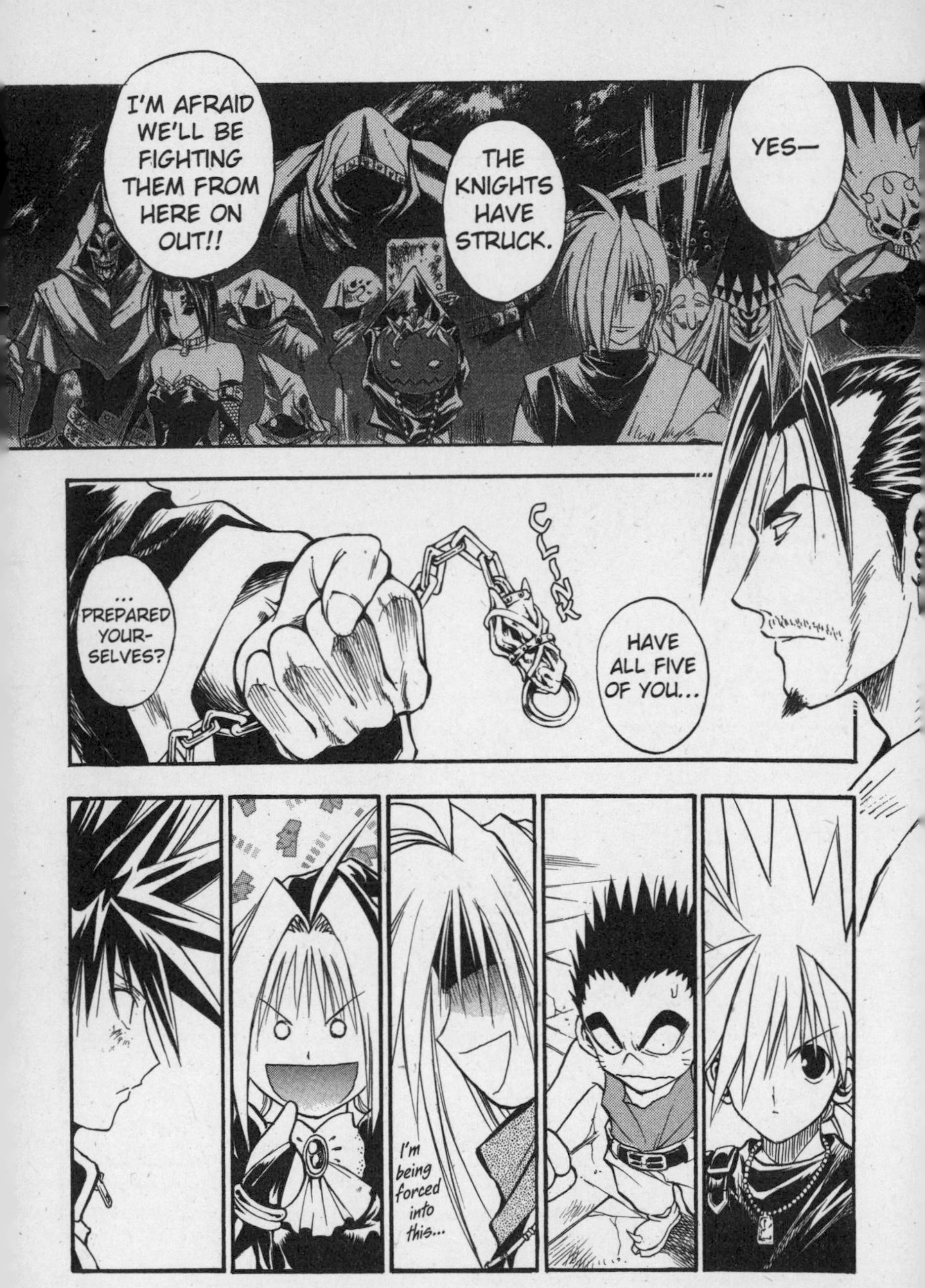
YES—
THE KNIGHTS HAVE STRUCK.
I'M AFRAID WE'LL BE FIGHTING THEM FROM HERE ON OUT!!
HAVE ALL FIVE OF YOU...
CLINK
...PREPARED YOUR-SELVES?
I'm being forced into this...

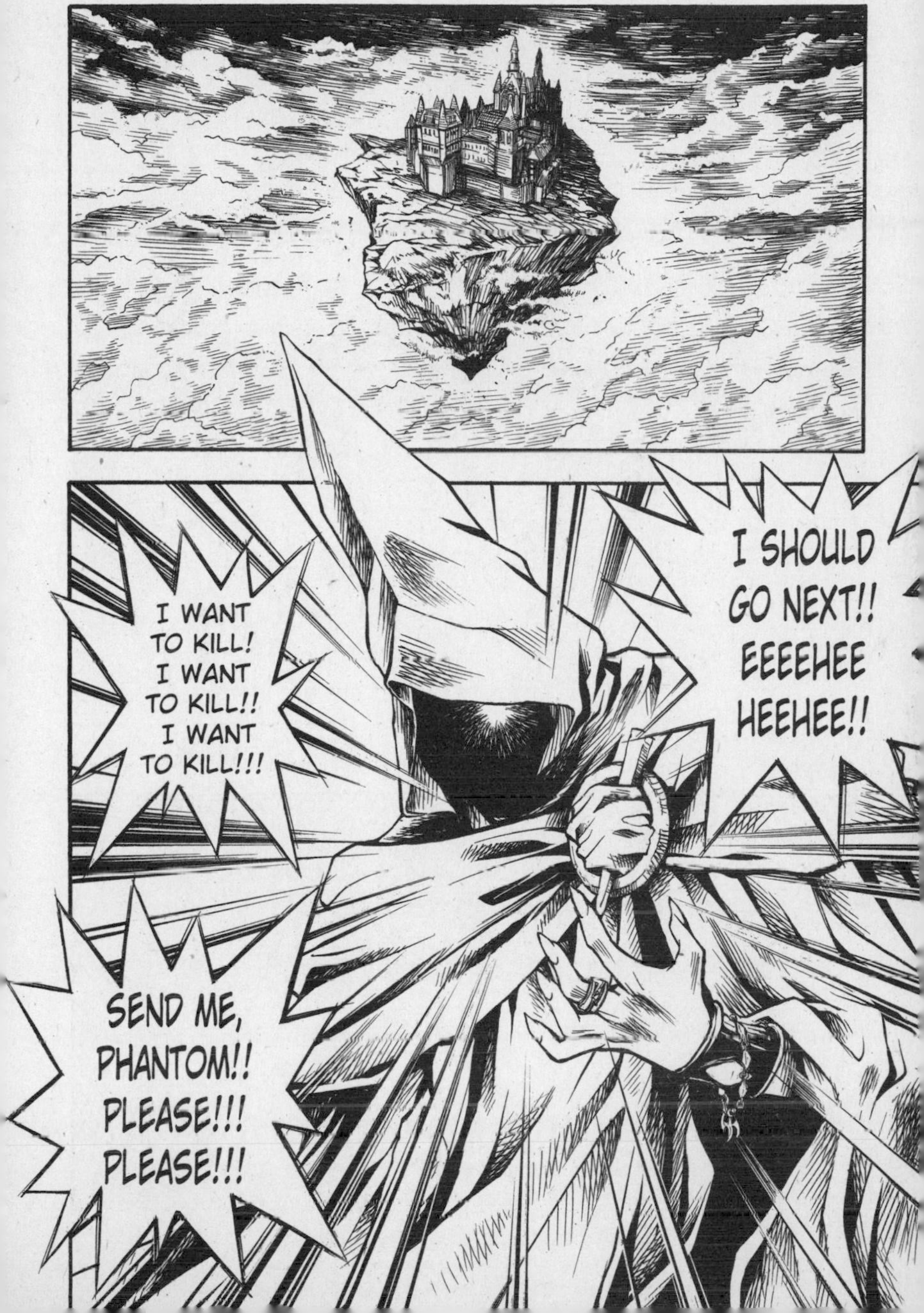
I SHOULD GO NEXT!! EEEEHEE HEEHEE!!
I WANT TO KILL! I WANT TO KILL!! I WANT TO KILL!!!
SEND ME, PHANTOM!! PLEASE!!! PLEASE!!!

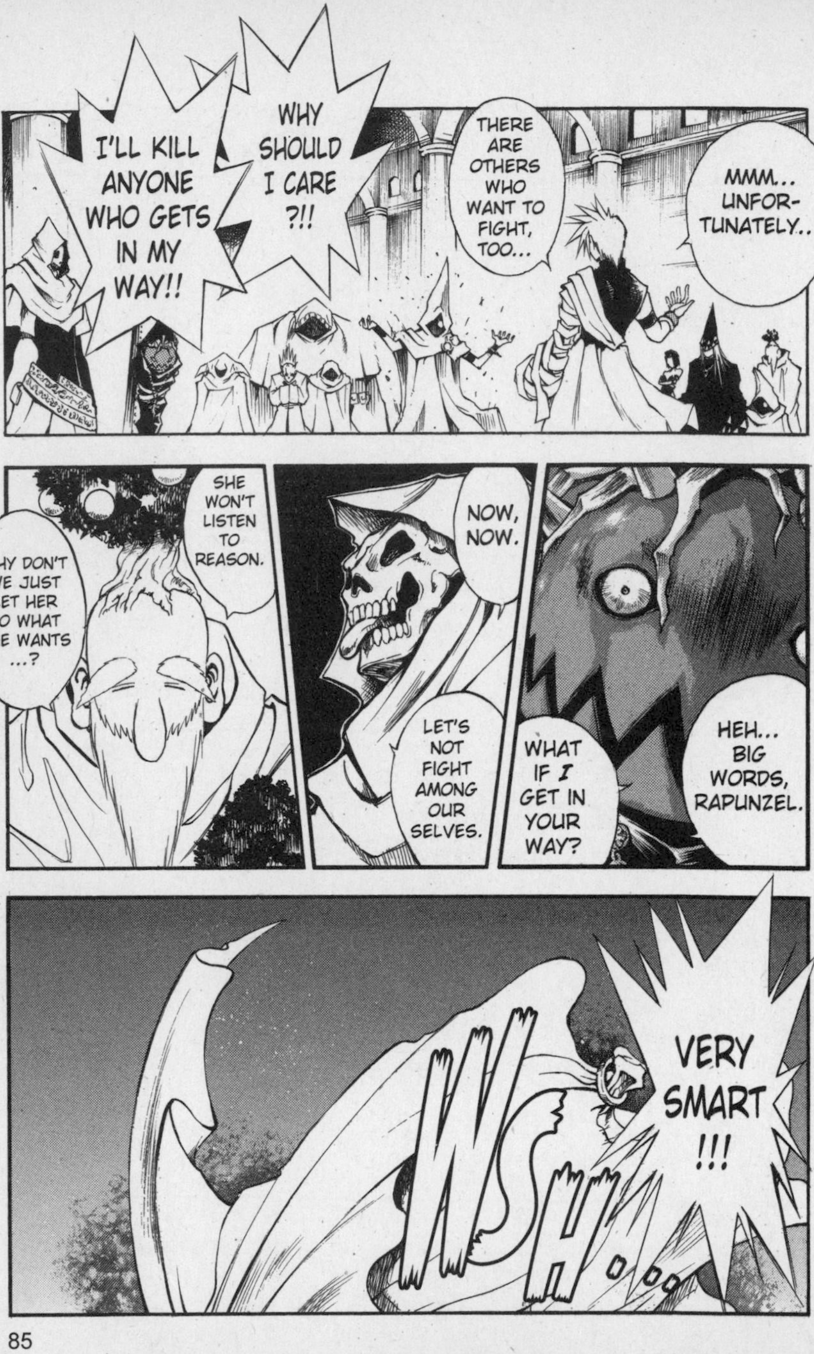
MMM... UNFORTUNATELY...
THERE ARE OTHERS WHO WANT TO FIGHT, TOO...
WHY SHOULD I CARE ?!!
I'LL KILL ANYONE WHO GETS IN MY WAY!!
HEH... BIG WORDS, RAPUNZEL.
WHAT IF I GET IN YOUR WAY?
NOW, NOW.
LET'S NOT FIGHT AMONG OUR SELVES.
SHE WON'T LISTEN TO REASON.
WHY DON'T WE JUST LET HER DO WHAT SHE WANTS ...?
VERY SMART !!!
WSH...

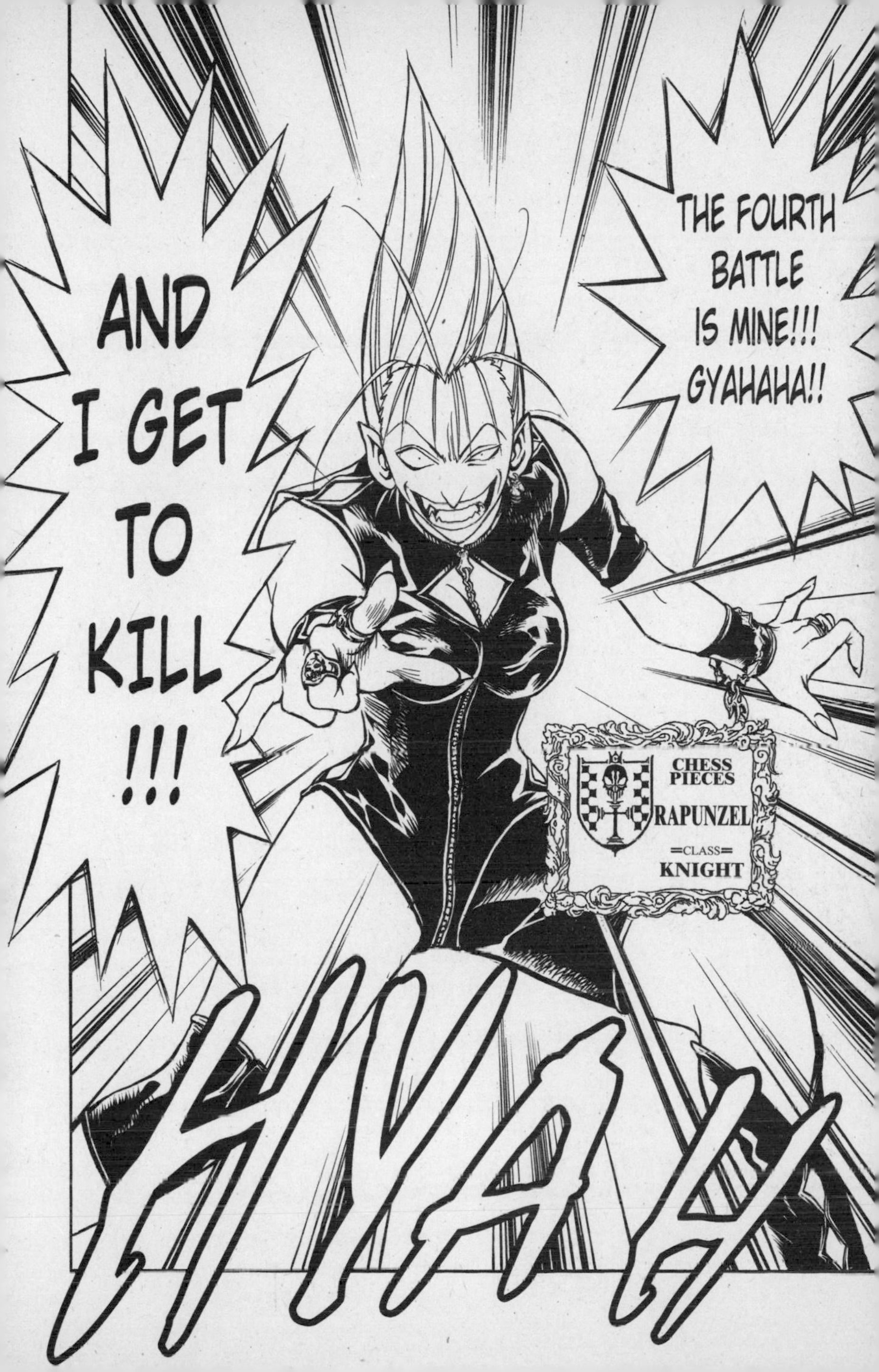
THE FOURTH BATTLE IS MINE!!! GYAHAHA!!
AND I GET TO KILL!!!
CHESS PIECES
RAPUNZEL
=CLASS=
KNIGHT
HYAH

AKT.69/
SHADOW BATTLES

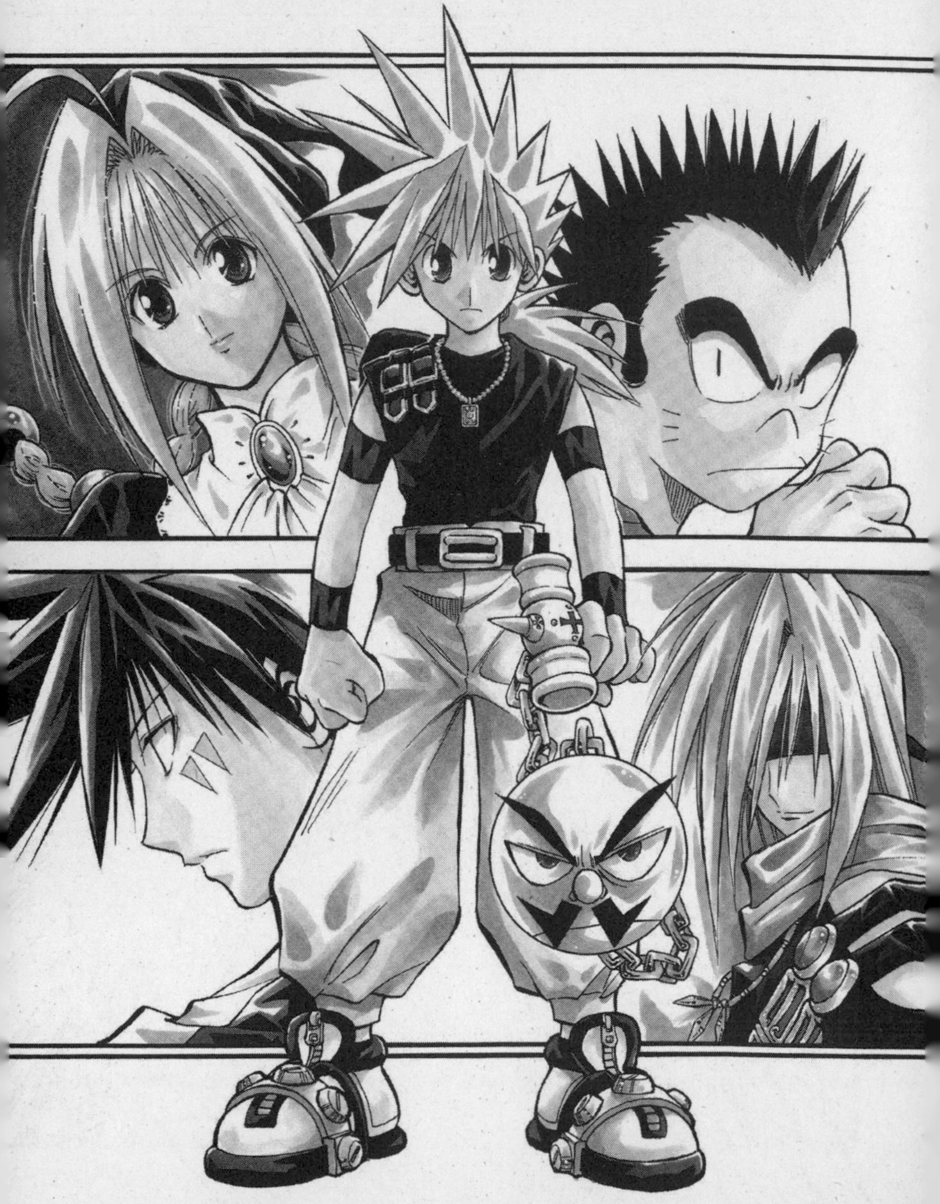

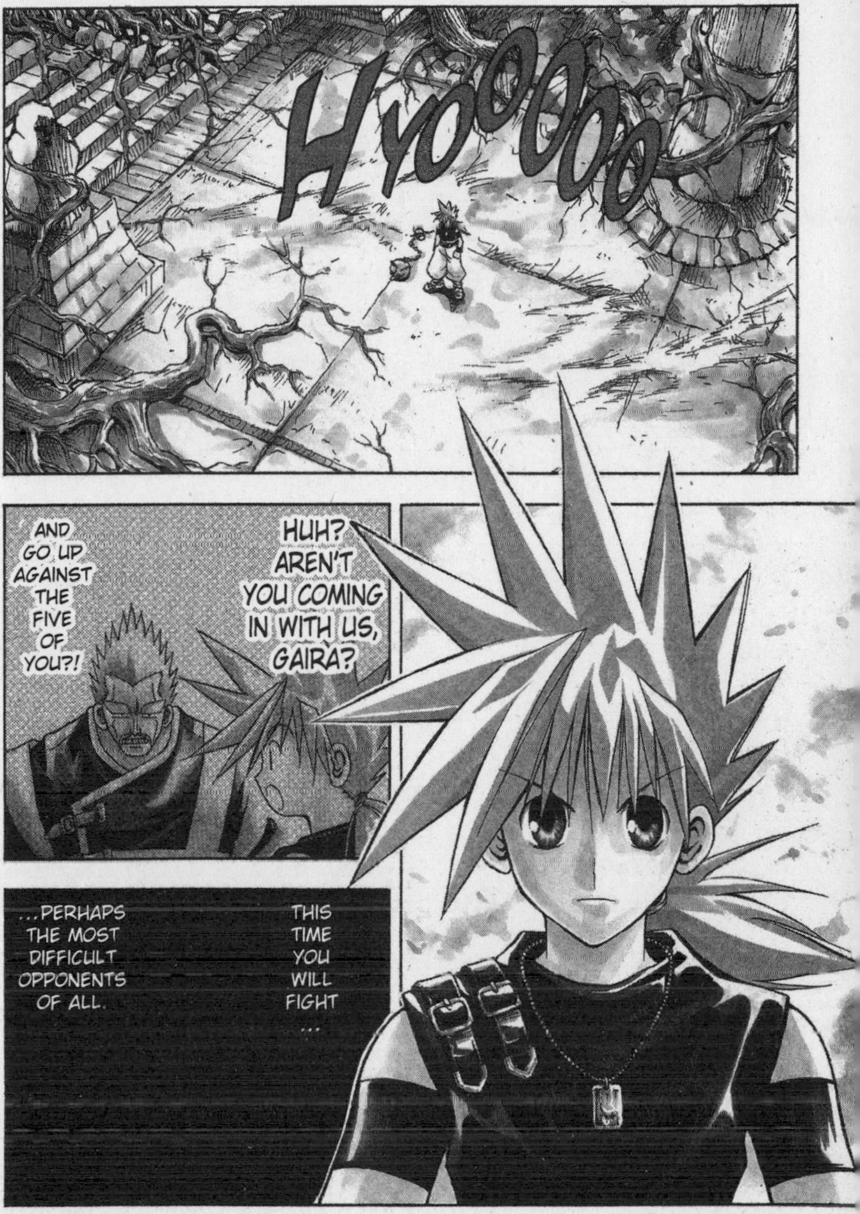
HYOOOOO
HUH? AREN'T YOU COMING IN WITH US, GAIRA?
AND GO UP AGAINST THE FIVE OF YOU?!
THIS TIME YOU WILL FIGHT ...
...PERHAPS THE MOST DIFFICULT OPPONENTS OF ALL.

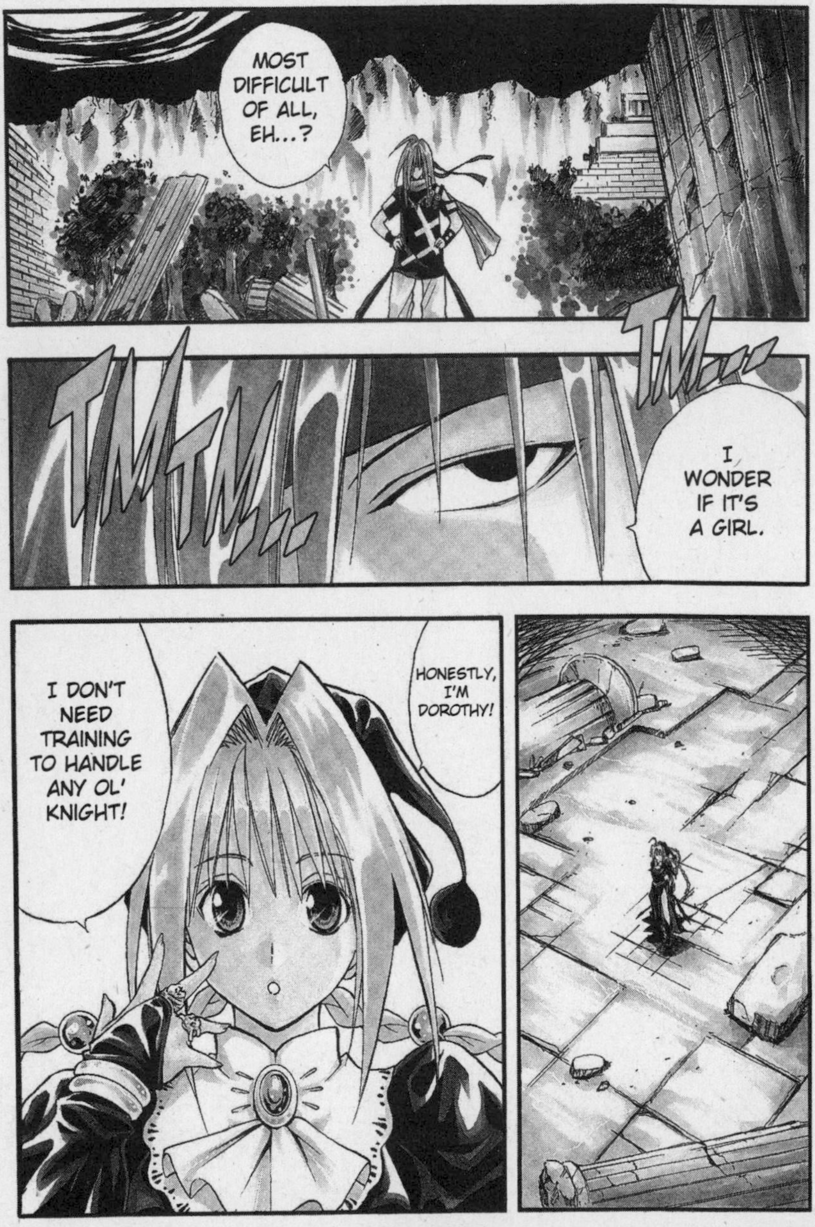
MOST DIFFICULT OF ALL, EH...?
TM...
I WONDER IF IT'S A GIRL.
TMTM...
HONESTLY, I'M DOROTHY!
I DON'T NEED TRAINING TO HANDLE ANY OL' KNIGHT!

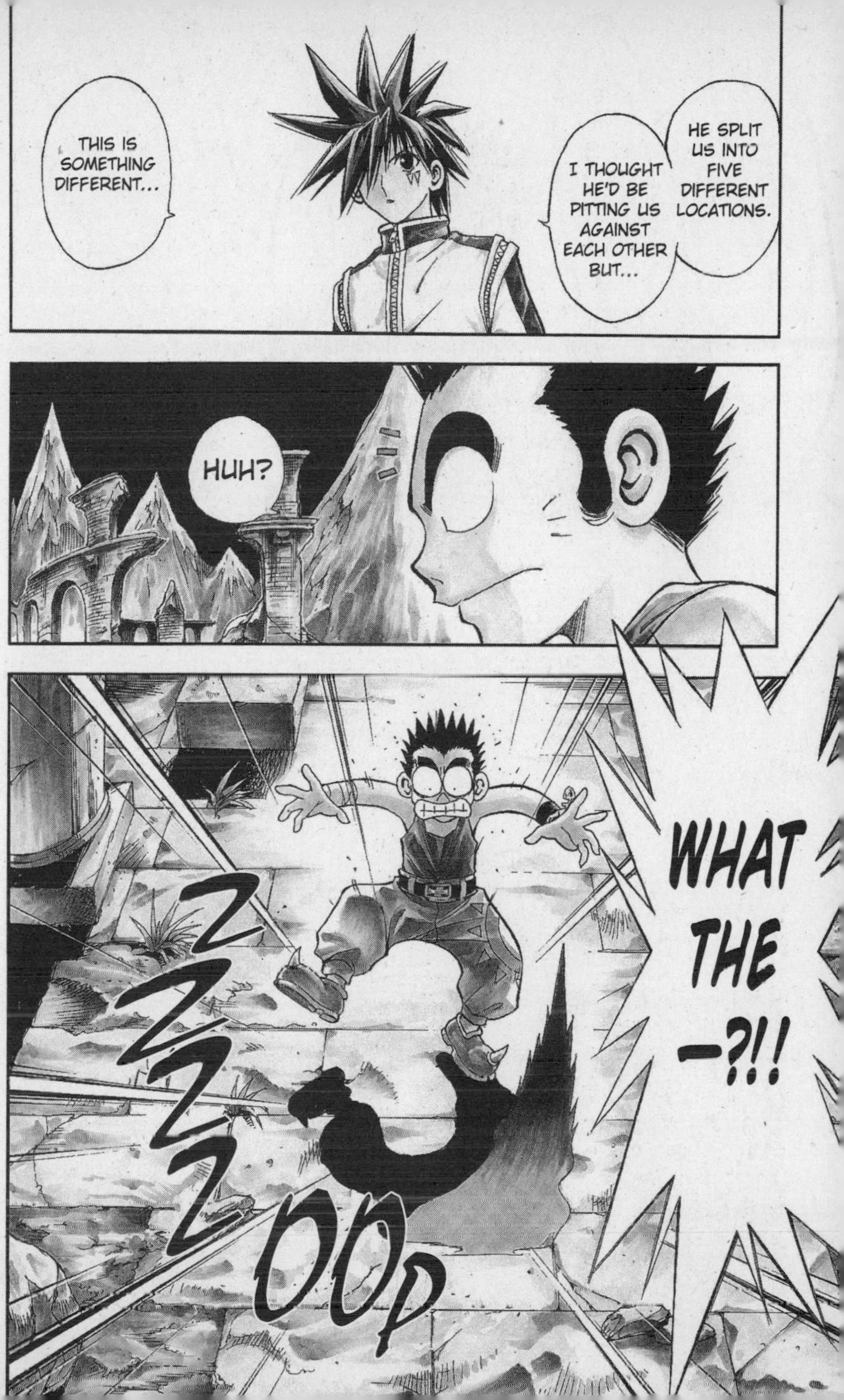
HE SPLIT US INTO FIVE DIFFERENT LOCATIONS.
I THOUGHT HE'D BE PITTING US AGAINST EACH OTHER BUT...
THIS IS SOMETHING DIFFERENT...
HUH?
WHAT THE —?!!
ZZZZOOP

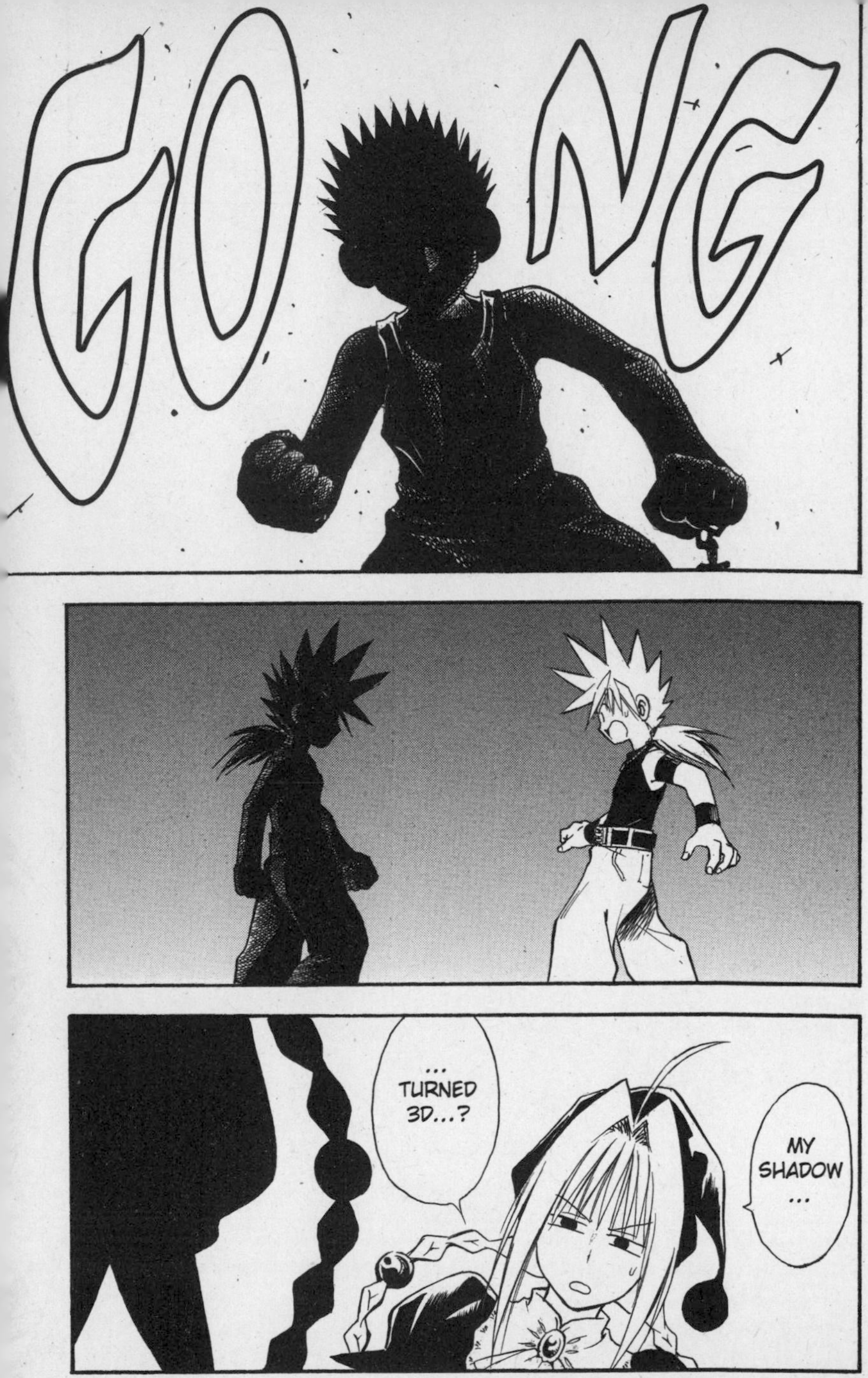
GONG
MY SHADOW ...
... TURNED 3D...?

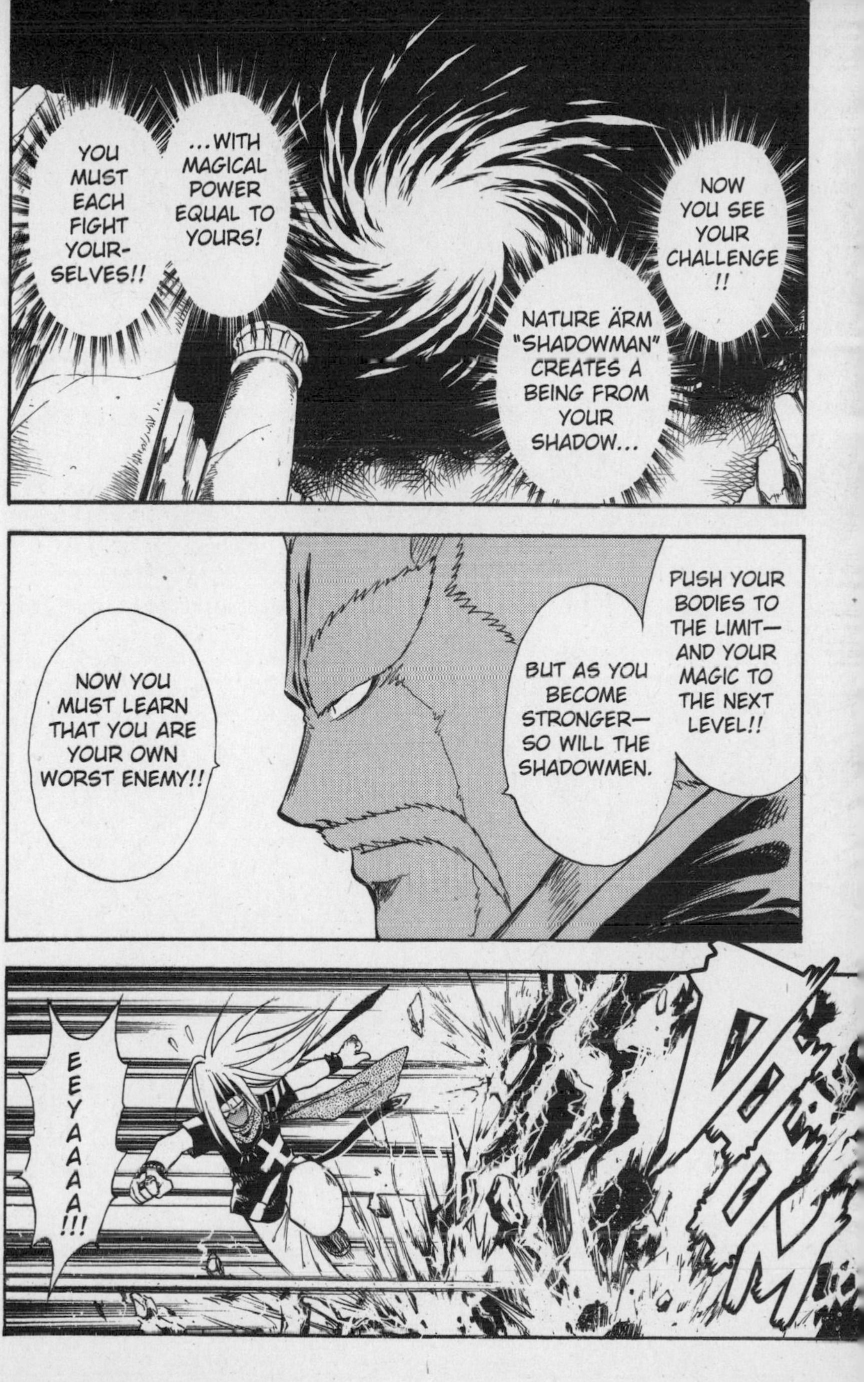
NOW YOU SEE YOUR CHALLENGE!!
NATURE ÄRM "SHADOWMAN" CREATES A BEING FROM YOUR SHADOW...
...WITH MAGICAL POWER EQUAL TO YOURS!
YOU MUST EACH FIGHT YOUR-SELVES!!
PUSH YOUR BODIES TO THE LIMIT—AND YOUR MAGIC TO THE NEXT LEVEL!!
BUT AS YOU BECOME STRONGER—SO WILL THE SHADOWMEN.
NOW YOU MUST LEARN THAT YOU ARE YOUR OWN WORST ENEMY!!
EEYAAAAA!!!

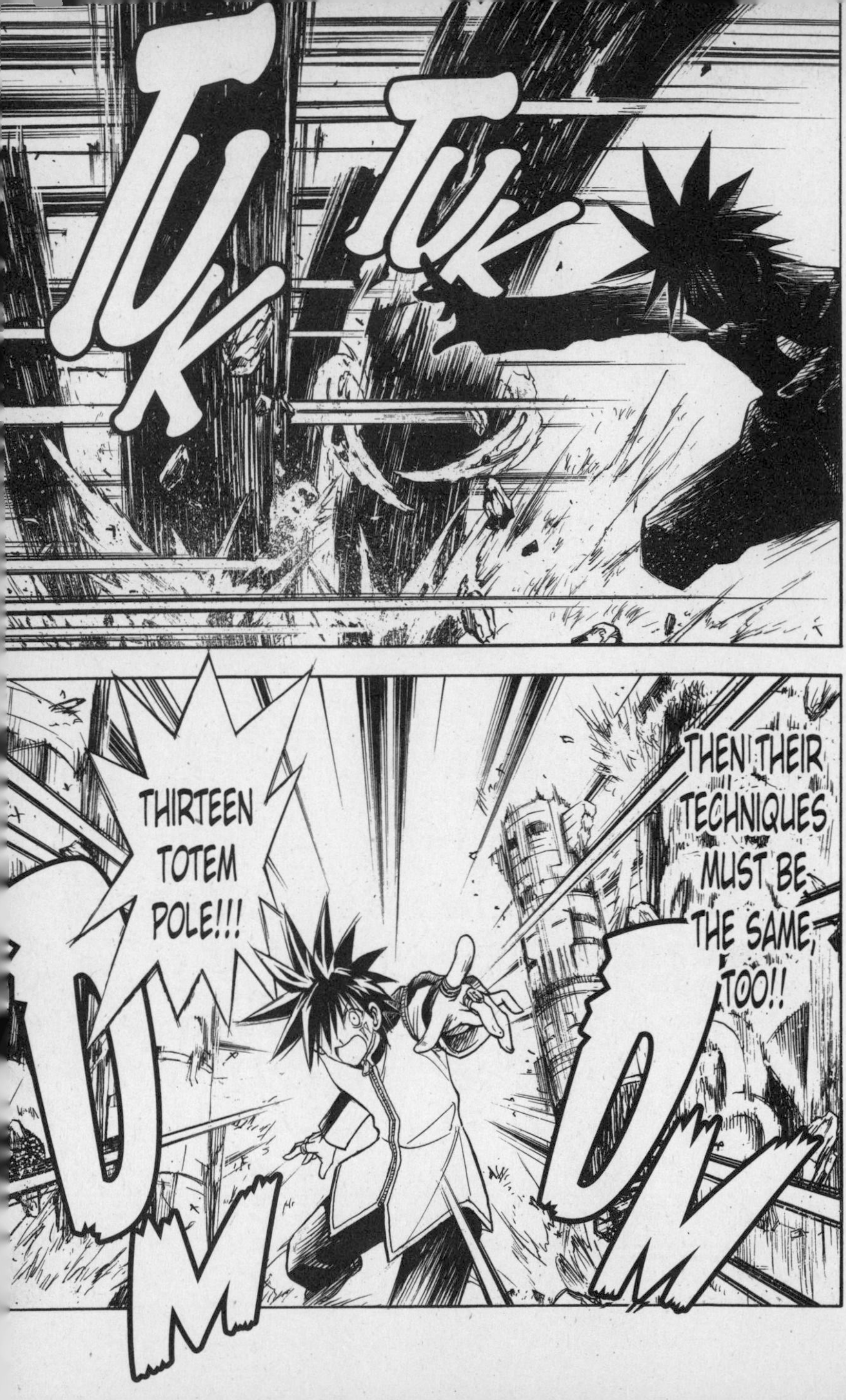
TUK TUK
THEN THEIR TECHNIQUES MUST BE THE SAME, TOO!!
THIRTEEN TOTEM POLE!!!
DOOM

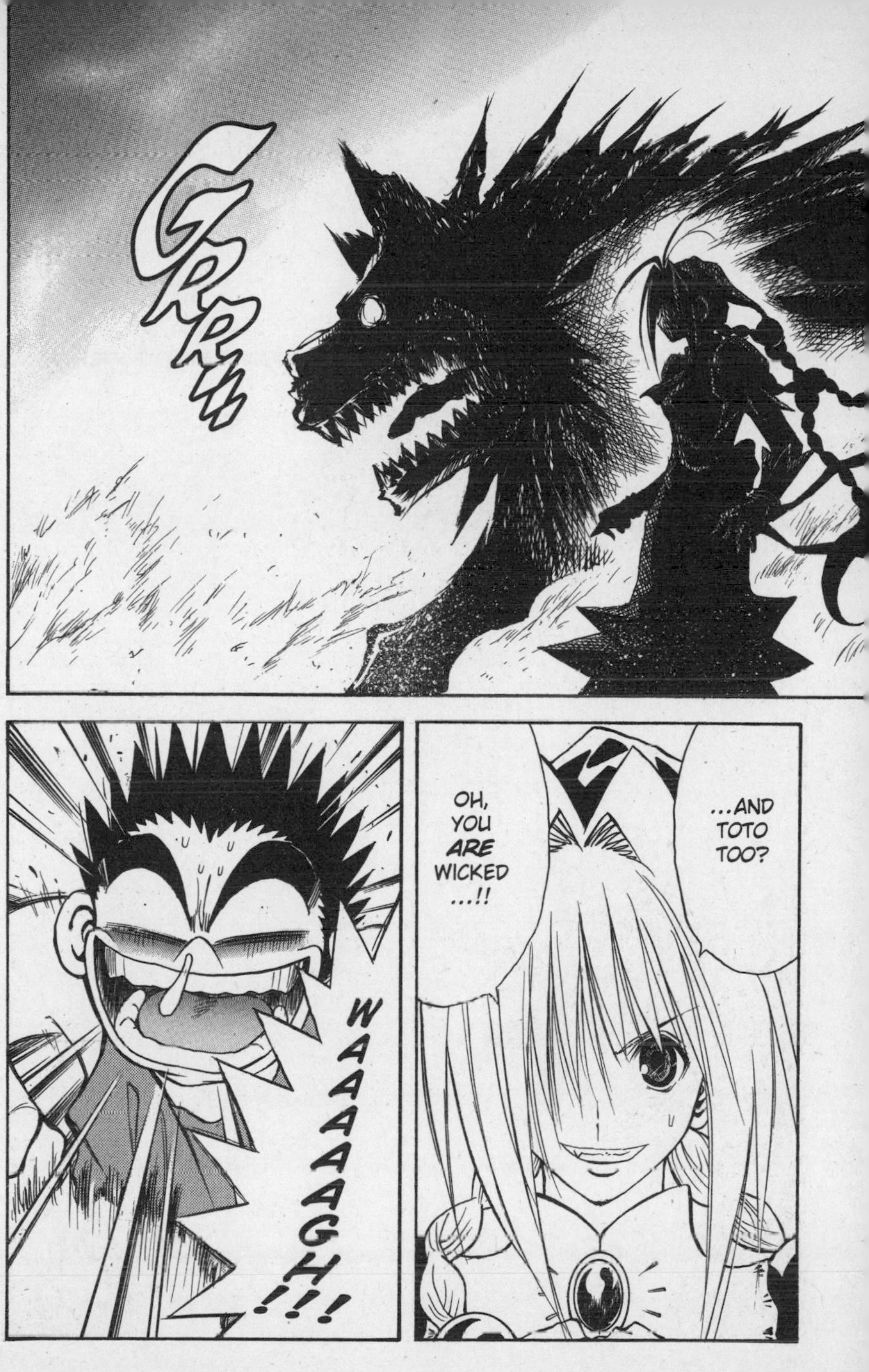
GRRR
...AND TOTO TOO?
OH, YOU ARE WICKED ...!!
WAAAAAAAGH!!!

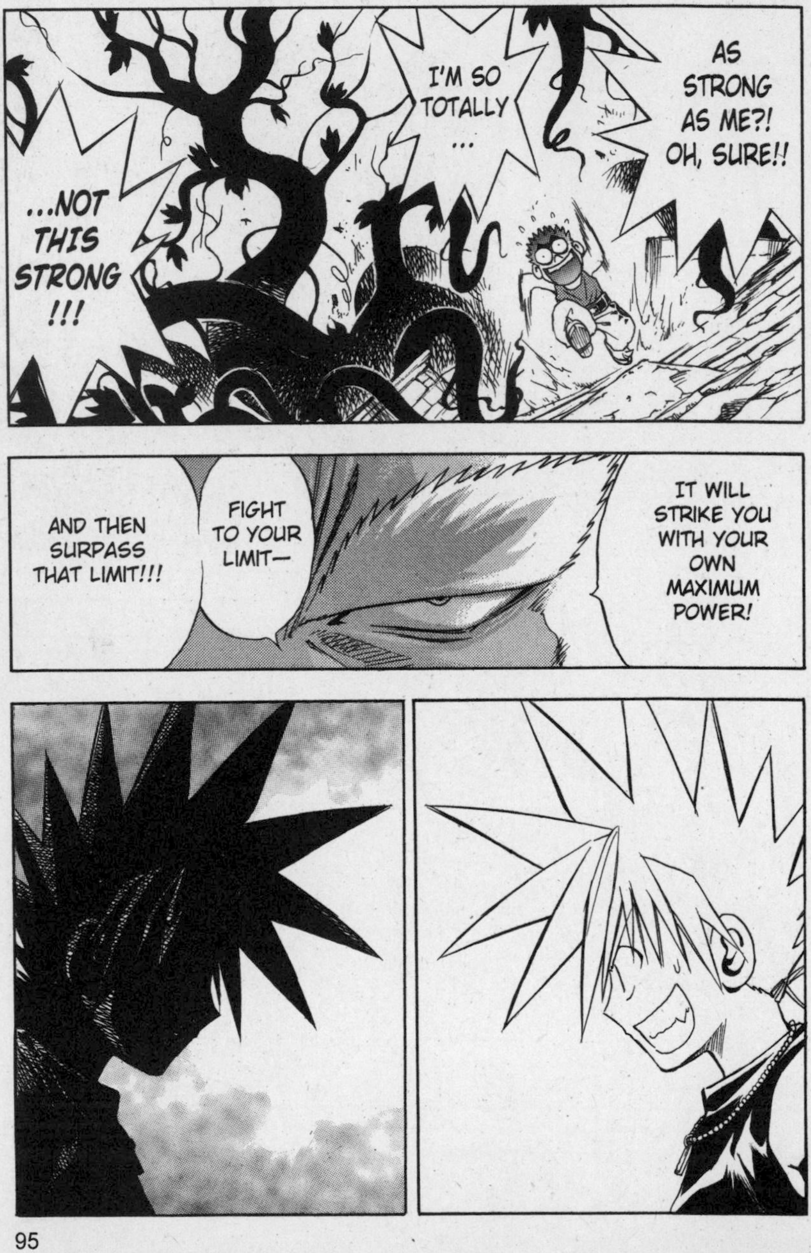
AS STRONG AS ME?! OH, SURE!!
I'M SO TOTALLY ...
...NOT THIS STRONG !!!
IT WILL STRIKE YOU WITH YOUR OWN MAXIMUM POWER!
FIGHT TO YOUR LIMIT—
AND THEN SURPASS THAT LIMIT!!!

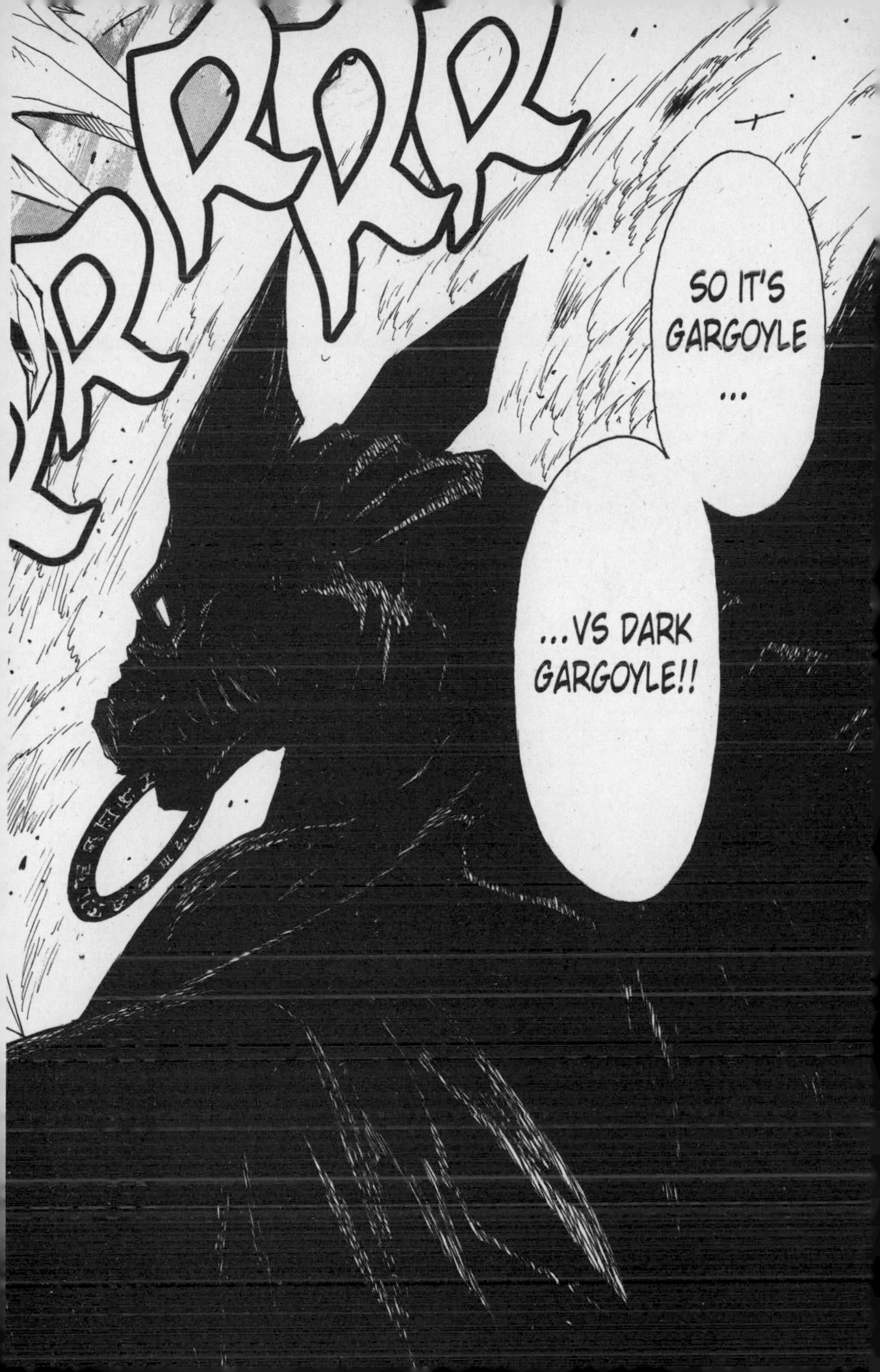
SO IT'S GARGOYLE ...
...VS DARK GARGOYLE!!

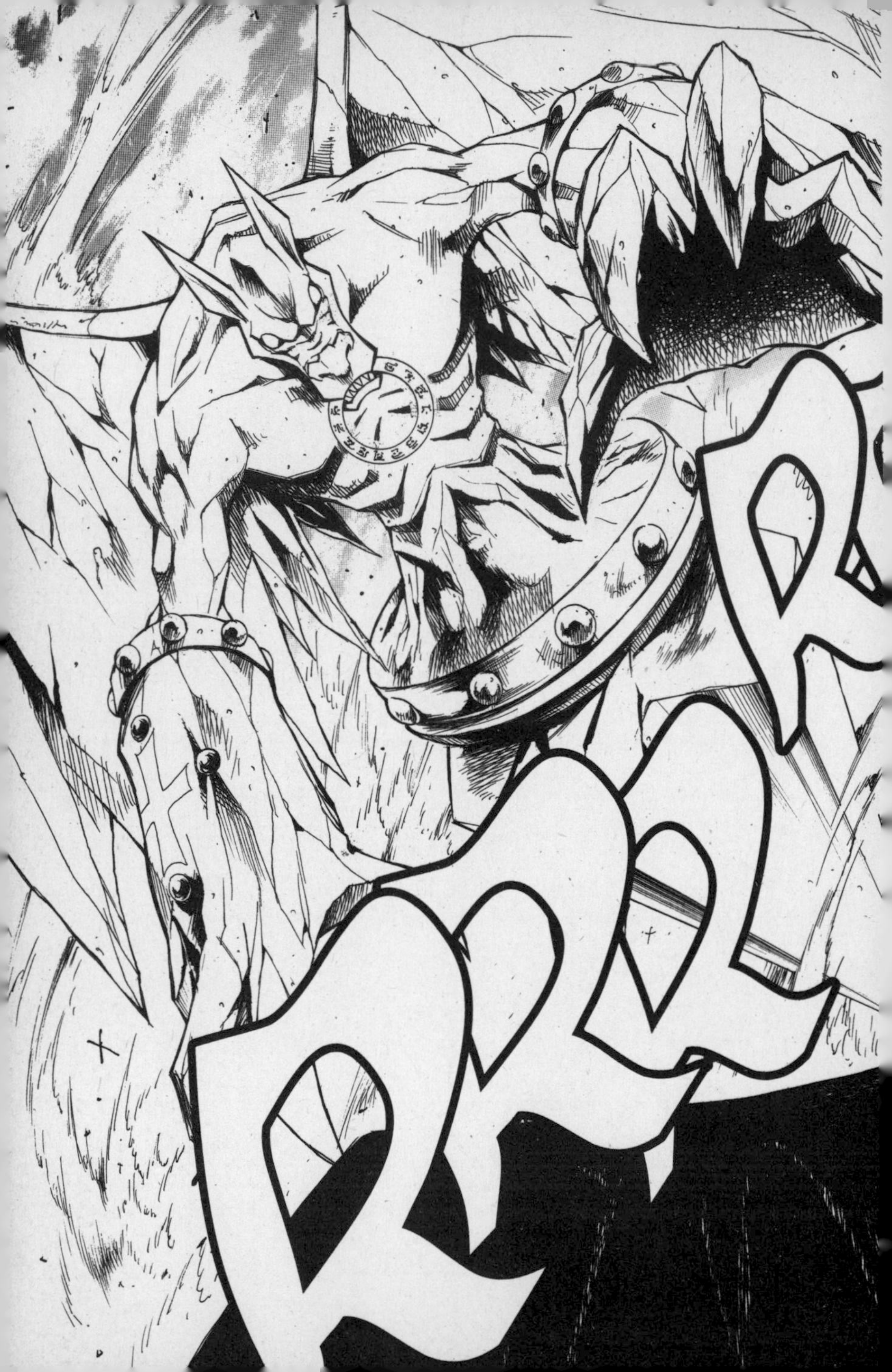
RRRR

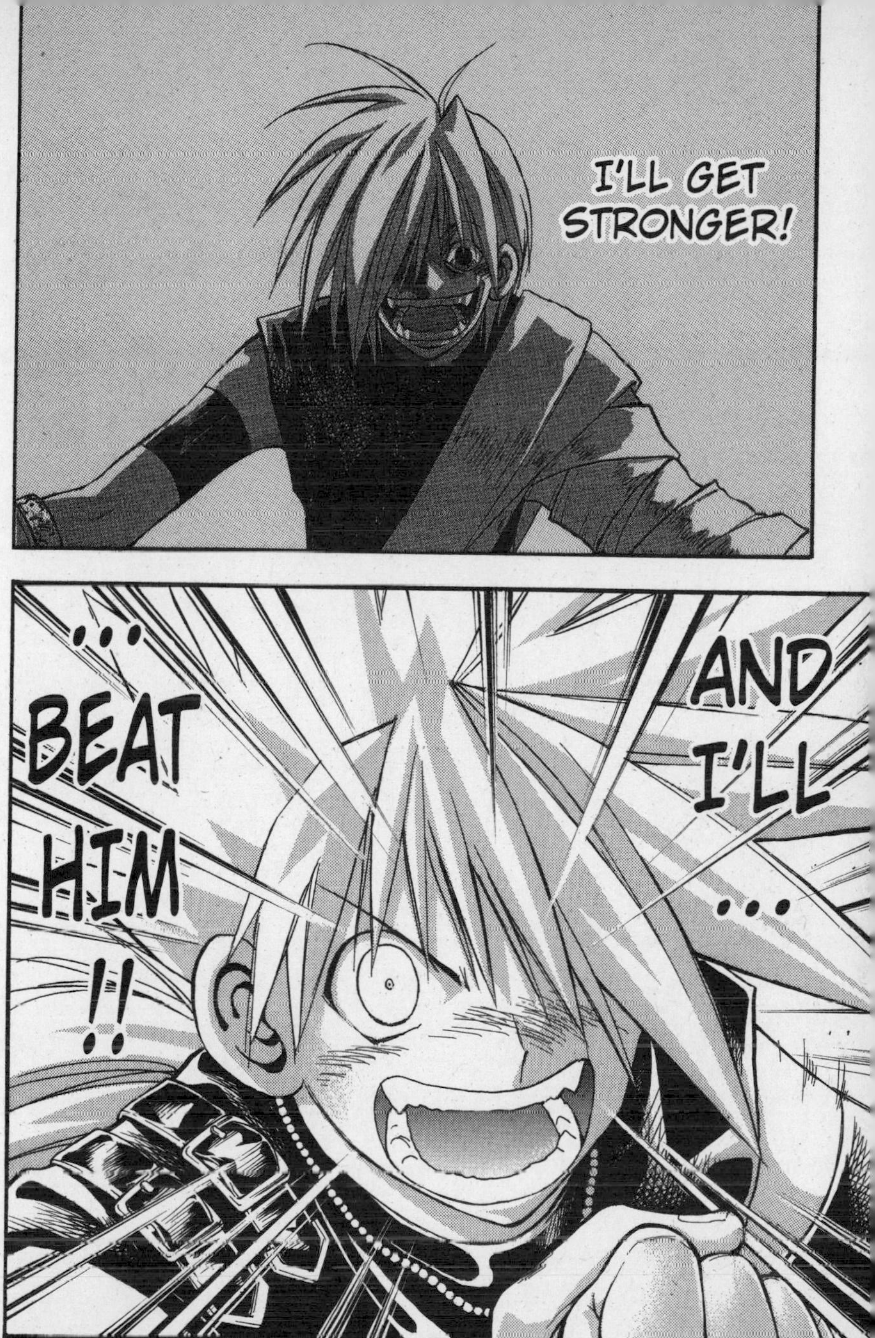
I'LL GET STRONGER!
AND I'LL...
...BEAT HIM!!

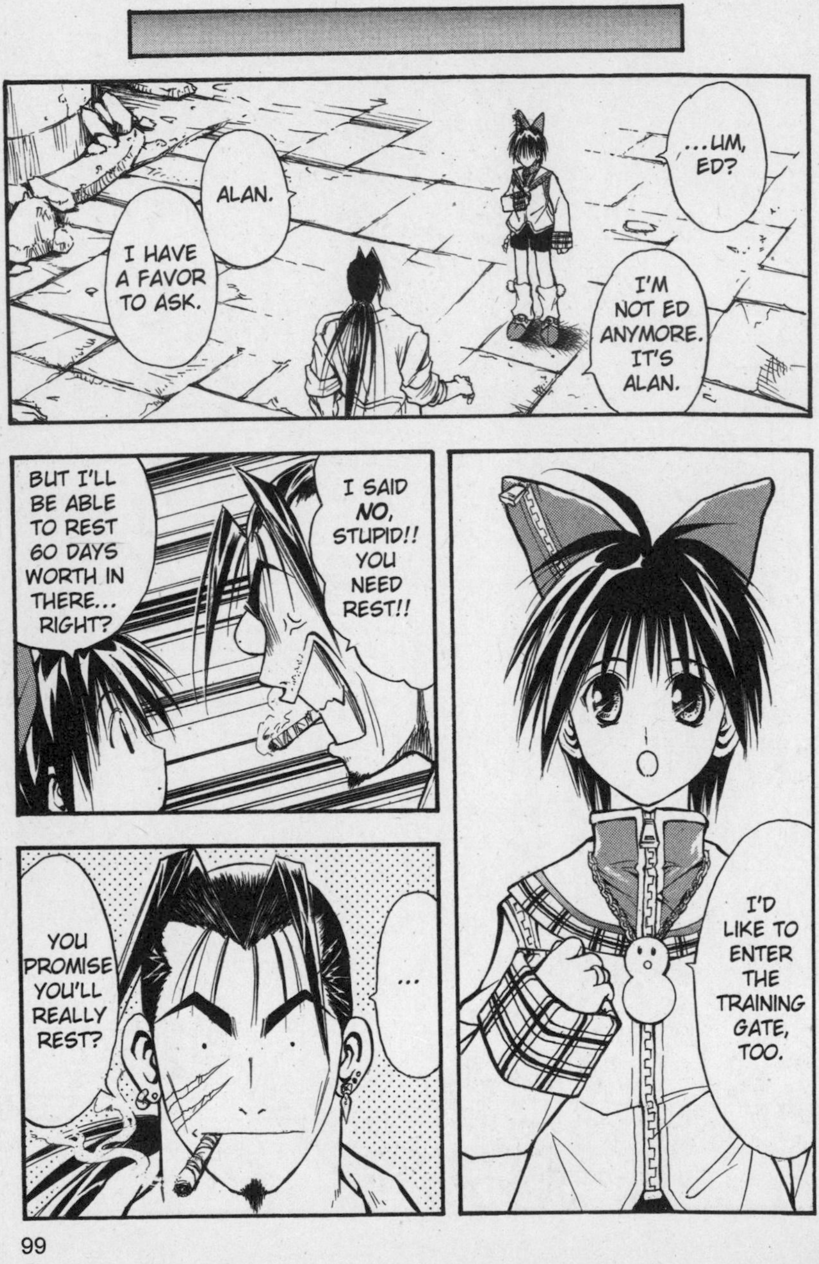
...UM, ED?
I'M NOT ED ANYMORE. IT'S ALAN.
ALAN.
I HAVE A FAVOR TO ASK.
I'D LIKE TO ENTER THE TRAINING GATE, TOO.
I SAID NO, STUPID!! YOU NEED REST!!
BUT I'LL BE ABLE TO REST 60 DAYS WORTH IN THERE... RIGHT?
...
YOU PROMISE YOU'LL REALLY REST?

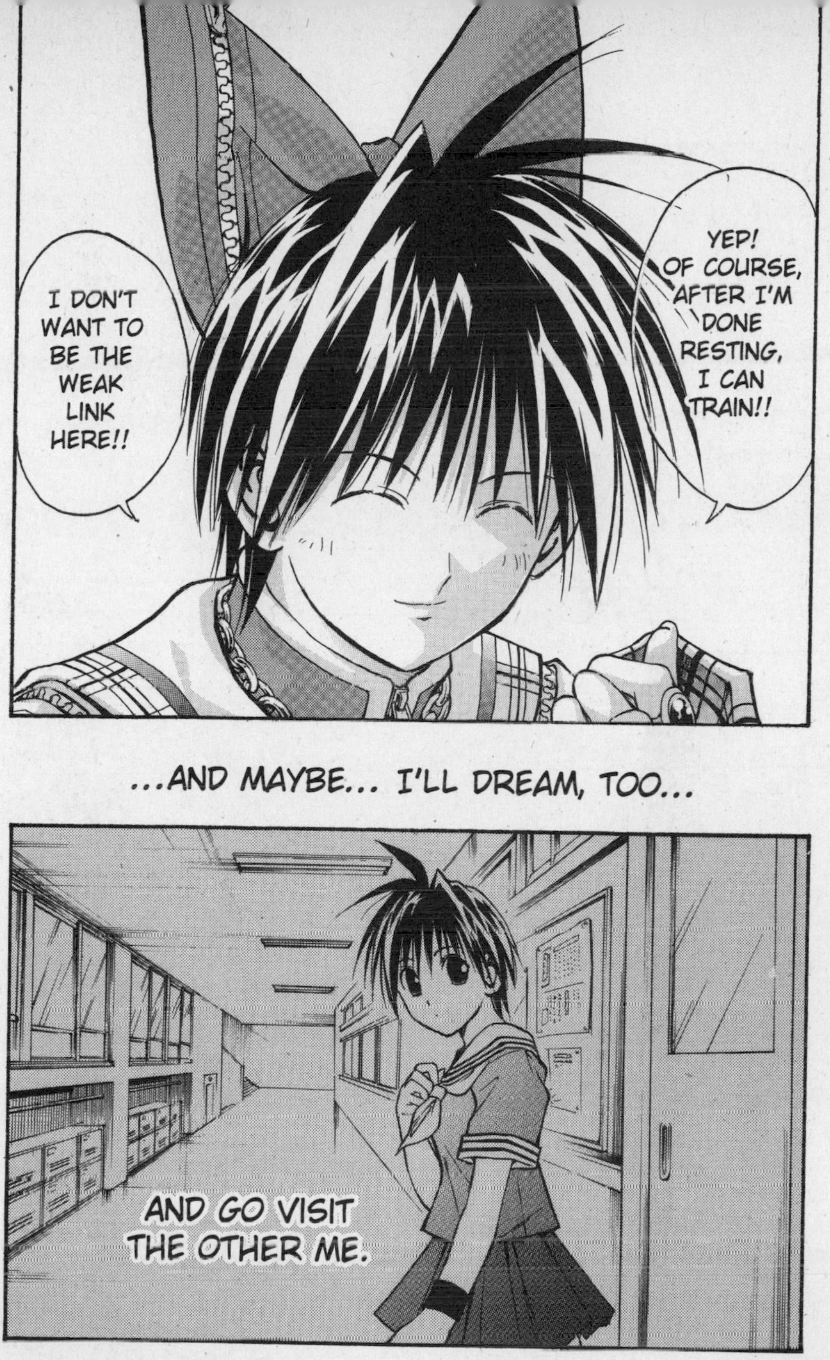
YEP! OF COURSE, AFTER I'M DONE RESTING, I CAN TRAIN!!
I DON'T WANT TO BE THE WEAK LINK HERE!!
...AND MAYBE... I'LL DREAM, TOO...
AND GO VISIT THE OTHER ME.

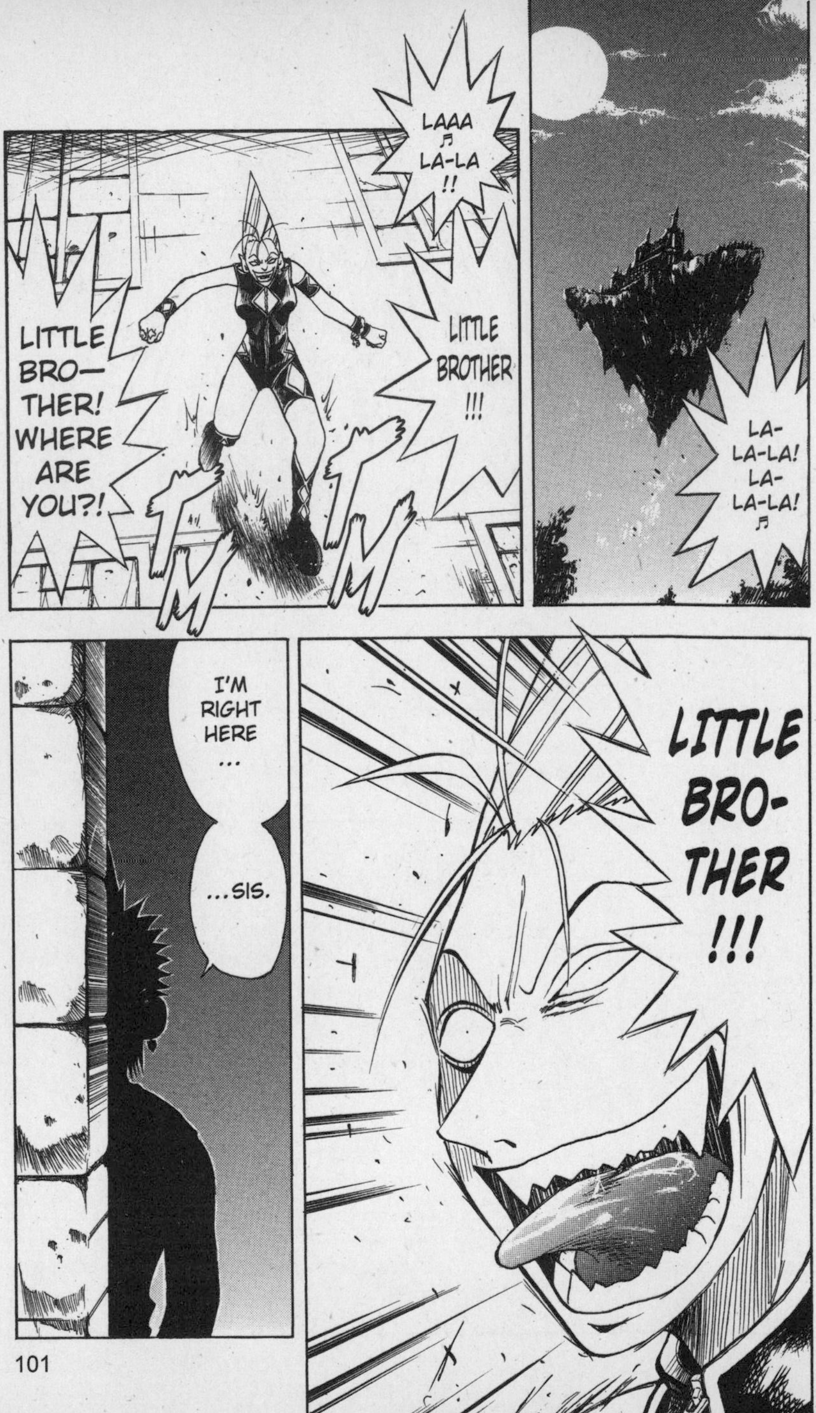
LAAA ♪ LA-LA !!
LA-LA-LA! LA-LA-LA! ♬
LITTLE BROTHER !!!
LITTLE BRO— THER! WHERE ARE YOU?!
LITTLE BRO-THER !!!
I'M RIGHT HERE ...
...SIS.

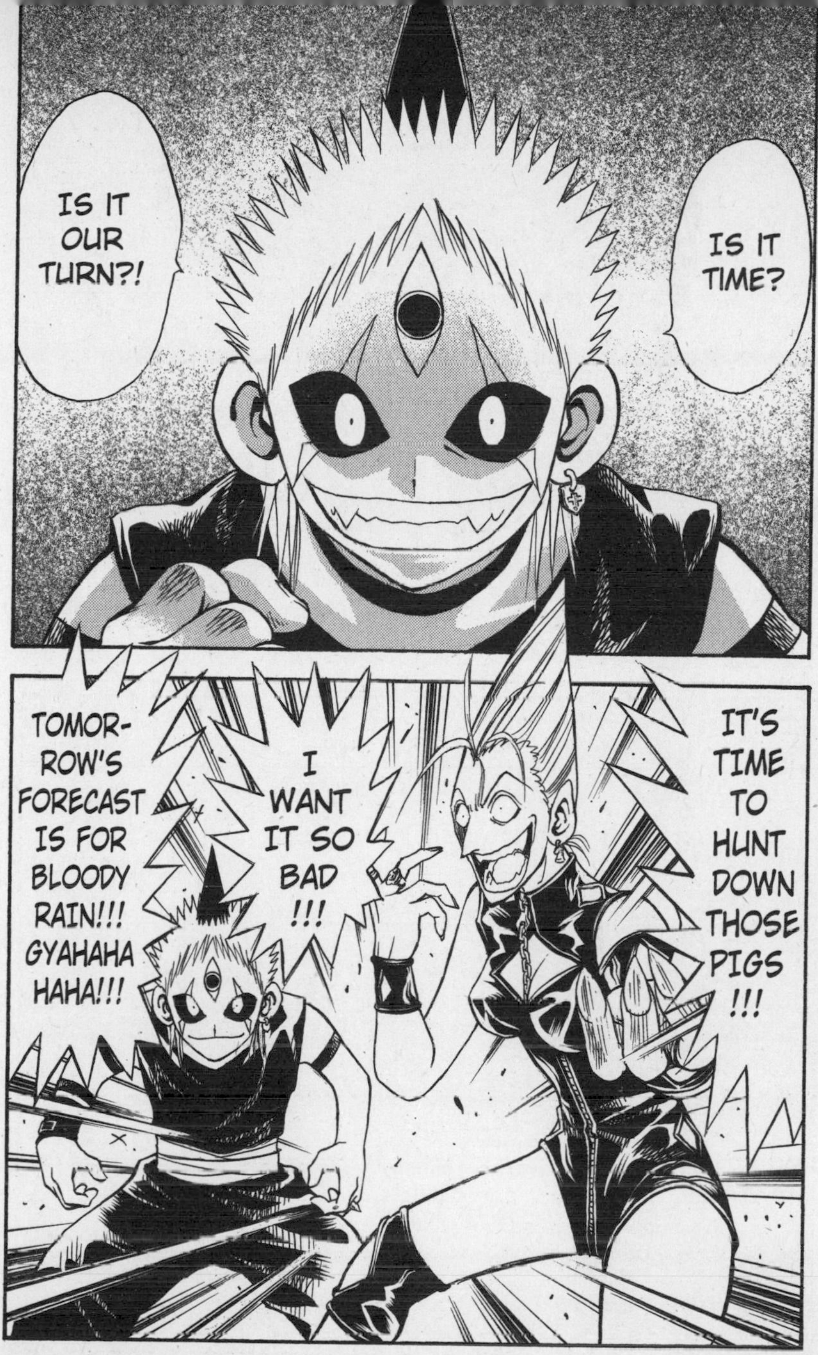
IS IT TIME?
IS IT OUR TURN?!
IT'S TIME TO HUNT DOWN THOSE PIGS!!!
I WANT IT SO BAD!!!
TOMOR-ROW'S FORECAST IS FOR BLOODY RAIN!!! GYAHAHA HAHA!!!

AKT.70/ SYNCHRONICITY

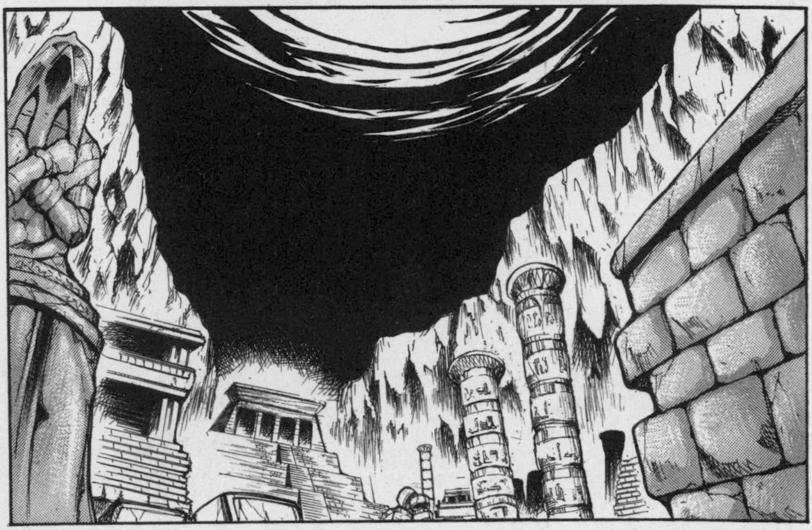

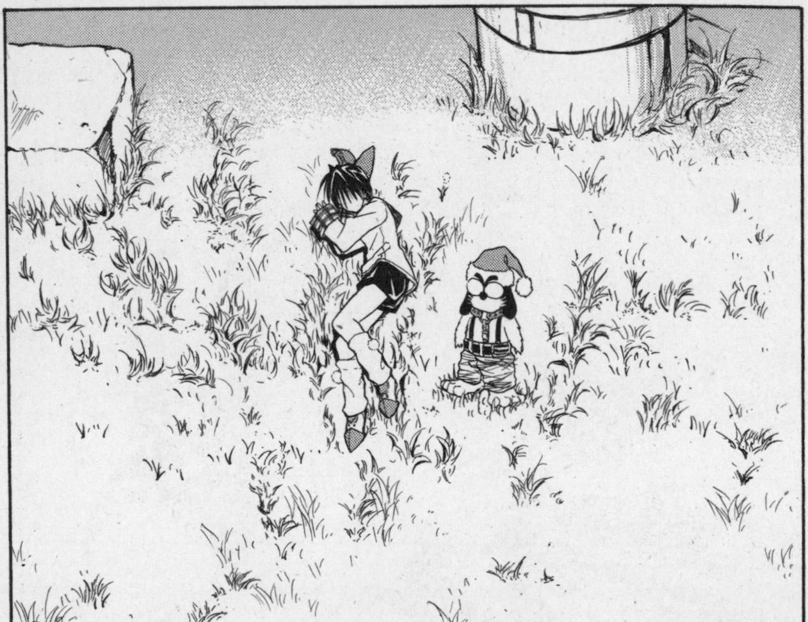

AKT.70/ SYNCHRONICITY

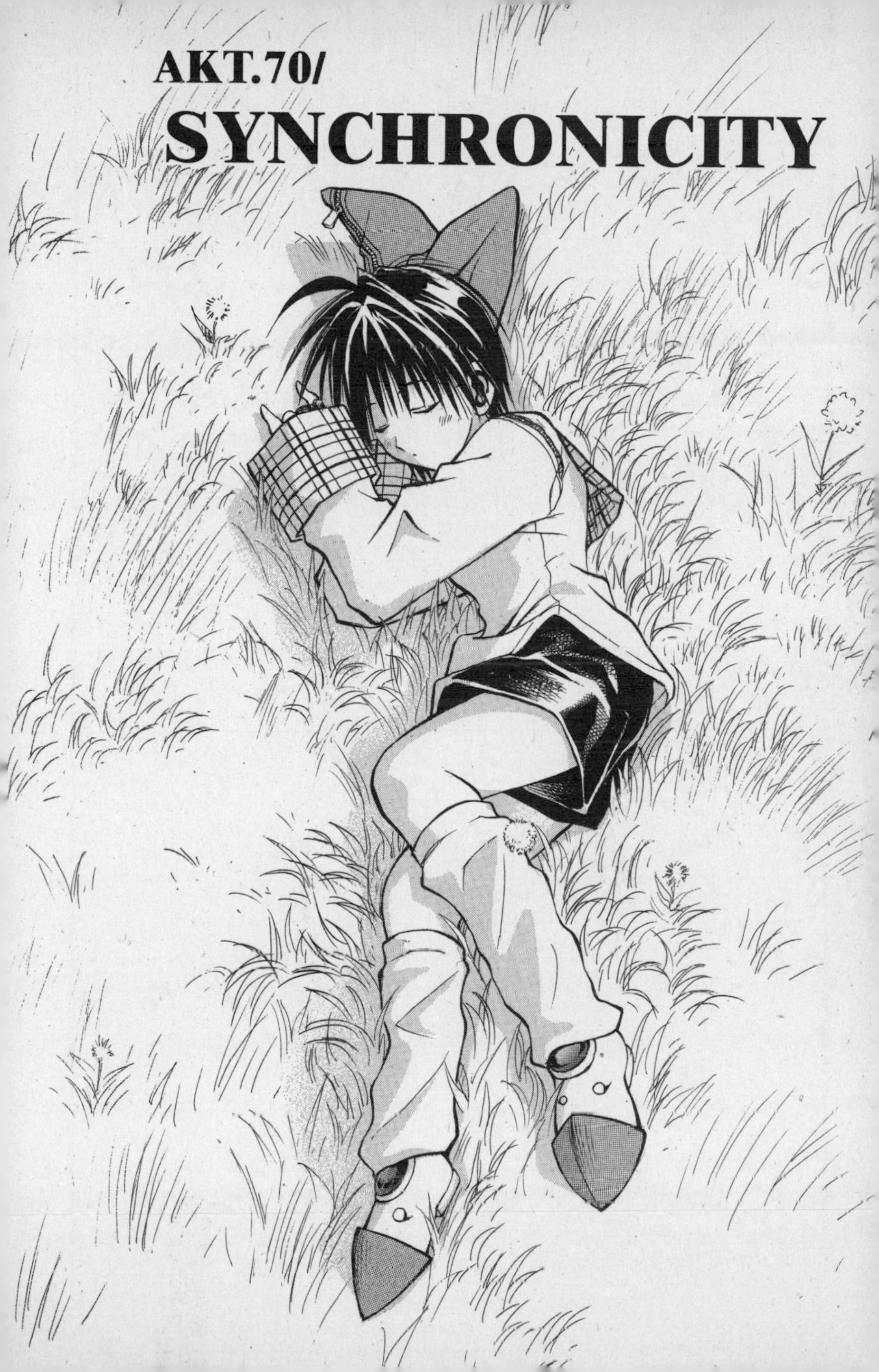

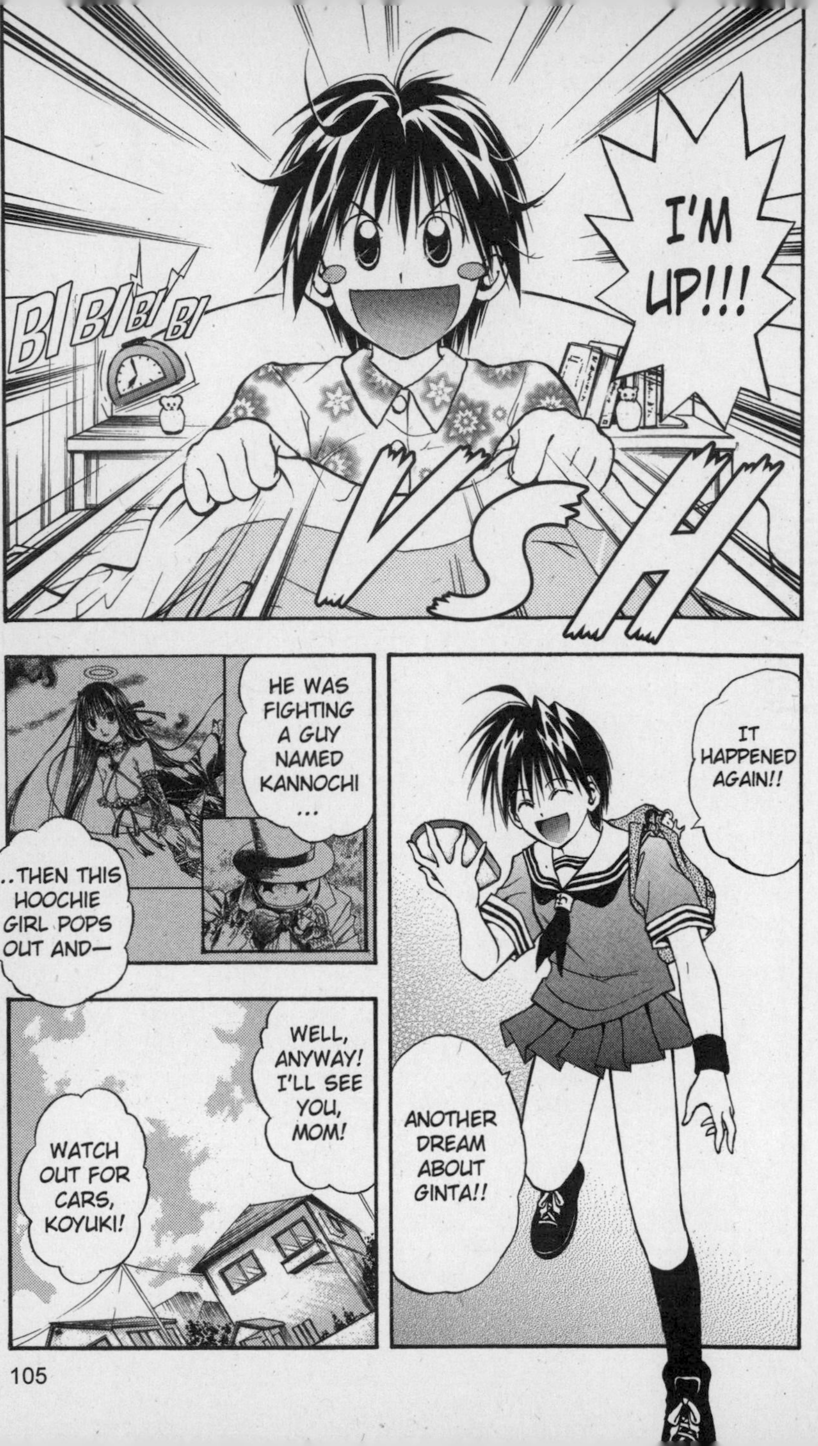
I'M UP!!!
BI BI BI BI
VSH
IT HAPPENED AGAIN!!
ANOTHER DREAM ABOUT GINTA!!
HE WAS FIGHTING A GUY NAMED KANNOCHI ...
...THEN THIS HOOCHIE GIRL POPS OUT AND—
WELL, ANYWAY! I'LL SEE YOU, MOM!
WATCH OUT FOR CARS, KOYUKI!

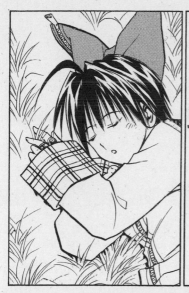

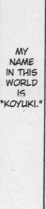

MY NAME IN THIS WORLD IS "KOYUKI."
I GO TO A PLACE CALLED "SCHOOL"...
WHERE MANY PEOPLE CONGRE-GATE FOR TRAINING...
...TO INCREASE THEIR MENTAL POWERS.

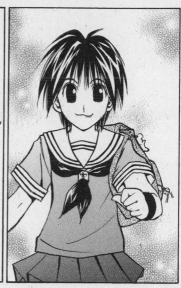

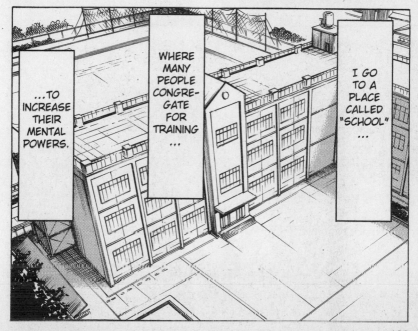

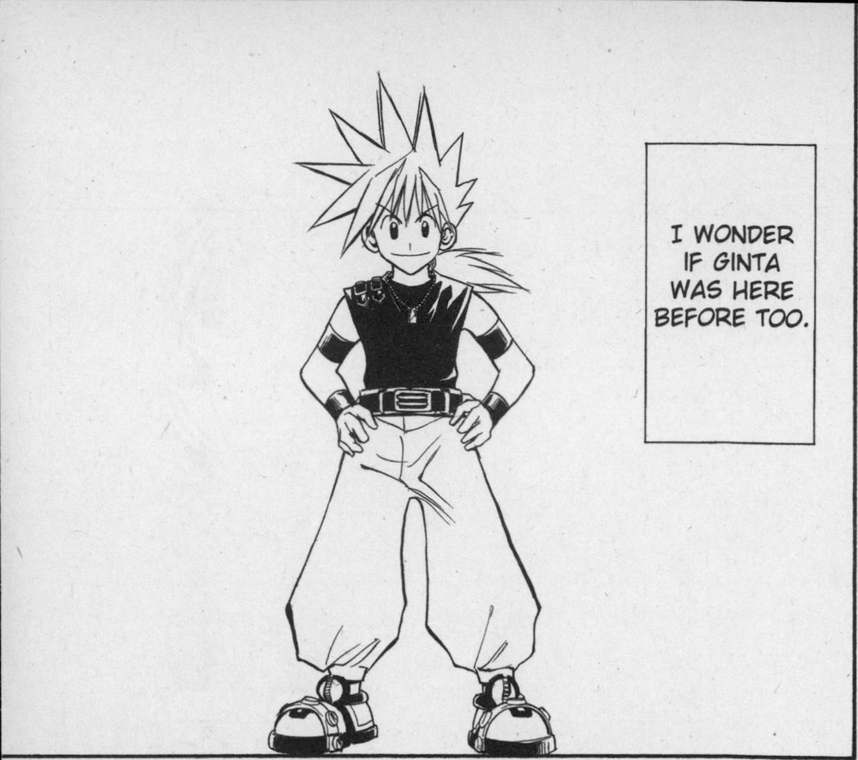
I WONDER IF GINTA WAS HERE BEFORE TOO.

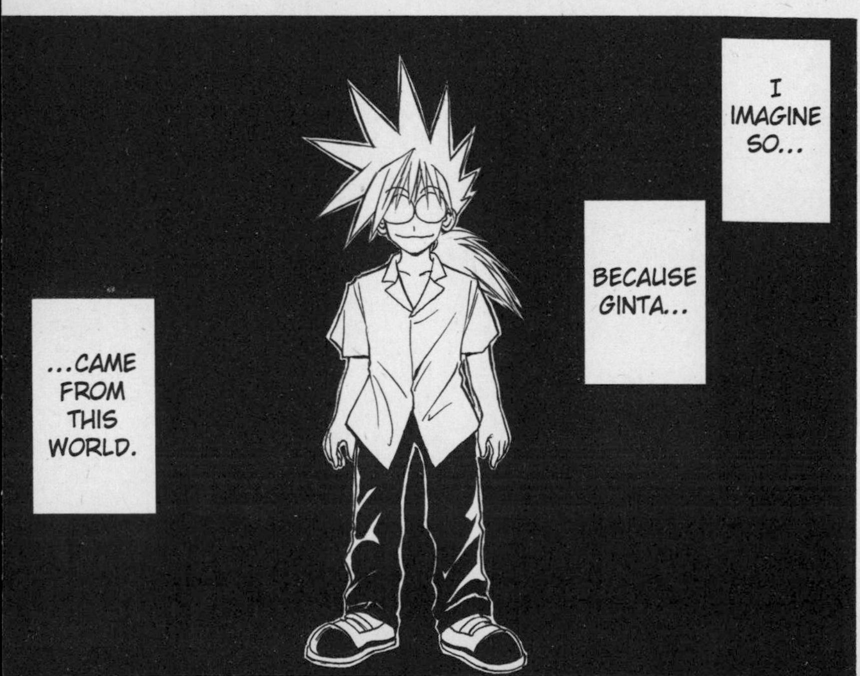
I IMAGINE SO...
BECAUSE GINTA...
...CAME FROM THIS WORLD.

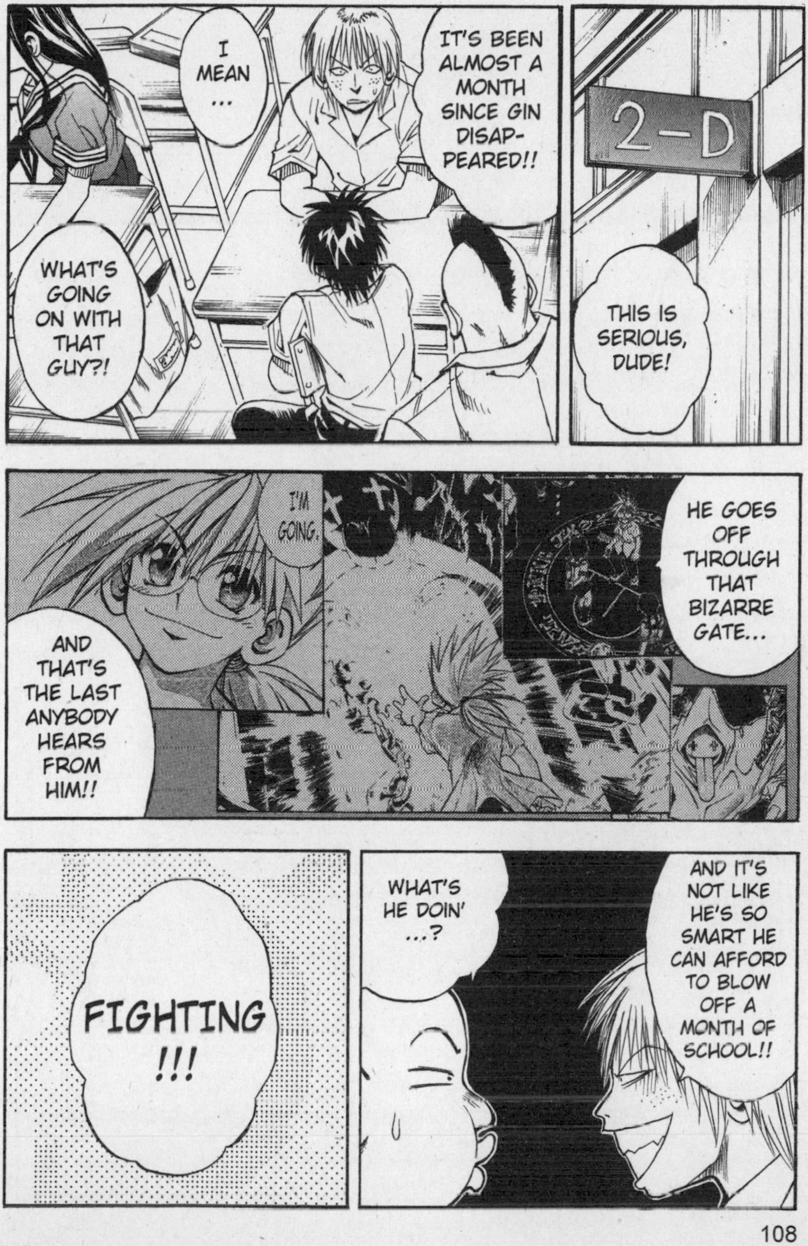
2-D
THIS IS SERIOUS, DUDE!
IT'S BEEN ALMOST A MONTH SINCE GIN DISAPPEARED!!
I MEAN ...
WHAT'S GOING ON WITH THAT GUY?!
HE GOES OFF THROUGH THAT BIZARRE GATE...
I'M GOING.
AND THAT'S THE LAST ANYBODY HEARS FROM HIM!!
AND IT'S NOT LIKE HE'S SO SMART HE CAN AFFORD TO BLOW OFF A MONTH OF SCHOOL!!
WHAT'S HE DOIN' ...?
FIGHTING !!!

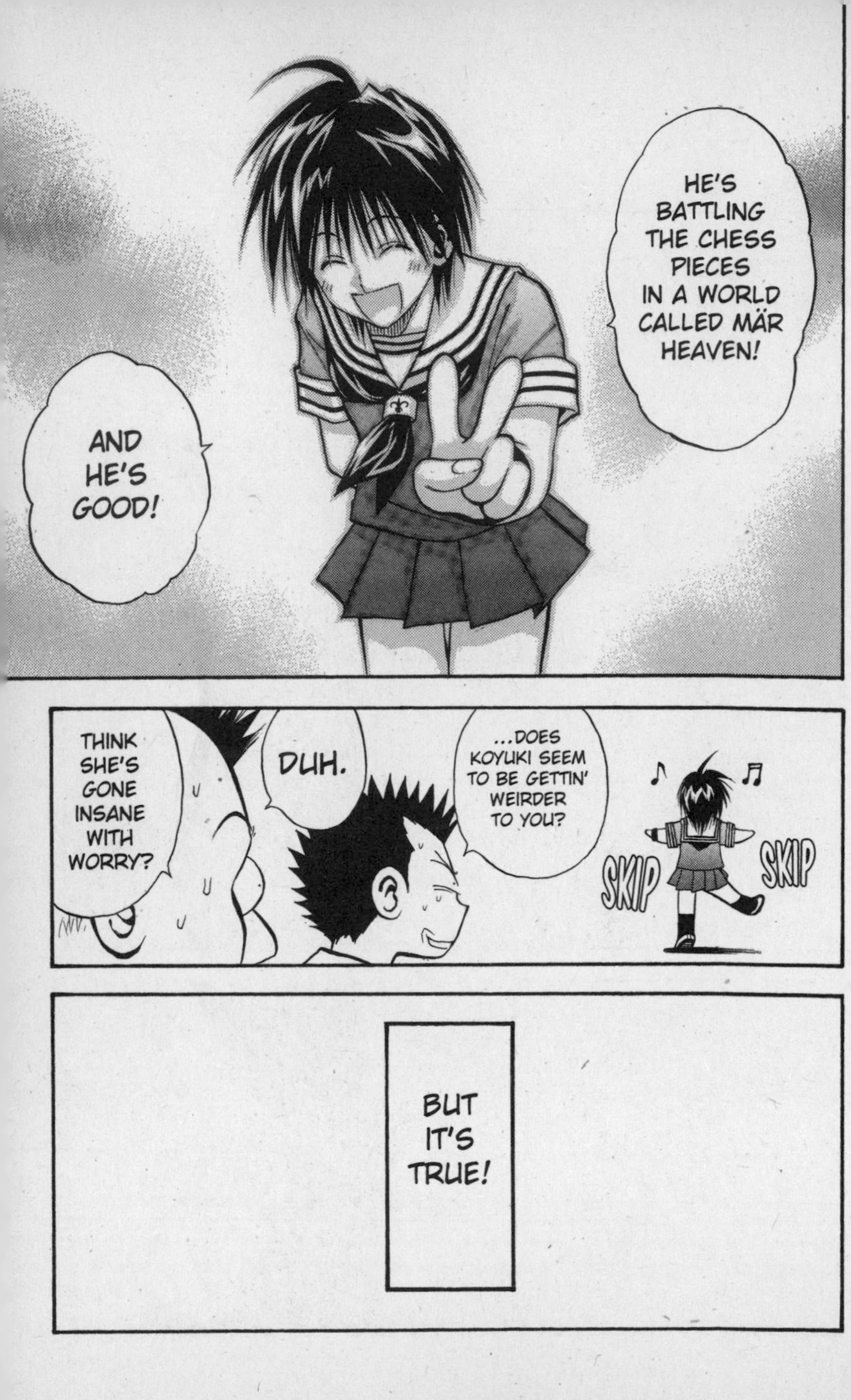
HE'S BATTLING THE CHESS PIECES IN A WORLD CALLED MÄR HEAVEN!
AND HE'S GOOD!
SKIP SKIP
...DOES KOYUKI SEEM TO BE GETTIN' WEIRDER TO YOU?
DUH.
THINK SHE'S GONE INSANE WITH WORRY?
BUT IT'S TRUE!

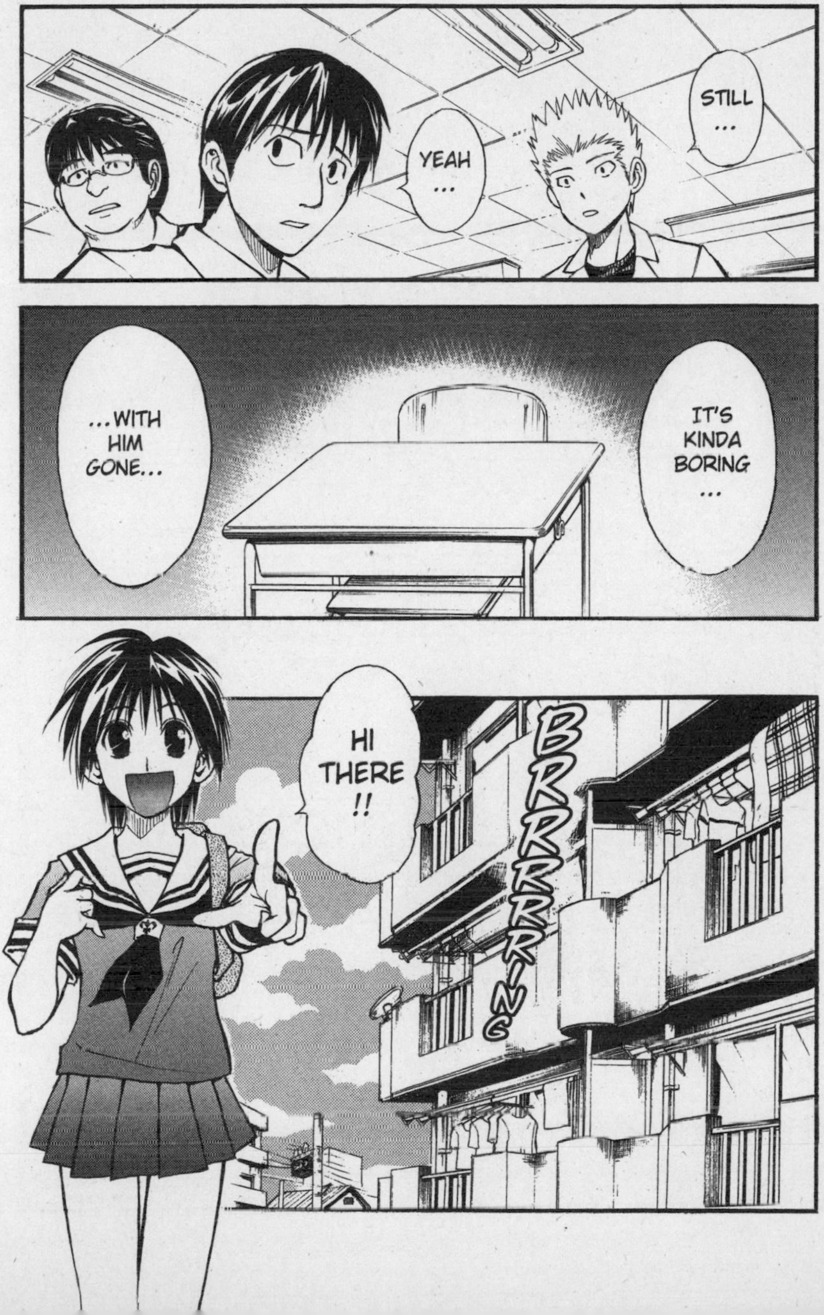
STILL ...
YEAH ...
IT'S KINDA BORING ...
...WITH HIM GONE...
BRRRRRING
HI THERE !!

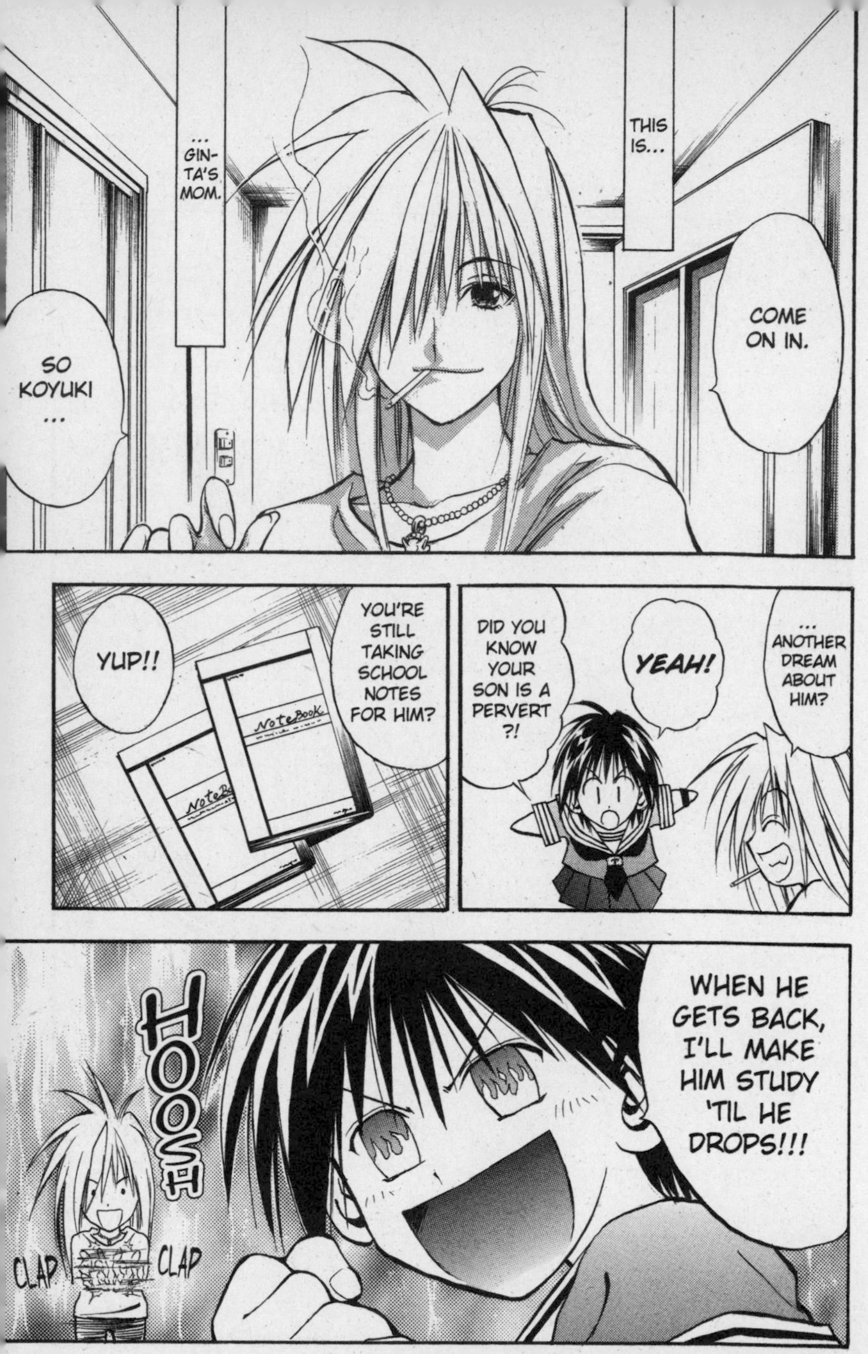
THIS IS...
...GIN-TA'S MOM.
COME ON IN.
SO KOYUKI ...
...ANOTHER DREAM ABOUT HIM?
YEAH!
DID YOU KNOW YOUR SON IS A PERVERT?!
YOU'RE STILL TAKING SCHOOL NOTES FOR HIM?
YUP!!
WHEN HE GETS BACK, I'LL MAKE HIM STUDY 'TIL HE DROPS!!!
HOOSH
CLAP CLAP

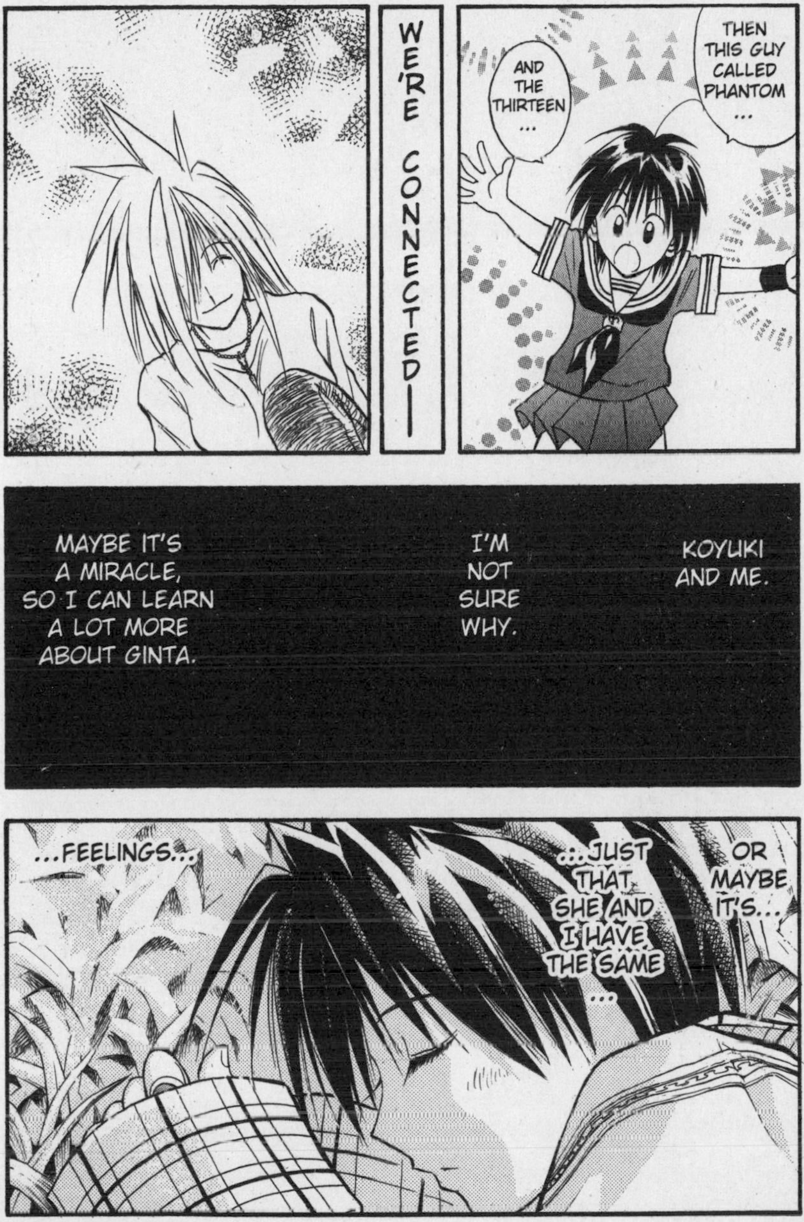
THEN THIS GUY CALLED PHANTOM ...
AND THE THIRTEEN ...
WE'RE CONNECTED—
KOYUKI AND ME.
I'M NOT SURE WHY.
MAYBE IT'S A MIRACLE, SO I CAN LEARN A LOT MORE ABOUT GINTA.
OR MAYBE IT'S...
...JUST THAT SHE AND I HAVE THE SAME ...
...FEELINGS...

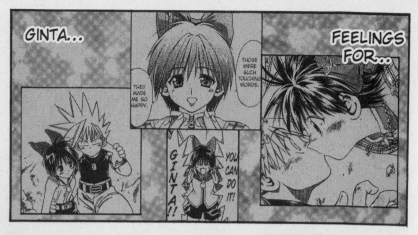

FEELINGS FOR...
THOSE WERE SUCH TOUCHING WORDS.
THEY MADE ME SO HAPPY.
YOU CAN DO IT!
GINTA!!
GINTA...
AHH!
A GOOD MORNING TO YOU, MY PRINCESS!!
BLINK
BUT ...
MORNING ...
...ED! ♬
HOW DOES HE FEEL ABOUT ME AND KOYUKI ...?

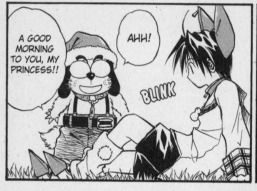

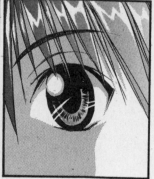

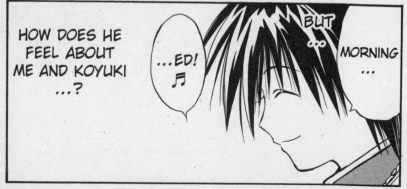

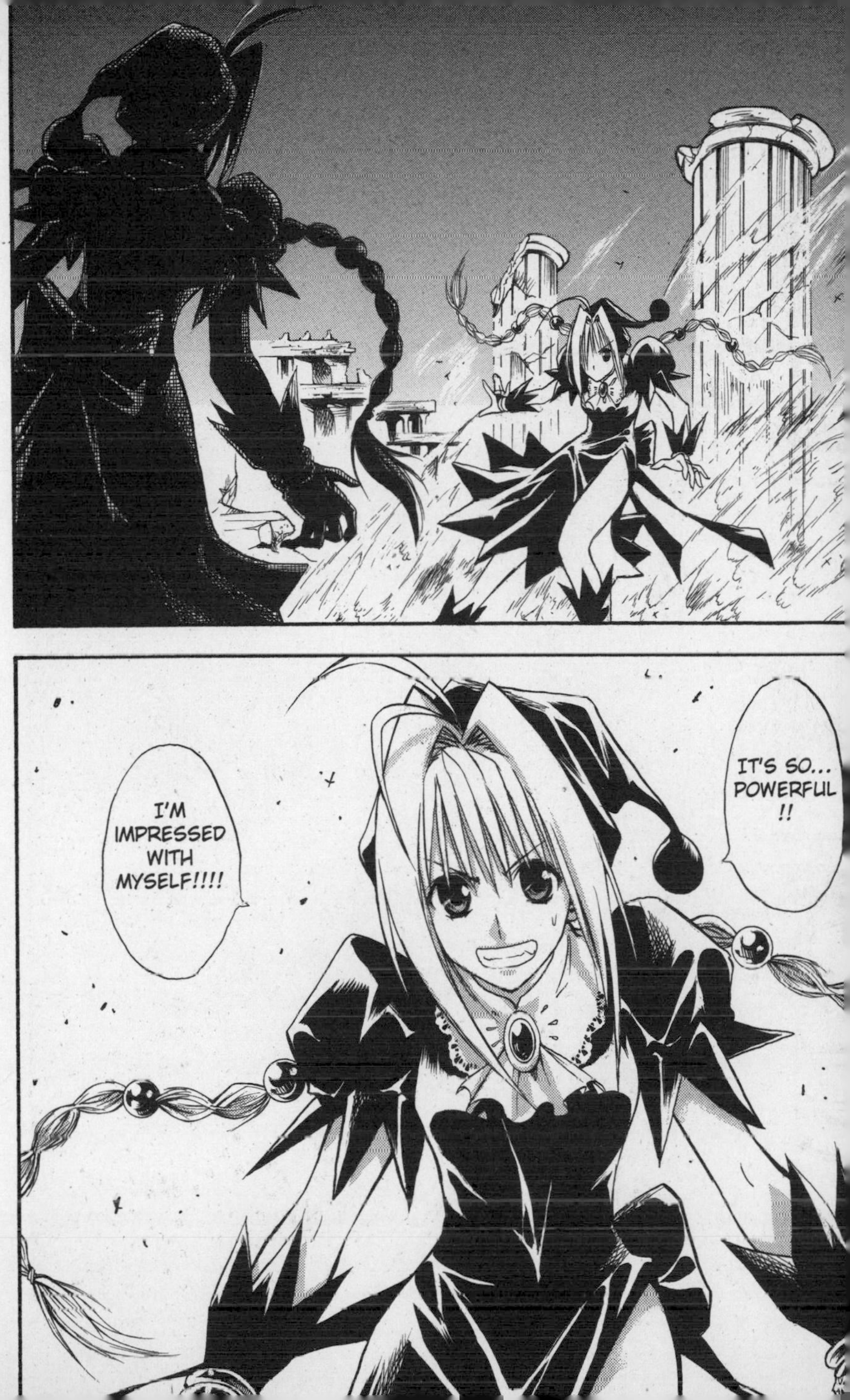
IT'S SO... POWERFUL !!
I'M IMPRESSED WITH MYSELF!!!!

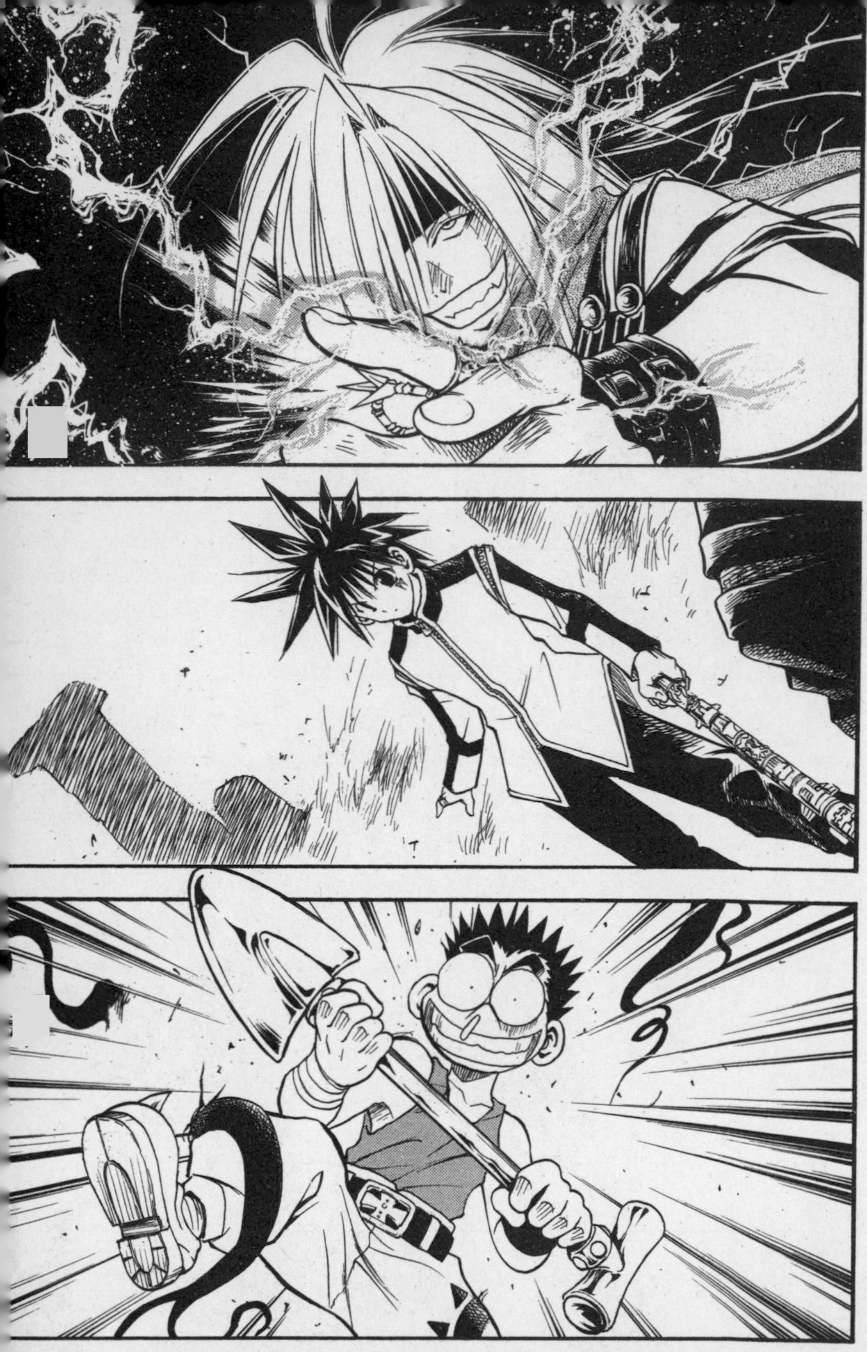

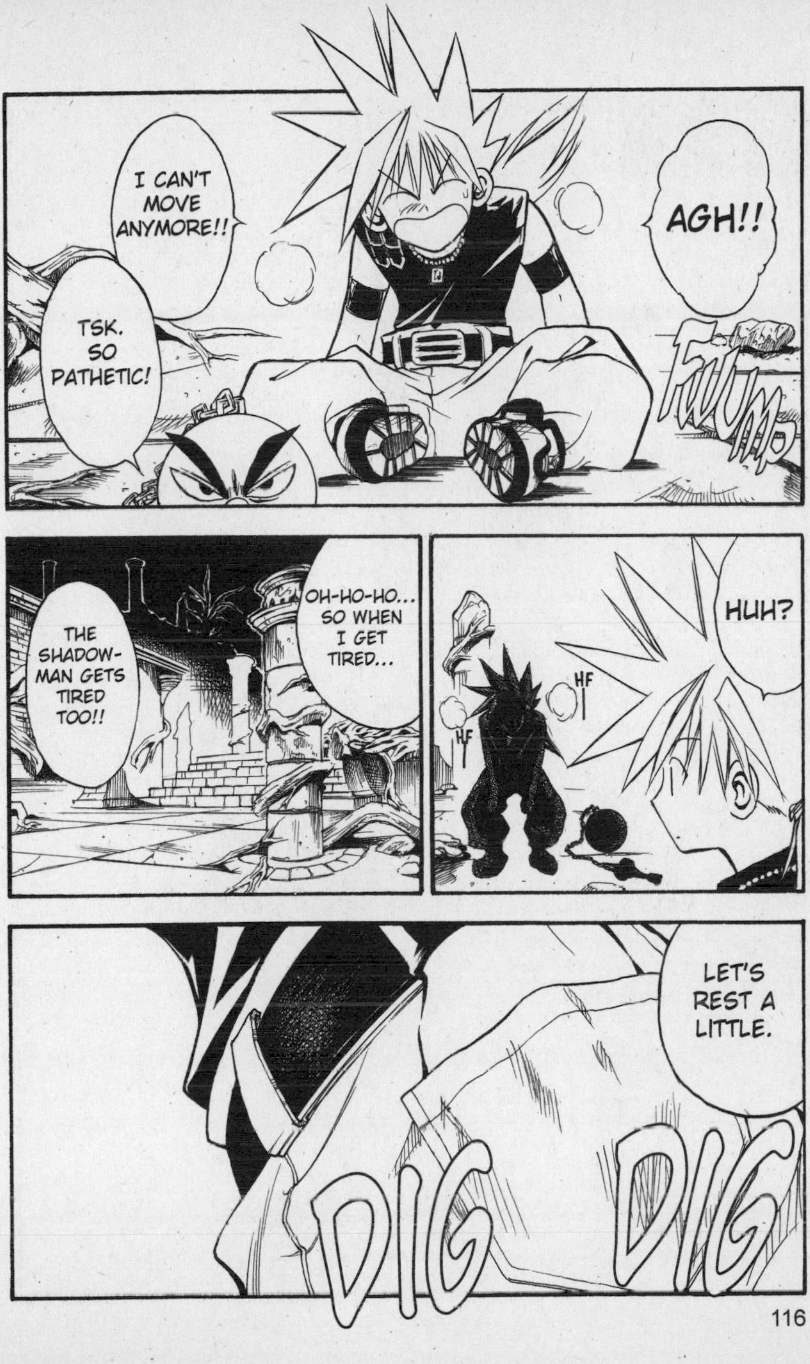
AGH!!
FWUMP
I CAN'T MOVE ANYMORE!!
TSK. SO PATHETIC!
HUH?
HF
HF
OH-HO-HO... SO WHEN I GET TIRED...
THE SHADOW-MAN GETS TIRED TOO!!
LET'S REST A LITTLE.
DIG
DIG

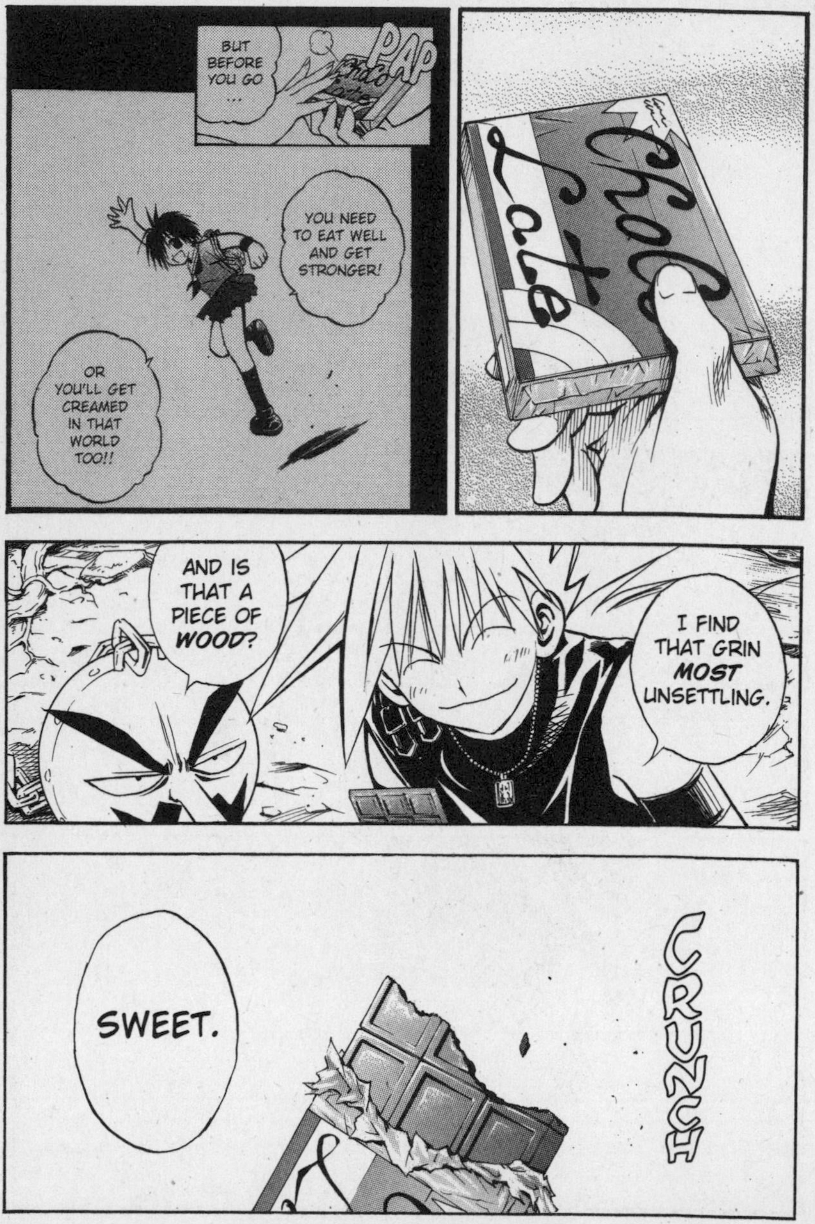

Choco
Late
PAP
BUT BEFORE YOU GO ...
YOU NEED TO EAT WELL AND GET STRONGER!
OR YOU'LL GET CREAMED IN THAT WORLD TOO!!
I FIND THAT GRIN **MOST** UNSETTLING.
AND IS THAT A PIECE OF **WOOD**?
CRUNCH
SWEET.

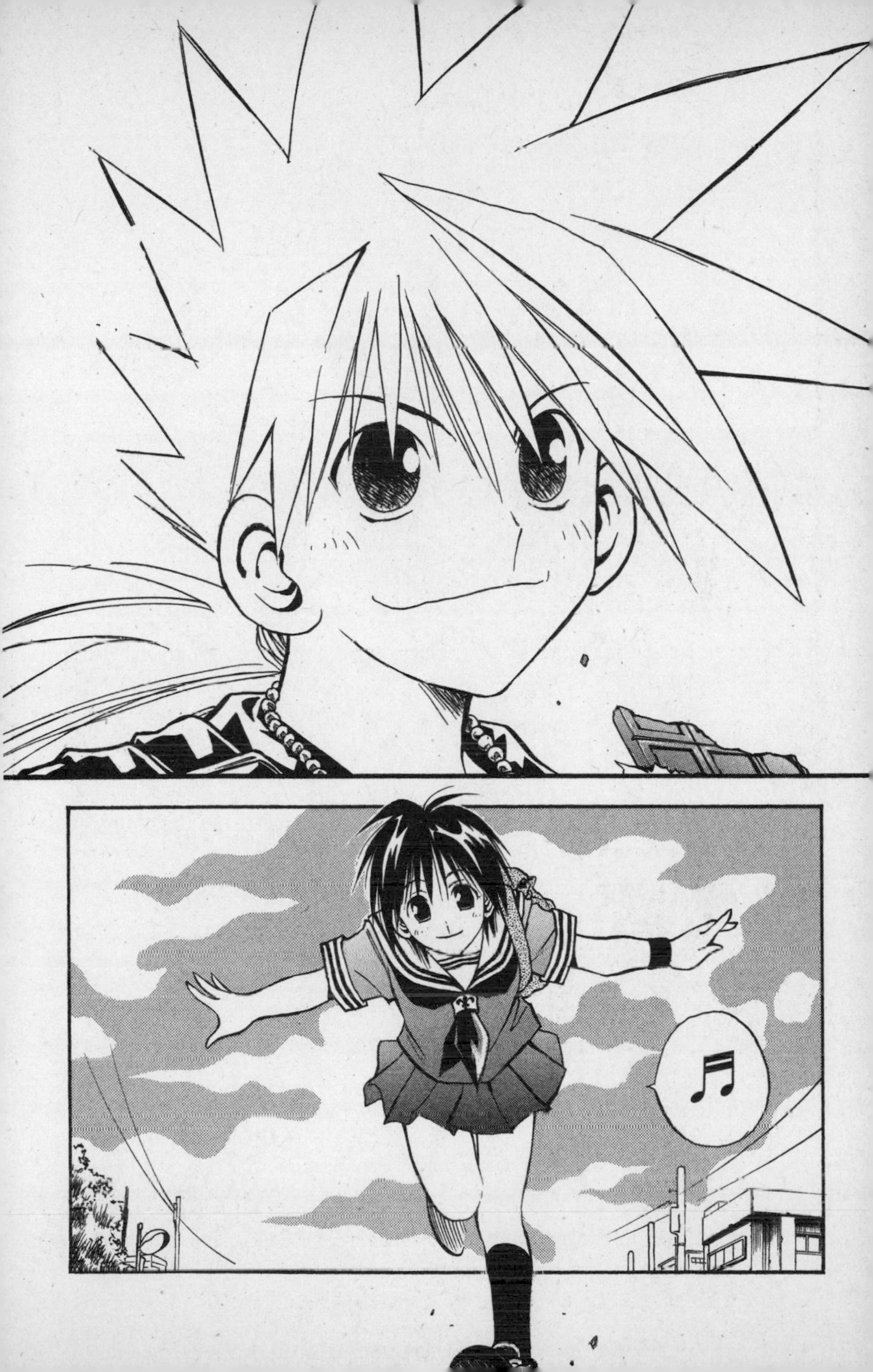
♬

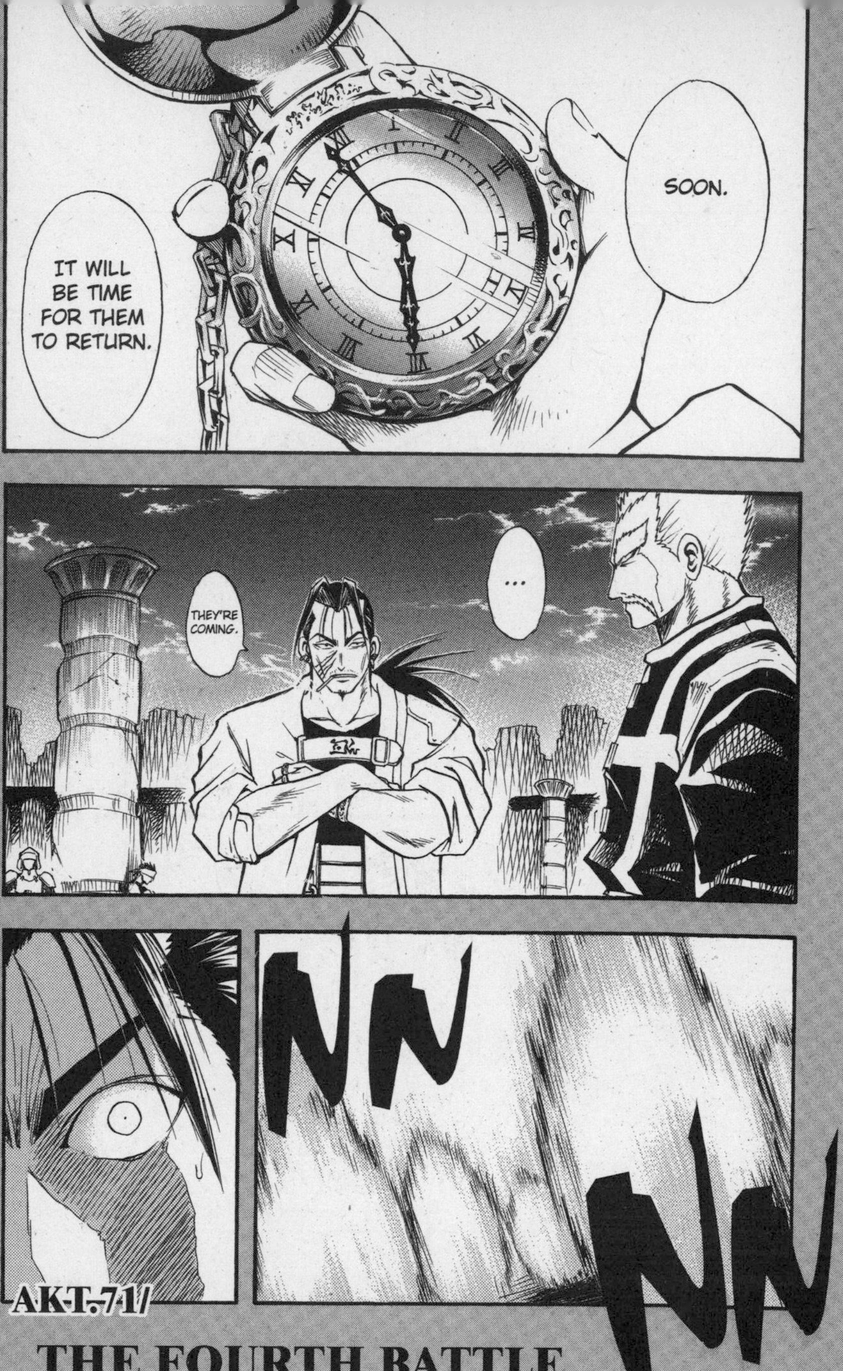
SOON.
IT WILL BE TIME FOR THEM TO RETURN.
...
THEY'RE COMING.
NN
NN

AKT.71/

THE FOURTH BATTLE

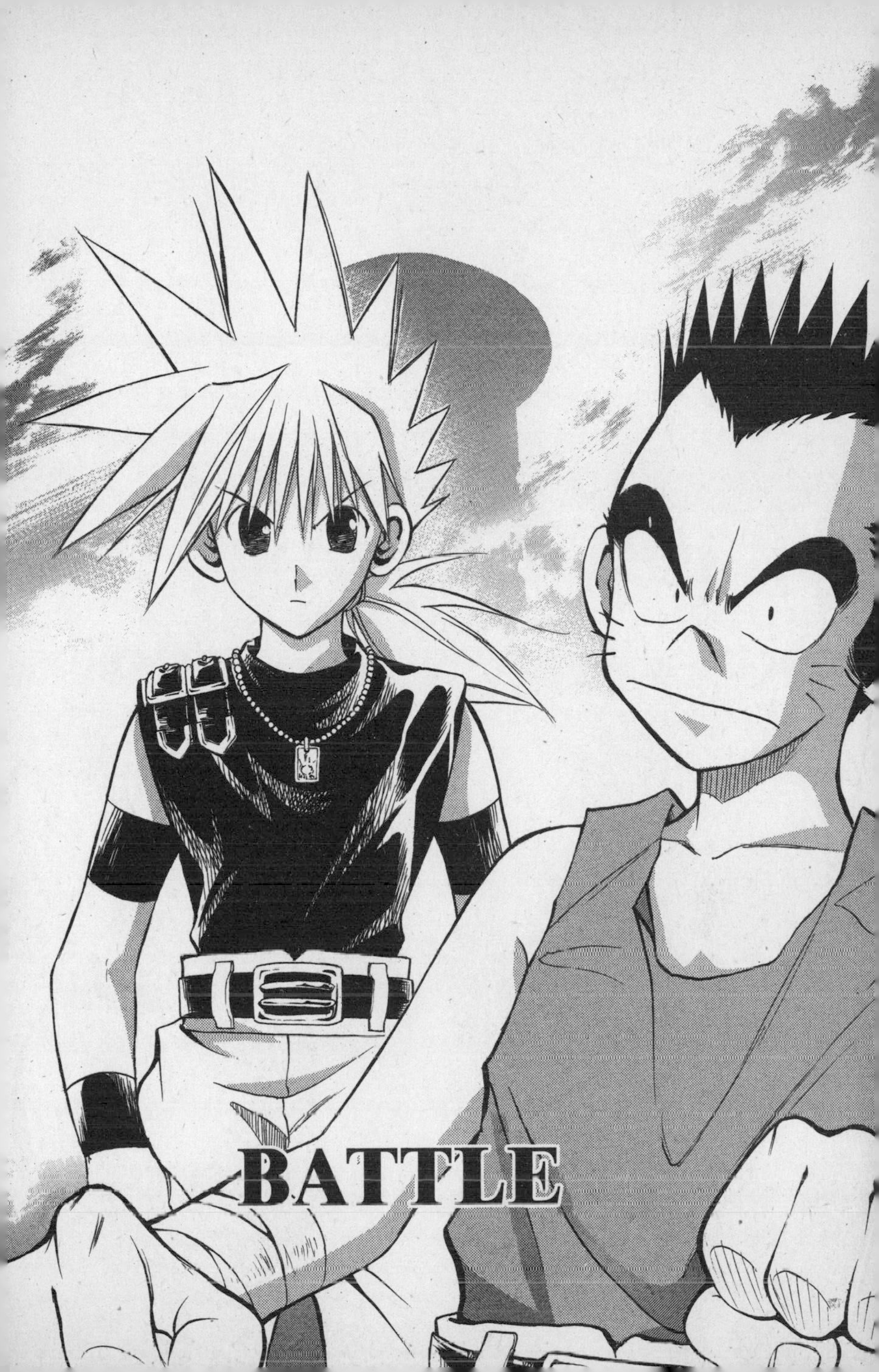
BATTLE

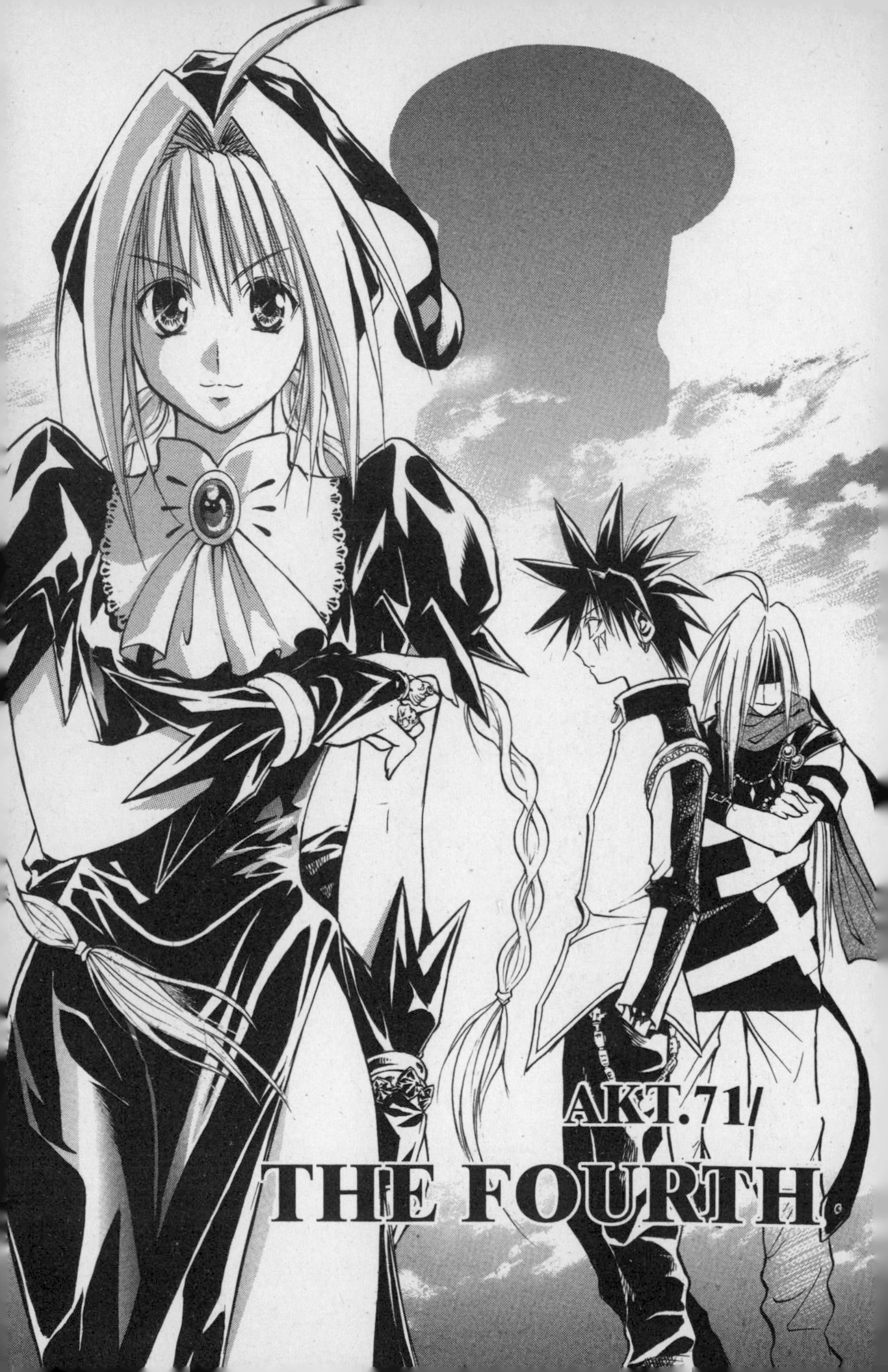
AKT. 71/
THE FOURTH

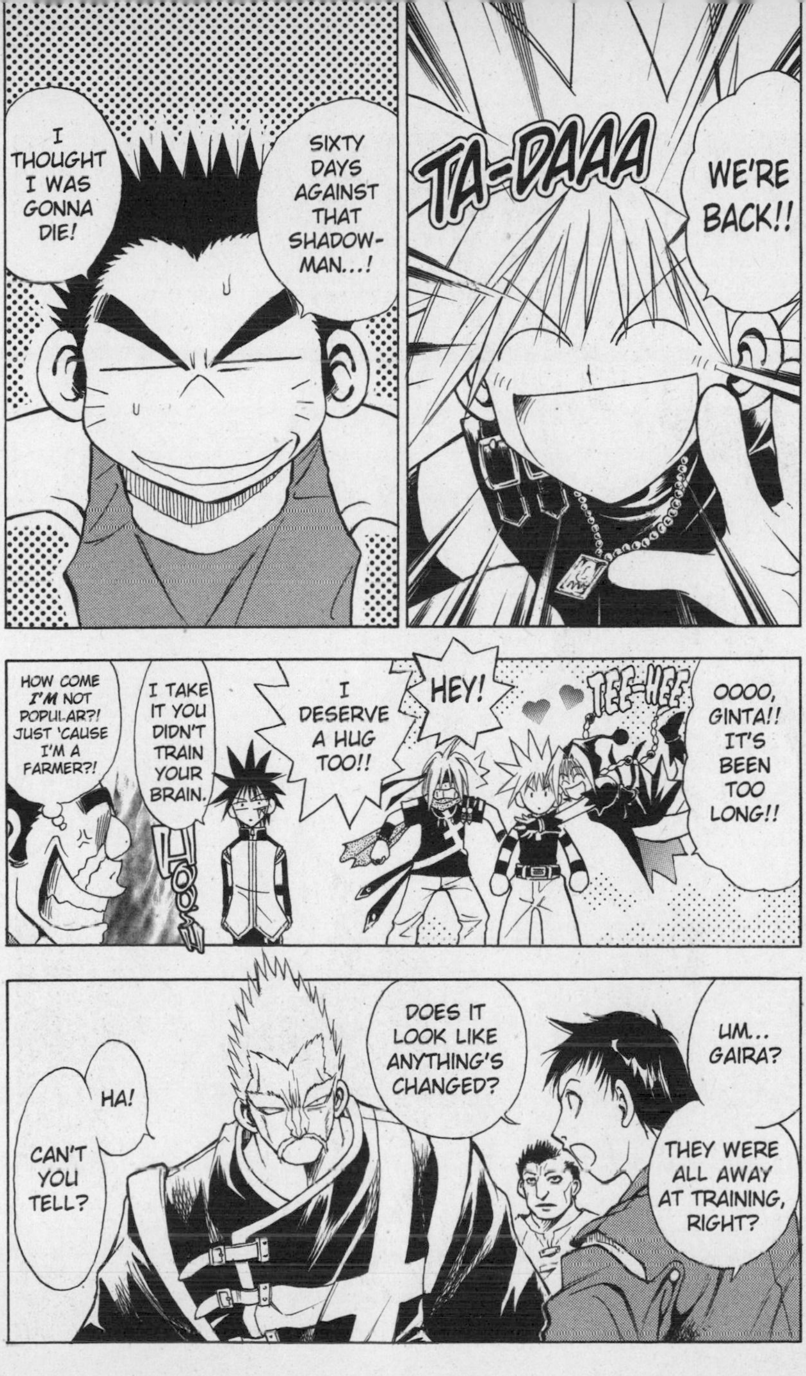
TA-DAAA
WE'RE BACK!!
SIXTY DAYS AGAINST THAT SHADOW-MAN...!
I THOUGHT I WAS GONNA DIE!
OOOO, GINTA!! IT'S BEEN TOO LONG!!
TEE-HEE
HEY!
I DESERVE A HUG TOO!!
I TAKE IT YOU DIDN'T TRAIN YOUR BRAIN.
HOW COME *I'M* NOT POPULAR?! JUST 'CAUSE I'M A FARMER?!
UM... GAIRA?
THEY WERE ALL AWAY AT TRAINING, RIGHT?
DOES IT LOOK LIKE ANYTHING'S CHANGED?
HA!
CAN'T YOU TELL?

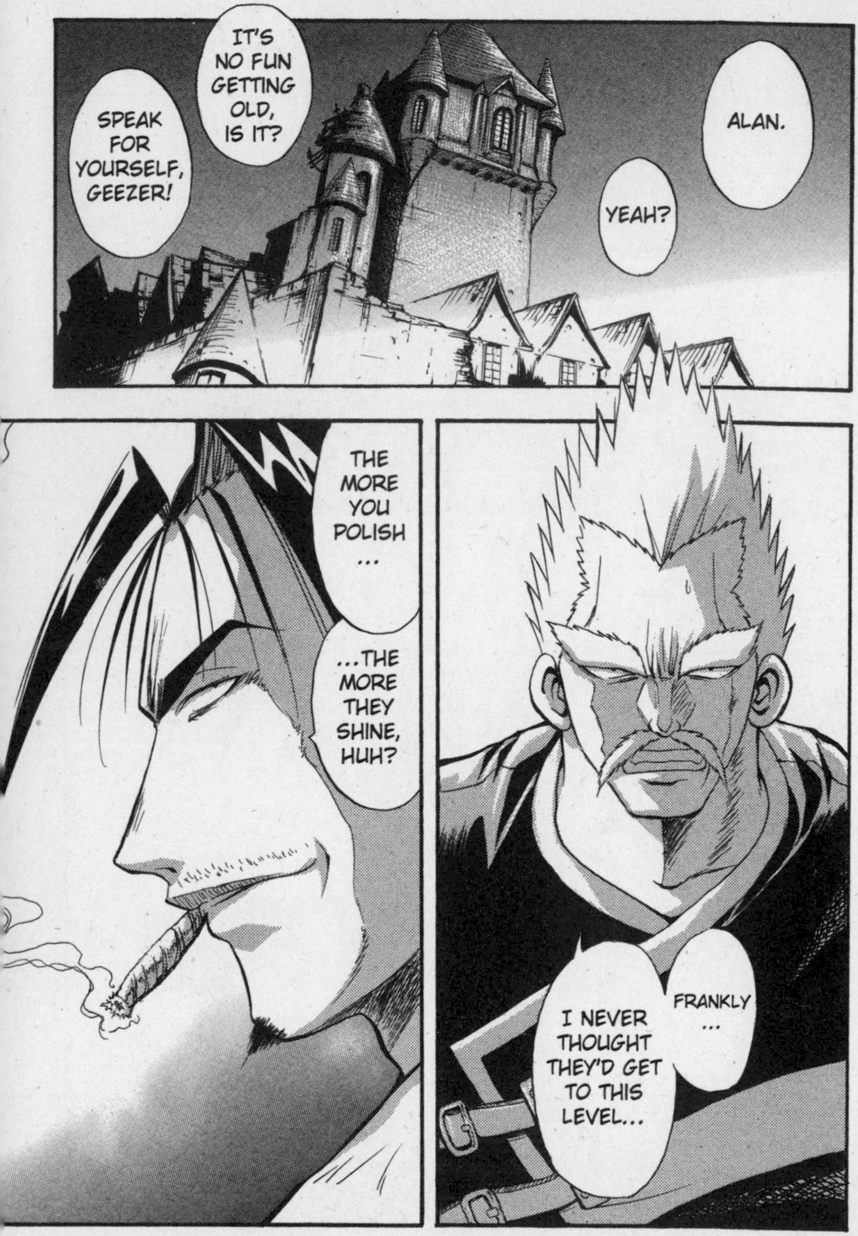
ALAN.
YEAH?
IT'S NO FUN GETTING OLD, IS IT?
SPEAK FOR YOURSELF, GEEZER!
FRANKLY...
I NEVER THOUGHT THEY'D GET TO THIS LEVEL...
THE MORE YOU POLISH...
...THE MORE THEY SHINE, HUH?

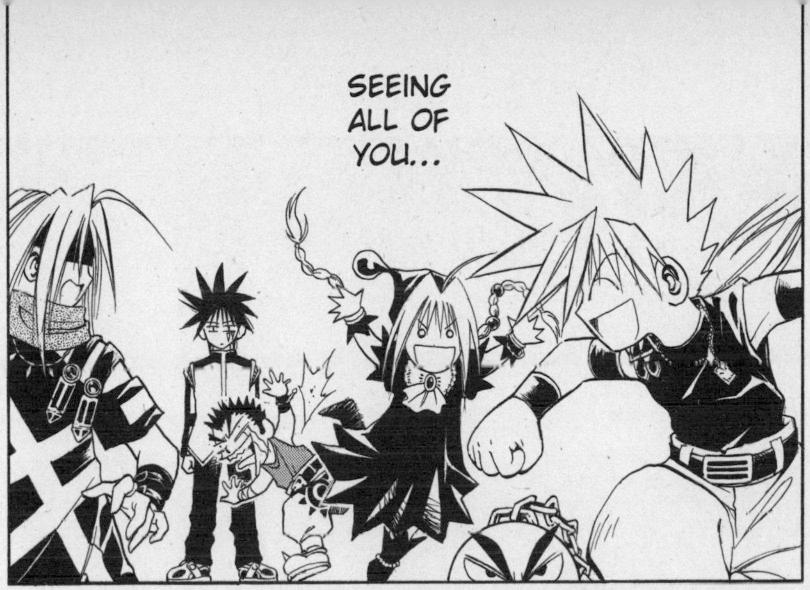
SEEING ALL OF YOU...

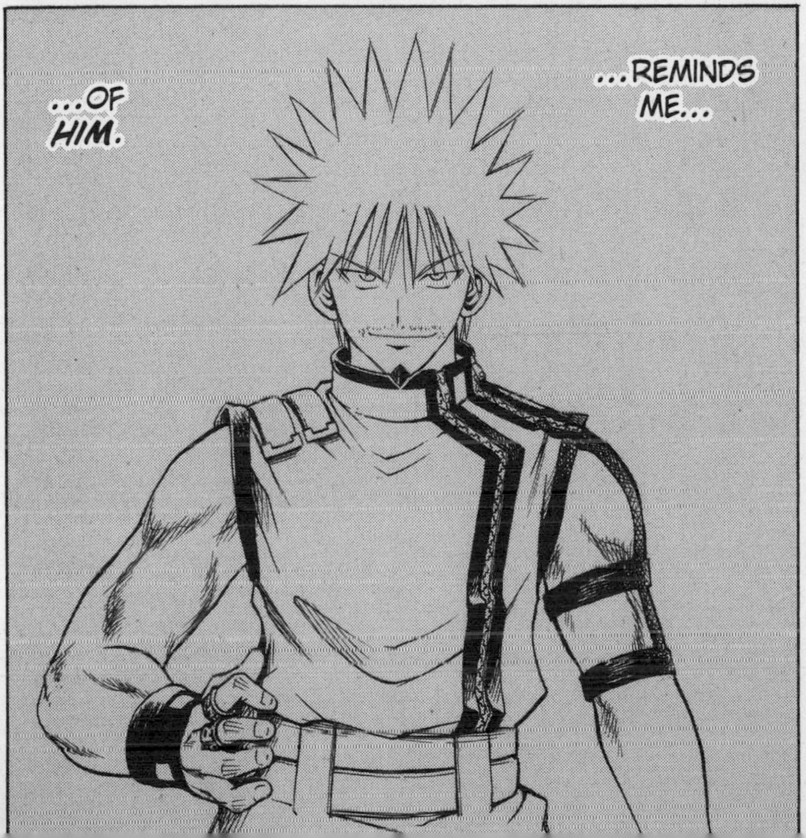
...REMINDS ME...
...OF HIM.

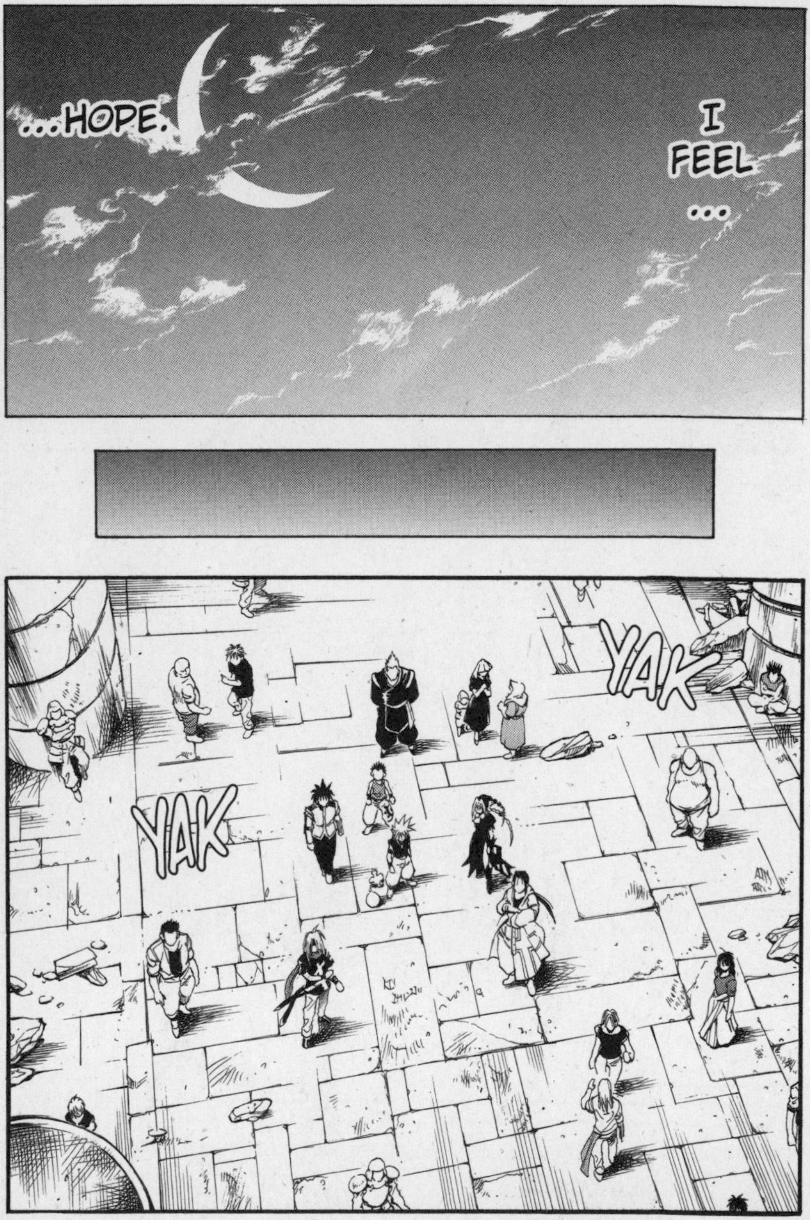
I FEEL ...
...HOPE.
YAK
YAK

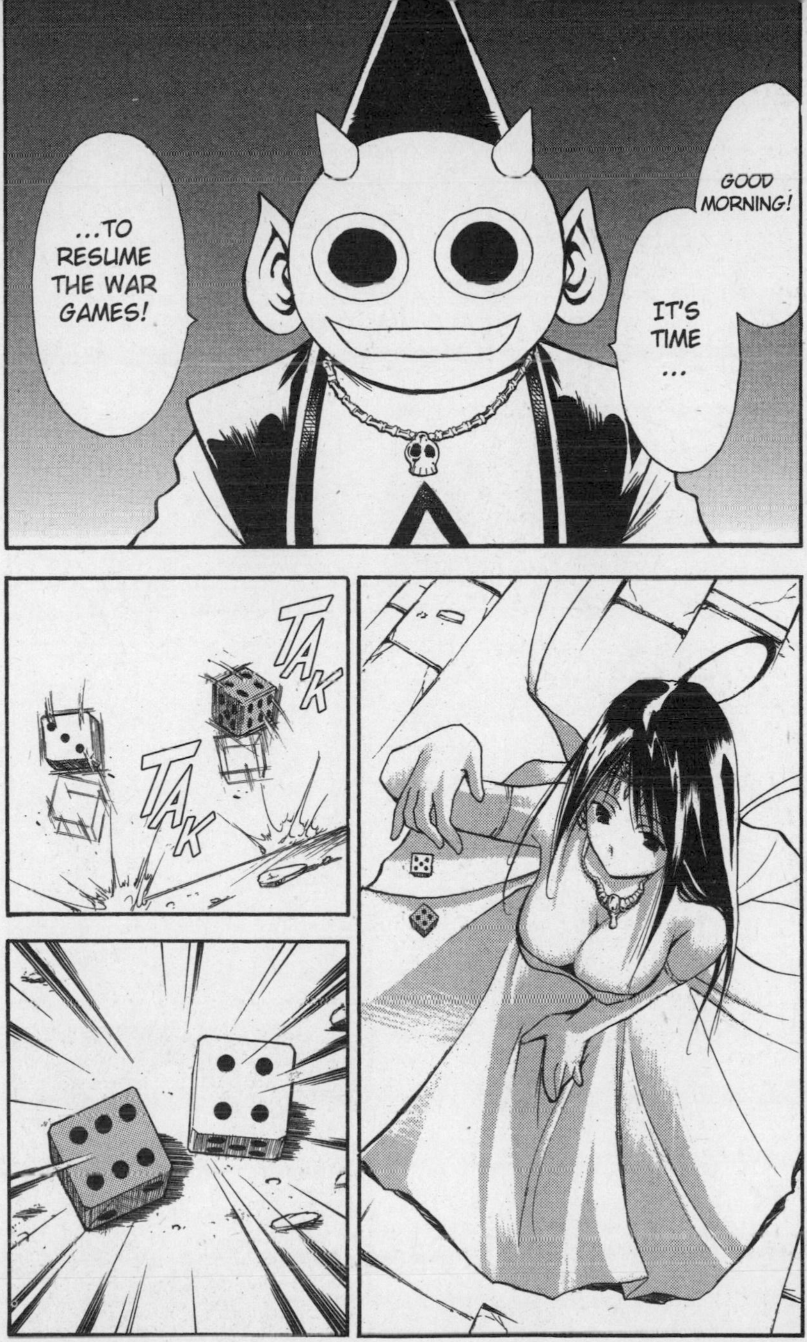
GOOD MORNING!
IT'S TIME ...
...TO RESUME THE WAR GAMES!
TAK
TAK

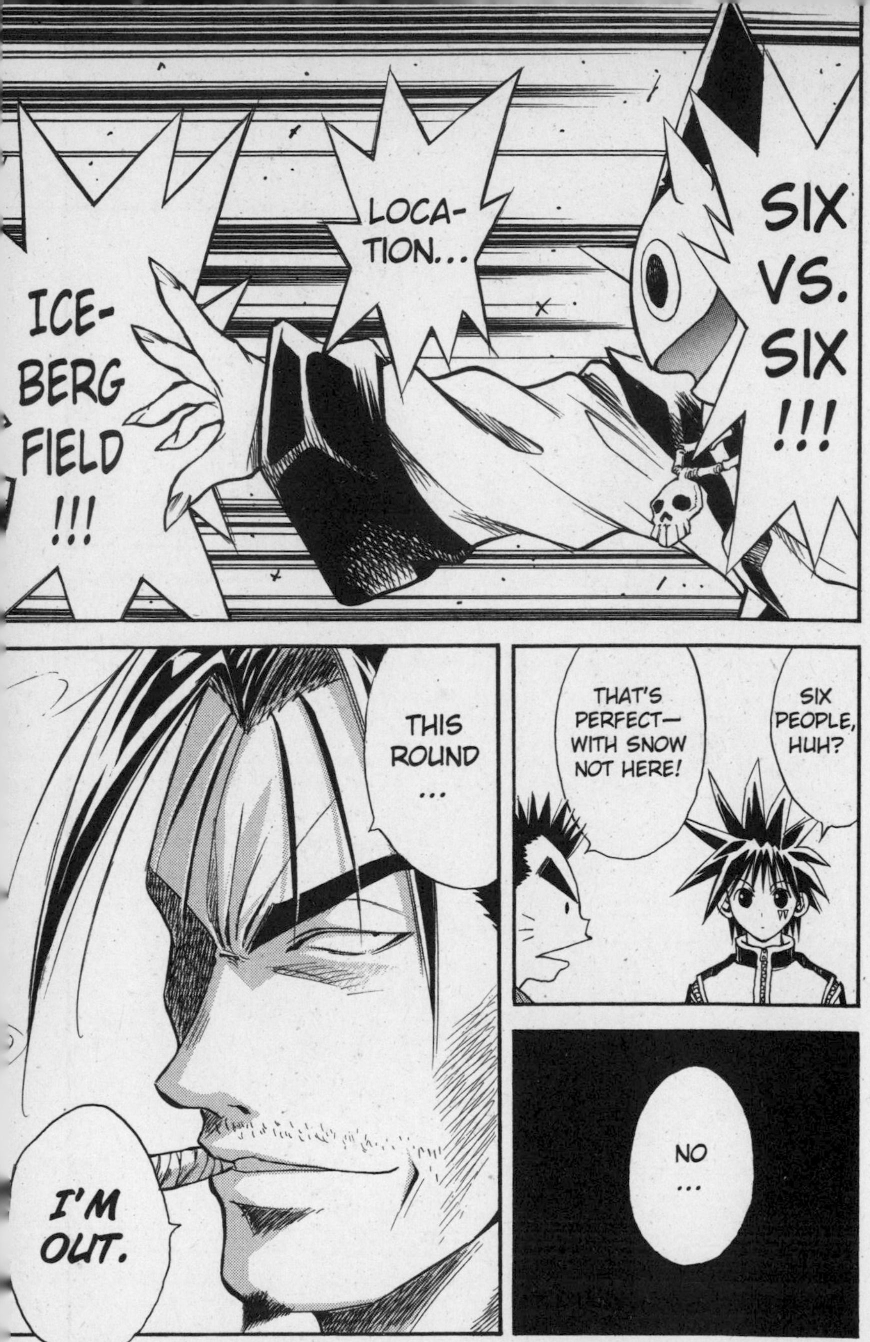
SIX VS. SIX!!!
LOCATION...
ICEBERG FIELD!!!
SIX PEOPLE, HUH?
THAT'S PERFECT—WITH SNOW NOT HERE!
NO ...
THIS ROUND ...
I'M OUT.

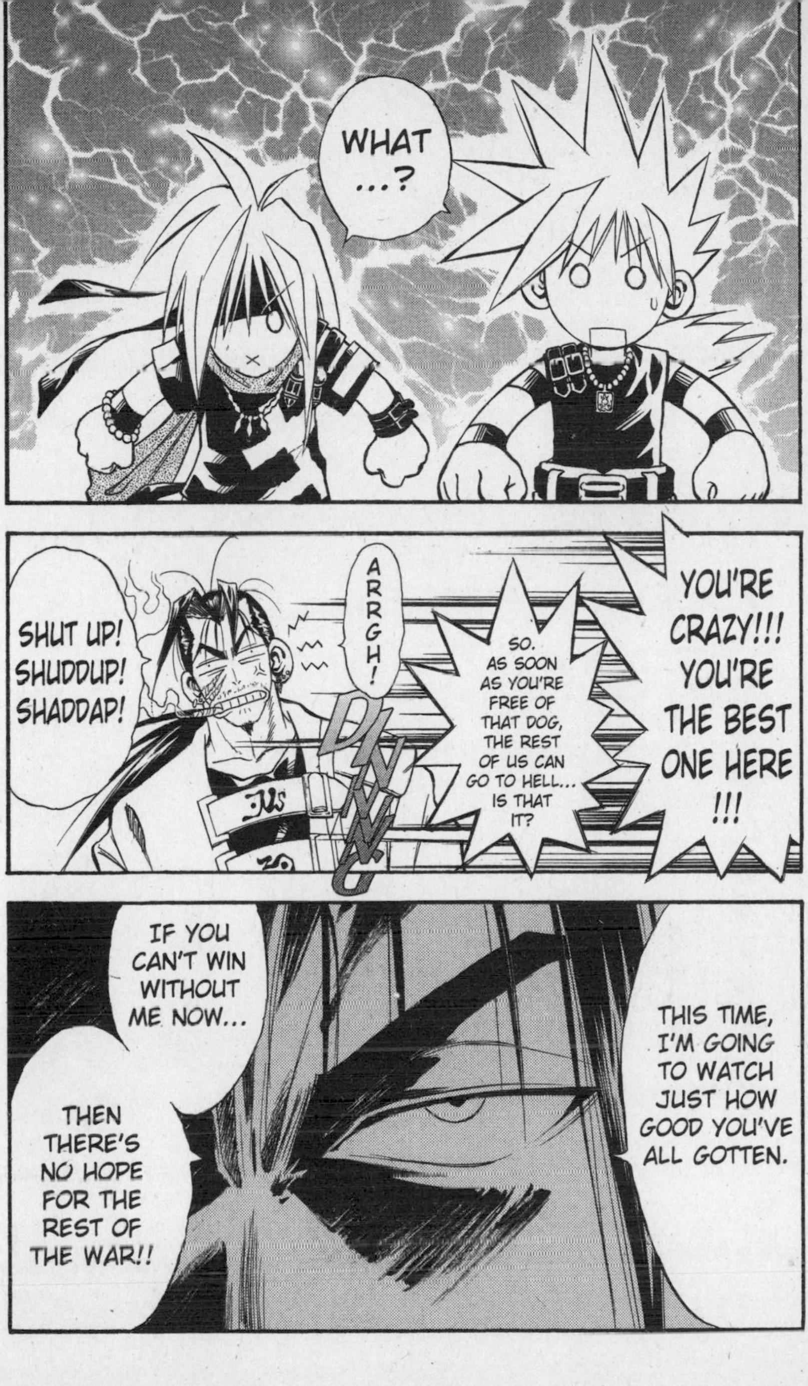
WHAT ...?
YOU'RE CRAZY!!! YOU'RE THE BEST ONE HERE !!!
SO. AS SOON AS YOU'RE FREE OF THAT DOG, THE REST OF US CAN GO TO HELL... IS THAT IT?
ARRGH!
SHUT UP! SHUDDUP! SHADDAP!
IF YOU CAN'T WIN WITHOUT ME NOW...
THEN THERE'S NO HOPE FOR THE REST OF THE WAR!!
THIS TIME, I'M GOING TO WATCH JUST HOW GOOD YOU'VE ALL GOTTEN.

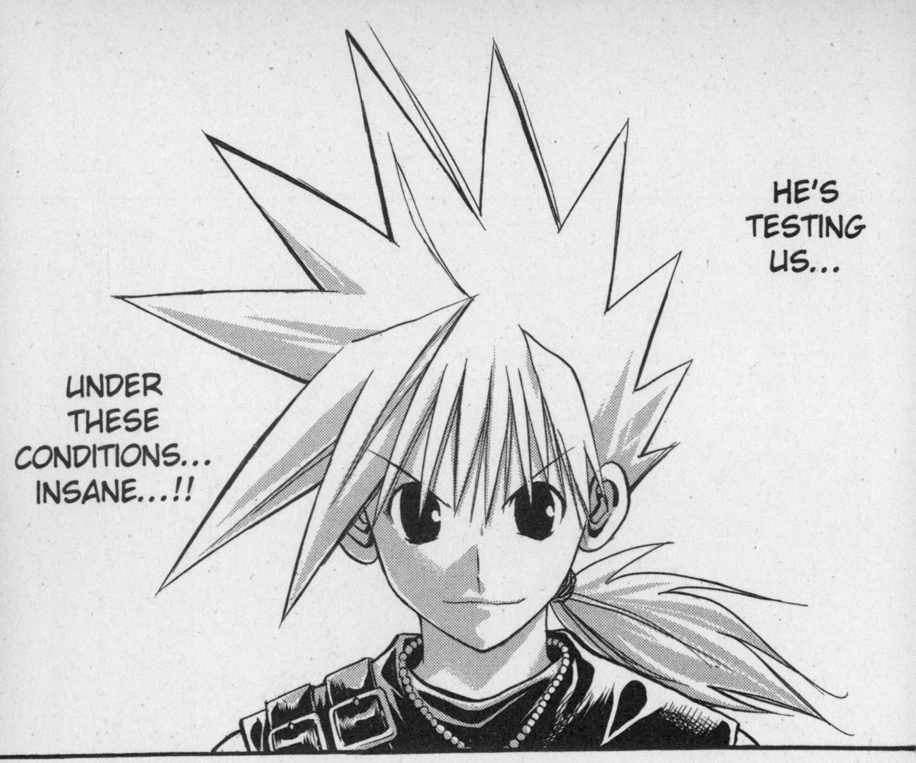
HE'S TESTING US...
UNDER THESE CONDITIONS... INSANE...!!
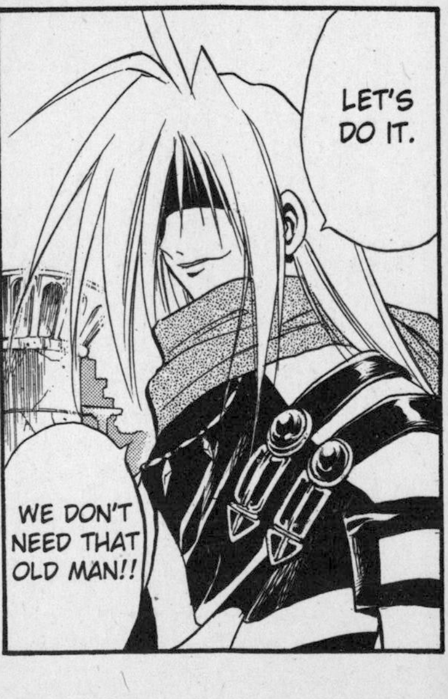
LET'S DO IT.
WE DON'T NEED THAT OLD MAN!!
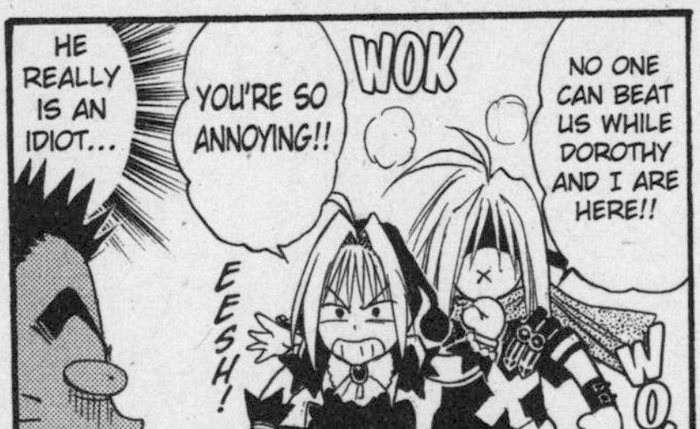
NO ONE CAN BEAT US WHILE DOROTHY AND I ARE HERE!!
WOK
WOK
YOU'RE SO ANNOYING!!
EESH!
HE REALLY IS AN IDIOT...
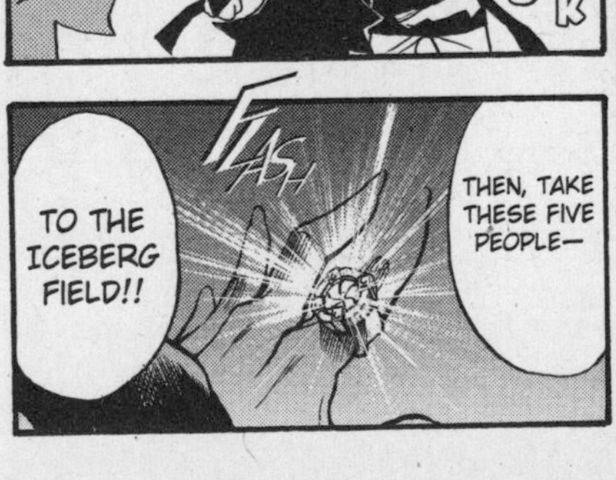
THEN, TAKE THESE FIVE PEOPLE—
FLASH
TO THE ICEBERG FIELD!!

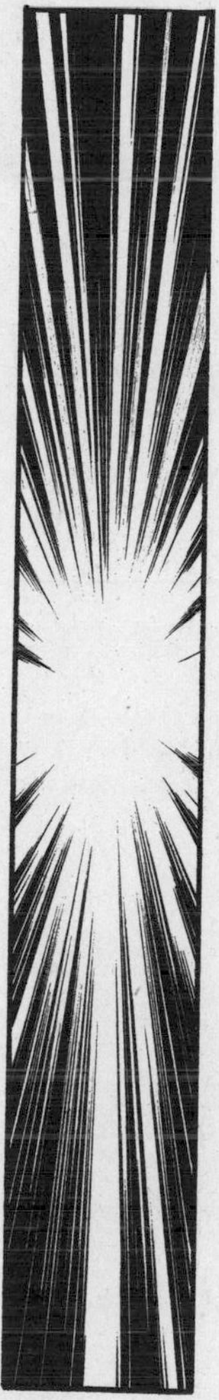

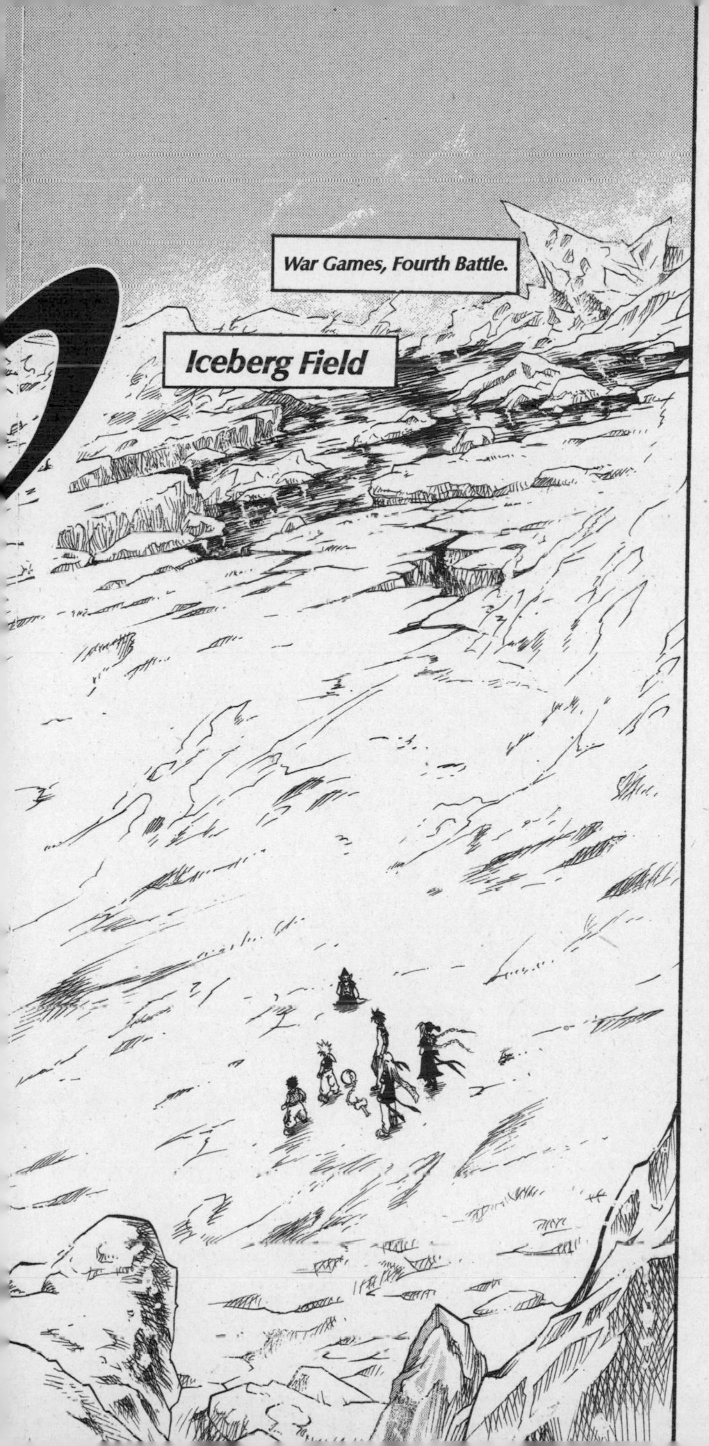
War Games, Fourth Battle.
Iceberg Field

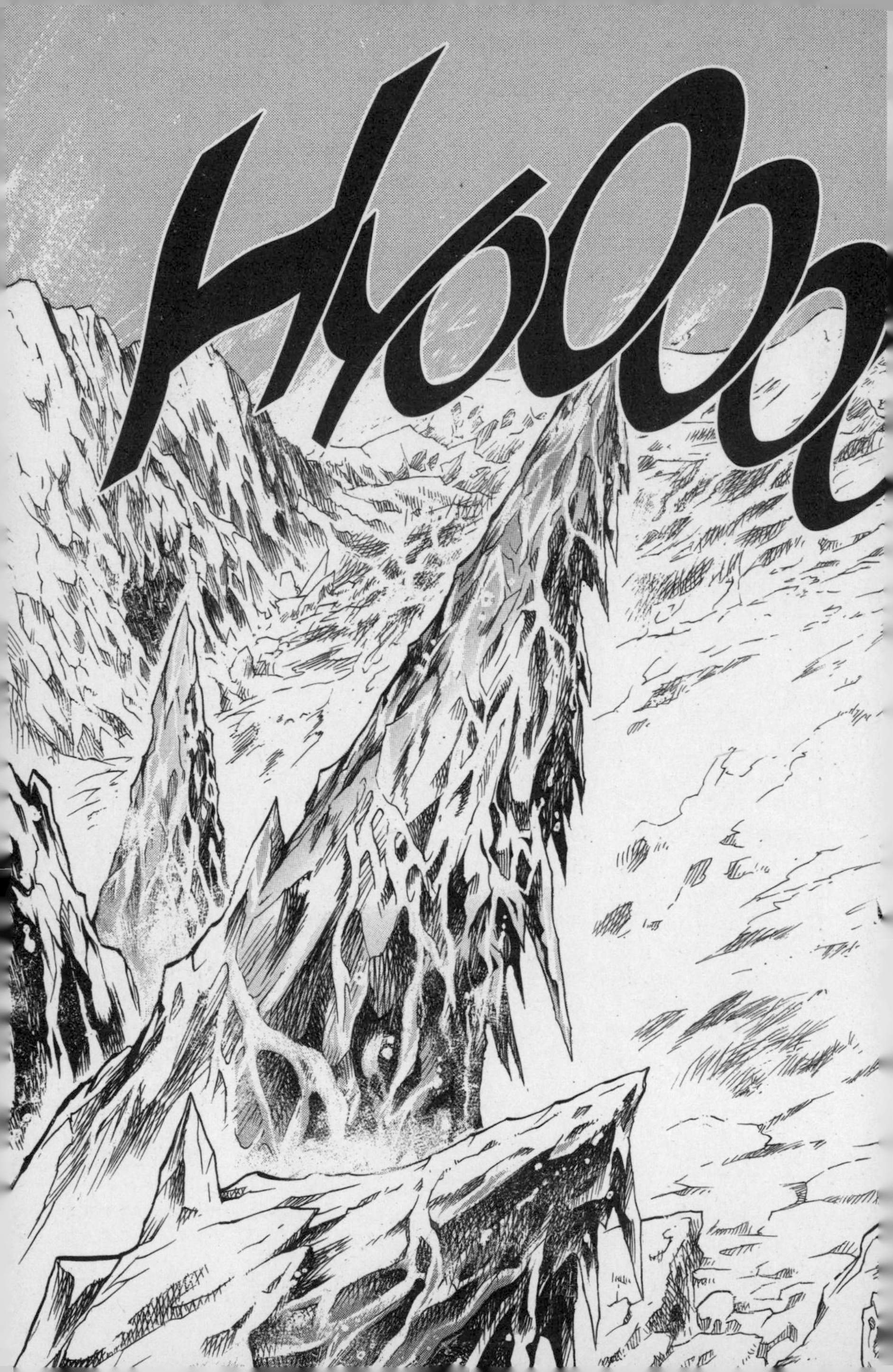
Hyoooo

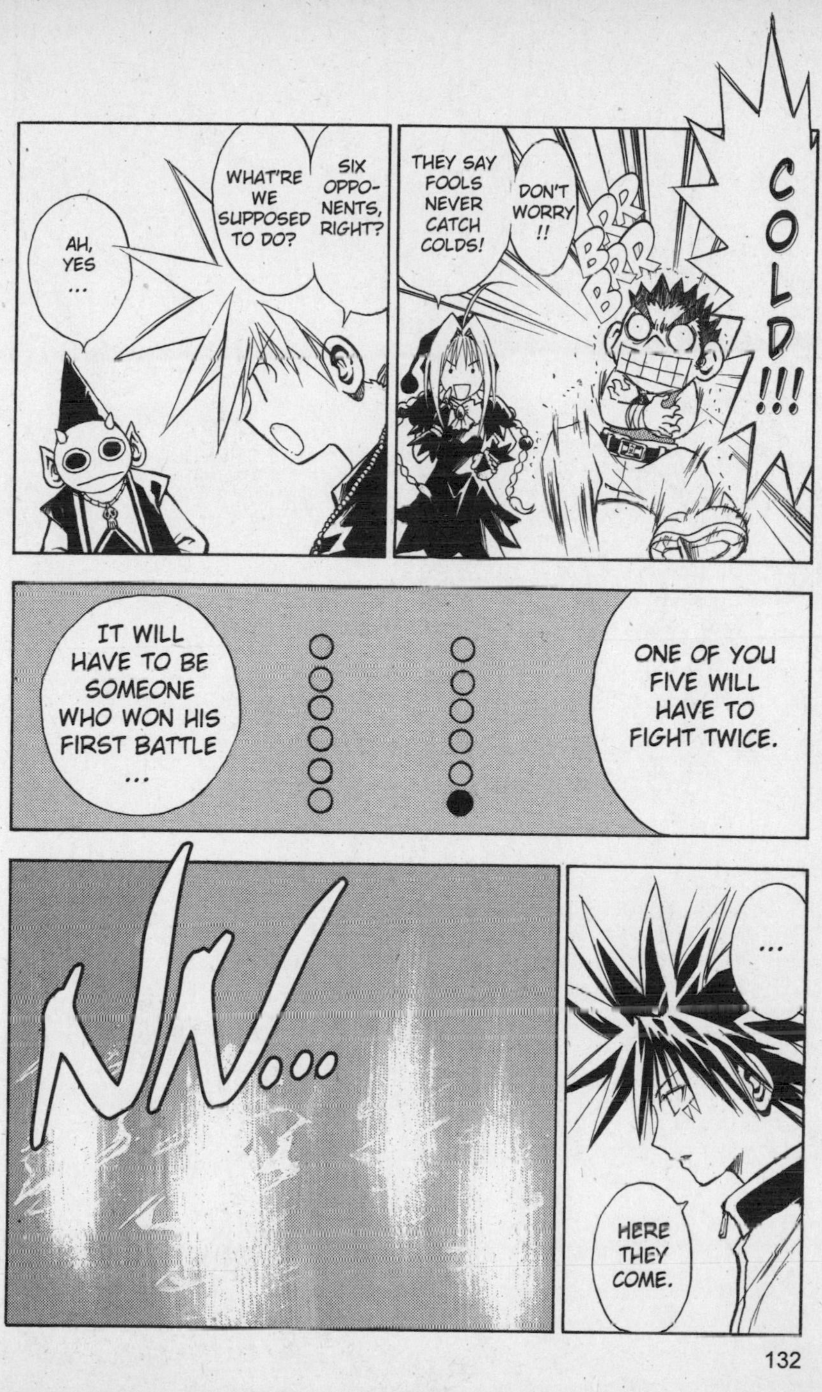
COLD!!!
BRR BRR BRR
DON'T WORRY!!
THEY SAY FOOLS NEVER CATCH COLDS!
SIX OPPONENTS, RIGHT?
WHAT'RE WE SUPPOSED TO DO?
AH, YES ...
ONE OF YOU FIVE WILL HAVE TO FIGHT TWICE.
IT WILL HAVE TO BE SOMEONE WHO WON HIS FIRST BATTLE ...
...
HERE THEY COME.
NN...

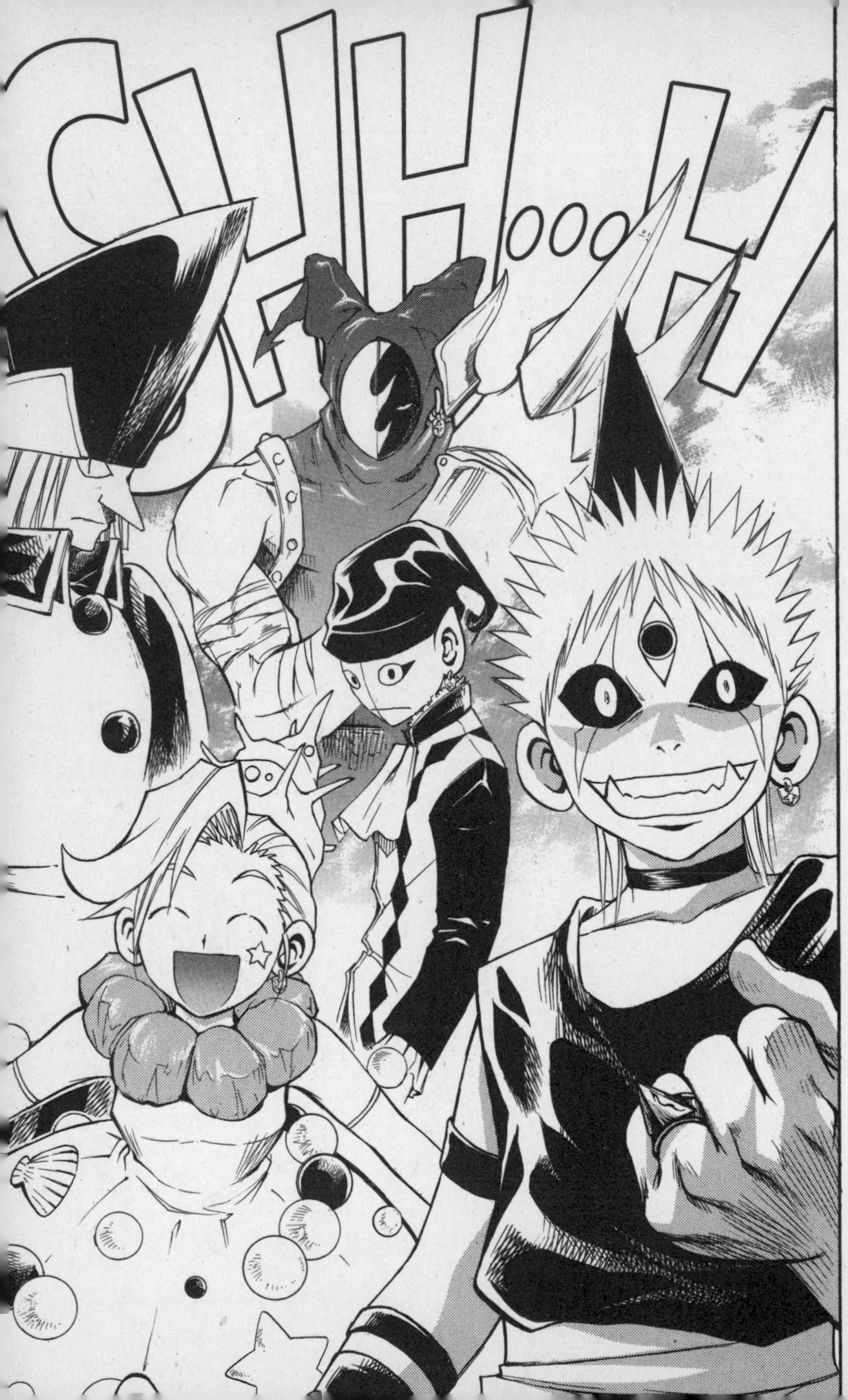
CHHOOOAH

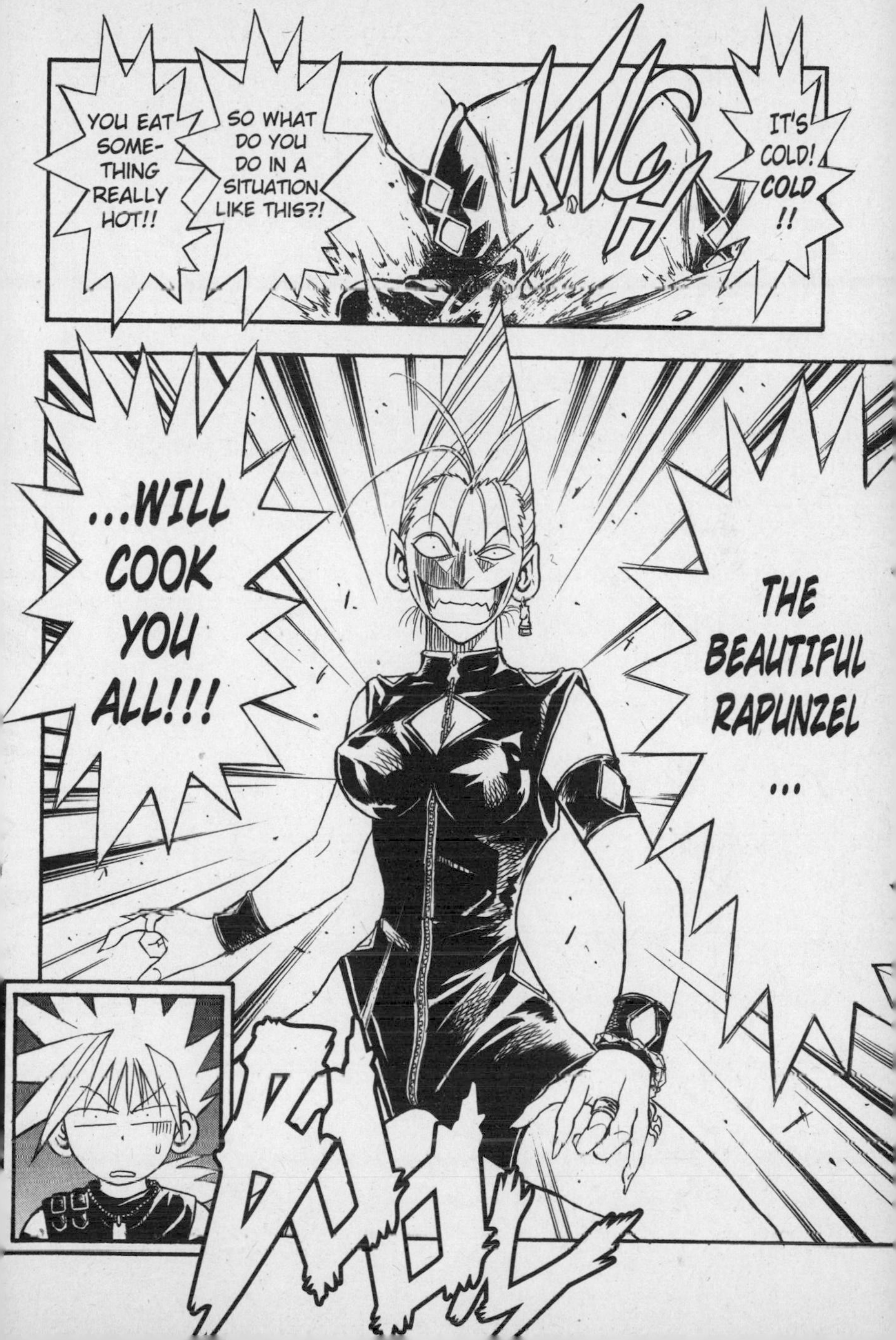
IT'S COLD! COLD !!
KNGH
SO WHAT DO YOU DO IN A SITUATION LIKE THIS?!
YOU EAT SOME-THING REALLY HOT!!
THE BEAUTIFUL RAPUNZEL ...
...WILL COOK YOU ALL!!!

AKT.72/ALVISS VS. MR. HOOK①

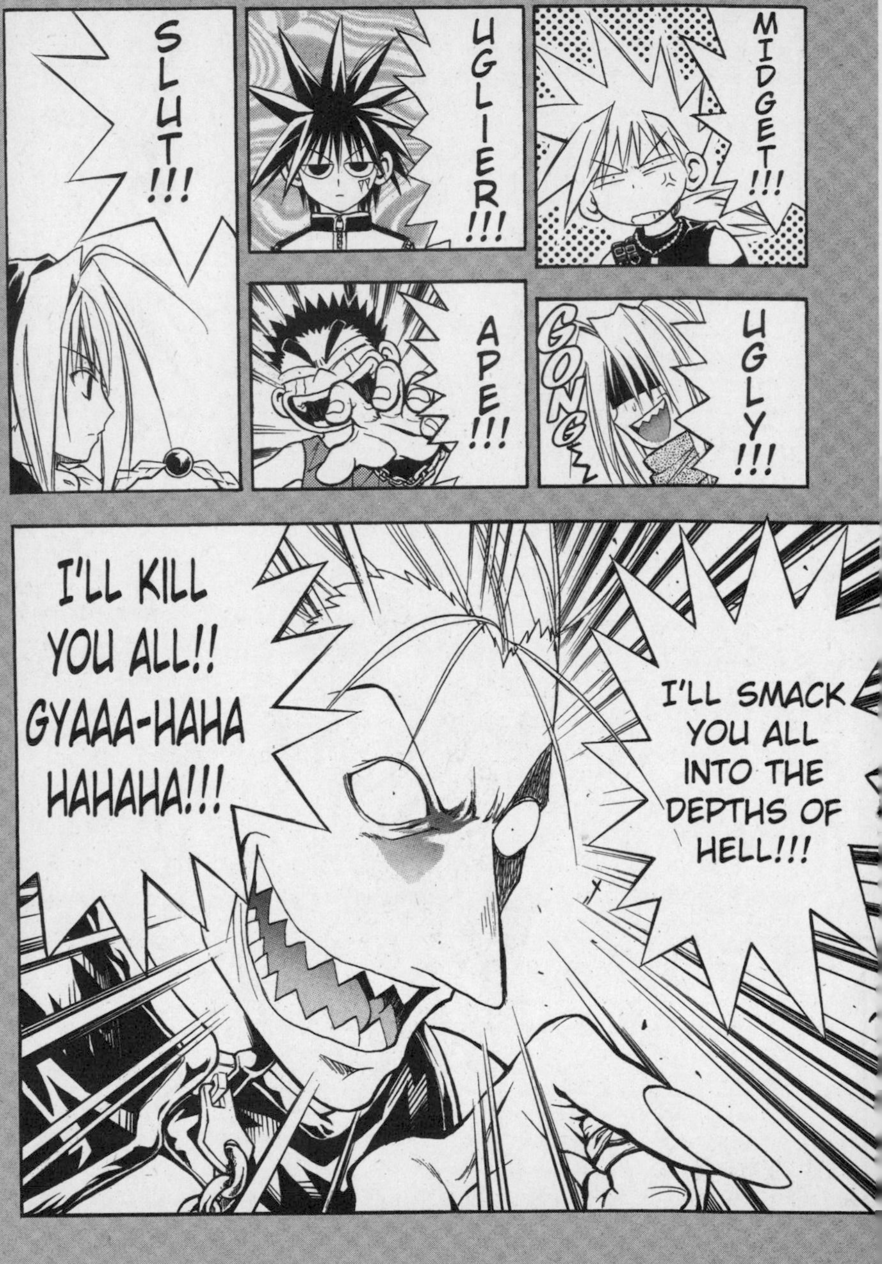
MIDGET!!!
UGLIER!!!
GONG
UGLY!!!
APE!!!
SLUT!!!
I'LL SMACK YOU ALL INTO THE DEPTHS OF HELL!!!
I'LL KILL YOU ALL!! GYAAA-HAHA HAHAHA!!!

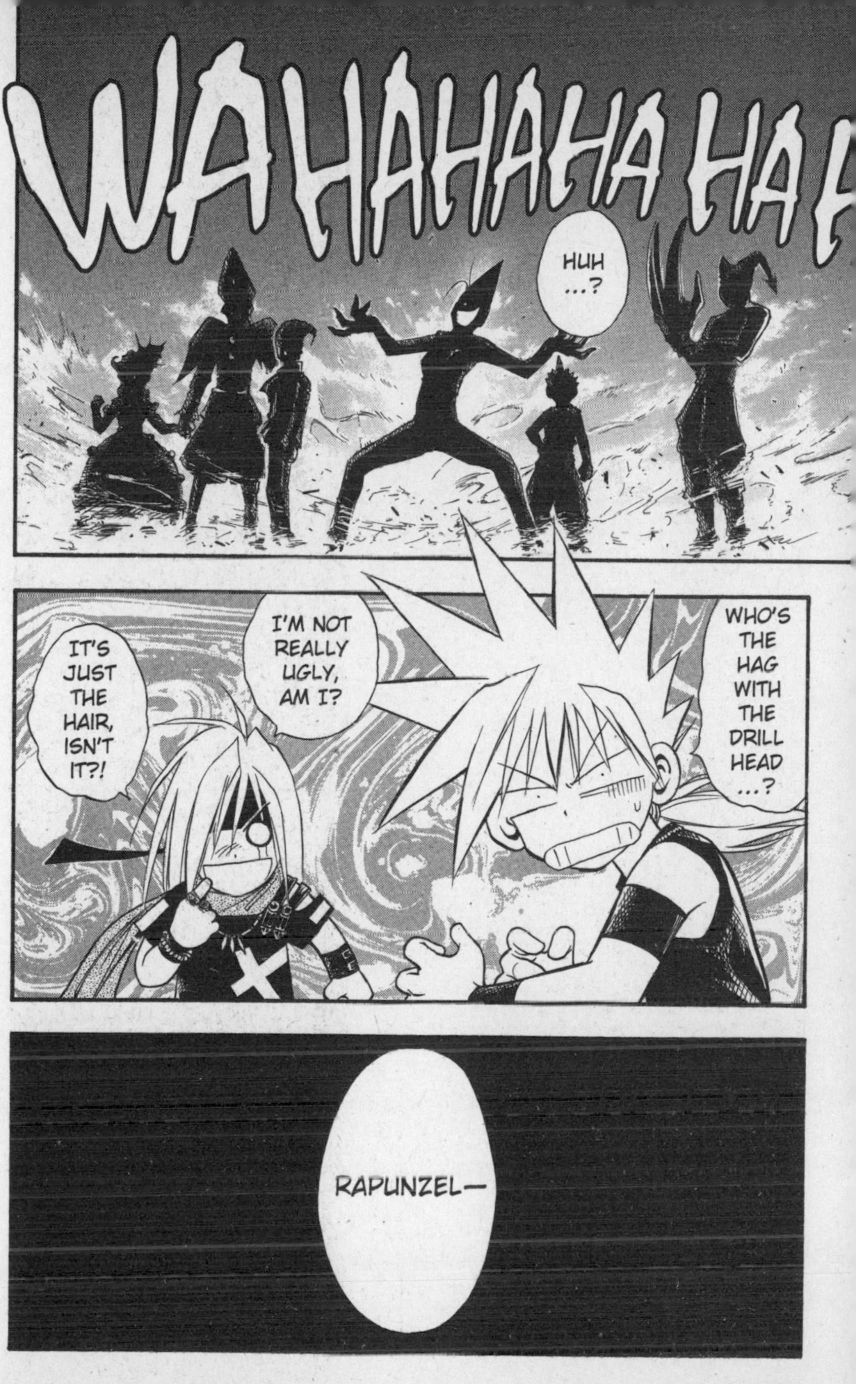
WAHAHAHA HA HA
HUH ...?
WHO'S THE HAG WITH THE DRILL HEAD ...?
I'M NOT REALLY UGLY, AM I?
IT'S JUST THE HAIR, ISN'T IT?!
RAPUNZEL—

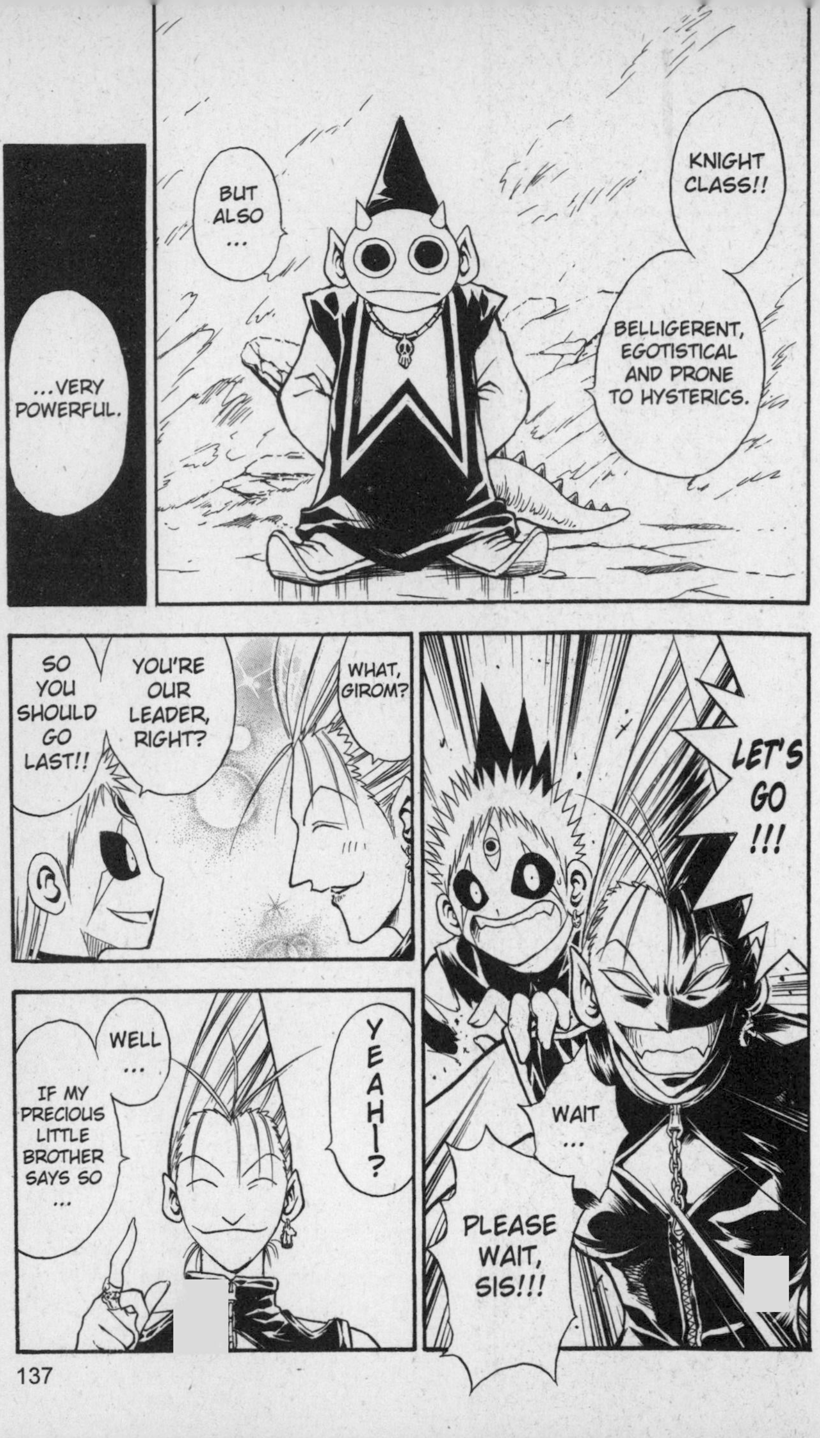
KNIGHT CLASS!!
BELLIGERENT, EGOTISTICAL AND PRONE TO HYSTERICS.
BUT ALSO ...
...VERY POWERFUL.
LET'S GO !!!
WAIT ...
PLEASE WAIT, SIS!!!
WHAT, GIROM?
YOU'RE OUR LEADER, RIGHT?
SO YOU SHOULD GO LAST!!
YEAH!?
WELL ...
IF MY PRECIOUS LITTLE BROTHER SAYS SO ...

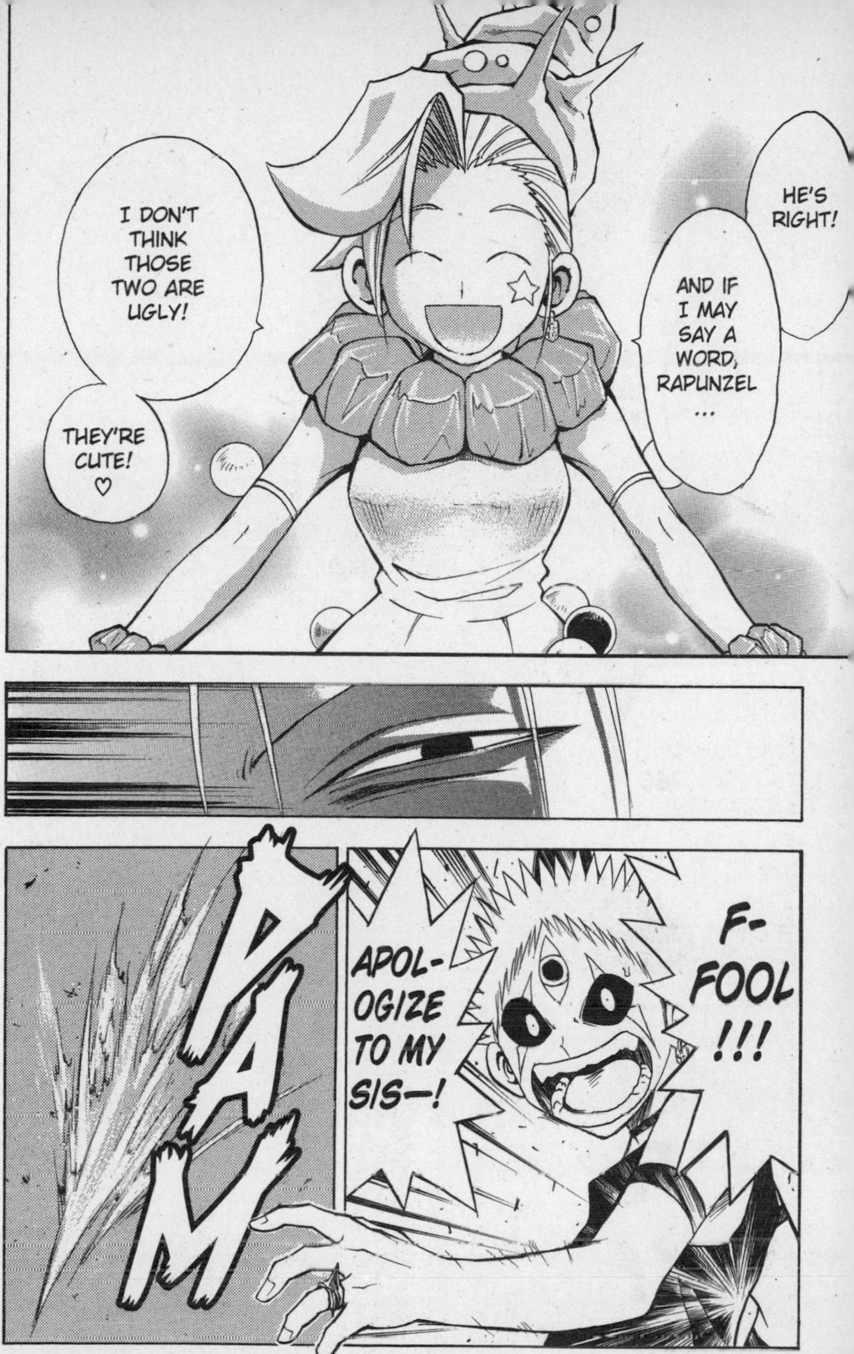
HE'S RIGHT!
AND IF I MAY SAY A WORD, RAPUNZEL ...
I DON'T THINK THOSE TWO ARE UGLY!
THEY'RE CUTE! ♡
F-FOOL!!!
APOLOGIZE TO MY SIS—!
BAM

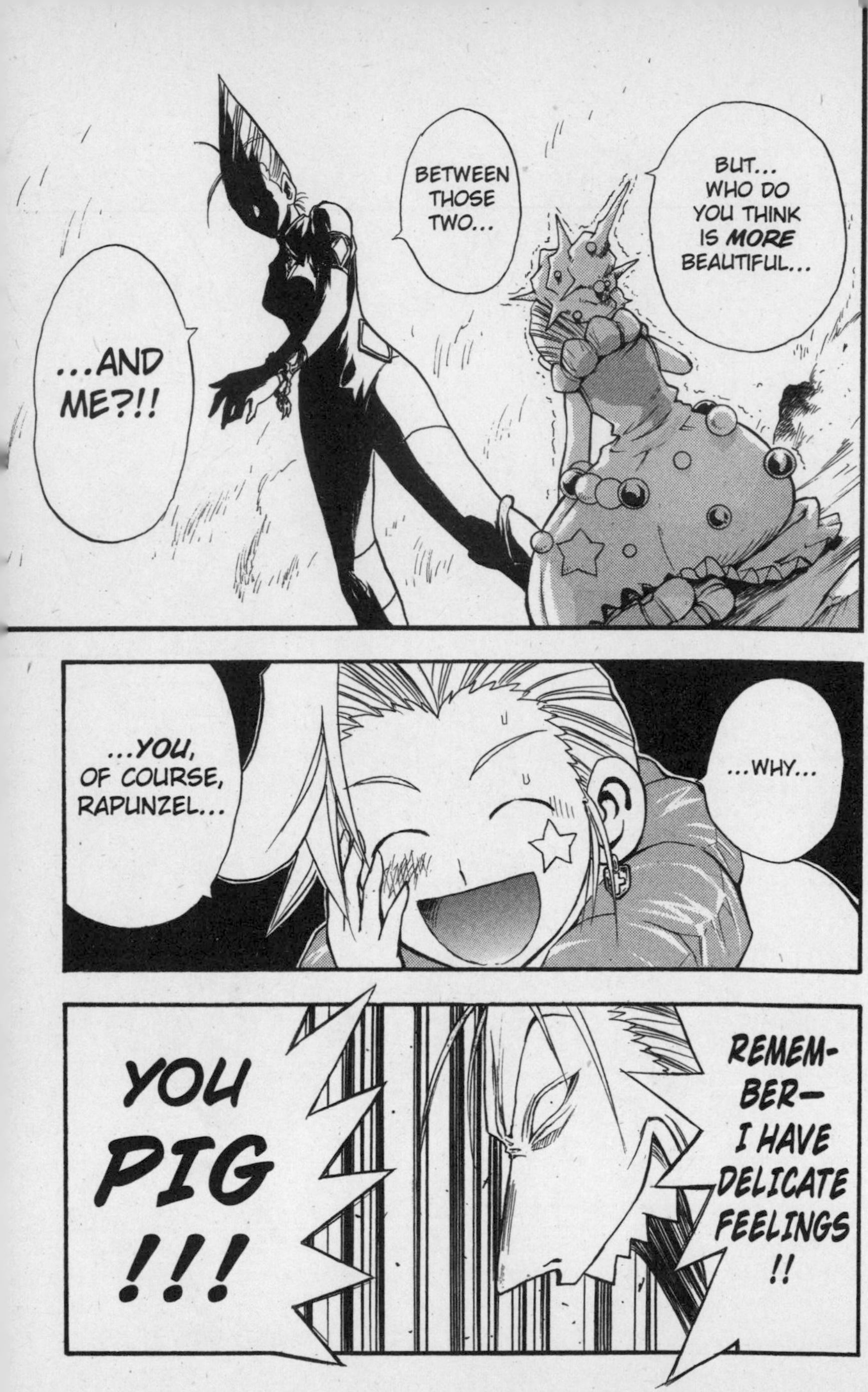
BUT... WHO DO YOU THINK IS MORE BEAUTIFUL...
BETWEEN THOSE TWO...
...AND ME?!!
...WHY...
...YOU, OF COURSE, RAPUNZEL...
REMEM-BER— I HAVE DELICATE FEELINGS !!
YOU PIG !!!

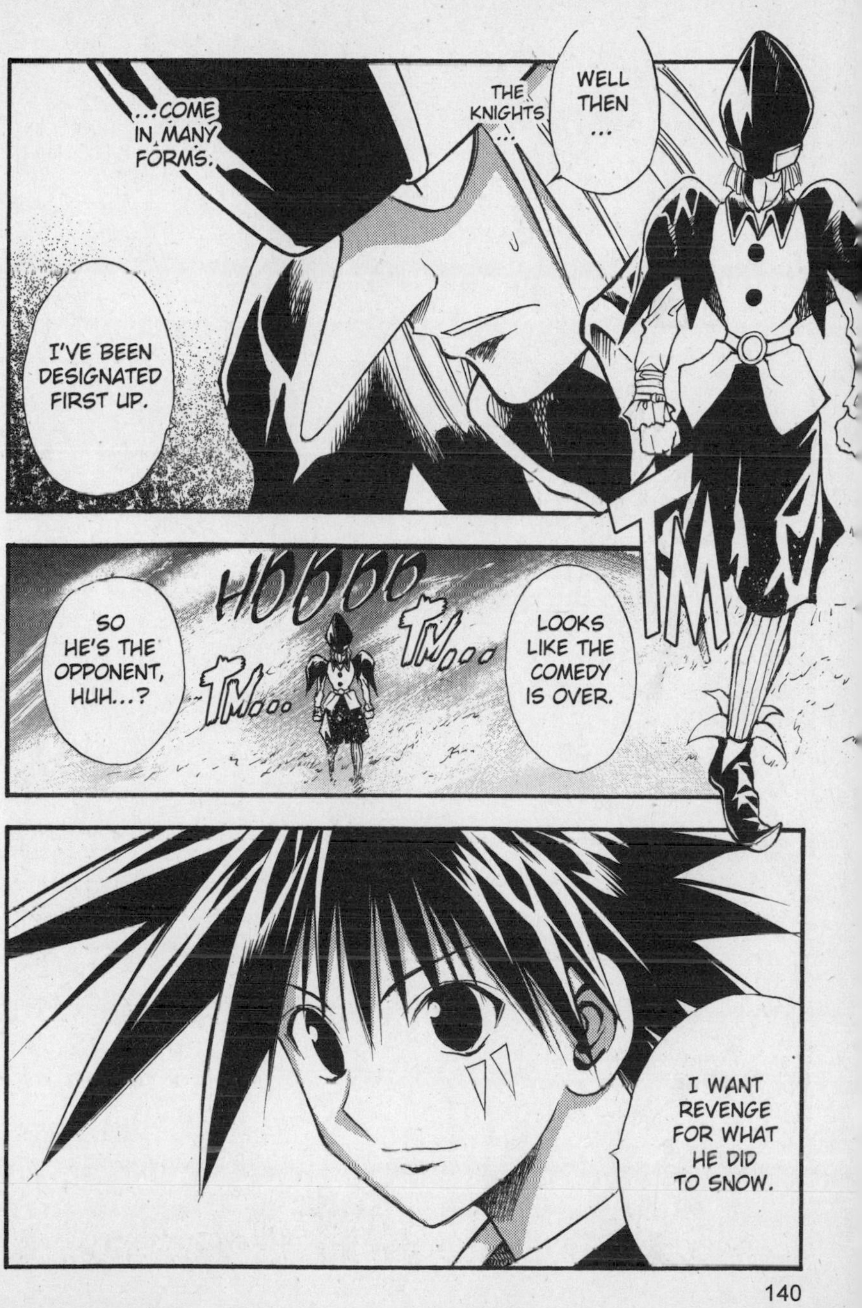
WELL THEN ...
THE KNIGHTS ...
...COME IN MANY FORMS.
I'VE BEEN DESIGNATED FIRST UP.
TMP
LOOKS LIKE THE COMEDY IS OVER.
TM...
HOOOOO
TM...
SO HE'S THE OPPONENT, HUH...?
I WANT REVENGE FOR WHAT HE DID TO SNOW.

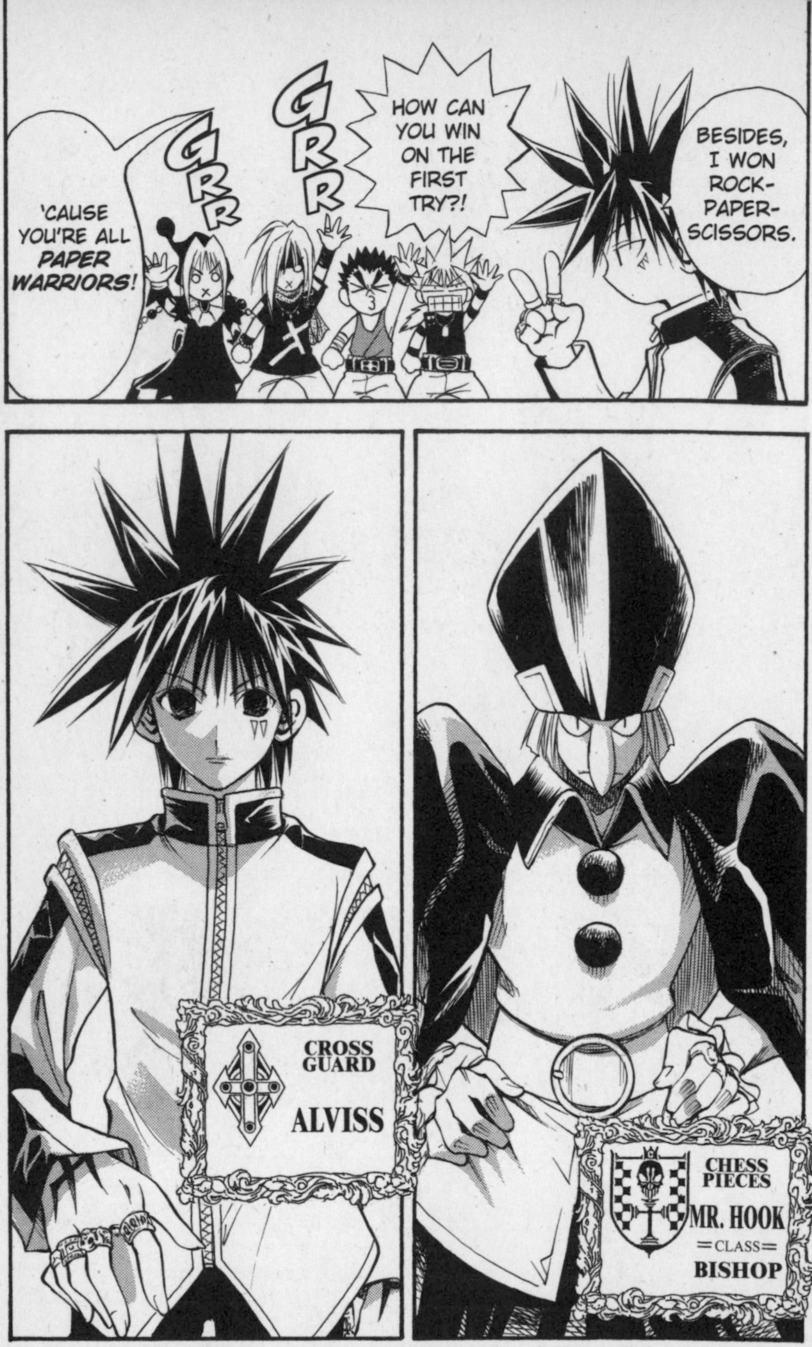
BESIDES, I WON ROCK-PAPER-SCISSORS.
HOW CAN YOU WIN ON THE FIRST TRY?!
GRR
GRR
'CAUSE YOU'RE ALL *PAPER WARRIORS!*
CHESS PIECES
MR. HOOK
=CLASS=
BISHOP
CROSS GUARD
ALVISS

AKT.72/ ALVISS VS. MR. HOOK①

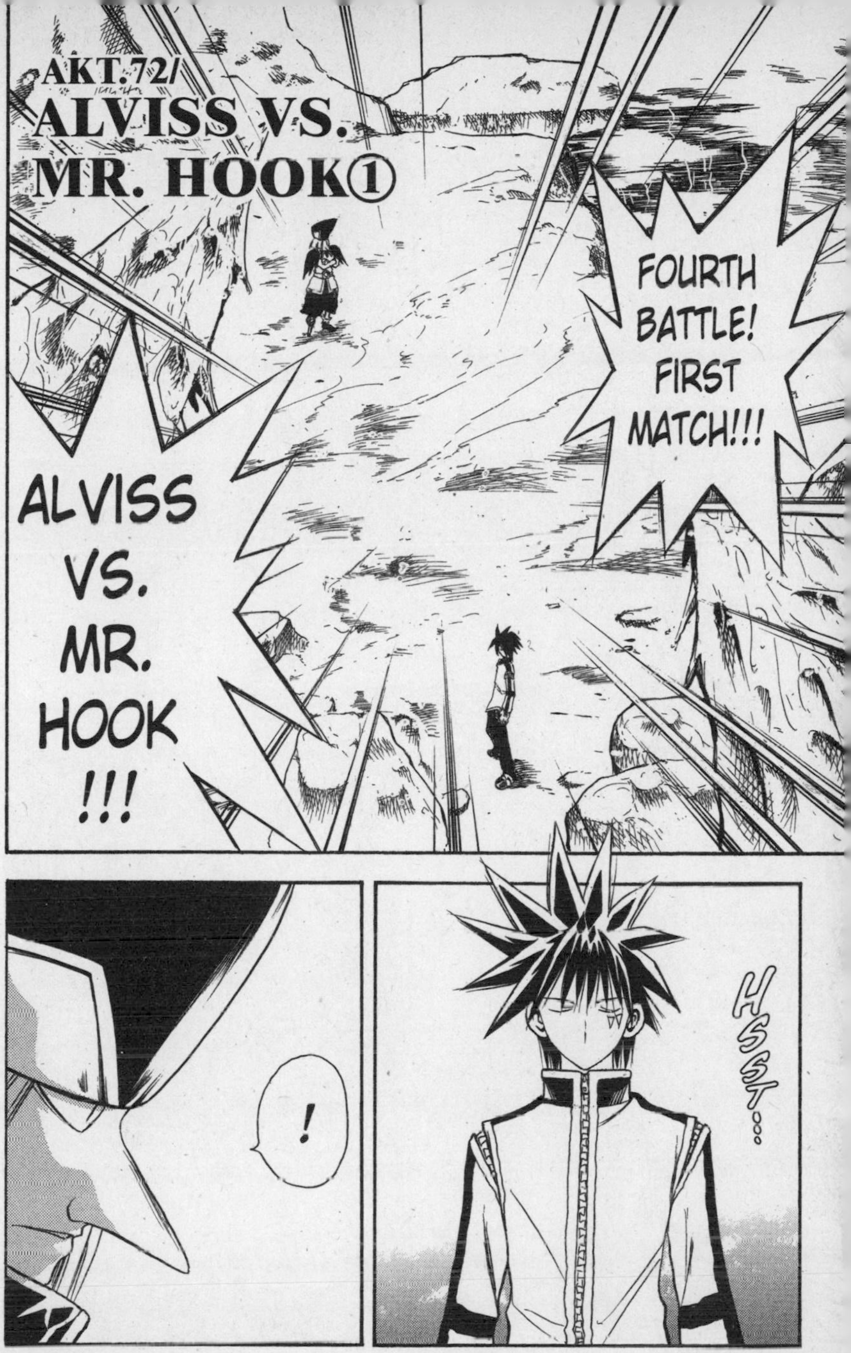

FOURTH BATTLE! FIRST MATCH!!!
ALVISS VS. MR. HOOK!!!
HSST...
!

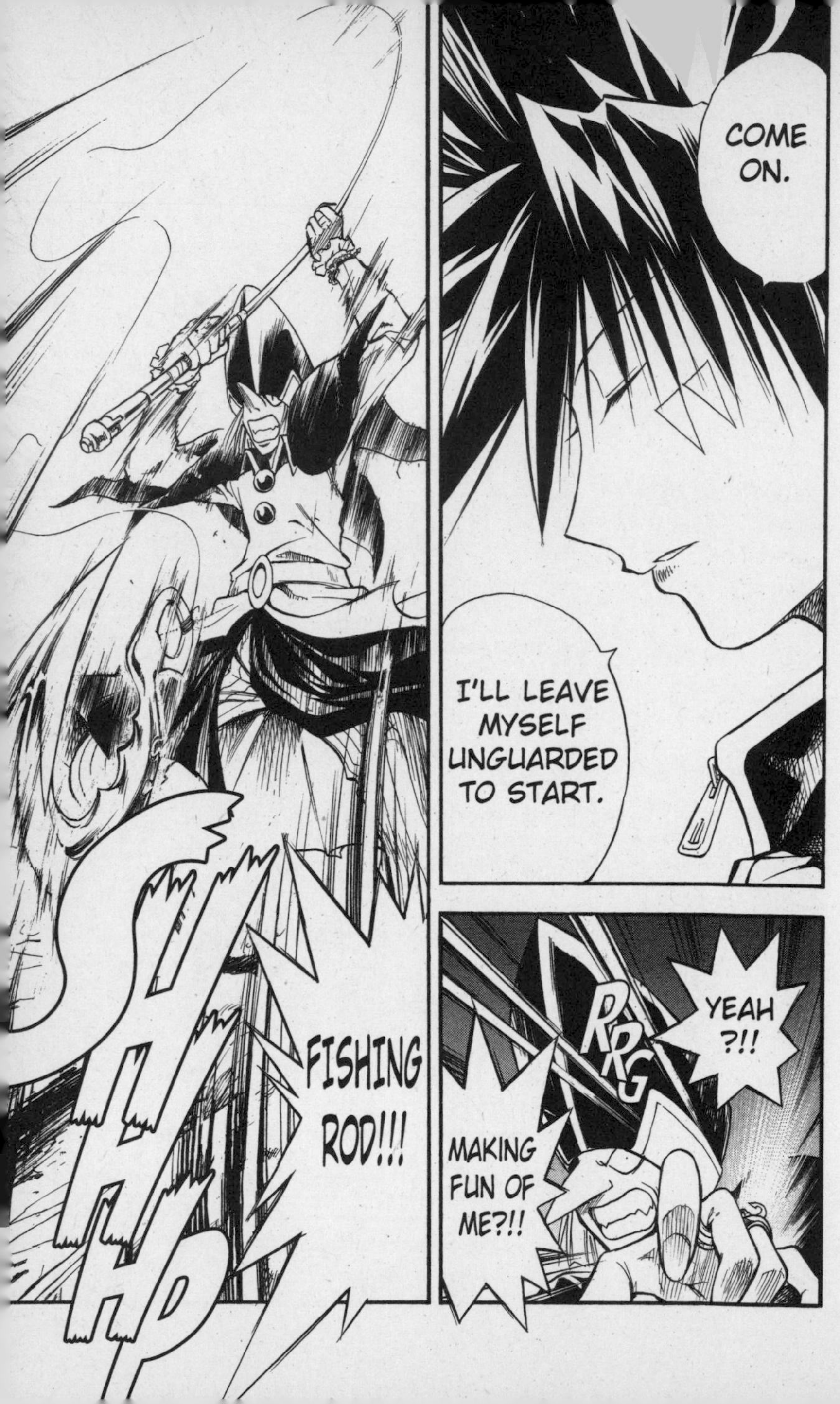
COME ON.
I'LL LEAVE MYSELF UNGUARDED TO START.
RRG
YEAH?!!
MAKING FUN OF ME?!!
FISHING ROD!!!
SHHP

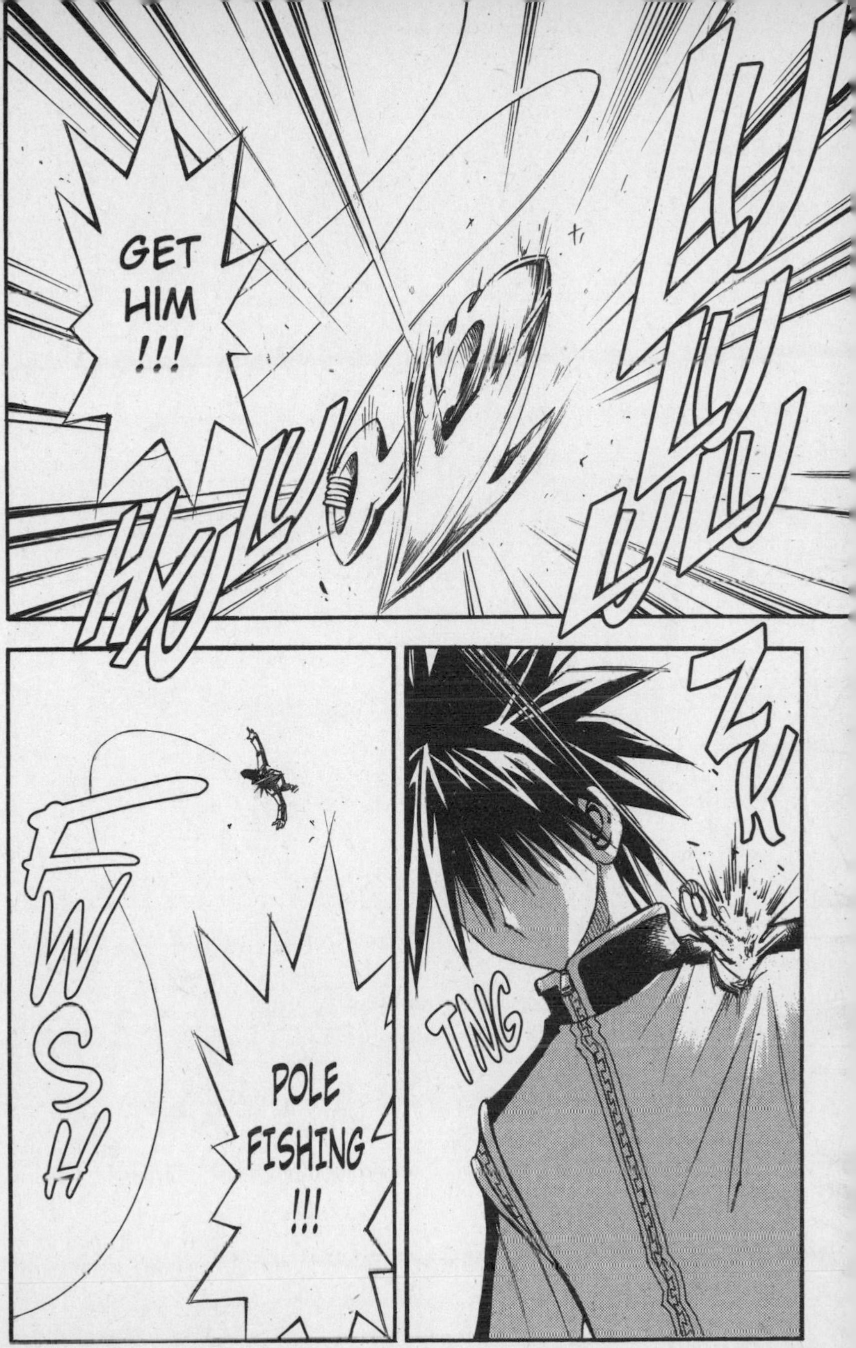
GET HIM !!!
ZK
TNG
POLE FISHING !!!
FWSH

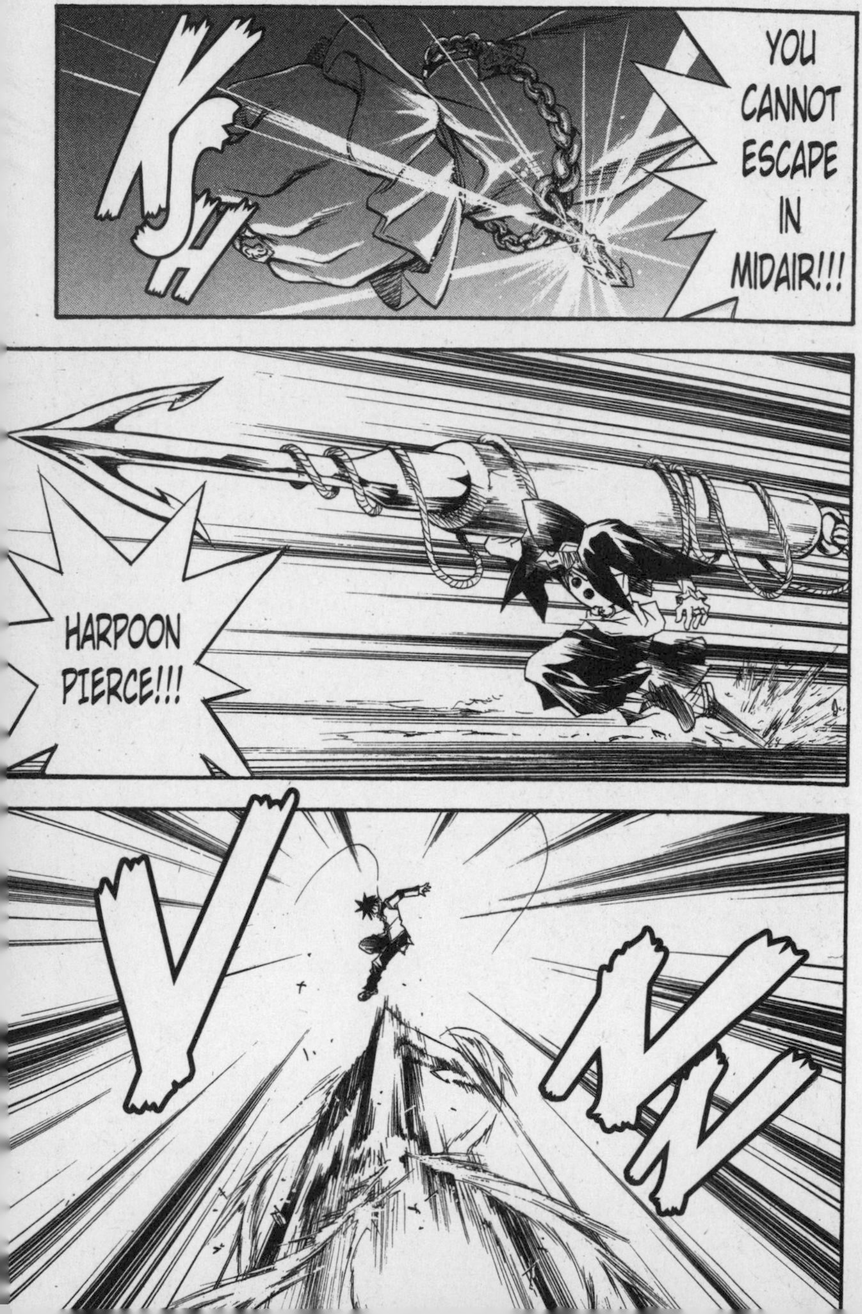
YOU CANNOT ESCAPE IN MIDAIR!!!
HARPOON PIERCE!!!

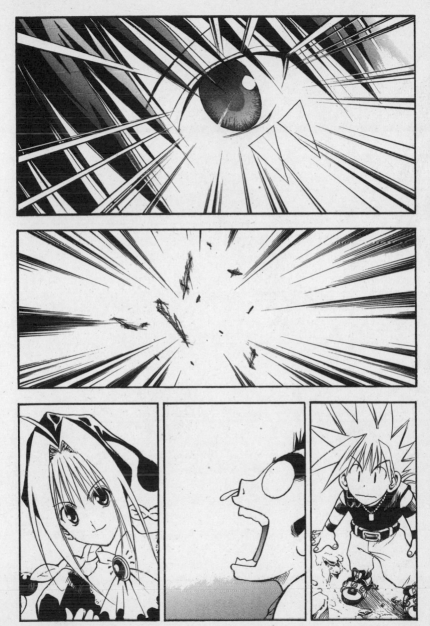

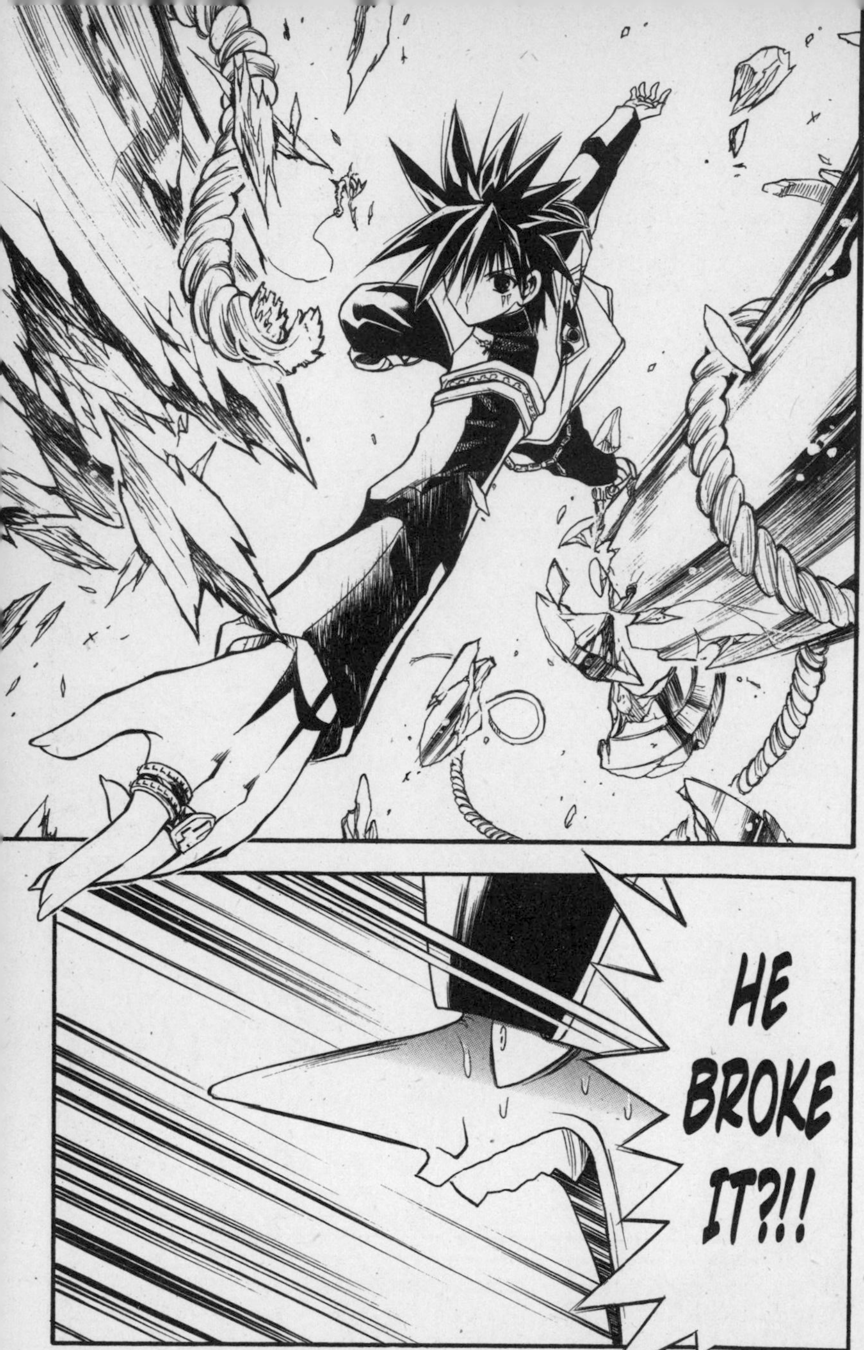
HE BROKE IT?!!

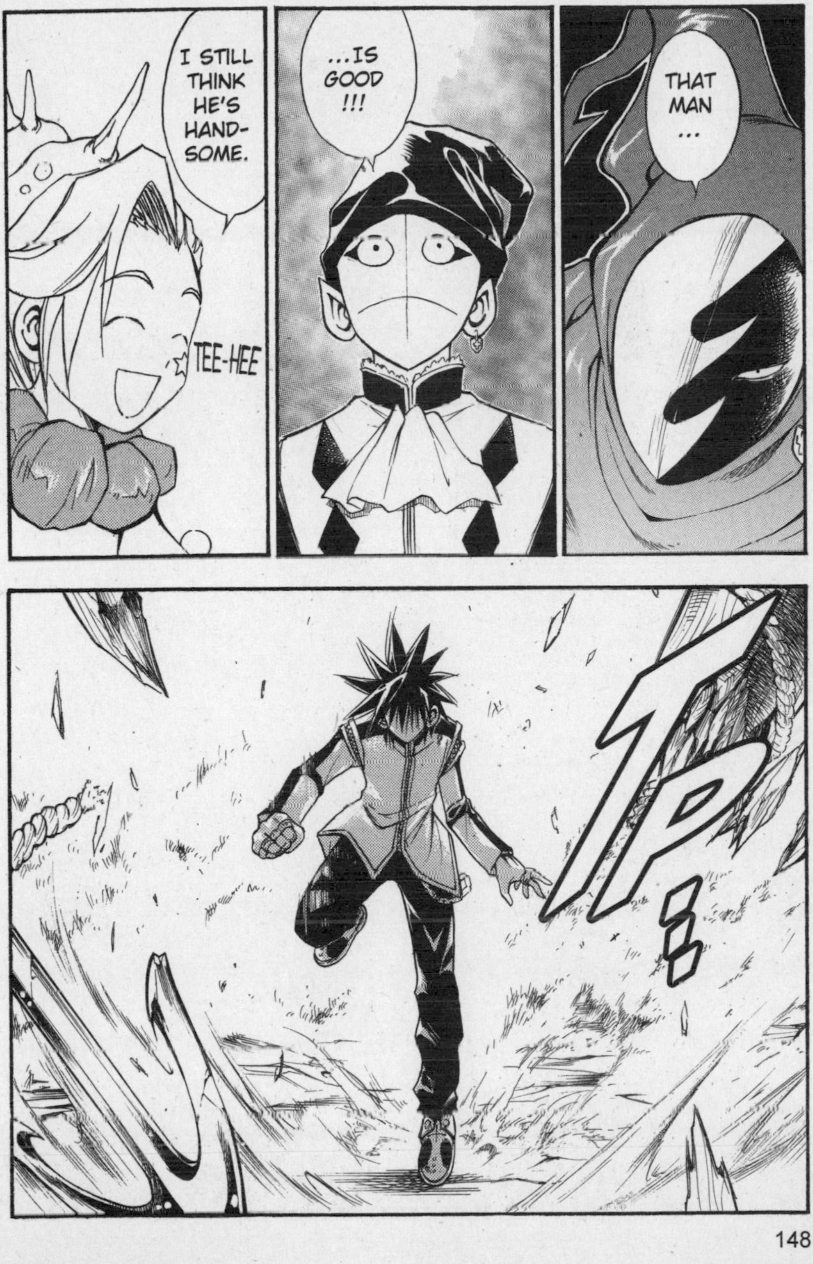
THAT MAN ...
...IS GOOD !!!
I STILL THINK HE'S HANDSOME.
TEE-HEE

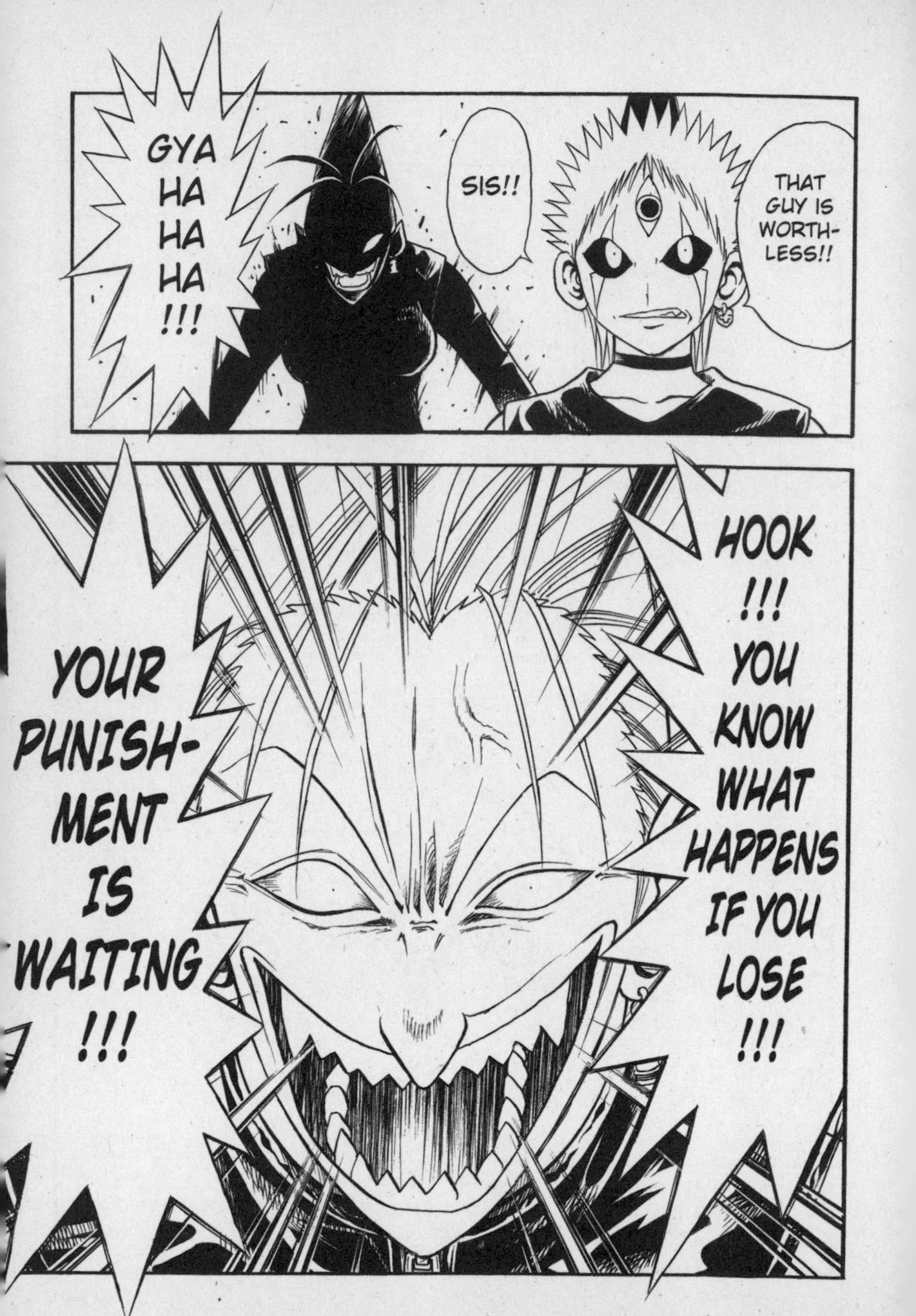
THAT GUY IS WORTHLESS!!
SIS!!
GYA HA HA HA!!!
HOOK!!! YOU KNOW WHAT HAPPENS IF YOU LOSE!!!
YOUR PUNISHMENT IS WAITING!!!

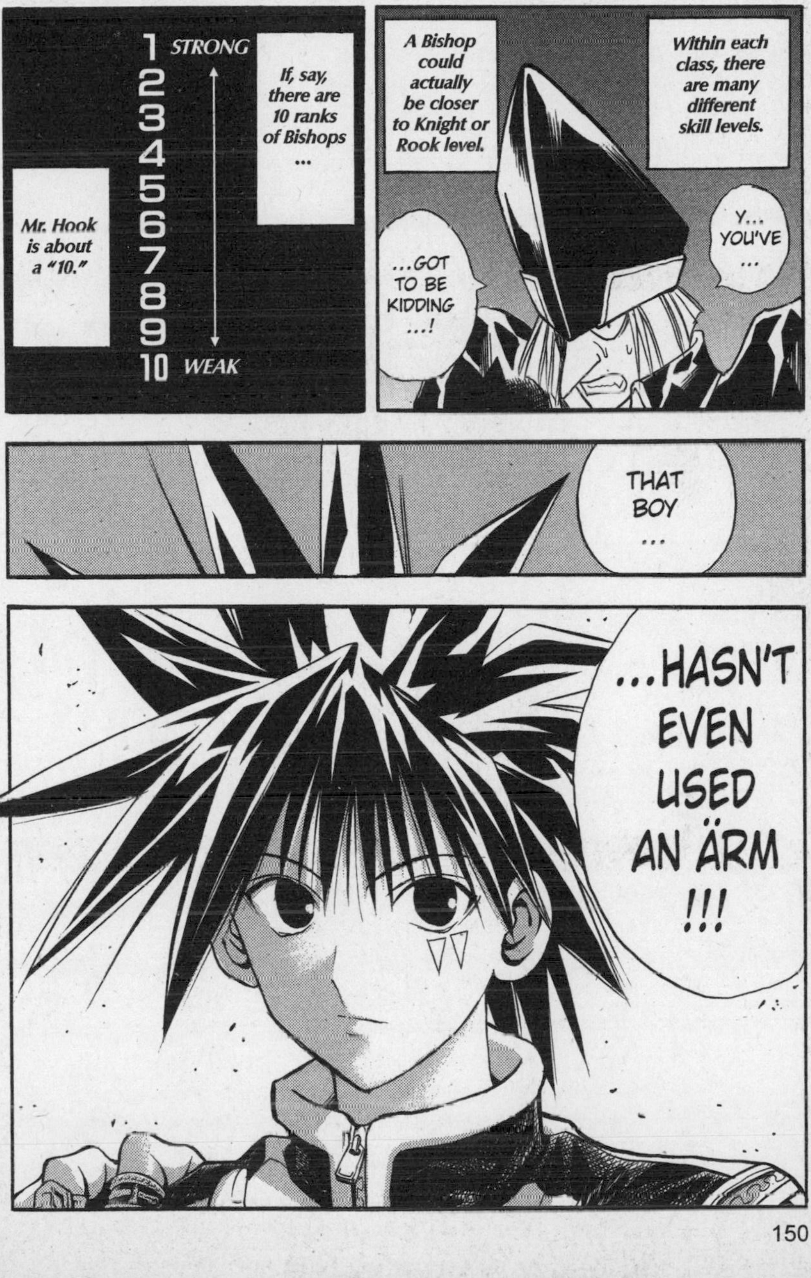
Within each class, there are many different skill levels.
A Bishop could actually be closer to Knight or Rook level.
Y... YOU'VE ...
...GOT TO BE KIDDING ...!
If, say, there are 10 ranks of Bishops ...
1 STRONG
2
3
4
5
6
7
8
9
10 WEAK
Mr. Hook is about a "10."
THAT BOY ...
...HASN'T EVEN USED AN ÄRM !!!

AKT.73/ALVISS VS. MR. HOOK②

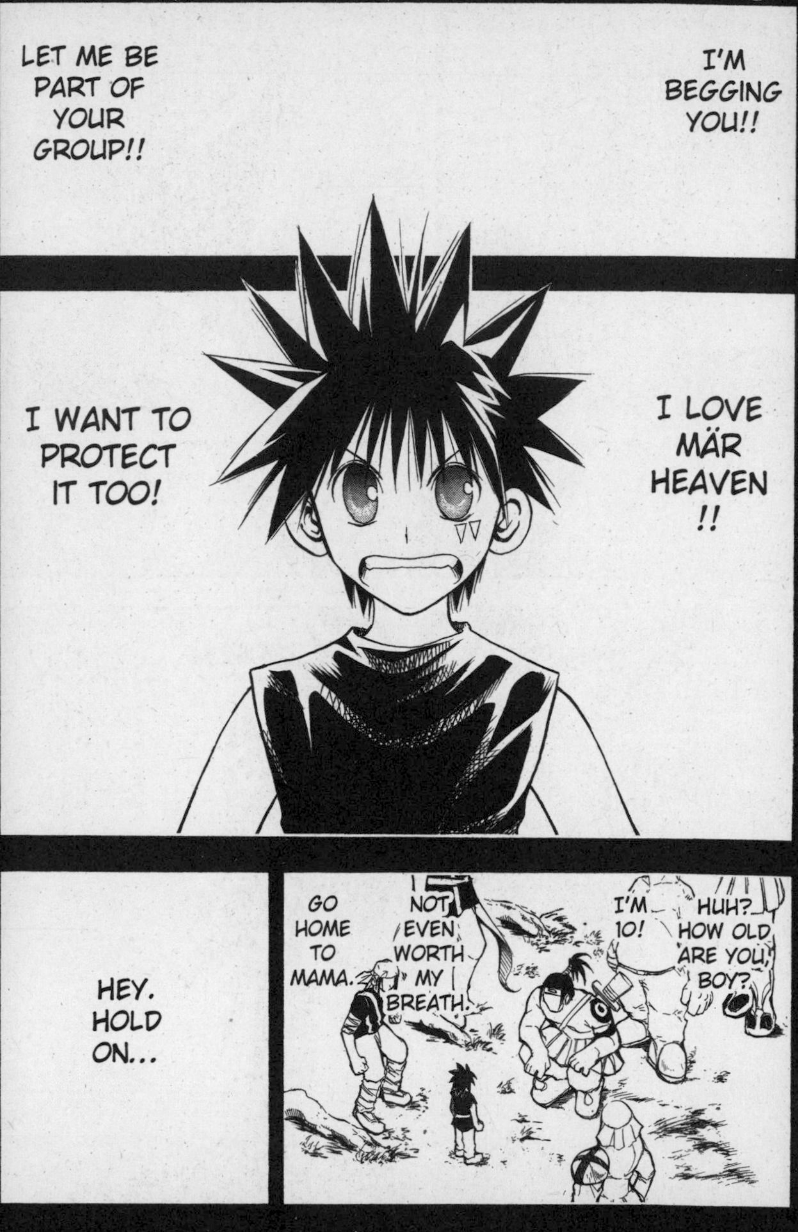
I'M BEGGING YOU!!
LET ME BE PART OF YOUR GROUP!!
I LOVE MÄR HEAVEN!!
I WANT TO PROTECT IT TOO!
HUH? HOW OLD ARE YOU, BOY?
I'M 10!
NOT EVEN WORTH MY BREATH.
GO HOME TO MAMA.
HEY. HOLD ON...

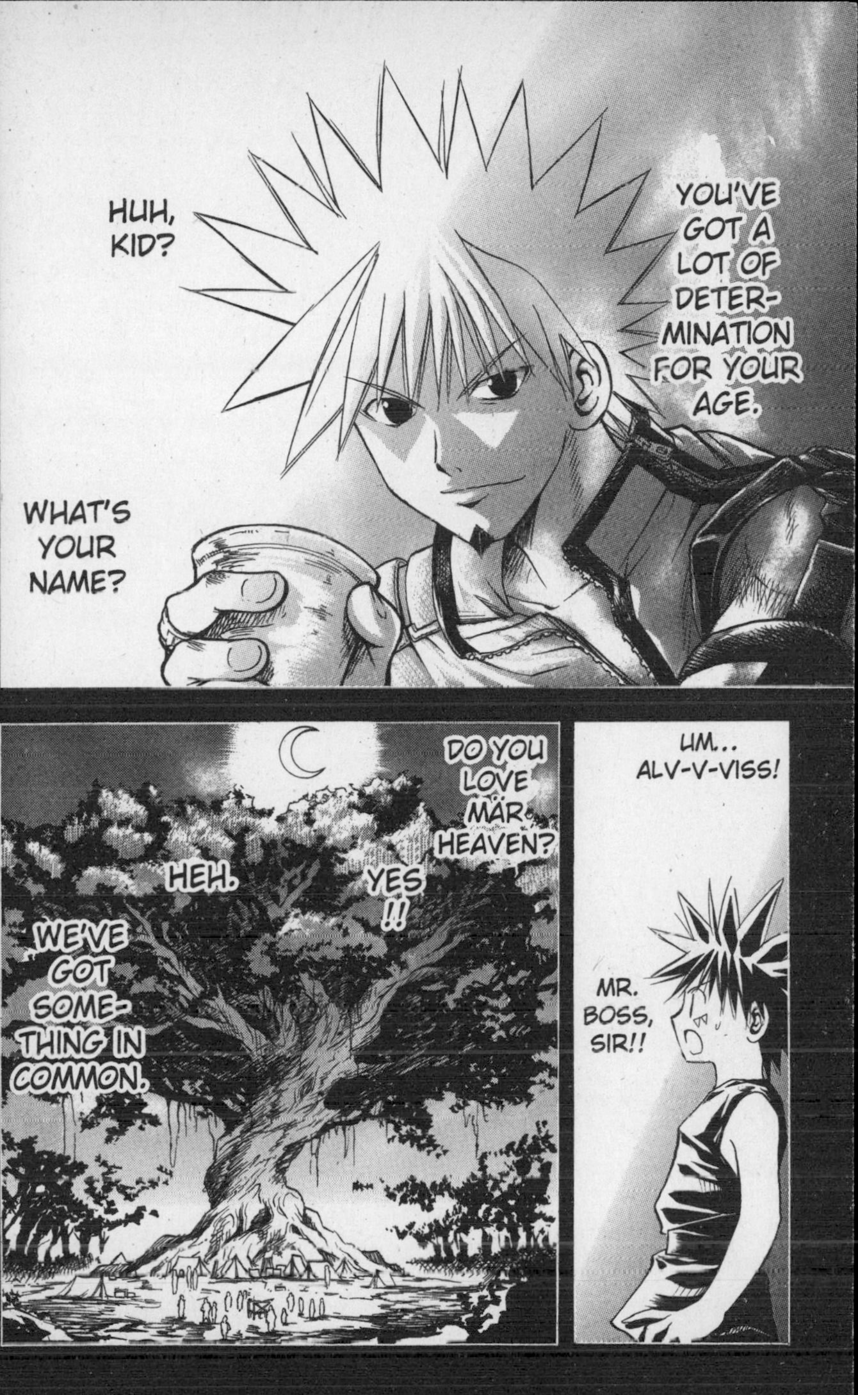
YOU'VE GOT A LOT OF DETER-MINATION FOR YOUR AGE.
HUH, KID?
WHAT'S YOUR NAME?
UM... ALV-V-VISS!
MR. BOSS, SIR!!
DO YOU LOVE MÄR HEAVEN?
YES!!
HEH.
WE'VE GOT SOME-THING IN COMMON.

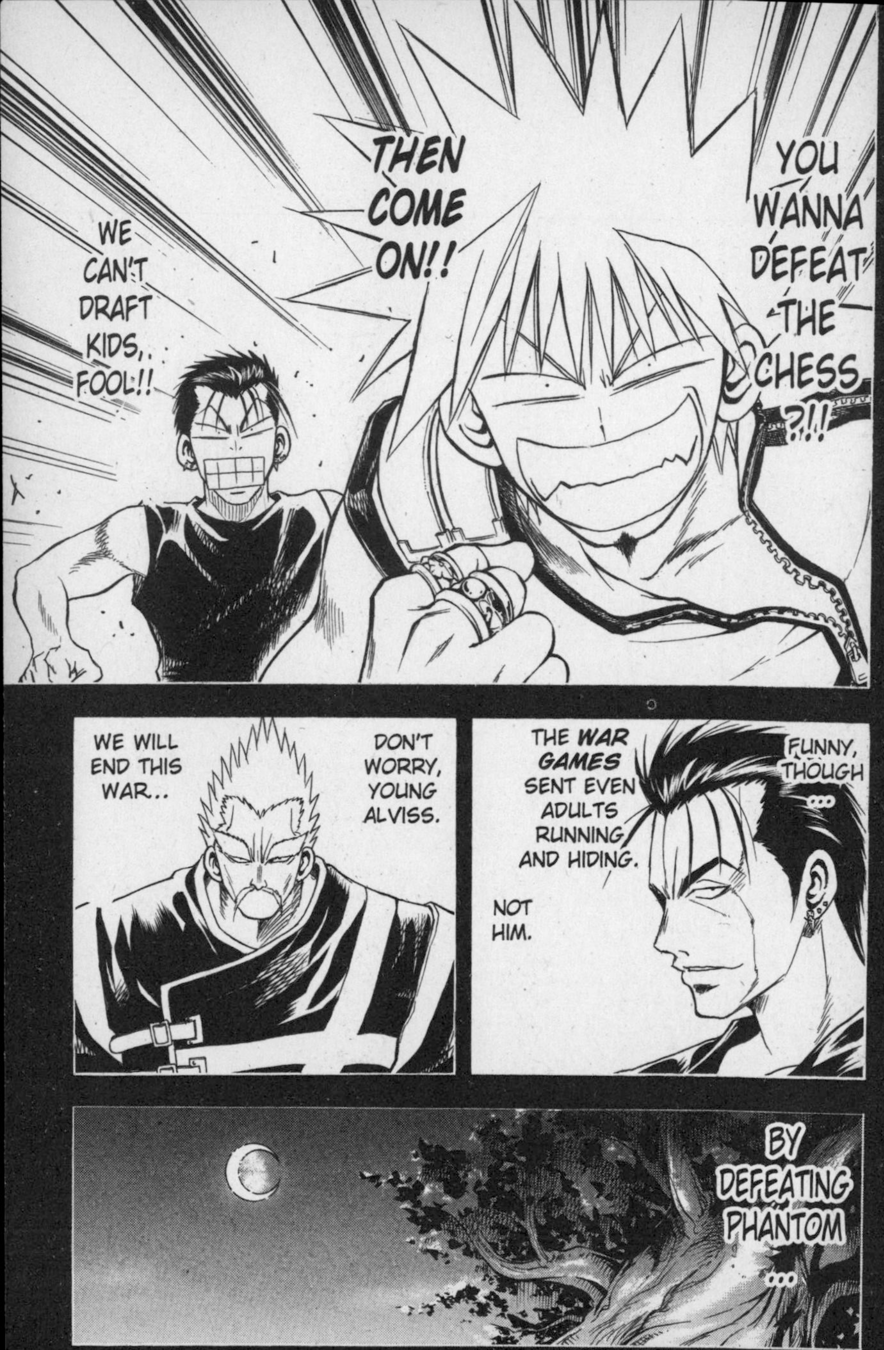
YOU WANNA DEFEAT THE CHESS?!!
THEN COME ON!!
WE CAN'T DRAFT KIDS, FOOL!!
FUNNY, THOUGH...
THE WAR GAMES SENT EVEN ADULTS RUNNING AND HIDING.
NOT HIM.
DON'T WORRY, YOUNG ALVISS.
WE WILL END THIS WAR..
BY DEFEATING PHANTOM...

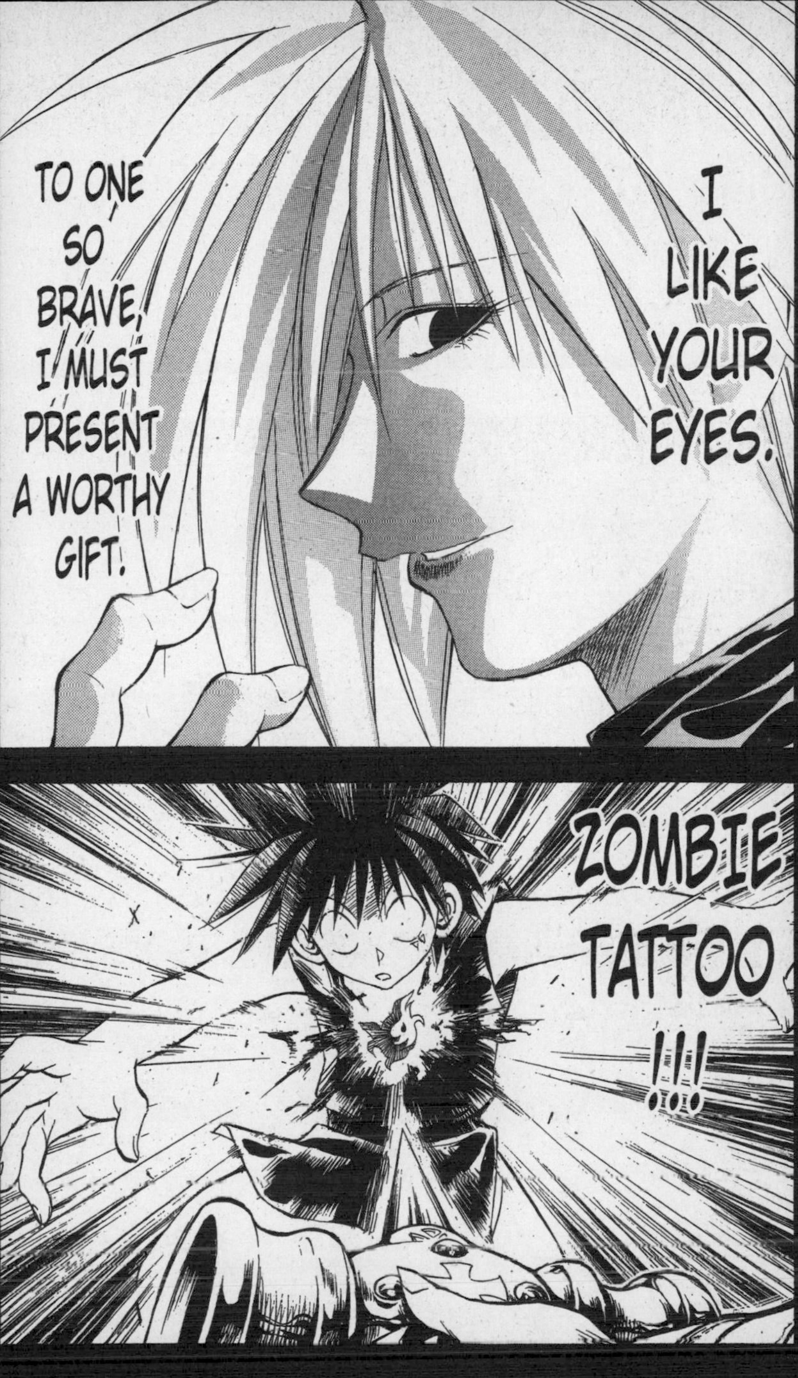
I LIKE YOUR EYES.
TO ONE SO BRAVE, I MUST PRESENT A WORTHY GIFT.
ZOMBIE TATTOO !!!

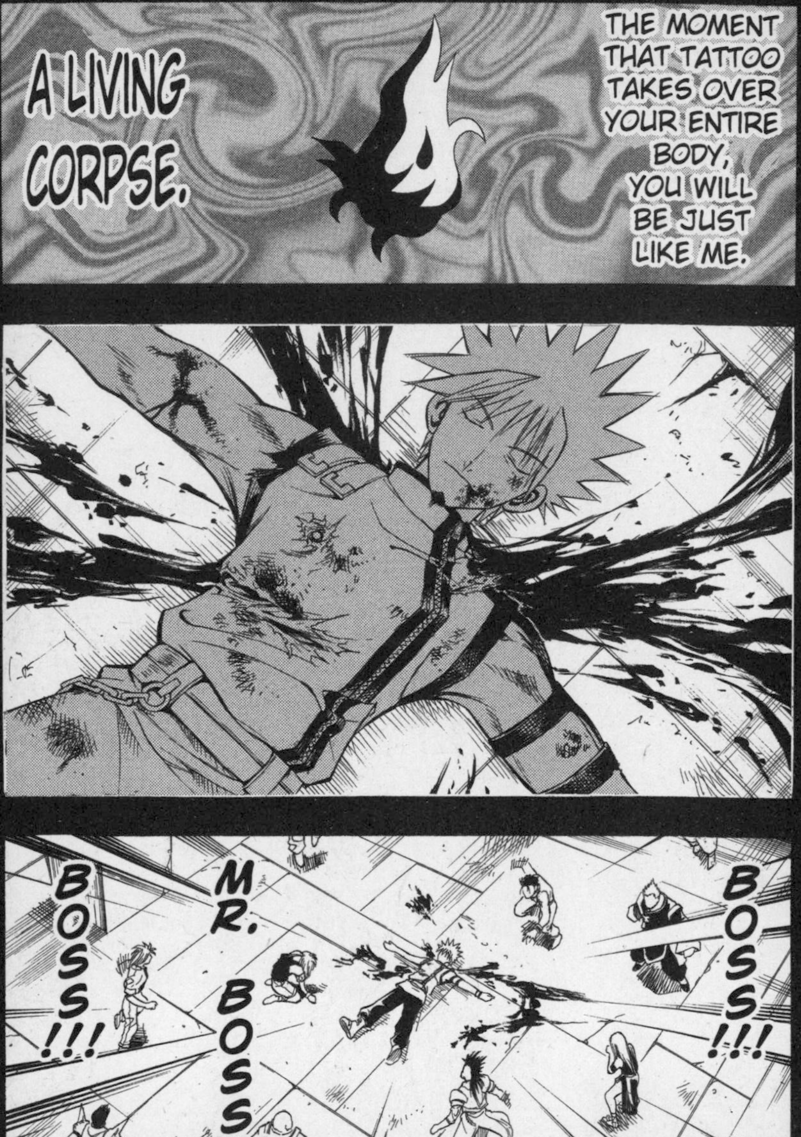
THE MOMENT THAT TATTOO TAKES OVER YOUR ENTIRE BODY, YOU WILL BE JUST LIKE ME.
A LIVING CORPSE.
BOSS!!!
MR. BOSS!!!
BOSS!!!

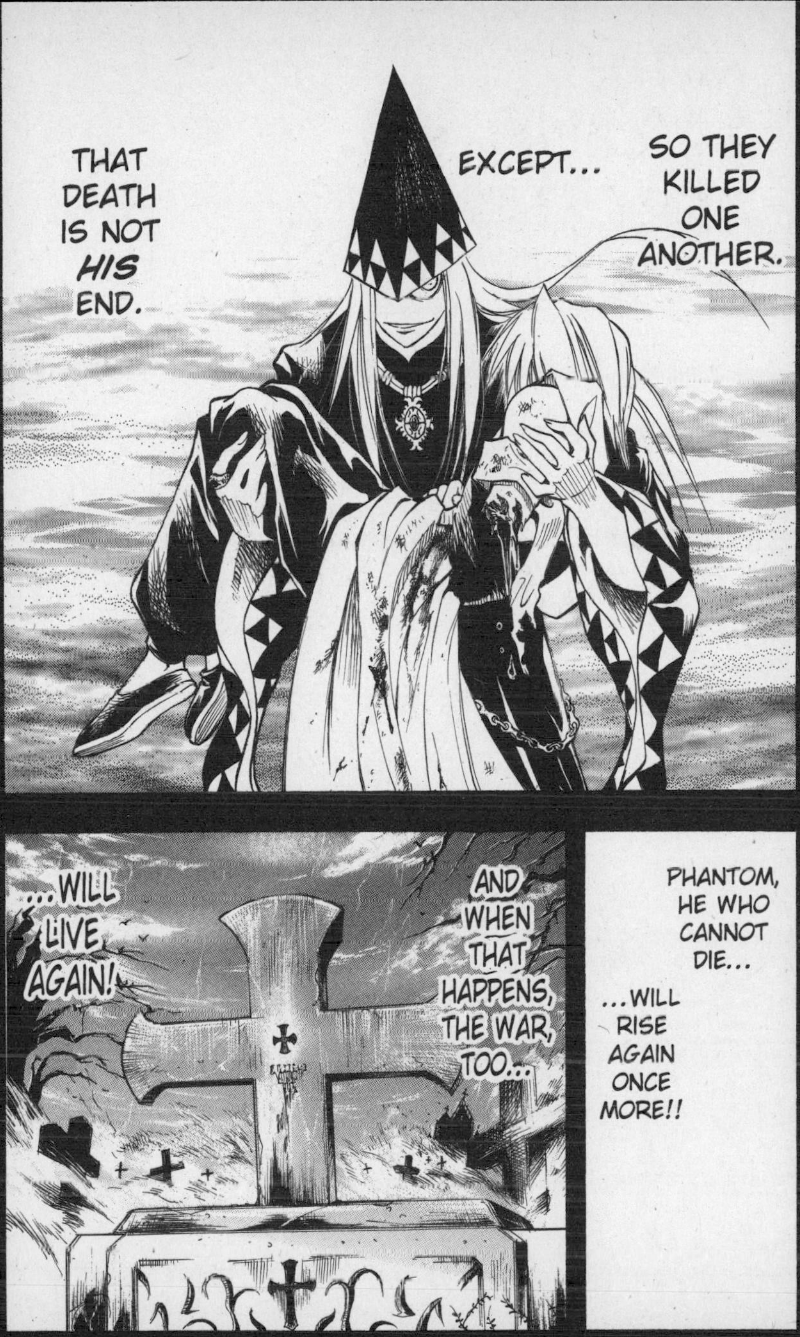
SO THEY KILLED ONE ANOTHER.
EXCEPT...
THAT DEATH IS NOT *HIS* END.
PHANTOM, HE WHO CANNOT DIE...
...WILL RISE AGAIN ONCE MORE!!
AND WHEN THAT HAPPENS, THE WAR, TOO...
...WILL LIVE AGAIN!

AKT.73/ ALVISS VS. MR. HOOK②

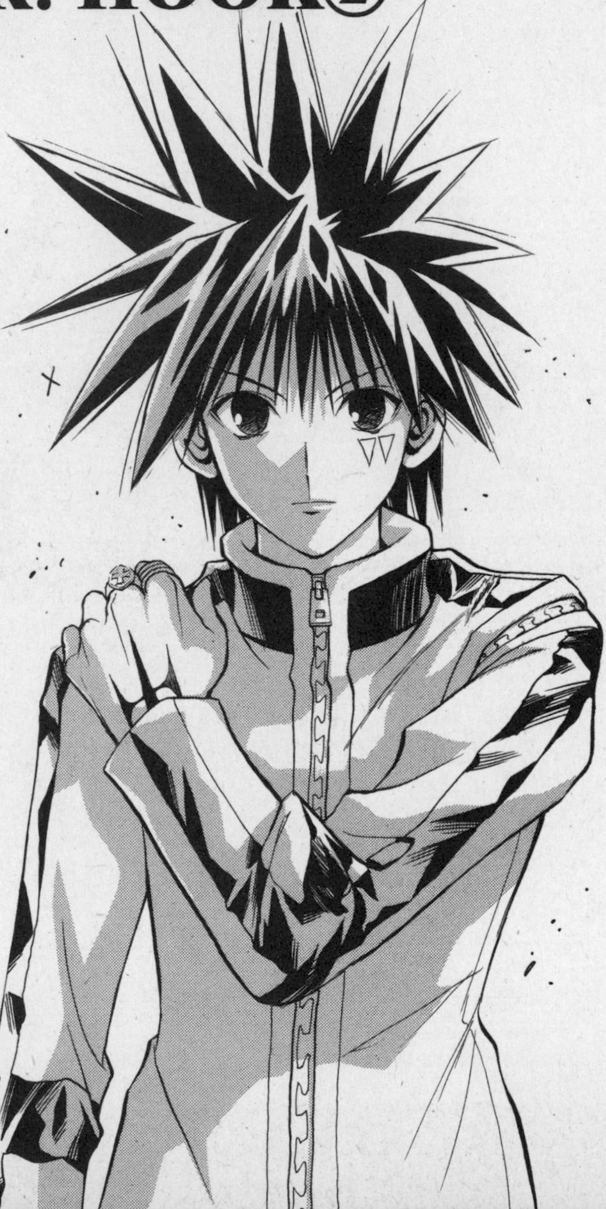

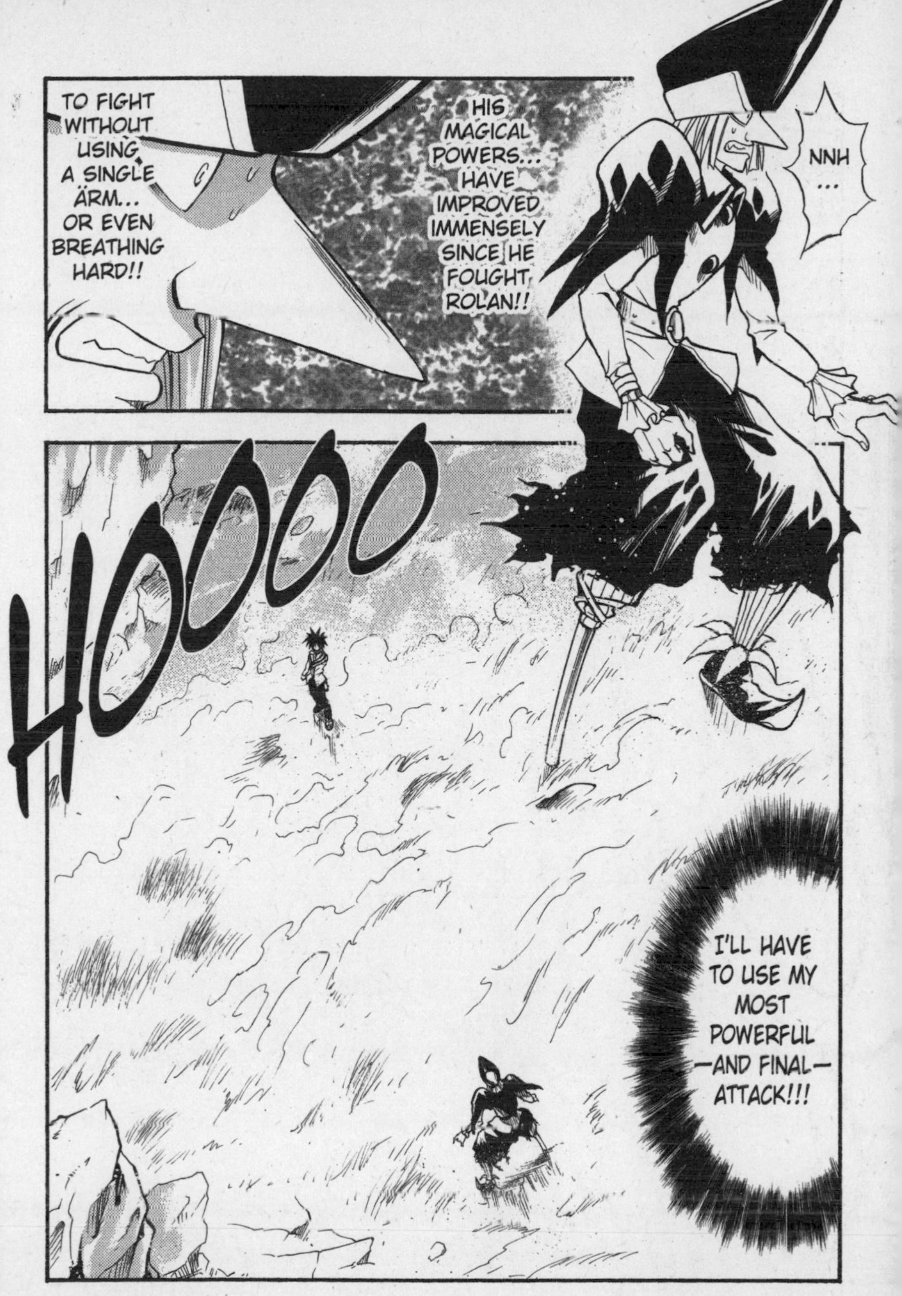
NNH ...
HIS MAGICAL POWERS... HAVE IMPROVED IMMENSELY SINCE HE FOUGHT ROLAN!!
TO FIGHT WITHOUT USING A SINGLE ÄRM... OR EVEN BREATHING HARD!!
HOOOOO
I'LL HAVE TO USE MY MOST POWERFUL —AND FINAL— ATTACK!!!

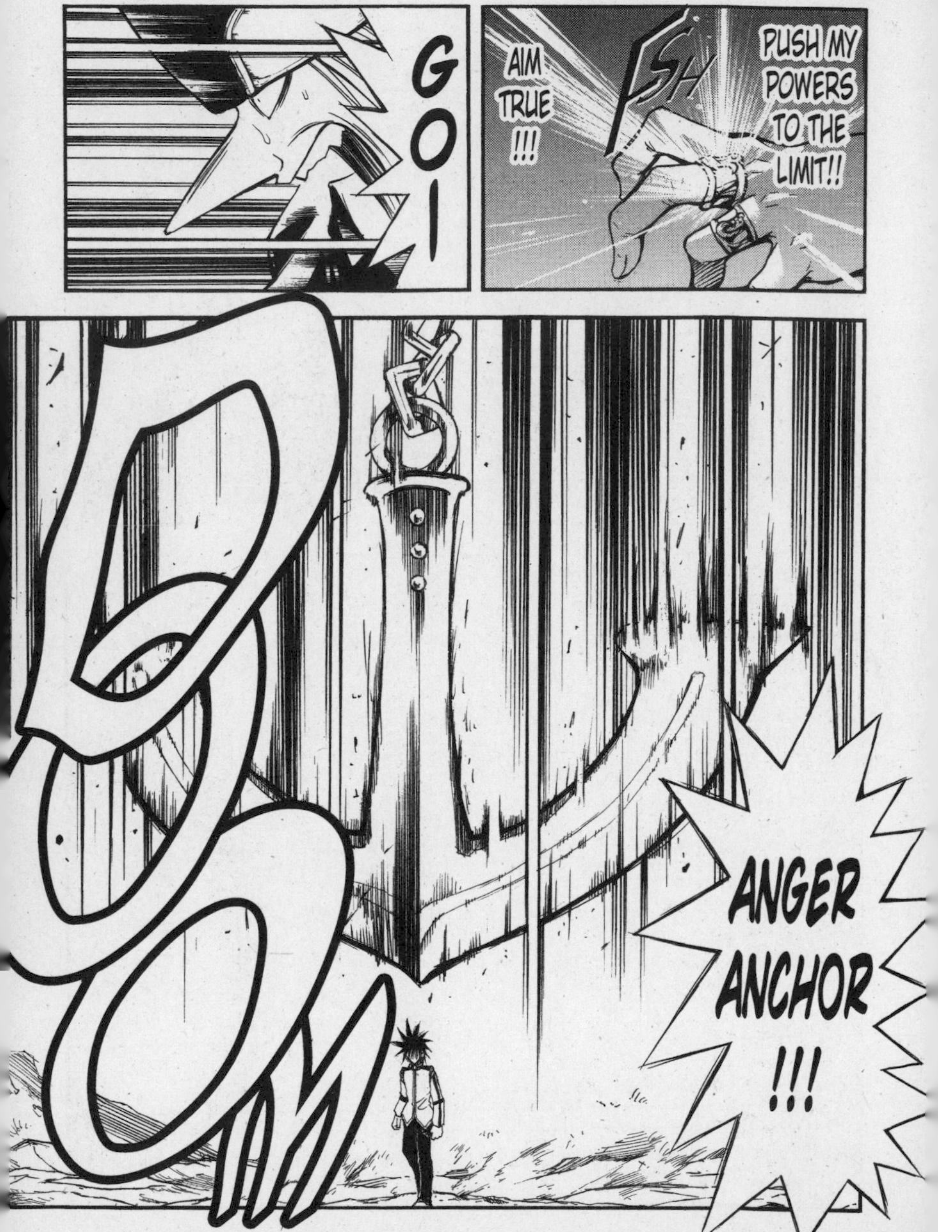
PUSH MY POWERS TO THE LIMIT!!
FSH
AIM TRUE!!!
GO!
ANGER ANCHOR!!!

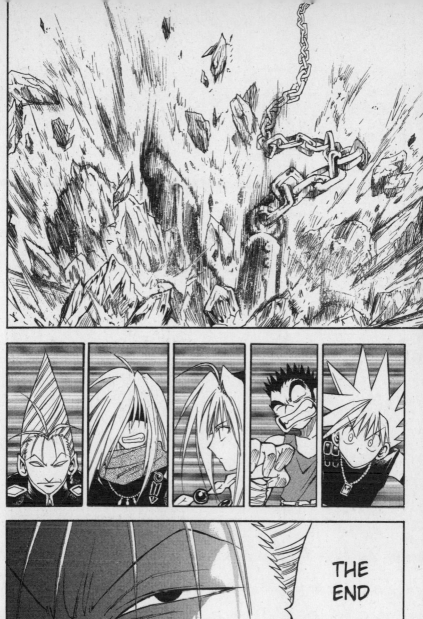

THE
END
...

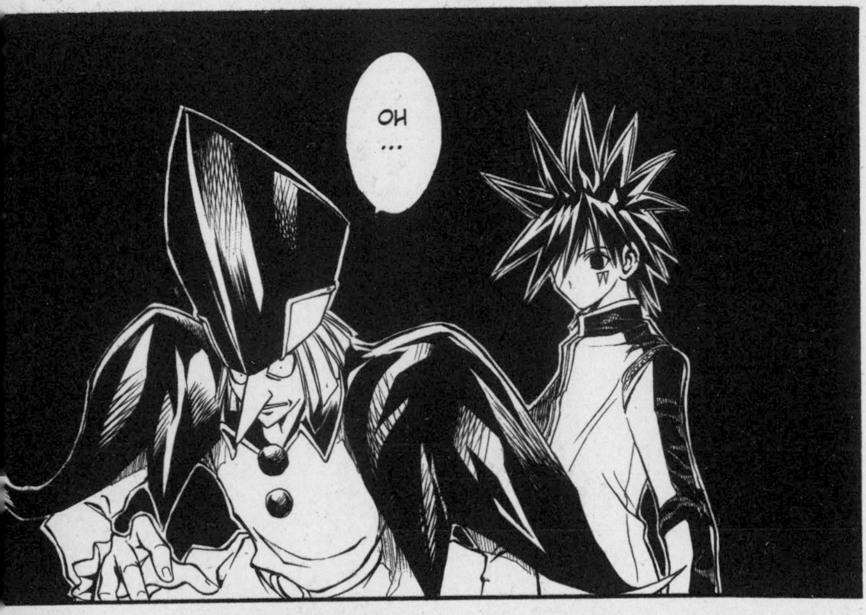
OH
...
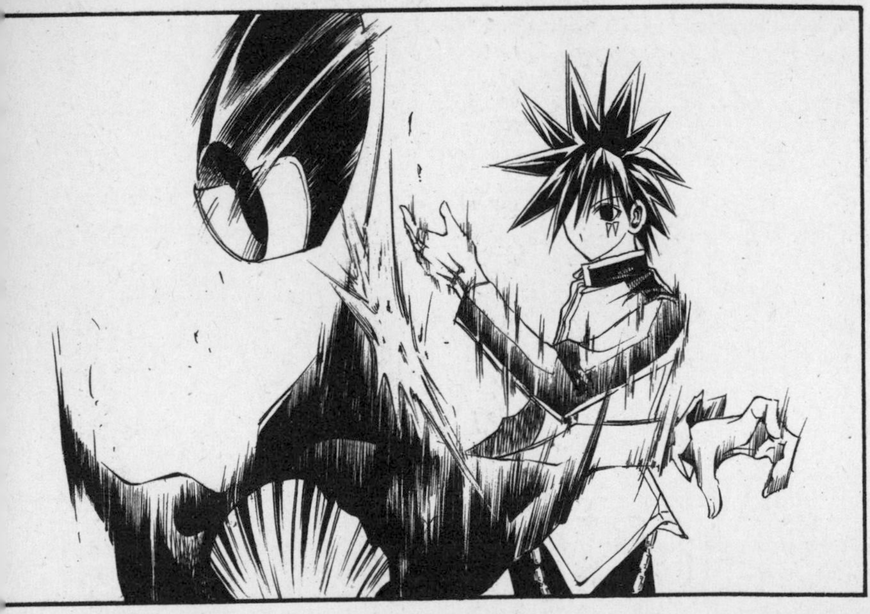

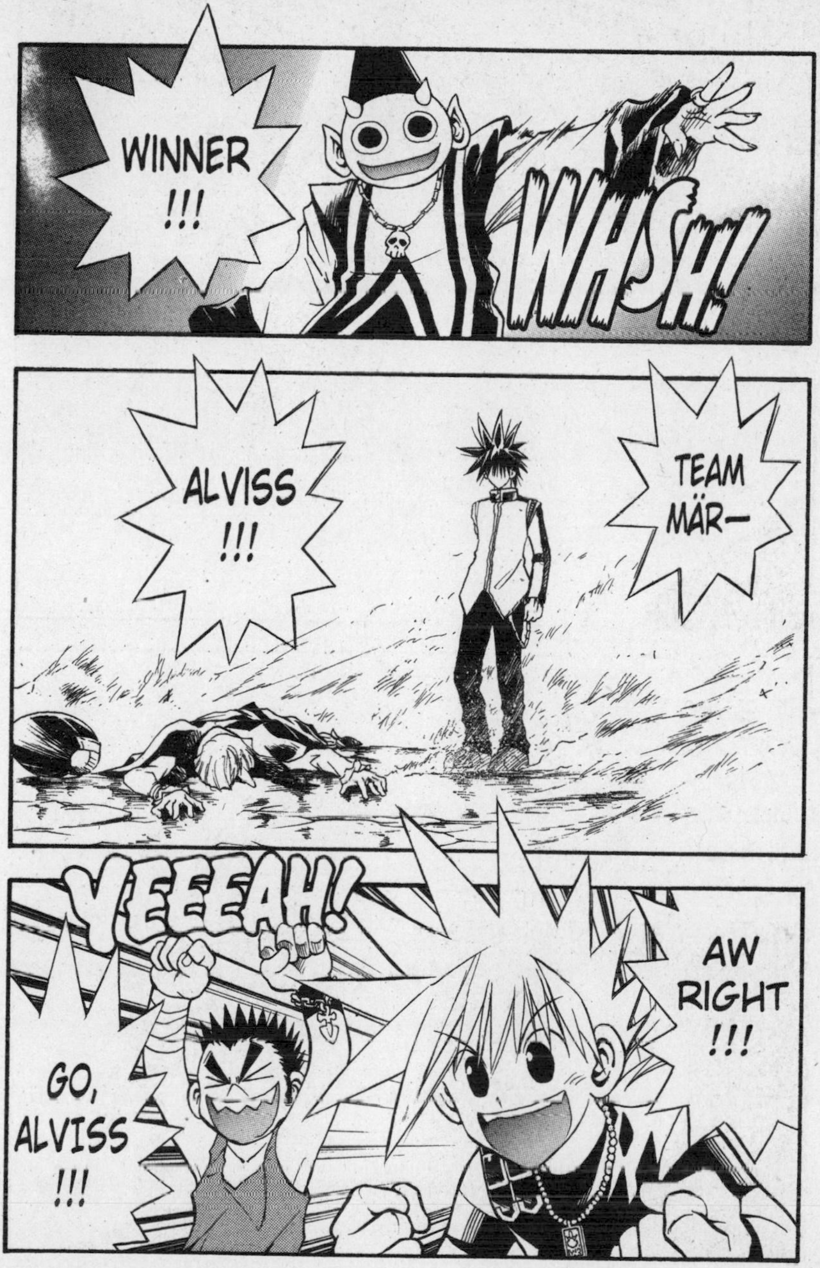
WINNER !!!
WASH!
TEAM MÄR—
ALVISS !!!
AW RIGHT !!!
YEEEAH!
GO, ALVISS !!!

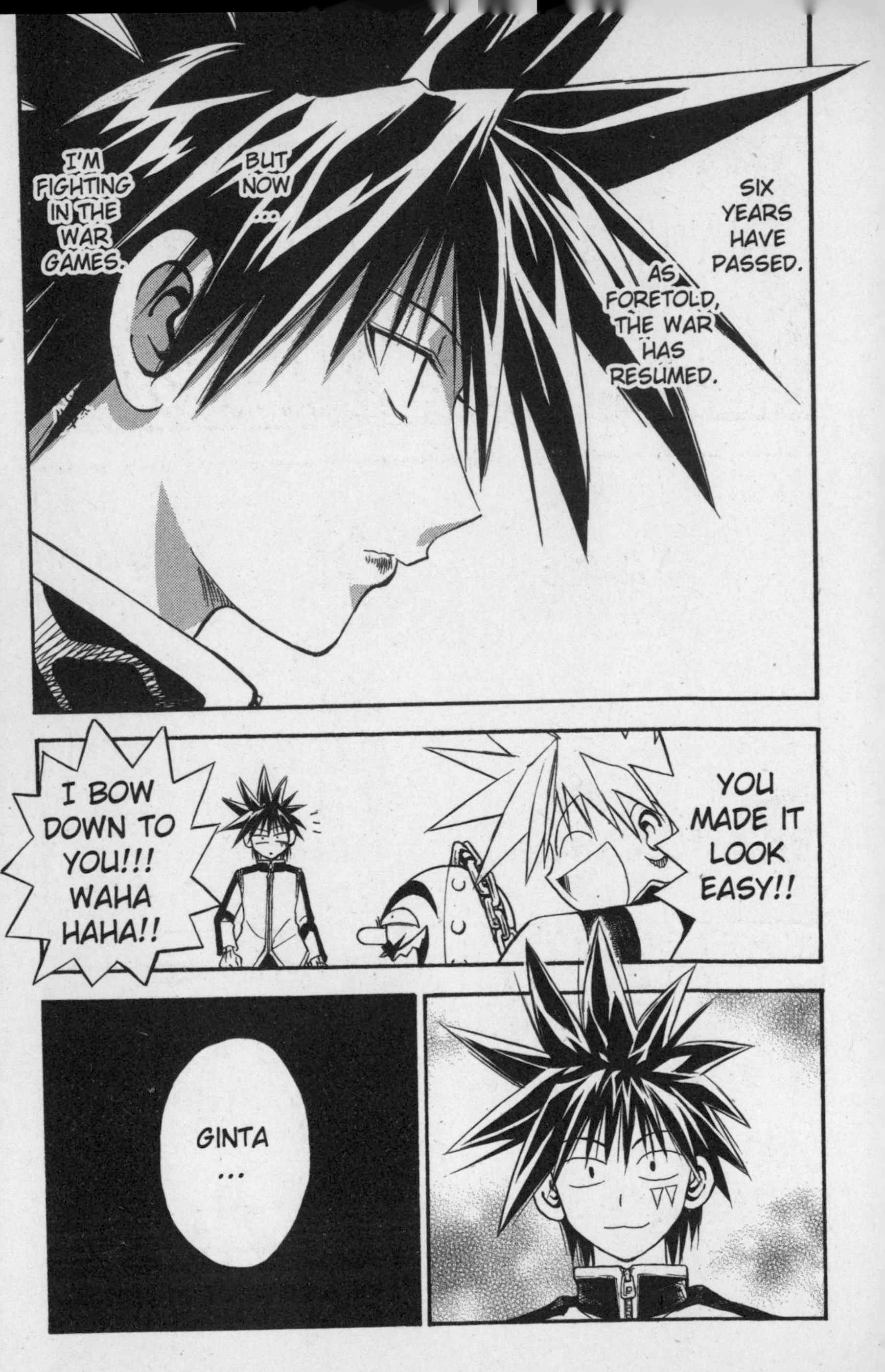
SIX YEARS HAVE PASSED.
AS FORETOLD, THE WAR HAS RESUMED.
BUT NOW...
I'M FIGHTING IN THE WAR GAMES.
YOU MADE IT LOOK EASY!!
I BOW DOWN TO YOU!!! WAHA HAHA!!
GINTA...

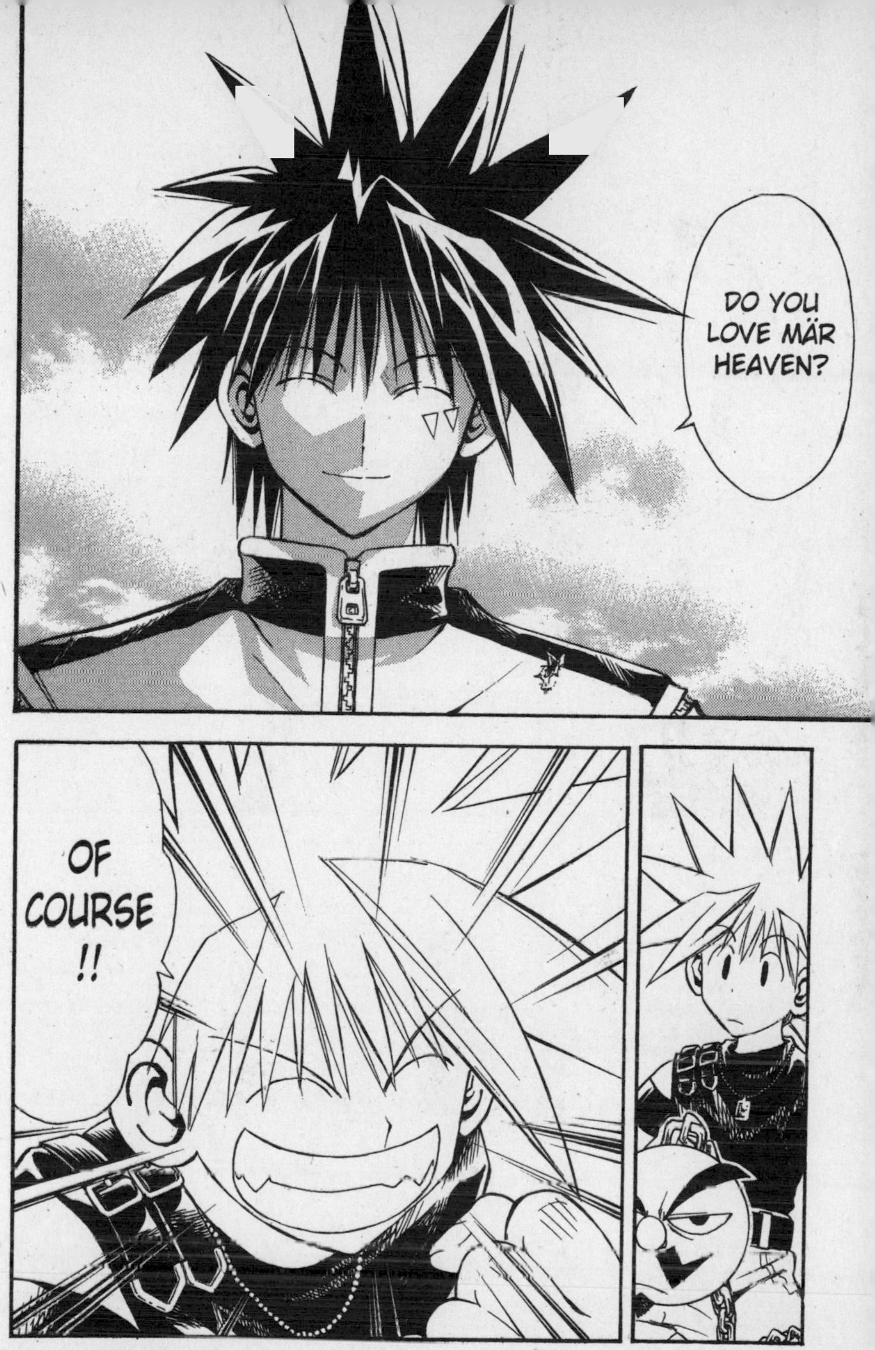
DO YOU LOVE MÄR HEAVEN?
OF COURSE !!

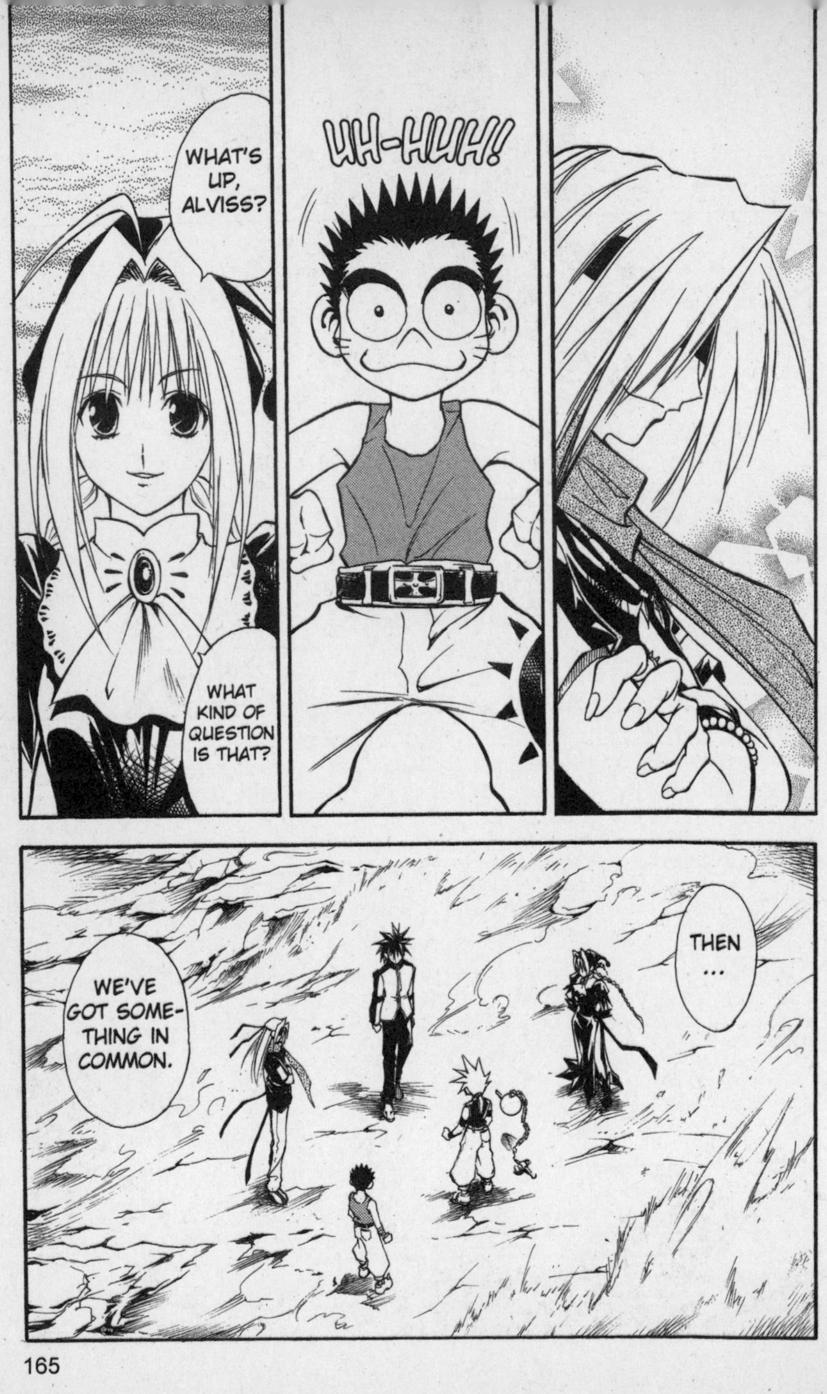
UH-HUH!
WHAT'S UP, ALVISS?
WHAT KIND OF QUESTION IS THAT?
THEN ...
WE'VE GOT SOME-THING IN COMMON.

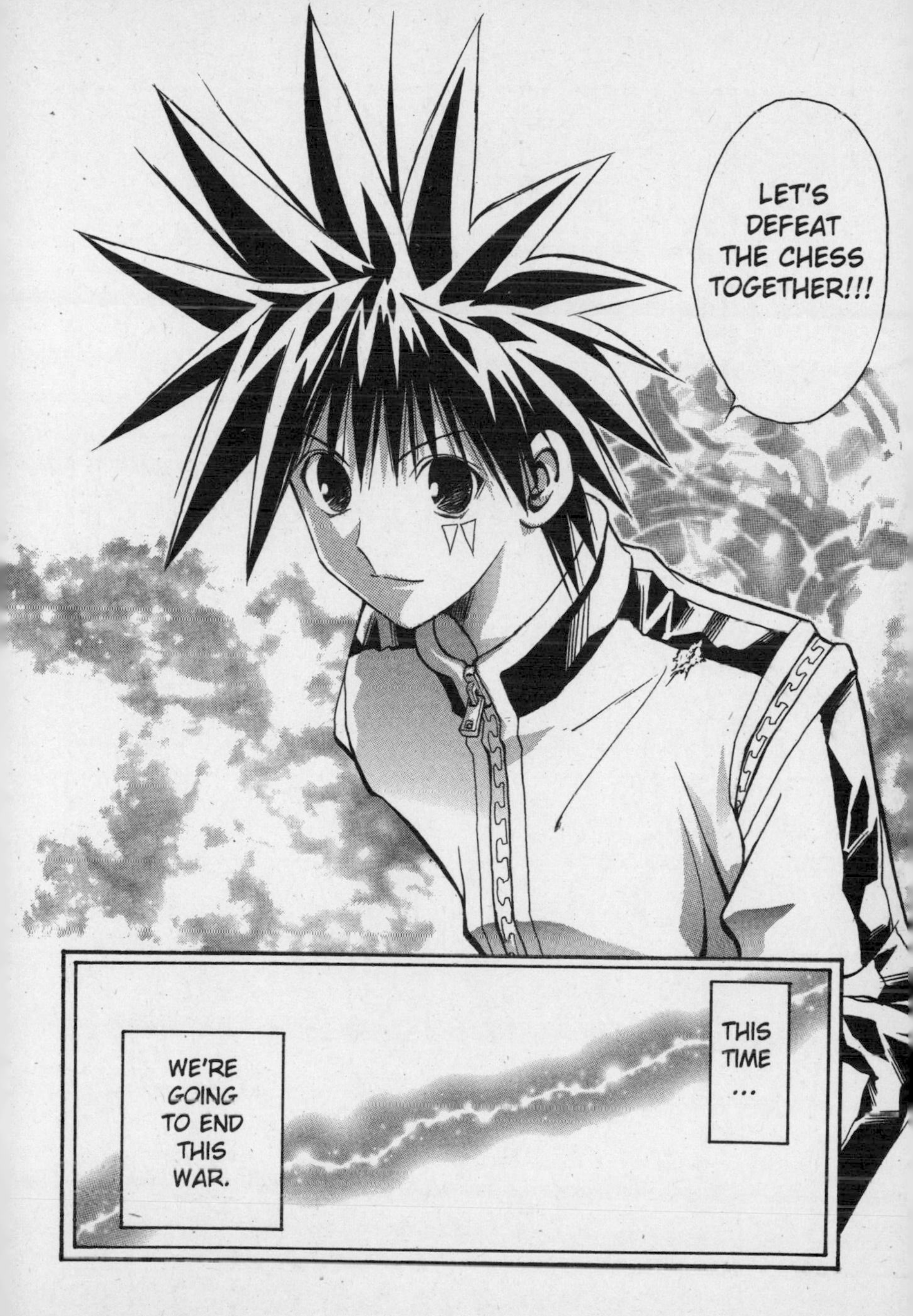
LET'S DEFEAT THE CHESS TOGETHER!!!
THIS TIME ...
WE'RE GOING TO END THIS WAR.

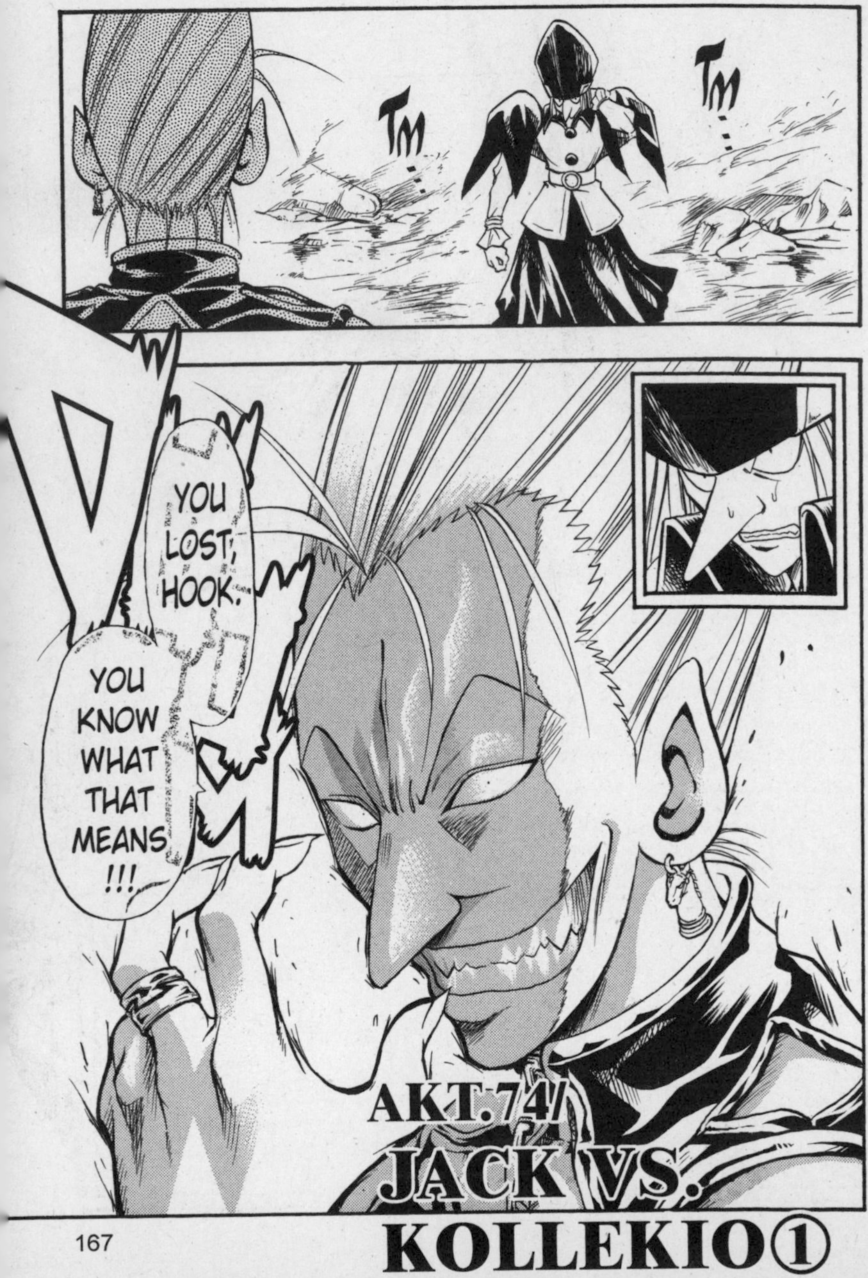
TM...
TM...
YOU LOST, HOOK.
YOU KNOW WHAT THAT MEANS!!!

AKT.74/ JACK VS. KOLLEKIO①

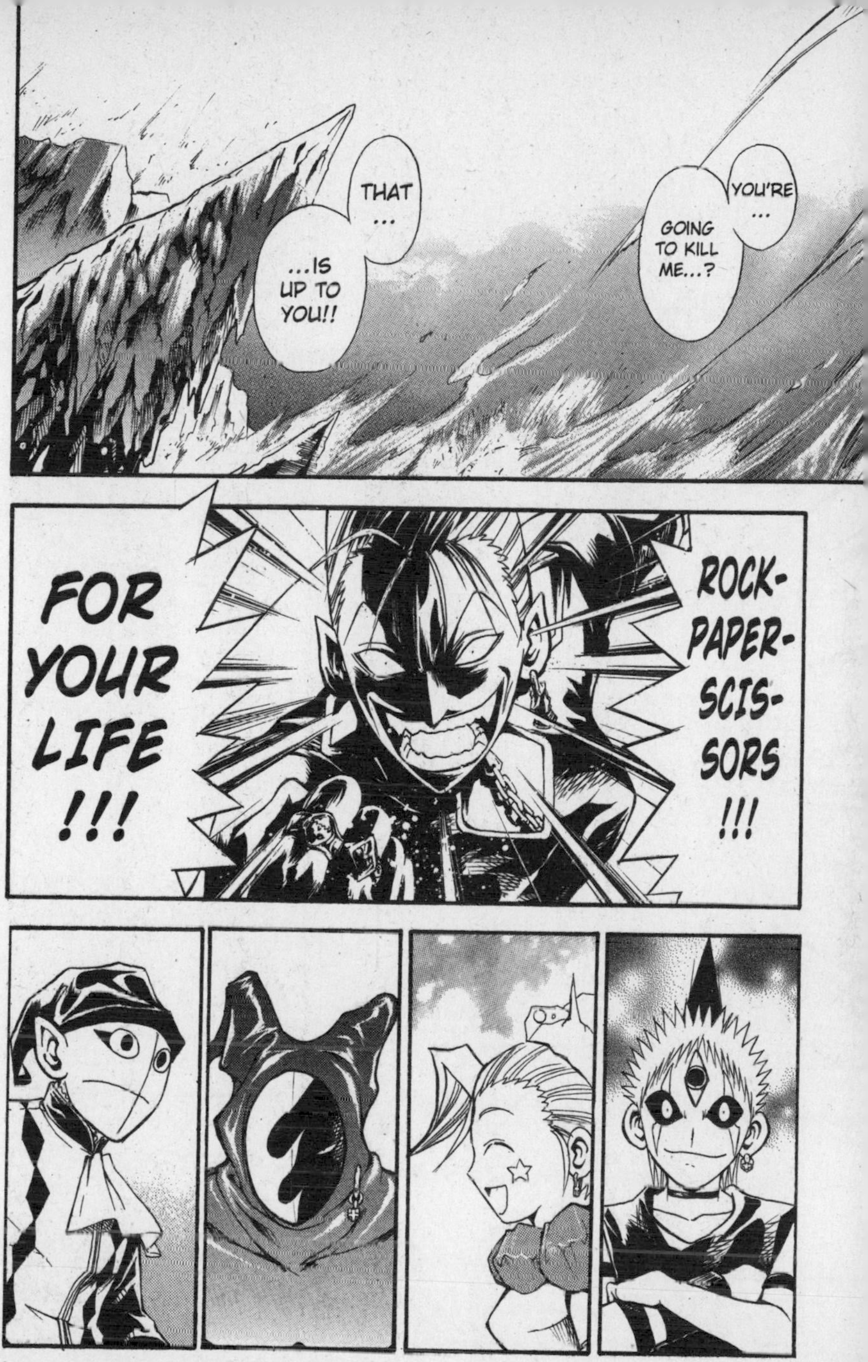
YOU'RE ...
GOING TO KILL ME...?
THAT ...
...IS UP TO YOU!!
ROCK-PAPER-SCIS-SORS !!!
FOR YOUR LIFE !!!

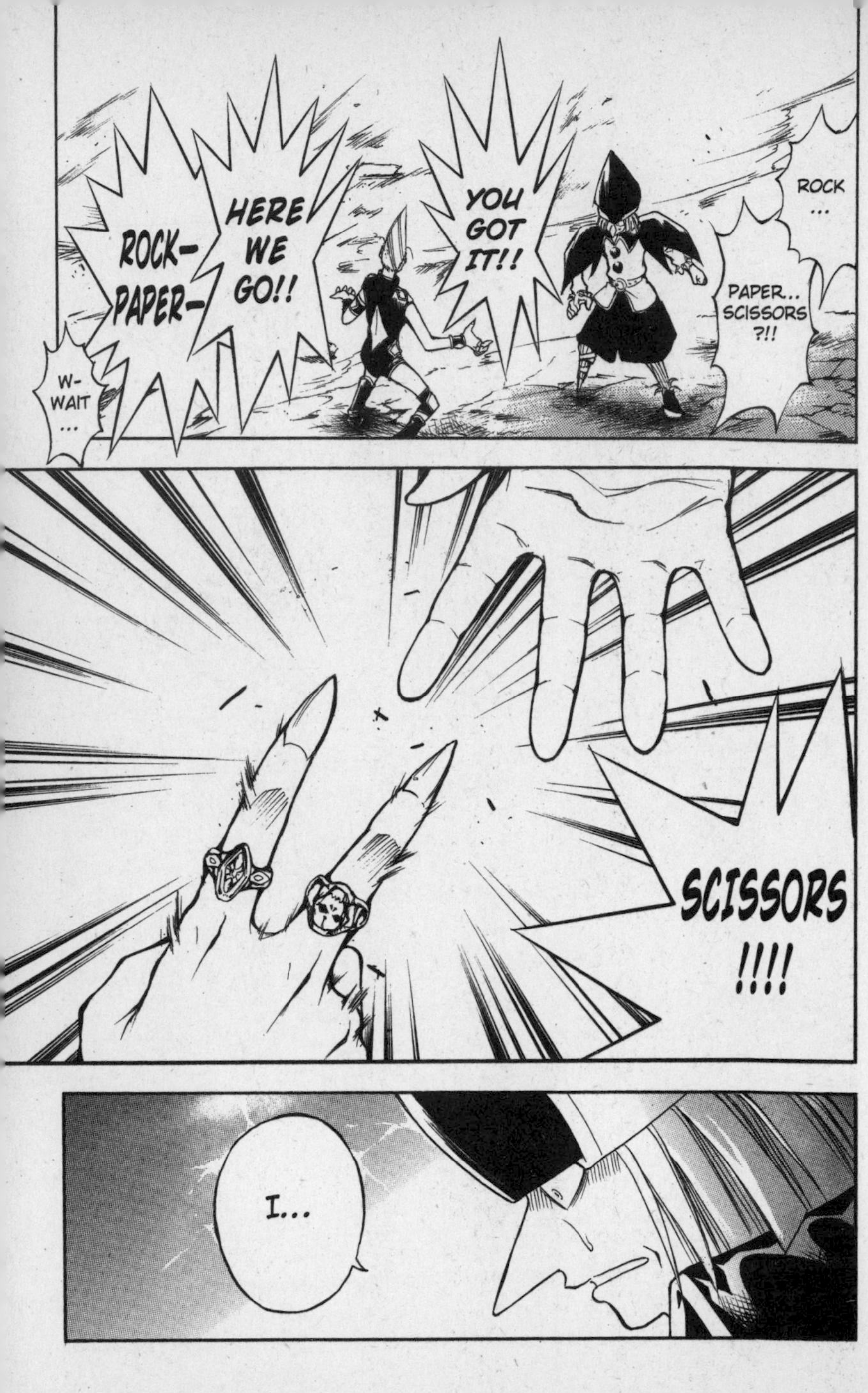
ROCK ... PAPER... SCISSORS ?!!
YOU GOT IT!!
HERE WE GO!!
ROCK-PAPER-
W-WAIT ...
SCISSORS !!!!
I...

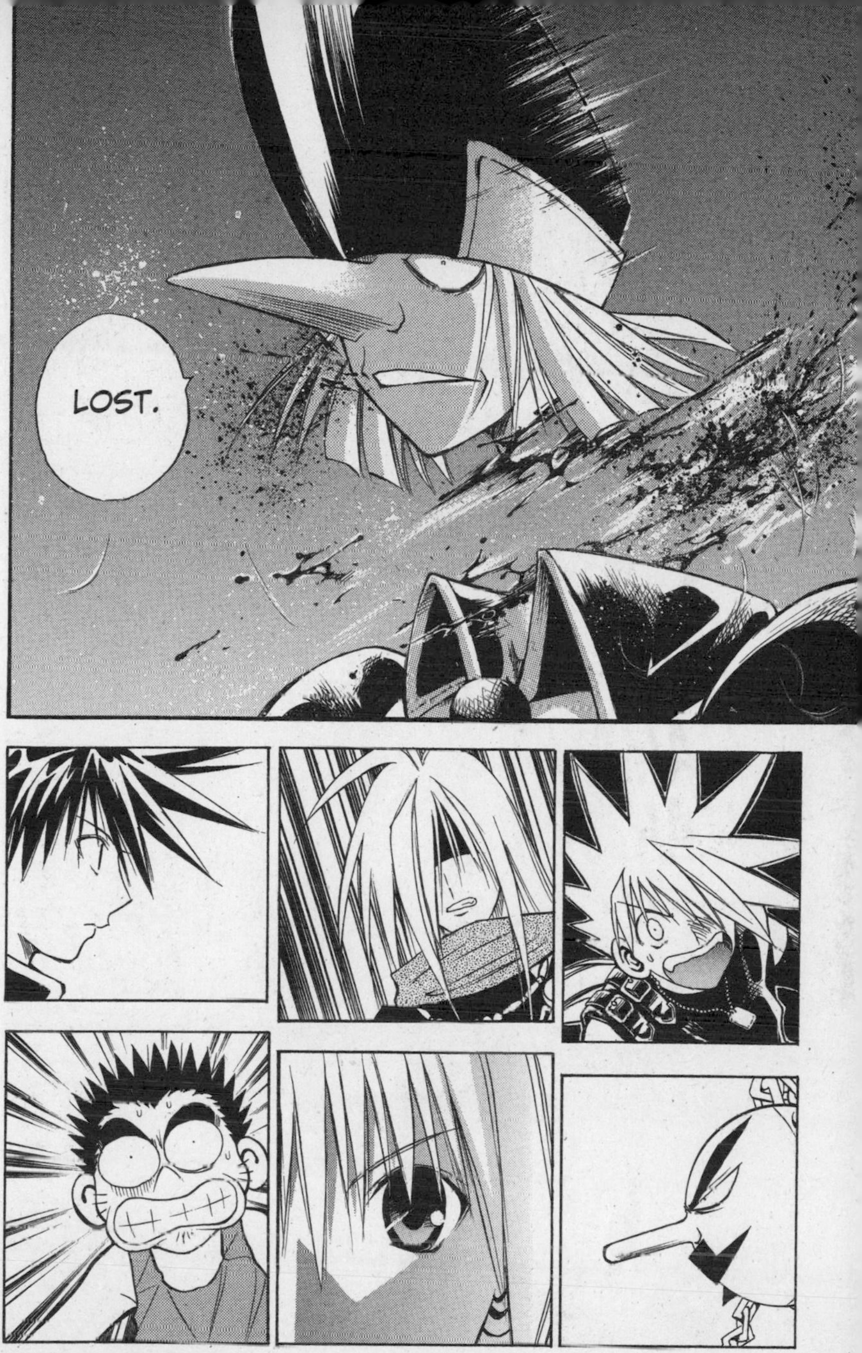
LOST.

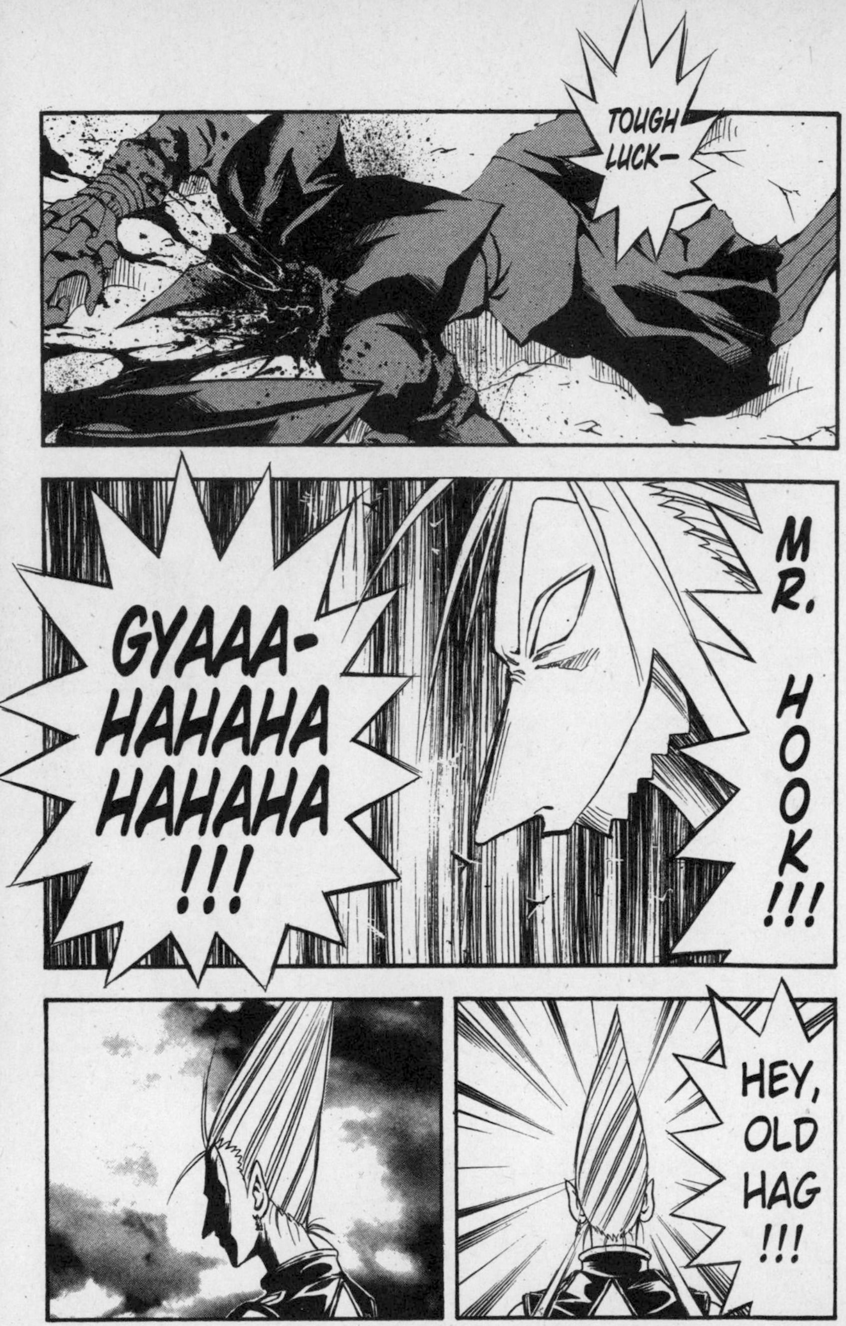
TOUGH LUCK—
MR. HOOK!!!
GYAAA-HAHAHA HAHAHA !!!
HEY, OLD HAG !!!

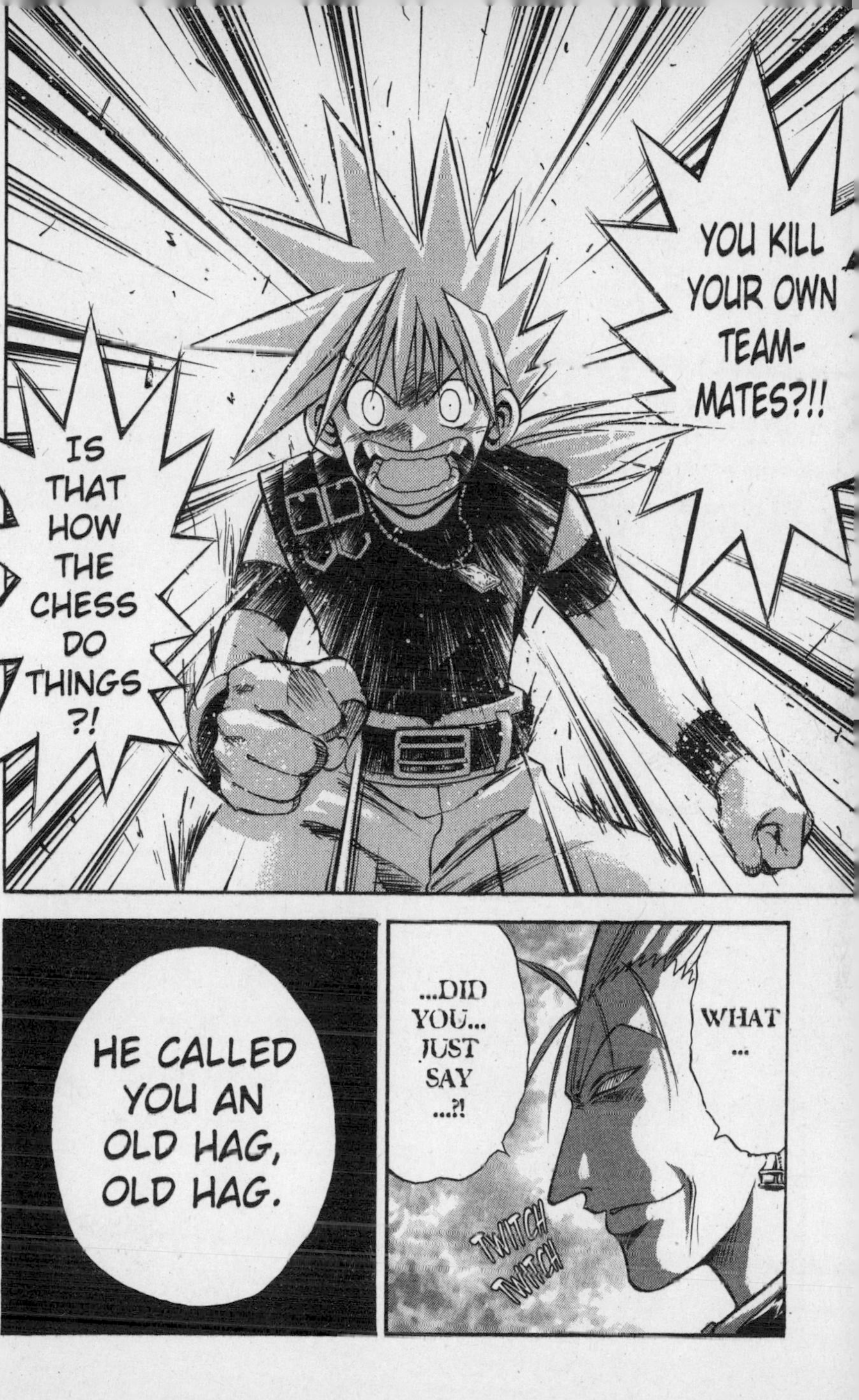
YOU KILL YOUR OWN TEAM-MATES?!!
IS THAT HOW THE CHESS DO THINGS ?!
WHAT ...
...DID YOU... JUST SAY ...?!
TWITCH TWITCH
HE CALLED YOU AN OLD HAG, OLD HAG.

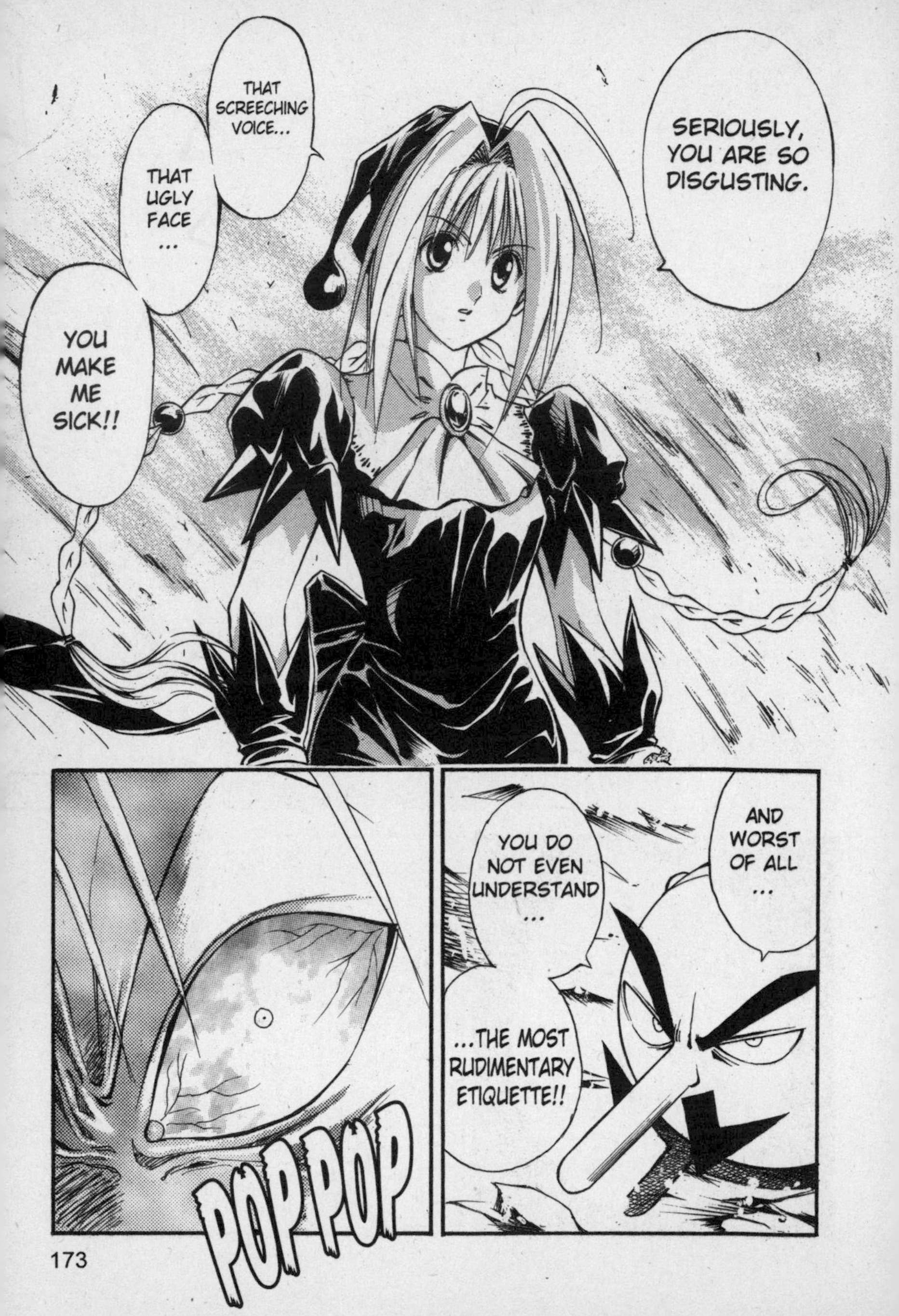

SERIOUSLY, YOU ARE SO DISGUSTING.
THAT SCREECHING VOICE...
THAT UGLY FACE ...
YOU MAKE ME SICK!!
AND WORST OF ALL ...
YOU DO NOT EVEN UNDERSTAND ...
...THE MOST RUDIMENTARY ETIQUETTE!!
POP POP

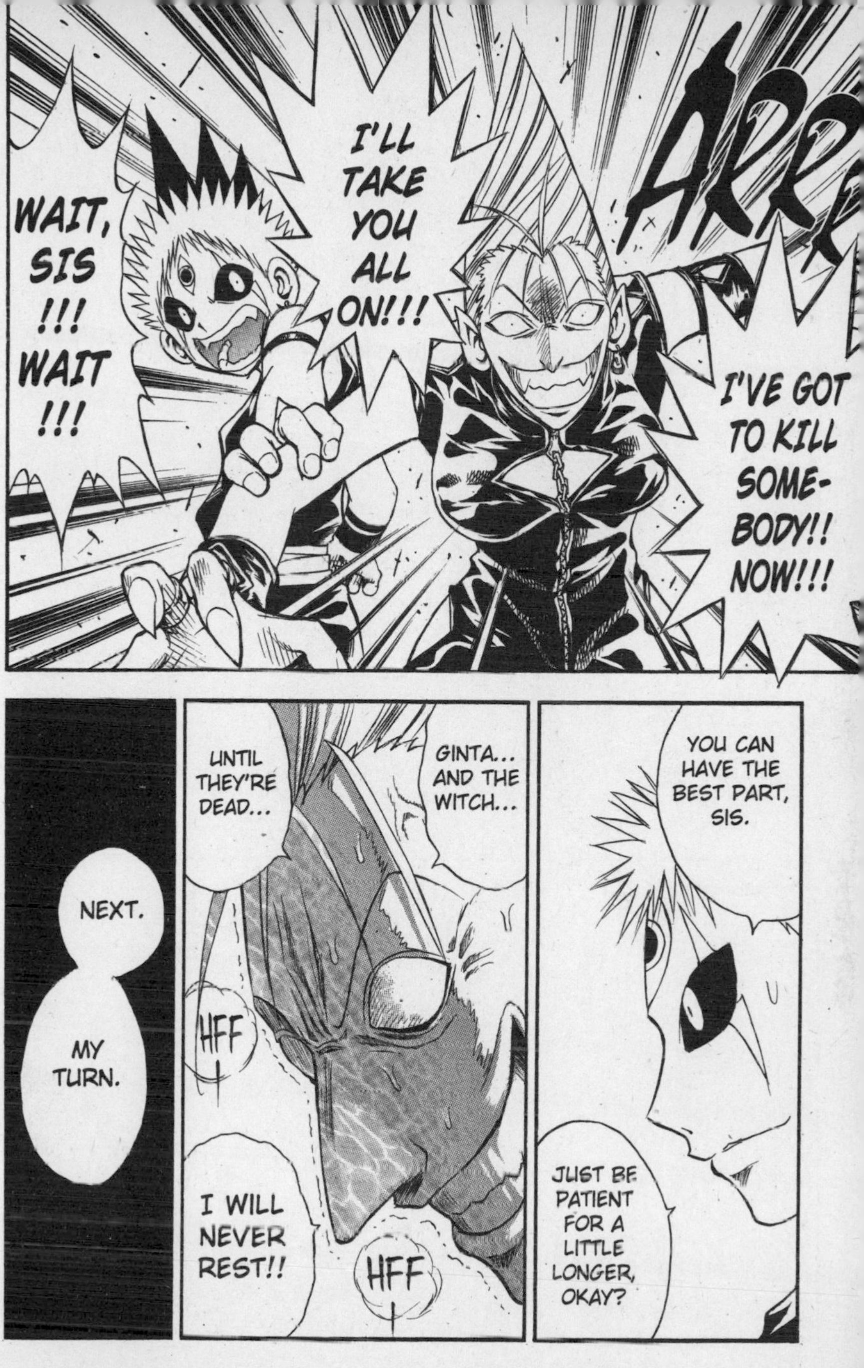
ARRR
I'VE GOT TO KILL SOME-BODY!! NOW!!!
I'LL TAKE YOU ALL ON!!!
WAIT, SIS!!! WAIT!!!
YOU CAN HAVE THE BEST PART, SIS.
JUST BE PATIENT FOR A LITTLE LONGER, OKAY?
GINTA... AND THE WITCH...
UNTIL THEY'RE DEAD...
HFF
I WILL NEVER REST!!
HFF
NEXT.
MY TURN.

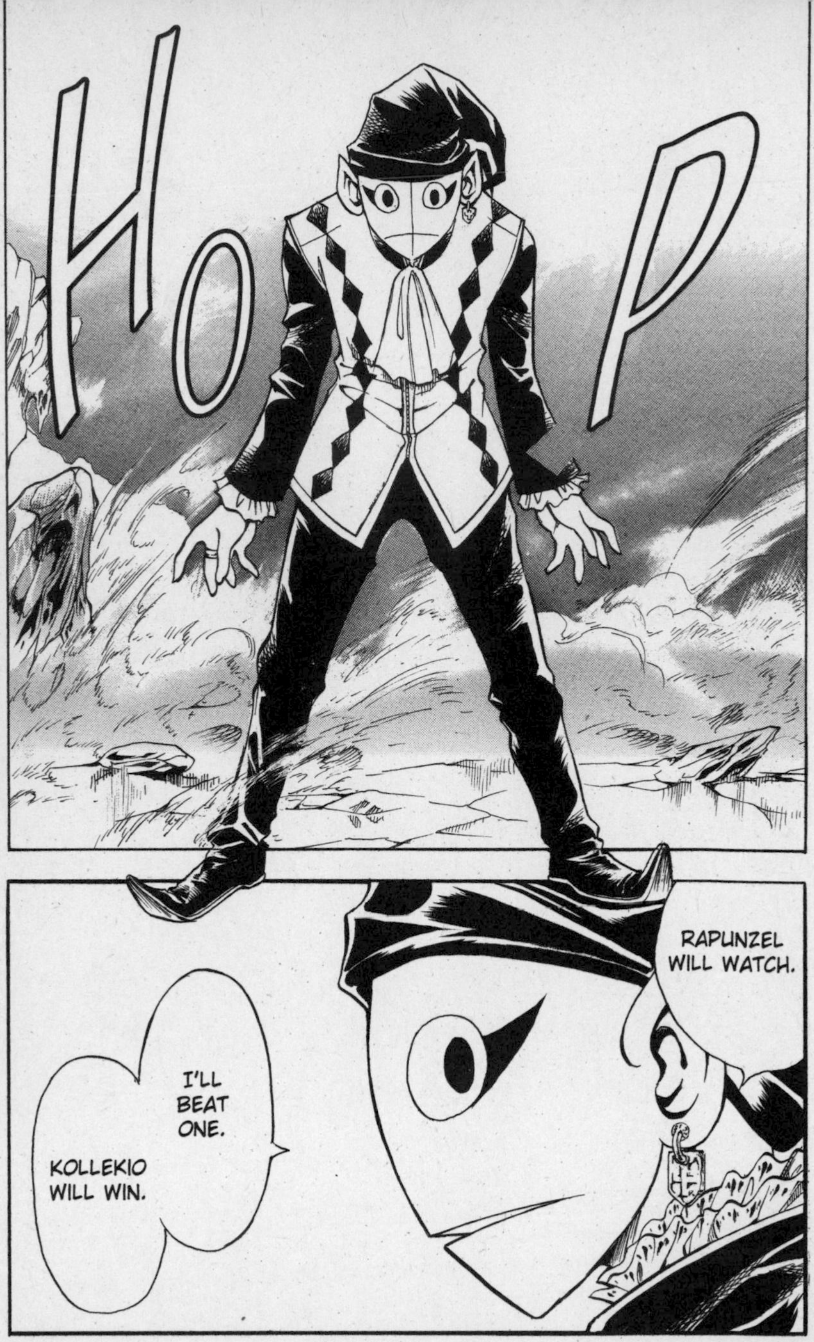
HOP
RAPUNZEL WILL WATCH.
I'LL BEAT ONE.
KOLLEKIO WILL WIN.

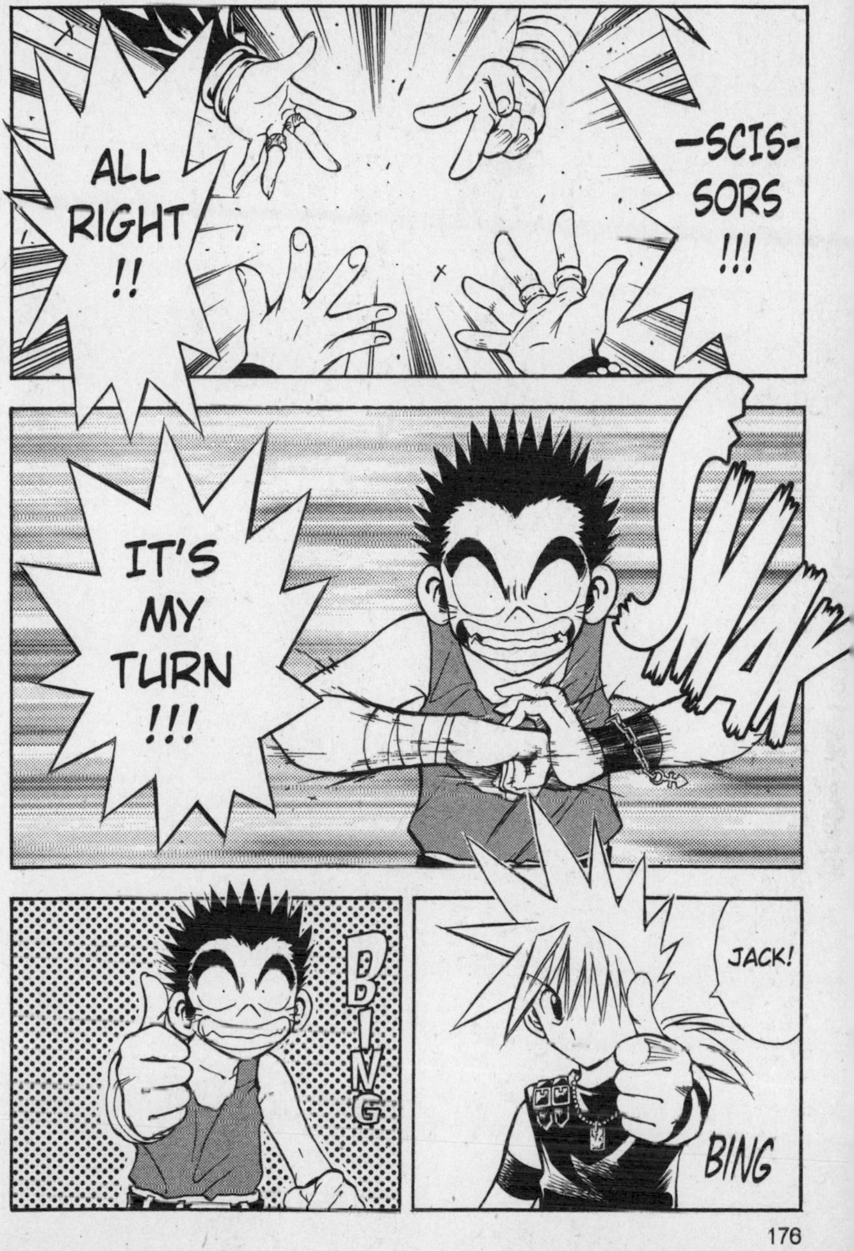
—SCIS-SORS !!!
ALL RIGHT !!
IT'S MY TURN !!!
JACK!
BING
BING

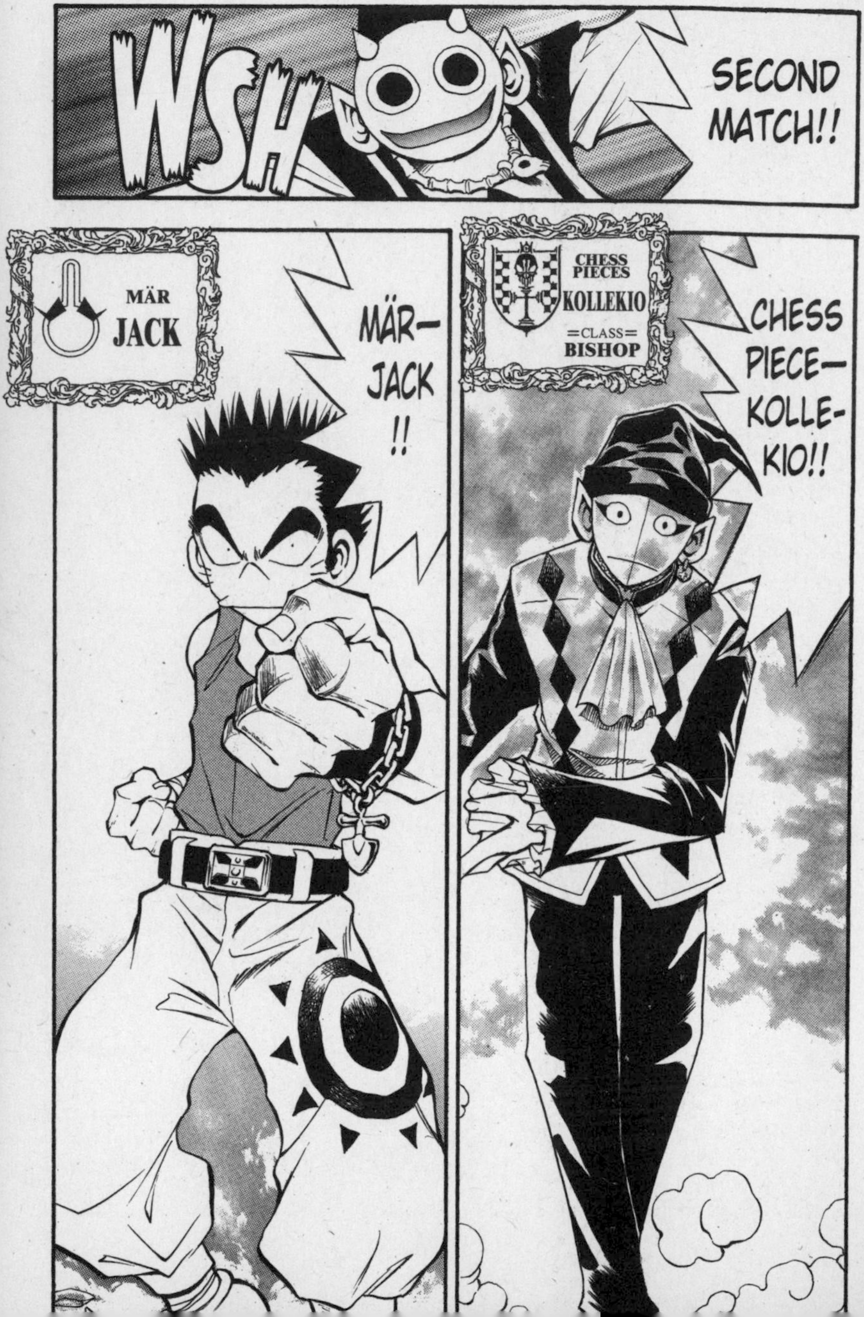
SECOND MATCH!!
WSH
CHESS PIECES
KOLLEKIO
=CLASS=
BISHOP
CHESS PIECE-KOLLE-KIO!!
MÄR
JACK
MÄR-JACK!!

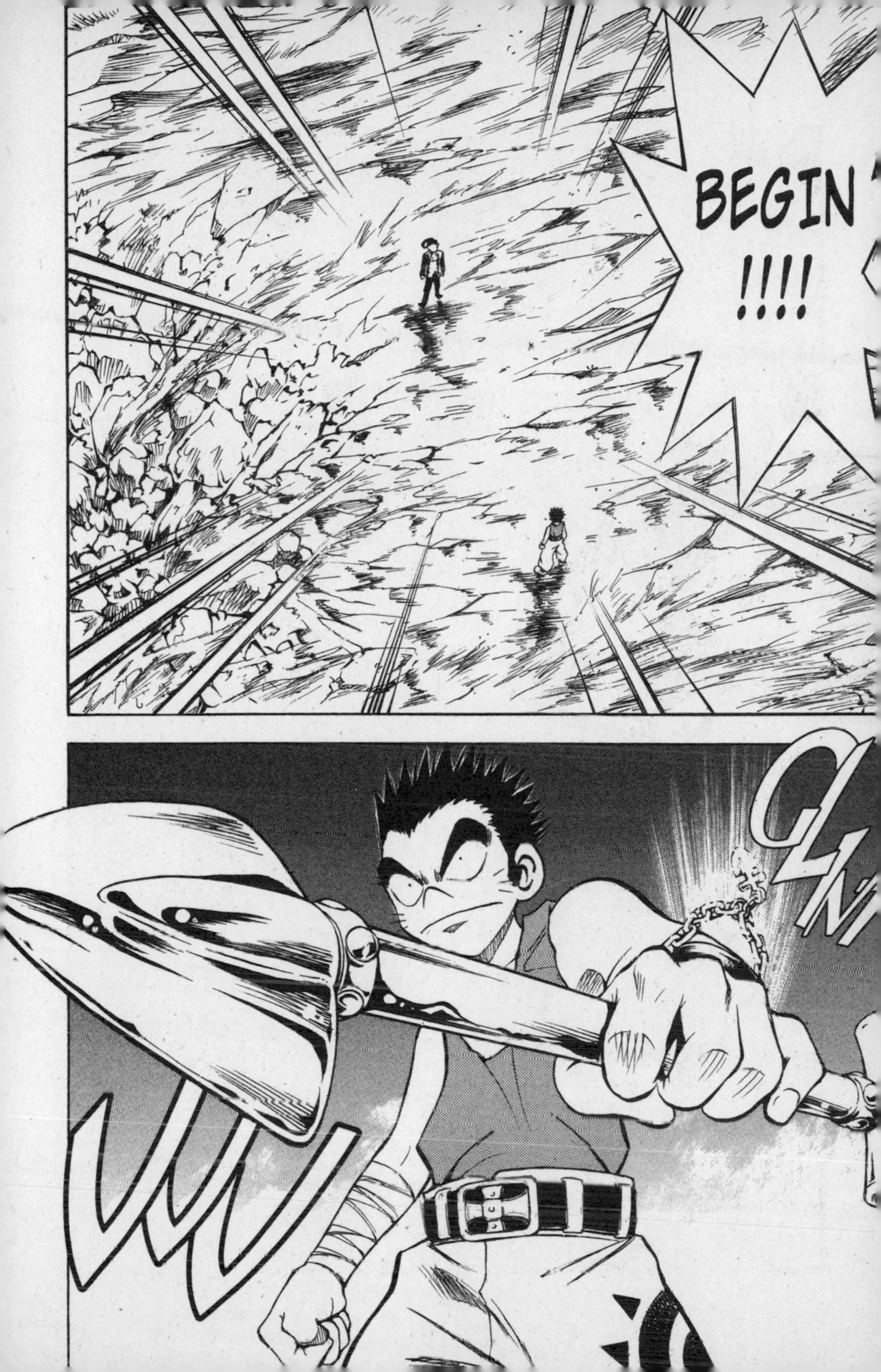
BEGIN !!!!

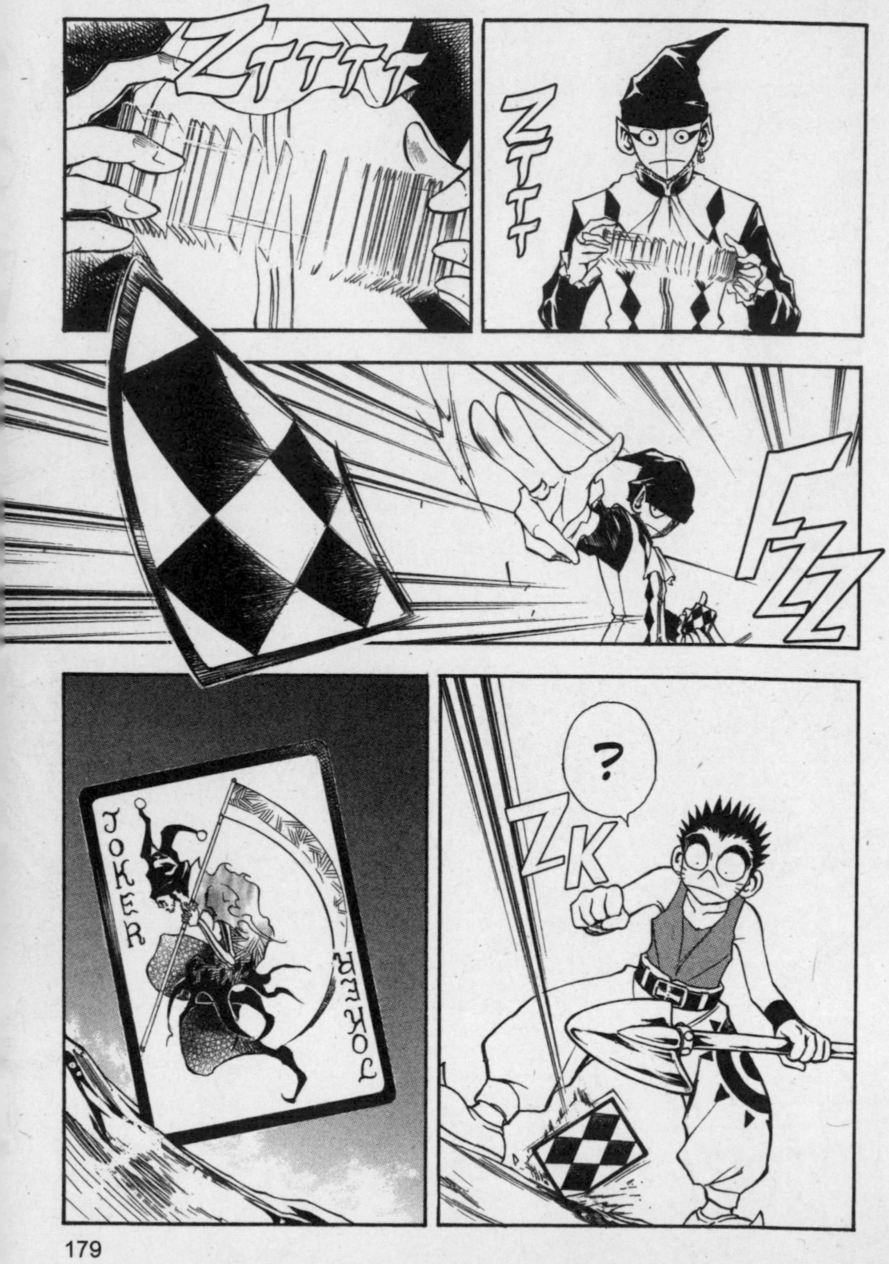
ZTTT
ZTTTTT
FZZ
?
ZK
JOKER
JOKER

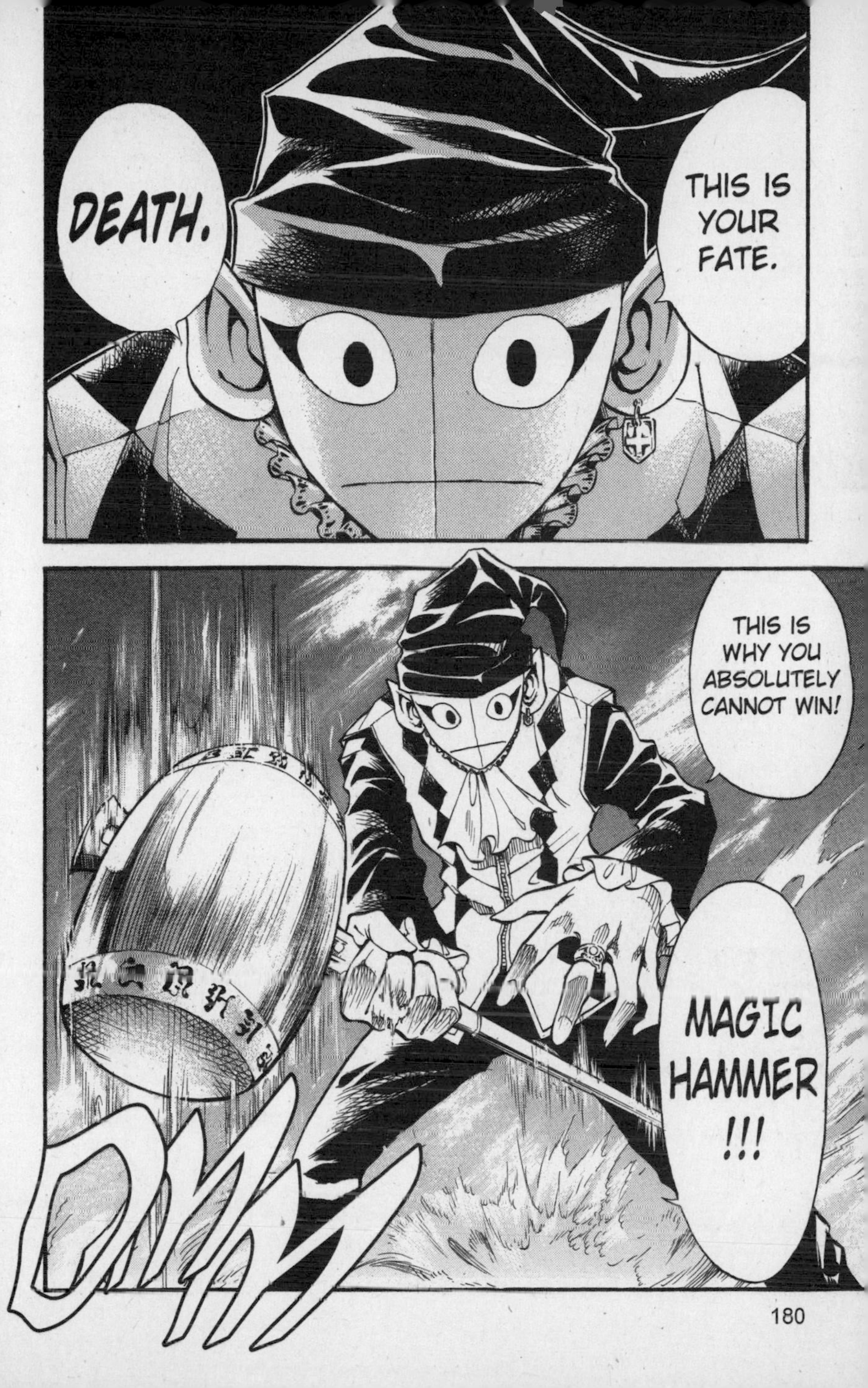
THIS IS YOUR FATE.
DEATH.
THIS IS WHY YOU ABSOLUTELY CANNOT WIN!
MAGIC HAMMER !!!

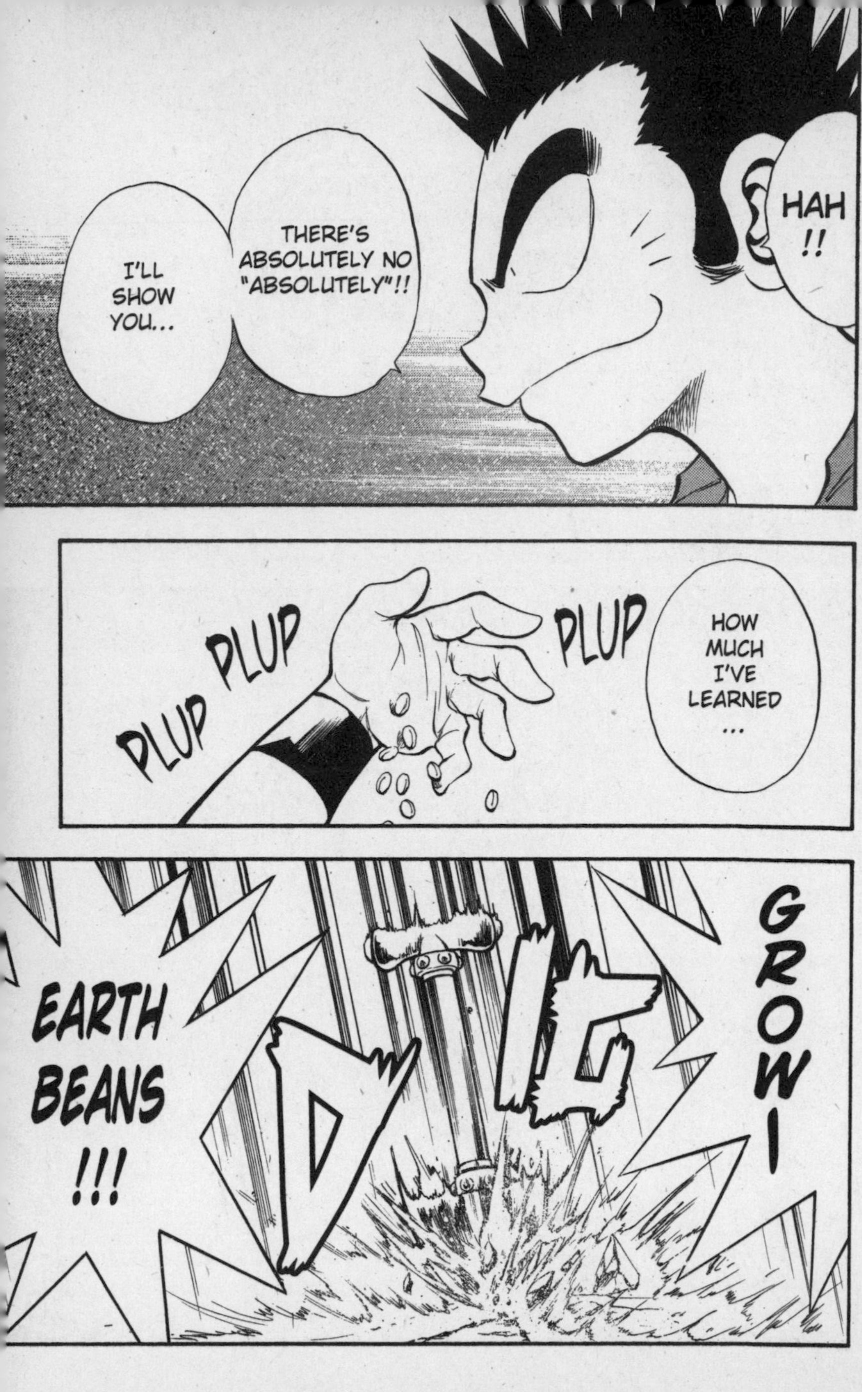
HAH !!
THERE'S ABSOLUTELY NO "ABSOLUTELY"!!
I'LL SHOW YOU...
HOW MUCH I'VE LEARNED ...
PLUP
PLUP
PLUP
GROW!
EARTH BEANS !!!

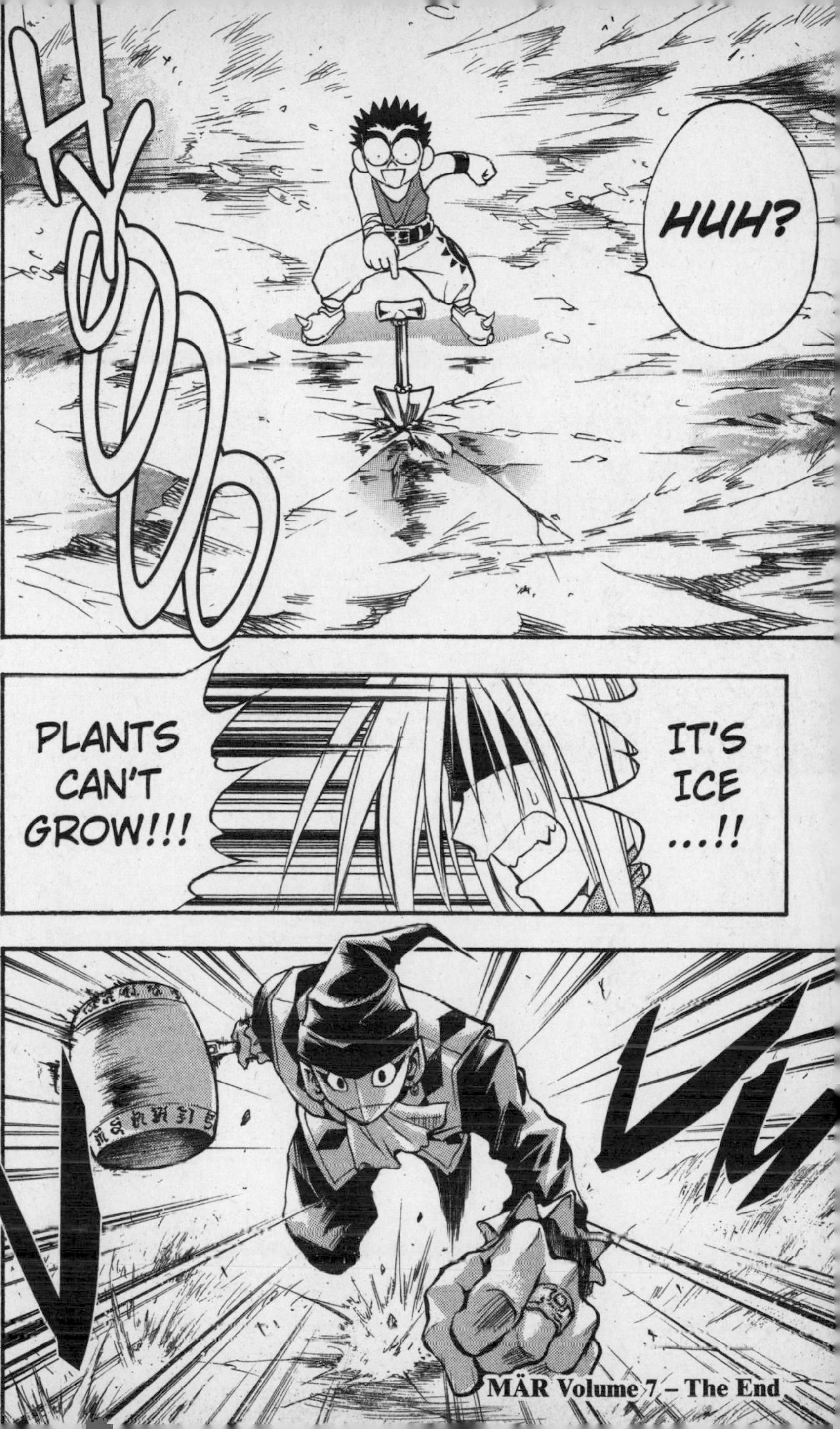
HUH?
IT'S ICE ...!!
PLANTS CAN'T GROW!!!
MÄR Volume 7 – The End

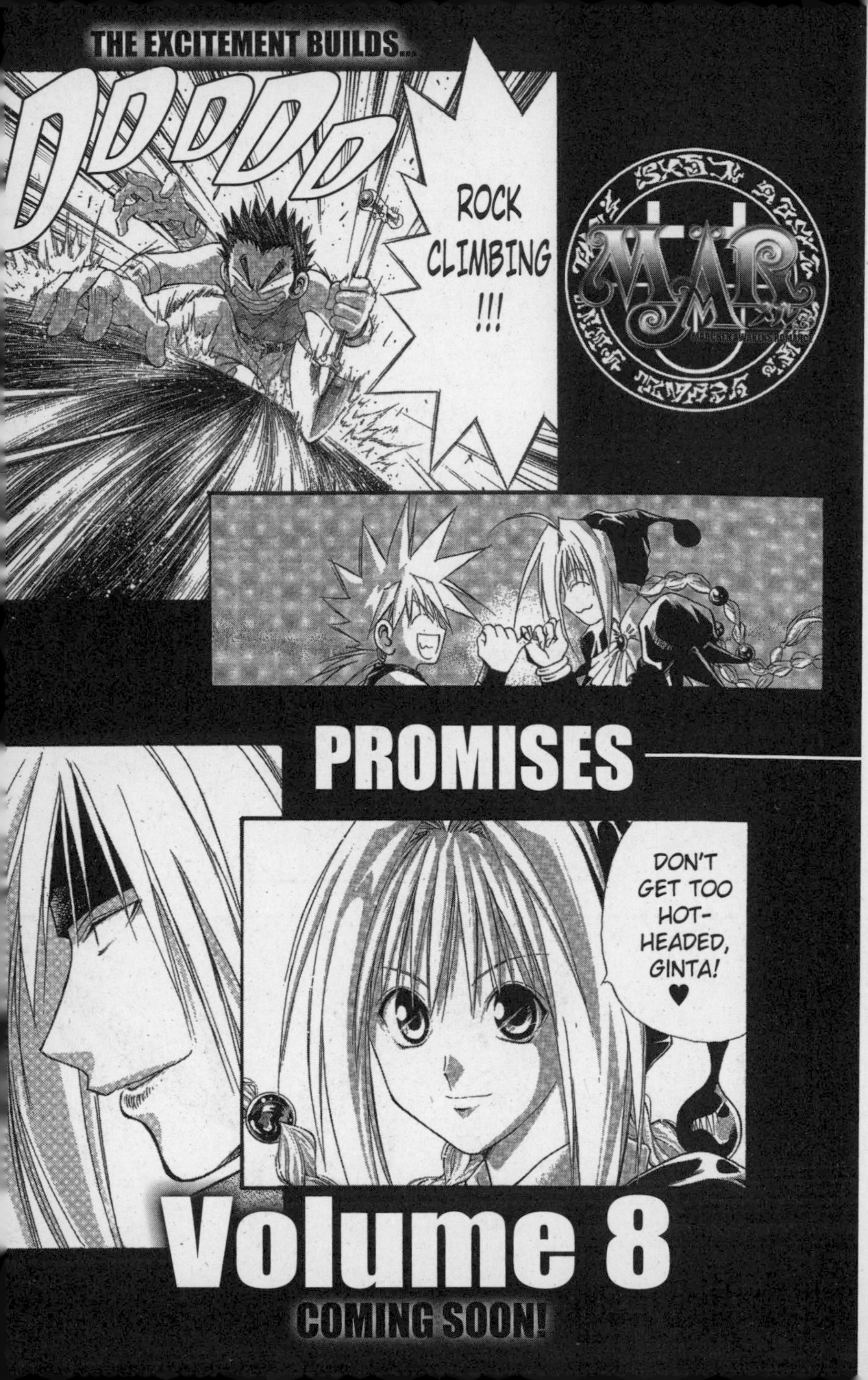
THE EXCITEMENT BUILDS...
DDDDD
ROCK CLIMBING!!!
PROMISES
DON'T GET TOO HOT-HEADED, GINTA! ♥
Volume 8
COMING SOON!

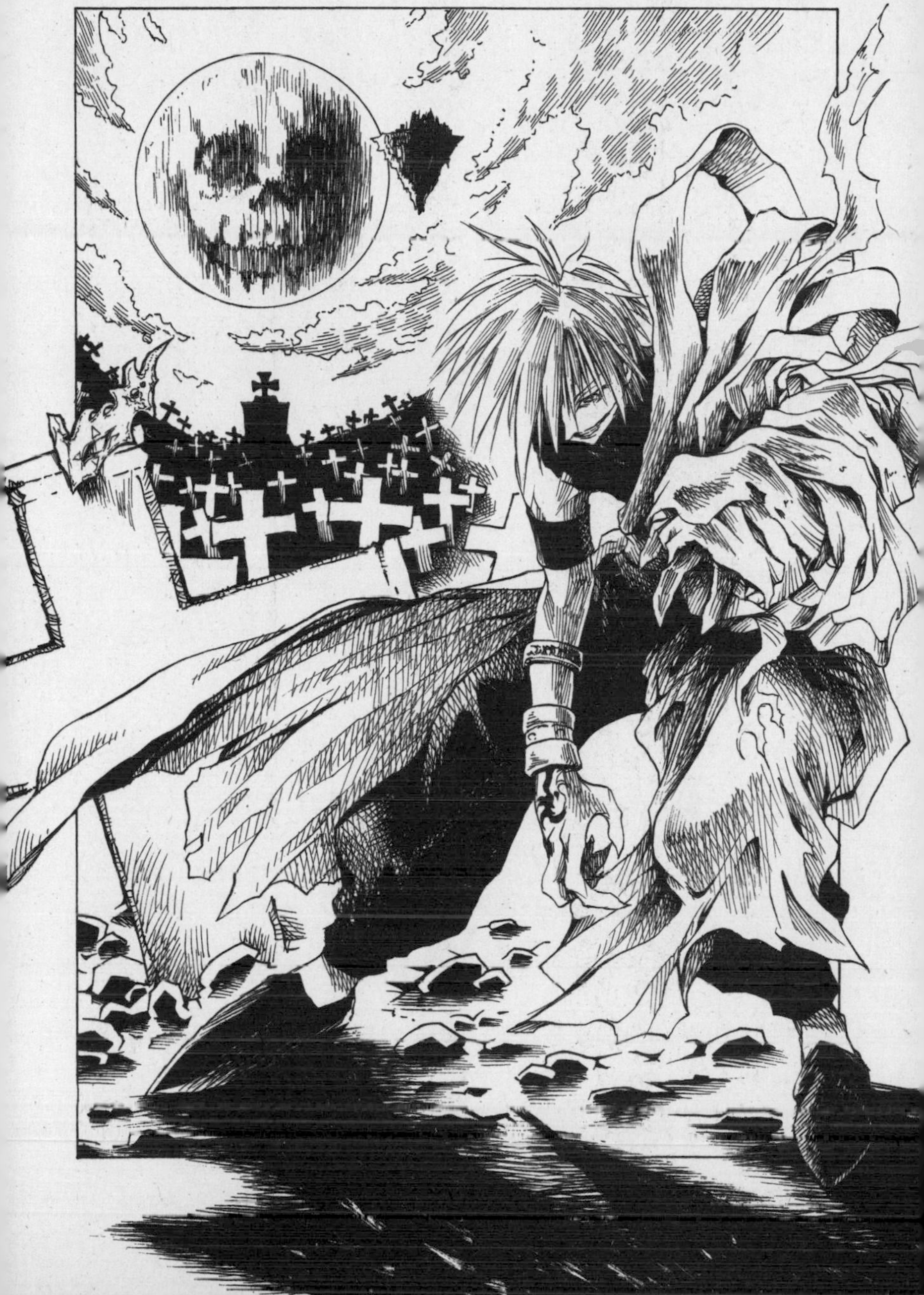

ACID VOMIT

Title lettering: Anzai
Written by: GB

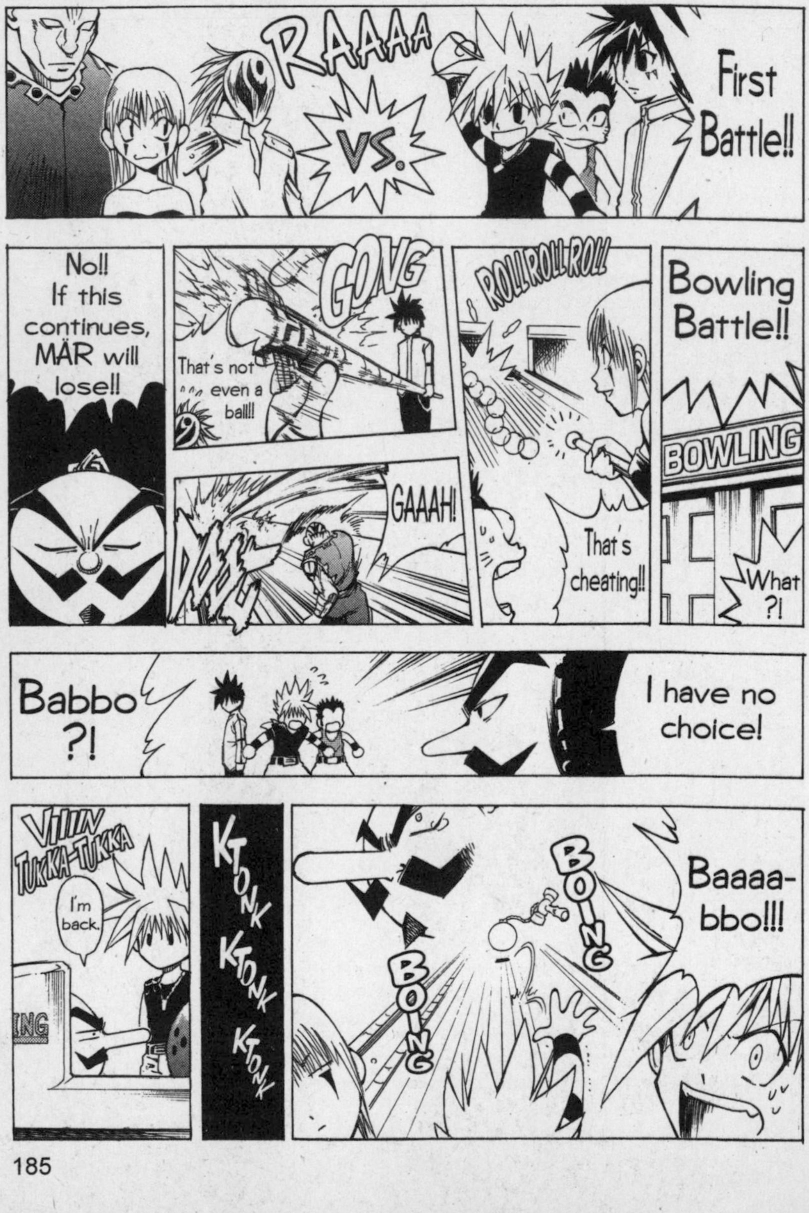

First Battle!!
RAAAA
VS.
Bowling Battle!!
BOWLING
What ?!
ROLLROLLROLL
That's cheating!!
GONG
That's not even a ball!!
GAAAH!
No!! If this continues, MÄR will lose!!
I have no choice!
Babbo ?!
Baaaa-bbo!!!
BOING
BOING
KTONK KTONK KTONK
VIIIIN TUKKA-TUKKA
I'm back.

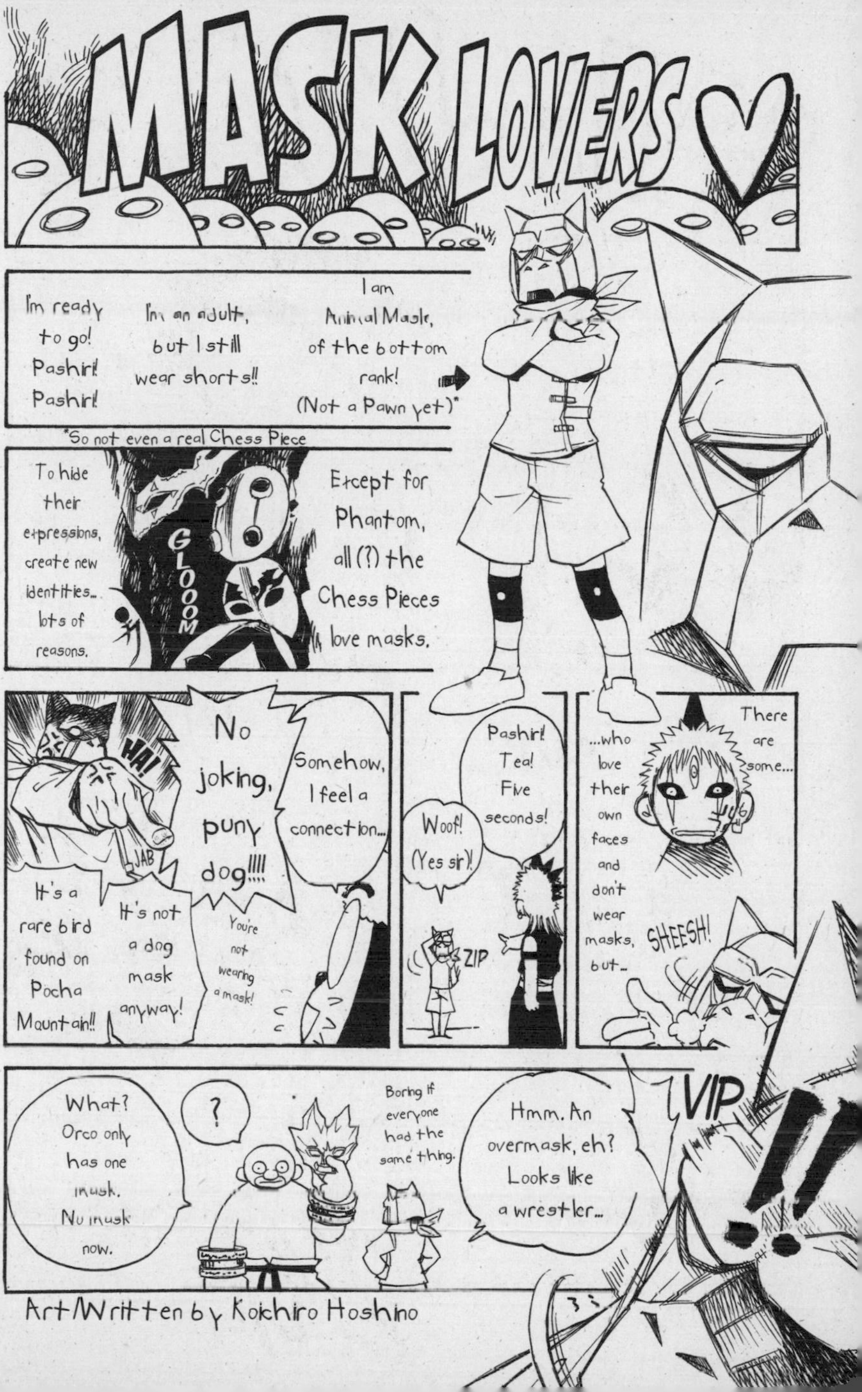
MASK LOVERS ♥
I am Animal Mask, of the bottom rank! (Not a Pawn yet)*
I'm an adult, but I still wear shorts!!
I'm ready to go! Pashiri! Pashiri!
*So not even a real Chess Piece
Except for Phantom, all (?) the Chess Pieces love masks.
GLOOOOM
To hide their expressions, create new identities... lots of reasons.
There are some...
...who love their own faces and don't wear masks, but...
SHEESH!
Pashiri! Tea! Five seconds!
Woof! (Yes sir)!
ZIP
Somehow, I feel a connection...
No joking, puny dog!!!!
WA!
JAB
You're not wearing a mask!
It's not a dog mask anyway!
It's a rare bird found on Pocha Mountain!!
VIP
!!
Hmm. An overmask, eh? Looks like a wrestler...
Boring if everyone had the same thing.
?
What? Orco only has one mask. No mask now.
Art/Written by Koichiro Hoshino

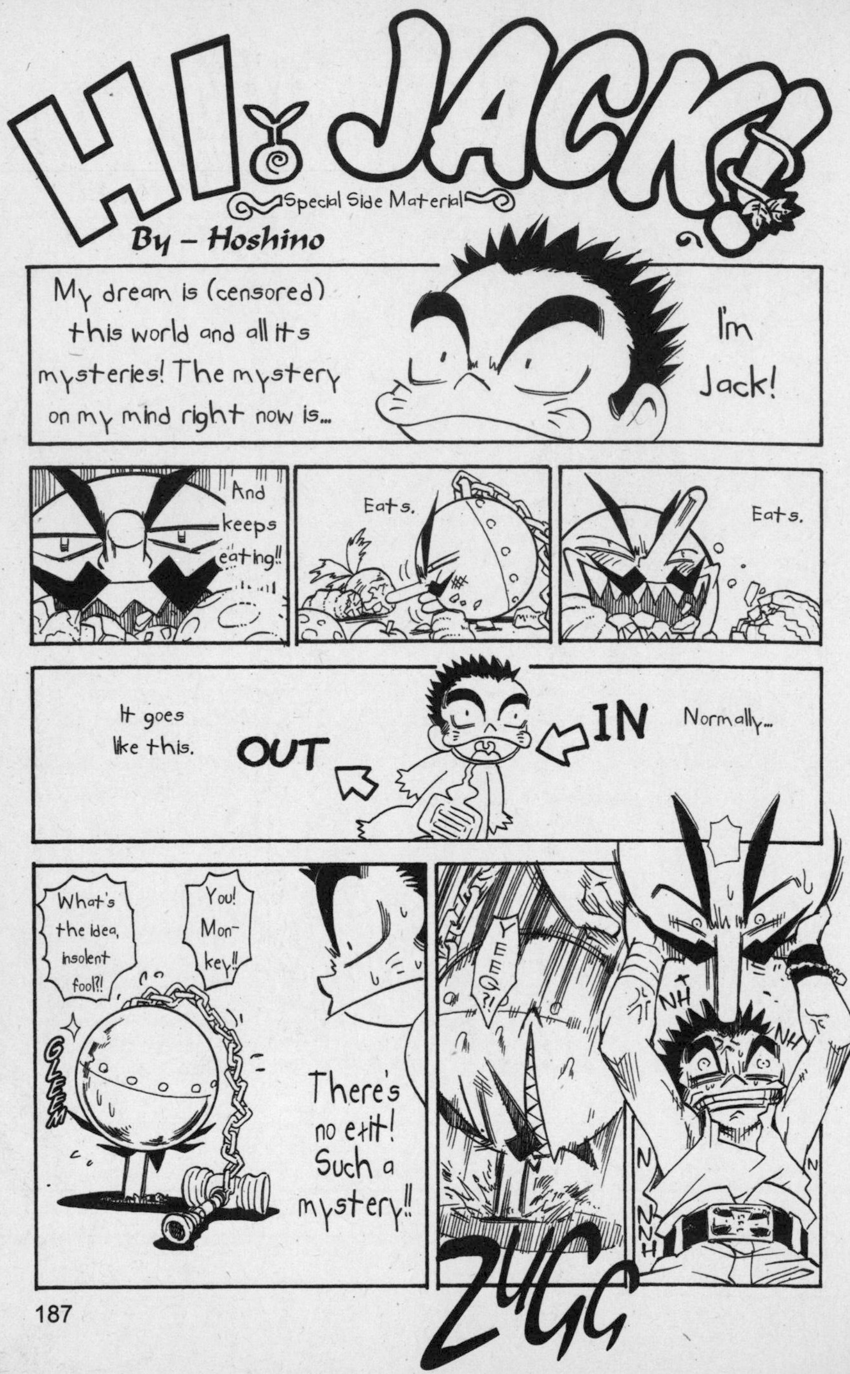
HI JACK!
Special Side Material
By – Hoshino
I'm Jack!
My dream is (censored) this world and all its mysteries! The mystery on my mind right now is...
Eats.
Eats.
And keeps eating!!
Normally...
IN
OUT
It goes like this.
NH
NH
N
N
NNNH
ZUGG
YEEG?!
You! Mon-key!!
What's the idea, insolent fool?!
There's no exit! Such a mystery!!
GLEEM

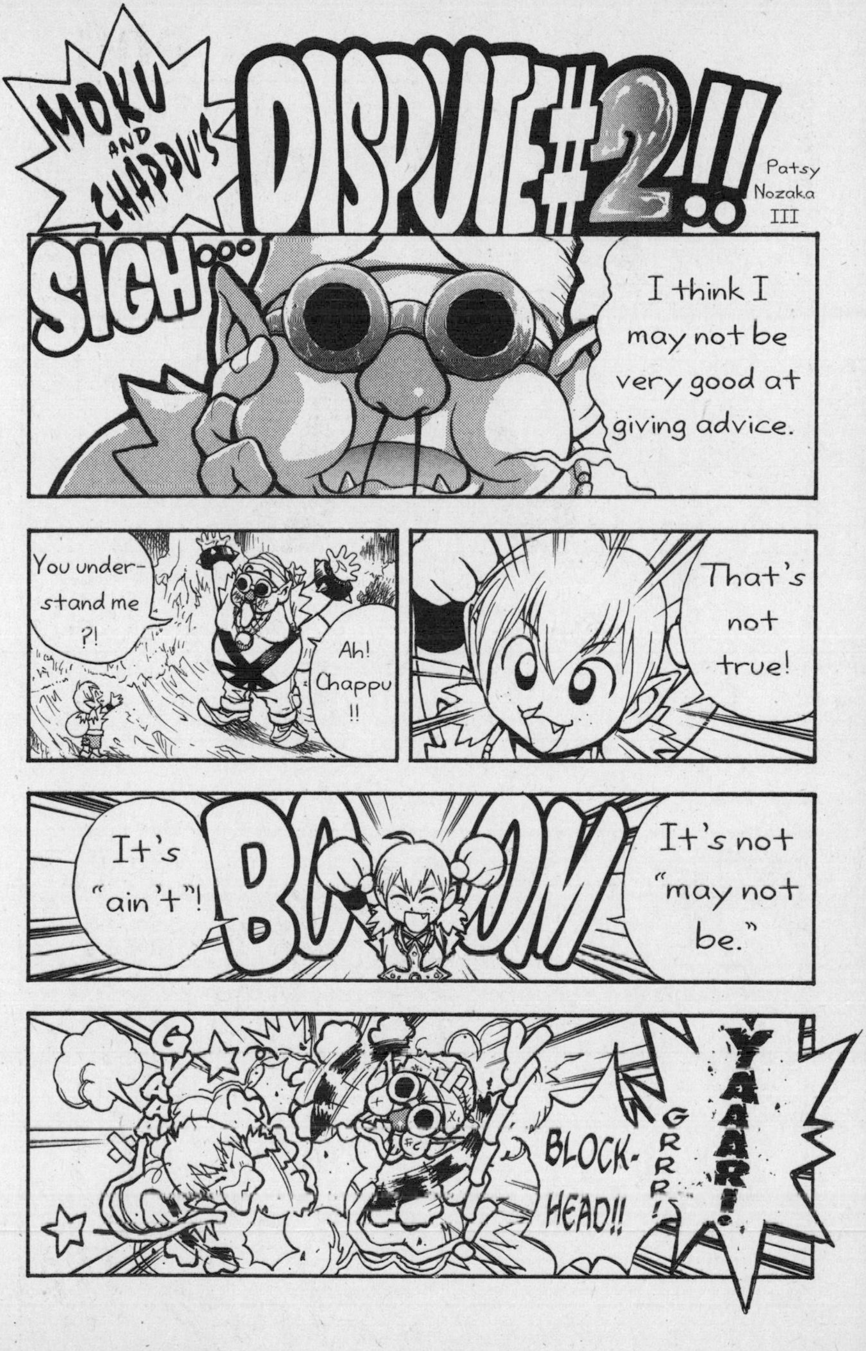
MOKU AND CHAPPU'S DISPUTE #2!!
Patsy Nozaka III
I think I may not be very good at giving advice.
SIGH...
That's not true!
Ah! Chappu!!
You under-stand me?!
It's not "may not be."
BOOM
It's "ain't"!
YAAAR!
GRRR!
BLOCK-HEAD!!

DOG

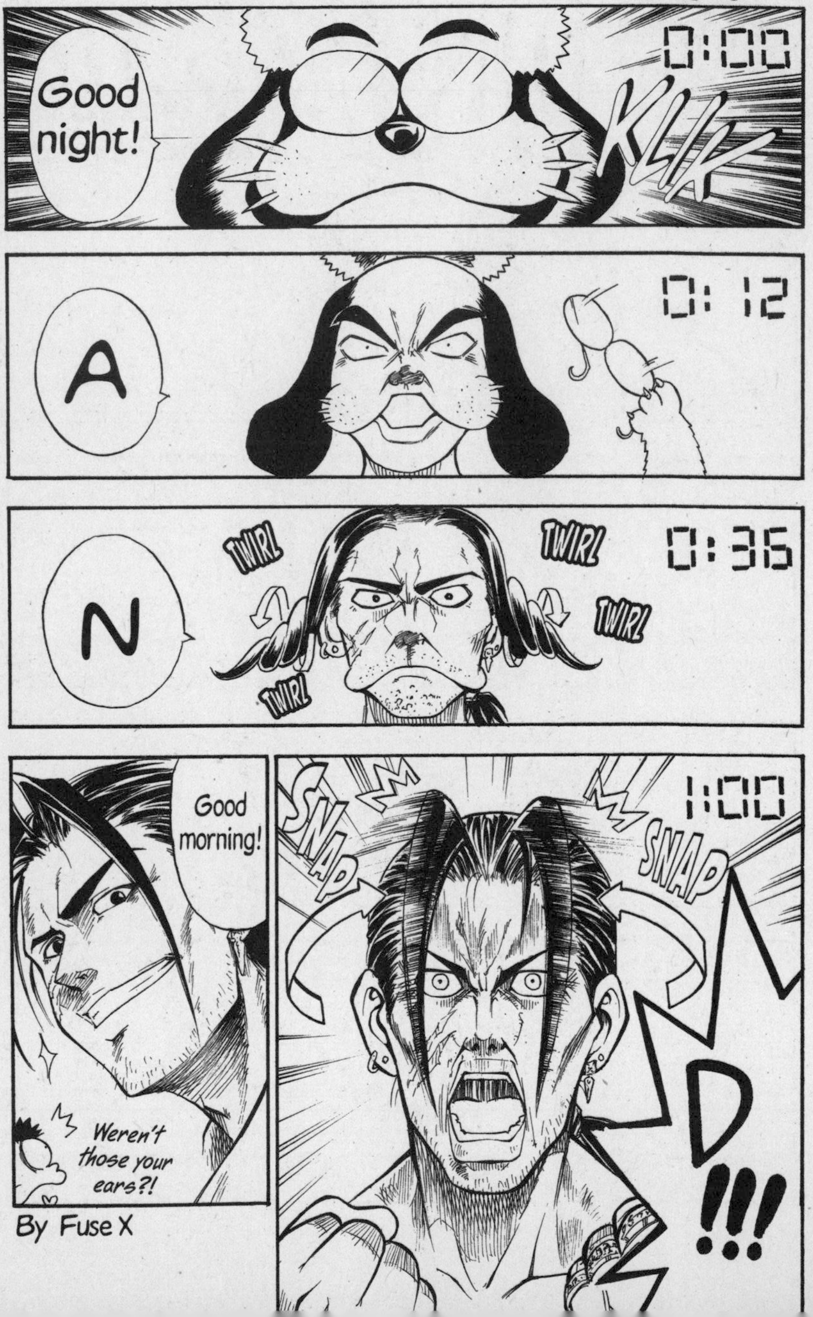
0:00
KLIK
Good night!
0:12
A
0:36
TWIRL
TWIRL
TWIRL
TWIRL
N
1:00
SNAP
SNAP
D!!!
Good morning!
Weren't those your ears?!

By Fuse X

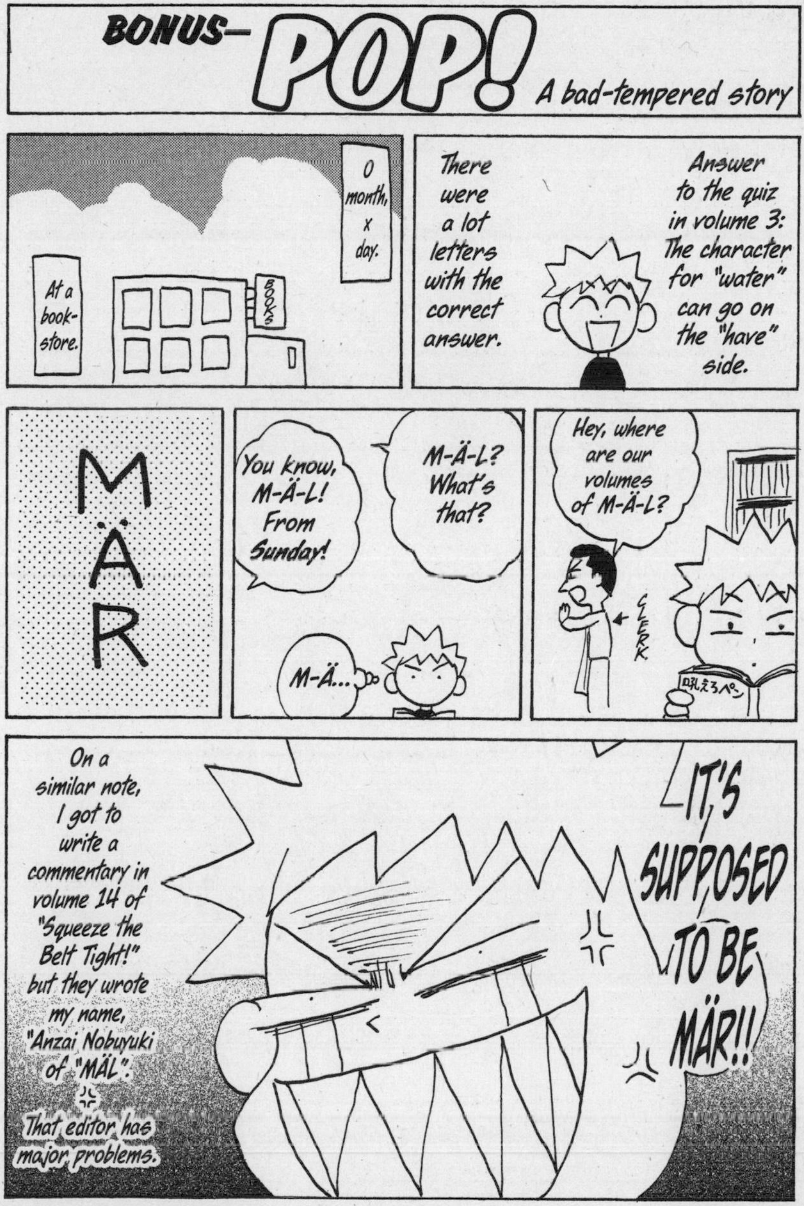
BONUS— POP!
A bad-tempered story
Answer to the quiz in volume 3: The character for "water" can go on the "have" side.
There were a lot letters with the correct answer.
0 month, x day.
BOOKS
At a book-store.
Hey, where are our volumes of M-Ä-L?
CLERK
M-Ä-L? What's that?
You know, M-Ä-L! From Sunday!
M-Ä...
MÄR
IT'S SUPPOSED TO BE MÄR!!
On a similar note, I got to write a commentary in volume 14 of "Squeeze the Belt Tight!" but they wrote my name, "Anzai Nobuyuki of "MÄL".
That editor has major problems.

LOVE MANGA?   LET US KNOW!

☐ Please do NOT send me information about VIZ Media products, news and events, special offers, or other information.

☐ Please do NOT send me information from VIZ Media's trusted business partners.

Name: _____

Address: _____

City:_____ State:_____ Zip:_____

E-mail: _____

☐ Male ☐ Female Date of Birth (mm/dd/yyyy): ___ / ___ / ___ (Under 13? Parental consent required)

What race/ethnicity do you consider yourself? (check all that apply)

☐ White/Caucasian   ☐ Black/African American   ☐ Hispanic/Latino

☐ Asian/Pacific Islander   ☐ Native American/Alaskan Native ☐ Other: _____

What VIZ Media title(s) did you purchase? (indicate title(s) purchased) _____

_____

What other VIZ Media titles do you own? _____

_____

Reason for purchase: (check all that apply)

☐ Special offer   ☐ Favorite title / author / artist / genre

☐ Gift   ☐ Recommendation   ☐ Collection

☐ Read excerpt in VIZ Media manga sampler   ☐ Other _____

Where did you make your purchase? (please check one)

☐ Comic store   ☐ Bookstore   ☐ Grocery Store

☐ Convention   ☐ Newsstand   ☐ Video Game Store

☐ Online (site:_____)   ☐ Other _____

How many manga titles have you purchased in the last year? How many were VIZ Media titles?
(please check one from each column)

MANGA	VIZ Media
☐ None	☐ None
☐ 1 – 4	☐ 1 – 4
☐ 5 – 10	☐ 5 – 10
☐ 11+	☐ 11+

How much influence do special promotions and gifts-with-purchase have on the titles you buy?
(please circle, with 5 being great influence and 1 being none)

1 2 3 4 5

Do you purchase every volume of your favorite series?

☐ Yes! Gotta have 'em as my own ☐ No. Please explain: ______________________

What kind of manga storylines do you most enjoy? (check all that apply)

☐ Action / Adventure
☐ Comedy
☐ Fighting
☐ Artistic / Alternative
☐ Science Fiction
☐ Romance (shojo)
☐ Sports
☐ Other ______________________
☐ Horror
☐ Fantasy (shojo)
☐ Historical

If you watch the anime or play a video or TCG game from a series, how likely are you to buy the manga? (please circle, with 5 being very likely and 1 being unlikely)

1 2 3 4 5

If unlikely, please explain: ______________________

Who are your favorite authors / artists? ______________________

____

What titles would like you translated and sold in English? ______________________

____

THANK YOU! Please send the completed form to:

NJW Research
42 Catharine Street
Poughkeepsie, NY 12601

Your privacy is very important to us. All information provided will be used for internal purposes only and will not be sold or otherwise divulged.